SOCIAL CONSTRUCTIVISM
AS A
PHILOSOPHY OF MATHEMATICS

SUNY Series in Science, Technology, and Society
Sal Restivo and Jennifer Croissant, Editors

and

SUNY Series, Reform in Mathematics Education
Judith Sowder, Editor

SOCIAL CONSTRUCTIVISM
AS A
PHILOSOPHY OF MATHEMATICS

PAUL ERNEST

STATE UNIVERSITY OF NEW YORK PRESS

Published by
State University of New York Press, Albany

For information, address State University of New York
Press, State University Plaza, Albany, N.Y. 12246

Production by E. Moore
Marketing by Nancy Farrell

Library of Congress Cataloging-in-Publication Data

Ernest, Paul.
    Social constructivism as a philosophy of mathematics / Paul
Ernest.
        p.   cm. — (SUNY series in science, technology, and society)
(SUNY series, reform in mathematics education)
    Includes bibliographical references and index.
    ISBN 0-7914-3587-3 (hardcover : alk. paper). — ISBN 0-7914-3588-1
(pbk. : alk. paper)
        1. Mathematics—Philosophy. 2. Constructivism (Philosophy)
I. Title. II. Series. III. Series: SUNY series, reform in
mathematics education.
    QA8.4.E76 1997
    510'.1—DC21   97-3515
                                                                        CIP

10 9 8 7 6 5 4 3 2 1

CONTENTS

TABLES AND FIGURES

ACKNOWLEDGMENTS

The following publishers have kindly given permission for the use of quotations for which they retain copyright. In each case I indicate within the text the relevant source and page references.

Basil Blackwell of Oxford has given permission to quote from *Philosophical Investigations* by Ludwig Wittgenstein, 1953, translated by G. E. M. Anscombe.

Harvard University Press of Cambridge, Massachusetts has given permission to quote from *Mind in Society* by Lev Vygotsky, 1978.

Massachusetts Institute of Technology Press, of Cambridge, Massachusetts and Basil Blackwell of Oxford have given permission to quote from the 1978 revised edition of *Remarks on the Foundations of Mathematics* by Ludwig Wittgenstein, translated by G. E. M. Anscombe.

Routledge of London has given permission to quote from *The Archaeology of Knowledge* by Michel Foucault, 1972.

I wish to express my gratitude to the Leverhulme Trust for supporting my initial work on this book through the award of a senior research fellowship for the period 1991–93.

I am very grateful to a number of people for kindly reading part or all of a draft of this book and offering helpful comments, criticisms or suggestions. These include David Bloor, Stephen I. Brown, Randall Collins, Bettina Dahl, Philip J. Davis, Ray Godfrey, Reuben Hersh, Vibeke Hølledig, Stefano Luzzato, Jakob L. Møller, Jacob Munter, Lene Nielsen, Alan Schoenfeld, Susanne Simoni, Ole Skovsmose, Robert S. D. Thomas, Lars H. Thomassen, Thomas Tymoczko and others.

Sal Restivo has been very encouraging throughout the development of this book and has influenced the final outcome considerably. I am also very grateful to the editorial staff at SUNY Press for the care they have taken in the preparation of the text for publication.

Finally, I wish to record my appreciation and thanks to Jill and our daughters Jane and Nuala for their love and support which sustained me, as always, while I worked on the book.

INTRODUCTION

Mathematics is one of the great cultural achievements of humankind. Every schooled person understands the rudiments of number and measures and sees the world through this quantifying conceptual framework. By these means mathematics provides the language of the socially all-important practices of work, commerce, and economics. In addition, digital computers and the full range of information technology applications are all regulated by and speak to each other exclusively in the language of mathematics, and they would not be possible without it. Thus mathematics is essential to the modern technological way of life and the social outlook that accompanies it.

In contrast, some of the deepest and most abstract speculations of the human mind concern the nature and relations of objects found only in the virtual reality of mathematics. Infinities, paradoxes, logical deduction, perfect harmonies, structures and symmetries, and many other concepts are all analyzed and explored definitively in mathematics. Thus mathematics provides the language of daring abstract thought. Related to this, mathematics is the language of certainty. For over two thousand years thinkers have regarded mathematics as the only self-subsistent area of thought that provides certainty, necessity, and absolute universal truth. So mathematics might be said to have, in addition to a mundane utilitarian role, an epistemological role, an ideological role, and even a mystical role in human culture

Despite being partly familiar to all, because of these contradictory aspects, mathematics remains an enigma and a mystery at the heart of human culture. It is both the language of the everyday world of commercial life and that of an unseen and perfect virtual reality. It includes both free-ranging ethereal speculation and rock-hard certainty. How can this mystery be explained? How can it be unraveled? The philosophy of mathematics is meant to cast some light on this mystery: to explain the nature and character of mathematics. However this philosophy can be purely technical, a product of the academic love of technique expressed in the foundations of mathematics or in philosophical virtuosity. Too often the outcome of philosophical inquiry is to provide detailed answers to the *how* questions of mathematical certainty and existence, taking for granted the received ideology of mathematics, but with too little attention to the deeper *why* questions. Thus, for example, there are still real controversies in the philosophy of mathematics over whether the history of mathematics has any bearing on its philosophy, and whether the experiences and practices of working mathematicians can shed any light on questions of mathematical knowledge. In the philosophy of science such questions have long been settled affirmatively. But this is not yet the case in the philosophy of mathematics. One of my goals in writing this book is to try to lift the veil and to demystify mathematics; to show that for all its wonder it remains a set of human practices, grounded, like everything else, in the material world we inhabit.

In the philosophy of mathematics a number of voices have been heard calling for a more naturalistic account of mathematics. In differing ways Davis and Hersh (1980), Kitcher (1984), Lakatos (1976), Tymoczko (1986a), Tiles (1991), Wittgenstein (1956), and others have argued for a critical re-examination of traditional presuppositions about the certainty of mathematical knowledge. Kitcher and Aspray (1988) suggest that these voices make up a new "maverick" tradition in the philosophy of mathematics which is concerned to accommodate current and past mathematical practices in a philosophical account of mathematics.

Outside of the philosophy of mathematics there has been more progress. First of all, a number of different traditions of thought in sociology, psychology, history and philosophy have been drawing on the central idea of the social construction of knowledge as a way of accounting for science and mathematics naturalistically. Second, a growing number of researchers have been drawing on other disciplines to account for the nature of mathematics, including Bloor (1976), Livingston (1986) and Restivo (1992), from sociology; Ascher (1991), D'Ambrosio (1985), Wilder (1981) and Zaslavsky (1973) from cultural studies and ethnomathematics; Rotman (1987, 1993) from semiotics, Aspray and Kitcher (1988), Joseph (1991) and Gillies (1992) from the history of mathematics, and Bishop (1988), Ernest (1991) and Skovsmose (1994) from education.

This book can be located at the intersection of these traditions. It draws its central explanatory scheme from the interdisciplinary social constructionist approaches currently burgeoning in the human sciences. It gains confidence from the parallels in multidisciplinary and multidimensional accounts of mathematics. But it draws its central concepts and inspiration from the emerging maverick tradition in the philosophy of mathematics.

The book begins with a strong critique of absolutist views of mathe-matical knowledge in the philosophy of mathematics (chap. 1) and traditional approaches to the philosophy of mathematics in general (chap. 2). It argues that the philosophy of mathematics needs to be reconceptualized and broad-ened to accommodate the social and historical factors mentioned above.

In the next part, the philosophies of Wittgenstein (chap. 3) and Lakatos (chap. 4) are critically reviewed and then used as a basis for an account of the social construction of mathematical knowledge (chap. 5). This involves redefining the concept of mathematical knowledge to include tacit and shared components, as well as developing an account of the "conversational" mech-anism for the social genesis and justification of mathematical knowledge. This is the generalized logic of mathematical discovery, extending Lakatos's heuristic.

Chapter 6 develops the central idea of conversation which underpins social constructivism. This requires breaking new ground in exploring the tex-tual basis of mathematical knowledge and the rhetorical functions of mathe-matical language and proof. The role of conversation in the formation of mind and in social construction of subjective knowledge of mathematics is also developed (chap. 7), together with the role of semiotic tools and rhetoric in the learning of mathematics. A surprising analogy is revealed between the social genesis and justification of "objective" mathematical knowledge, on the one hand, and that of subjective mathematical knowledge, on the other. It is argued that the philosophy of mathematics must consider the social con-struction of the individual mathematician and her/his creativity, if it is to account for mathematical knowledge naturalistically.

The book concludes by evaluating its proposals in the light of its cri-tique of the philosophy of mathematics and argues that, contrary to traditional perceptions, a socially constructed mathematics has a vital social responsibil-ity to bear (chap. 8).

Followers of my work will know that I have been working on social constructivism for more than a decade, and it will come as no surprise that this account builds on an earlier version (Ernest 1991). The greatest similarities between the two versions occur in chapters 1 and 2 of this book, where I felt it was necessary to go over and improve the arguments against absolutism in the philosophy of mathematics and for the reconceptualization of the field. In addition to the goal of making the argument self-contained, there is enough novelty in these chapters to justify including them in their own right, even for seasoned readers of the earlier work. For example, there is a new argument that a reconceptualized philosophy of mathematics should offer an account of the learning of mathematics and its role in the onward transmission of math-ematical knowledge.

The present work is not merely an extension and elaboration of the earlier version of social constructivism in Ernest (1991). In addition to being almost three times the length there are a number of significant conceptual differences between this and the earlier version, including the following improvements:

1. Deeper analyses of Wittgenstein's and Lakatos's thought
2. Less reliance on language as an explicit foundation of subjective knowledge of mathematics, with more emphasis on tacit knowledge, and on language and rhetoric in accounting for "objective" mathematical knowledge
3. Recognition of the semiotic basis of mathematics and mathematical knowledge
4. A shift from a Piagetian/constructivist view of mind to a social view based on Mead, Vygotsky, and others (see also Ernest 1994b)
5. Greater recognition of the culture-boundedness of all knowledge, and the necessity of identifying its material basis
6. A diminished concern to maintain the boundaries between history, sociology, psychology and the philosophy of mathematics

CHAPTER 1

A CRITIQUE OF ABSOLUTISM IN THE PHILOSOPHY OF MATHEMATICS

Historically, mathematics has long been viewed as the paradigm of infallibly secure knowledge. Euclid and his colleagues first constructed a magnificent logical structure around 2,300 years ago in the *Elements*, which at least until the end of the nineteenth century was taken as the paradigm for establishing incorrigible truth. Descartes ([1637] 1955) modeled his epistemology directly on the method and style of geometry. Hobbes claimed that "geometry . . . is the only science . . . bestow[ed] on [hu]mankind" (Hobbes [1651] 1962, 77). Newton in his *Principia* and Spinoza in his *Ethics* used the form of the *Elements* to strengthen their claims of systematically expounding the truth.[1] This logical form reached its ultimate expression in *Principia Mathematica*, in which Whitehead and Russell (1910–13) reapplied it to mathematics, while paying homage to Newton with their title. As part of the logicist program, *Principia Mathematica* was intended to provide a rigorous and certain foundation for all of mathematical knowledge. Thus mathematics has long been taken as the source of the most infallible knowledge known to humankind, and much of this is due to the logical structure of its presentation and justification.

With this background, a philosophical inquiry into mathematics raises questions including: What is the basis for mathematical knowledge? What is the nature of mathematical truth? What characterizes the truths of mathematics? What is the justification for their assertion? Why are the truths of mathematics necessary truths? How absolute is this necessity?

THE NATURE OF KNOWLEDGE

The question, What is knowledge? lies at the heart of philosophy, and mathematical knowledge plays a special part. The standard philosophical answer, which goes back to Plato, is that knowledge is justified true belief. To put it differently, propositional knowledge consists of propositions which are accepted (i.e., believed), provided there are adequate grounds fully available to the believer for asserting them (Sheffler 1965; Chisholm 1966; Woozley 1949). This way of putting it avoids presupposing the truth of what is known, although traditional accounts require it, by referring instead to adequate grounds, which also include the justificatory element. The phrase "fully available" circumvents the difficulty caused when the adequate grounds exist but are not in the cognizance of the believer.[2]

Knowledge is classified on the basis of the grounds for its assertion. A *priori* knowledge consists of propositions which are asserted on the basis of reason alone, without recourse to observations of the world. Here reason consists of the use of deductive logic and the meanings of terms, typically to be found in definitions. In contrast, empirical or *a posteriori* knowledge consists of propositions asserted on the basis of experience, that is, based on observations of the world (Woozley 1949). This basis refers strictly to the empirical *justificatory* basis of a posteriori knowledge, not its genesis. Indeed, such knowledge may be initially generated by pure thought, whilst a priori knowledge, such as that of mathematics, may be first generated by induction from empirical observation. Such origins are immaterial; only the grounds for asserting the knowledge matter. This distinction is first to be found in Kant ([1781] 1961), but also occurs implicitly in earlier work, such as in Leibniz ("truths of reason" versus "truths of fact") and Hume ("matters of fact" versus "matters of reason"), Vico ("verum" or a priori truth versus "certum" or the empirical), as well as being anticipated by Plato.

Kant not only distinguishes a priori and a posteriori knowledge, on the basis of the means of verification used to justify them, but also distinguishes between *analytic* and *synthetic* propositions. A proposition is *analytic* if it follows from the law of contradiction, that is, if its denial is logically inconsistent.[3] Kant argued that mathematical knowledge is synthetic *a priori*, since it is based on reason, not empirical facts, but does not follow from the law of contradiction alone. The standard view in epistemology (see Feigl and Sellars 1949, for example) is that Kant was wrong and mathematics is analytic, and that the analytic can be identified with the *a priori* and the synthetic with the *a posteriori*. According to this view, mathematical theorems add nothing to knowledge which is not implicitly contained in the premises *logically*, although *psychologically* the theorems may be novel.

The debate is not straightforward, for a number of reasons. First of all, Kant believed in a universal logic, whereas now we recognize alternative systems in logic (Haack 1974, 1978). He also believed that mathematical theories such as Euclidean geometry and arithmetic are the necessary logical outcomes of reason. (Non-Euclidean geometry and nonstandard arithmetics were simply not possible in his system.) He concluded that although the truths of mathematics are necessary, they do not follow from the law of contradiction, but from the forms that human understanding takes, by its very nature.

A number of modern philosophers have agreed with Kant, at least so far as to dissent from the received view that identifies the analytic with the *a priori* and the synthetic with the *a posteriori*. Hintikka (1973) argues that some mathematical proofs require the addition of auxiliary elements or concepts, and hence add something unforeseen and logically novel to the mathematical knowledge. Since such proofs do not rest on the law of contradiction alone, he argues that they are synthetic, in both senses, as well as *a priori*. Brouwer and Wittgenstein (as I shall show below and in chap. 3, respectively) similarly accept that some mathematical knowledge is both synthetic and *a priori*. Finally, some others, such as Quine (1953b, 1970) and White argue that "the analytic and the synthetic [is] an untenable dualism" (White 1950). Their view is that the boundary between the two classes cannot be fixed determinately. Quine (1960) goes on to elaborate his view that mathematical and empirical scientific knowledge cannot be neatly partitioned into the analytic and synthetic. He argues that the whole of language is a "vast verbal structure," and it is not possible to separate out those parts which have empirical import from those that do not; "this structure of interconnected sentences is a single connected fabric including all sciences, and . . . logical truths" (Quine 1960, 12).

These subtleties and dissenting views notwithstanding, according to the received view mathematical knowledge is classified as *a priori* knowledge, since it consists of propositions asserted on the basis of reason alone. Reason includes deductive logic and definitions which are used, in conjunction with an assumed set of mathematical axioms or postulates, as a basis from which to infer mathematical knowledge. Thus the foundation of mathematical knowledge, that is, the grounds for asserting the truth of mathematical propositions, consists of deductive proof, together with the assumed truth of any premises employed. Apart from the assumed truth of the premises, there is another fundamental way in which mathematical proof depends on truth. The essential underpinning feature of a correct or valid deductive proof is the transmission of truth, that is, truth value is preserved.

Truth in Mathematics

It is often the case in mathematics that the definition of truth is assumed to be clear-cut, unambiguous, and unproblematic. While this is often justifiable as a simplifying assumption, the fact is that it is incorrect and that the meaning of the concept of truth in mathematics has changed significantly over time. I wish to distinguish among three truth-related concepts used in mathematics.

The traditional view of mathematical truth. First of all, there is the traditional view that a mathematical truth is a general statement which not only correctly describes all its instances in the world (as would a true empirical generalization) but is *necessarily* true of its instances. Implicitly underpinning this view is the assumption that mathematical theories have an intended interpretation, often an idealization of some aspect of the world. The key feature of this view is the association of an intended interpretation with a theory. Thus number theory refers to the domain of natural numbers, geometry refers to ideal objects in space, calculus largely refers to functions of the real line, and so on. To be true in this first sense (I will denote it by "truth$_1$") is to be true in the intended interpretation. The mode of expression I have used depends of course upon a modern way of thinking, for it requires prizing open mathematical signs to separate the signifiers (formal mathematical symbols) from the signified (the intended meanings). Truth$_1$ treats mathematical signs as integral; only one interpretation is built in.

Truth$_1$ is analogous to naive realism, a view of truths as statements which accurately describe a state of affairs in some fixed realm of discourse. According to this view, the terms involved in expressing the truth name objects in the intended universe of discourse, and the true statement as a whole describes the relationship that holds between these denotations. In essence, this is the naive correspondence theory of truth.

Such a view of mathematical truth was widespread, dominant even, until the middle and end of the nineteenth century. For example De Morgan commenting on Peacock's new generalized formal algebra described it as made up of "symbols bewitched . . . running about the world in search of meaning" (1835, 311). What he objected to was the severance of algebraic symbols from their generalized arithmetical meanings (Richards 1987). Without such fixed and determinate meanings, mathematical propositions could not express their intended meanings, let alone truths. Similarly, Frege had a sophisticated and philosophically well elaborated view that the theorems of arithmetic are true in its intended interpretation, the domain of natural number. Again, this is the notion of truth$_1$.

Mathematical truth as satisfiability. Secondly, there is the modern view of the truth of a mathematical statement relative to a background mathematical theory: the statement is satisfied by some interpretation or model of the theory. I shall term this second conception "truth$_2$." According to this (and the following) view, mathematical theories are open to multiple interpretations, that is, possible worlds. Truth in this sense consists merely in being true (i.e., satisfied, following Tarski 1936) in one of these possible worlds; that is, in having a model. Thus truth$_2$ is represented by Tarski's explication of truth, which forms the basis of model theory. A proposition is true$_2$ relative to a given mathematical theory if there is some interpretation of the theory which satisfies the proposition, irrespective of the other properties of the interpretation, such as resemblance to some original intended interpretation. (This interpretation must include an assignment of objects and relations of appropriate type to the extralogical symbols, as well as an assignment of values from the universe of discourse to the variable letters of the proposition.)

Truth$_2$ probably originates with Hilbert's work on geometry. Hilbert detached geometrical notions such as 'point, line, and plane' from their original physical (or ideal) interpretations, and argued instead that they could be interpreted as 'table, chair, and beer-mug', provided that what resulted was a model of the axioms of geometry. It has been suggested that Tarski's theory of truth originates in algebra, by analogy with a set of roots satisfying an equation. Likewise, the assignment of values to the components of a proposition satisfies it when it makes it true.

Truth$_2$ is anticipated by Leibniz's notion of 'true in a possible world', which he contrasted with 'true in all possible worlds' (Barcan Marcus 1967).

Logical truth or validity in mathematics. Thirdly, there is the modern view of the logical truth or validity of a mathematical statement relative to a background theory: the statement is satisfied by *all* interpretations or models of the theory. Thus the statement is true in all of these representations of possible worlds. I shall denote this conception of truth by 'truth$_3$'. Evidently truth$_3$ more or less corresponds to Leibniz's notion of 'true in all possible worlds'. This is also one of the notions explicated by Tarski's theory of mathematical truth as 'logical validity'.

Truth$_3$ can be established by logical deduction from the background theory if the theory is represented by a first-order axiom set, as Gödel's (1930) completeness theorem establishes. For a given theory, Truths$_3$ (the set of propositions which are true in the sense of truth$_3$) is a subset (usually a proper subset) of Truths$_2$. Incompleteness arises, as Gödel ([1931] 1967) proved, in most mathematical theories as there are true$_1$ sentences (i.e., satisfied in the intended model) which are not true$_3$ (i.e., true in *all* models).

Thus not only does the concept of truth have multiple meanings, but crucial mathematical issues hinge upon this ambiguity. The modern mathematical views of truth (truth$_2$ and truth$_3$) differ in meaning and properties from the traditional mathematical view of truth$_1$ and the everyday naive notion which resembles it. Historically, the transition from truth$_1$ to the modern notions was highly problematic, as Richards (1980, 1989) shows in her studies. Even the correspondence between such mathematically (and philosophically) great thinkers as Frege (1980) and Hilbert shows disagreements and sometimes a lack of understanding that may be attributed to Frege's use of truth$_1$ and Hilbert's use of truth$_2$.

A consequence of this is that the traditional problem of establishing the indubitable foundations of mathematical truth has changed in meaning, as the definition of truth employed has changed. The relationship between the three notions explicated above is as follows (assuming a given background mathematical theory). Given any proposition P, if P is $true_3$, then P is also $true_1$; and if P is $true_1$, it is also $true_2$. Thus to claim that a statement is $true_2$ is much weaker than $truth_1$ or $truth_3$.

Although there are these complexities in the mathematical concept of truth, one way to vouchsafe it has remained at the center of mathematics for more than two millennia, that is, mathematical proof. This ties in with the discussion of truth, because as mentioned above provability (relative to a given set of axioms) is equivalent to $truth_3$ (Gödel 1930). Similarly, it follows from a contrapositive argument that consistency (relative to a given set of axioms) is equivalent to $truth_2$.

Proof in Mathematics

Since proof constitutes the means of justifying knowledge in mathematics, it is important to analyze how it does this. The proof of a mathematical proposition is a finite sequence of statements ending in the given proposition, which sequence ideally satisfies the following property.[4] Each statement is an axiom drawn from a previously stipulated set of axioms, or is derived by a rule of inference from one or more statements occurring earlier in the sequence. The term *set of axioms* should be understood broadly, to include whatever statements are admitted into a proof without demonstration, including axioms, postulates, and definitions.

This account describes a "primitive" and ideal proof, one in which all of the assumptions are primitive, that is, basic assumptions, and all of the inferences are justified by specified rules. In a "derived" proof some of these assumptions are themselves the results of earlier proofs. A derived proof can, in principle, be turned into a primitive proof simply by incorporating within it the proofs of all nonprimitive assumptions, and iterating this procedure until no nonprimitive assumptions remain. Thus there is no loss of generality in considering only primitive proofs.[5] However the assumption that all proofs can be rendered as ideal proofs, that is, as based on logical or mathematical rules of inference, is not so easily discharged.[6]

The idea underpinning the notion of proof is that of truth transmission. If the axioms adopted are taken to be true, and if the rules of inference infallibly transmit truth (i.e., true premises necessitate a true conclusion), then the theorem proved must also be true. For there is an unbroken and undiminished flow of truth from the axioms transmitted through the proof to the conclusion. With this in mind, the modern definitions of the logical connectives are understood in terms of truth tables. Thus, an implication statement P→Q is true if, and only if, it cannot be the case that P is true and Q is false. Thus to safeguard the transmission of truth in proof, the shared content or causal link between antecedent and consequent sometimes found in the everyday language usage of implication statements is sacrificed.

As a simple example of a mathematical proof I will analyze a proof of the statement 1 + 1 = 2 in the axiomatic system of Peano arithmetic. This proof requires as assumptions a number of definitions and axioms, as well as logical rules of inference. These assumptions are the definitions of 1 and 2 as successors of 0 and 1, respectively, axioms specifying the properties of addition recursively, and logical rules stating that (1) two equal terms have the same properties and (2) a general property of numbers applies to any particular number. Based on these assumptions, 1 + 1 = 2 can be proved in ten steps.[7] Each equation in the proof either is a specified assumption or is derived from earlier parts of the proof by applying rules of inference. Since the assumptions are assumed to be true, and the rules transmit truth, every equation in the sequence is equally true, including 1 + 1 = 2. The proof establishes 1 + 1 = 2 as an item of mathematical knowledge or truth, according to the previous analysis, for the deductive proof provides a legitimate warrant for asserting the statement.[8] Furthermore it is a priori knowledge, since it is asserted on the basis of reason alone.

However, what has not yet been made clear are the grounds for the assumptions made in the proof. These are of two types: mathematical and logical assumptions. The mathematical assumptions used are the definitions and the axioms. The logical assumptions are the rules of inference used, which are part of the overall proof theory, as well as the underlying syntax of the formal language. Although not specified here, this syntax is not negligible. It includes the categories of symbols, and the inductively defined rules of combination (e.g., for terms and sentences) and of transformation (e.g., substitution of individual terms in formulas).

I consider first the mathematical assumptions. Explicit mathematical definitions are unproblematic, since they are eliminable in principle. Thus every occurrence of the defined terms 2 and 1 can be replaced by what is abbreviated (the successors of 1 and 0, respectively), until these terms are completely eliminated. The result is an abbreviated proof of "the successor of zero plus the successor of zero = the successor of the successor of zero," which represents 1 + 1 = 2 in other words. Although explicit definitions are eliminable in principle—that is, they do not entail any additional logical assumptions—they play an important (probably essential) role in human knowing. However, in the present context I am concerned to minimize assumptions, to reveal the irreducible assumptions on which mathematical knowledge and its justification rests.

If the definitions had not been explicit, such as in Peano's original inductive definition of addition (Heijenoort 1967), which are specified in the example as basic axioms (Ernest 1991, 5), then the definitions would not be eliminable in principle. This case is analogous to that of an axiom. In other words, a basic assumption would have been made and would have to be acknowledged as such.

I have now disposed of all the categories of assumption that are eliminable. The axioms in the proof are not eliminable. They must either be assumed as self-evident axiomatic (or otherwise warranted) truths or simply retain the status of unjustified, tentative assumptions, adopted to permit the development of the mathematical theory under consideration. The logical assumptions, that is, the rules of inference (part of the overall proof theory) and the logical syntax, are assumed as part of the underlying logic and are part of the mechanism needed for the application of reason. Thus in proofs of mathematical theorems, such as in the example under discussion, logic is assumed as an unproblematic foundation for the justification of knowledge.

In summary, the elementary mathematical truth $1 + 1 = 2$ depends for its justification on a mathematical proof.[9] This, in turn, depends on assuming a number of basic mathematical statements (axioms), as well as on the underlying logic. In general, mathematical knowledge consists of statements justified by proofs, which depend on mathematical axioms (and an underlying logic).

This account of mathematical knowledge is essentially that which has been accepted for at least 2,300 years. Early presentations of mathematical knowledge, such as Euclid's *Elements*, are susceptible to the above description and differ from it only by degree. In Euclid, as above, mathematical knowledge is established by the logical deduction of theorems from axioms and postulates (which I include among the axioms). The underlying logic is left unspecified (other than the statement of some axioms concerning the equality relation). The axioms are not regarded as temporarily adopted assumptions, held only for the construction of the theory under consideration. The axioms are considered to be basic truths which need no justification, beyond their own self evidence (Blanché 1966).[10]

Because of this, the account claims to provide absolute grounds for mathematical knowledge. For if the axioms are truths and logical proof preserves truth, then any theorems derived from them must also be truths. This reasoning is implicit, not explicit, in Euclid. However, this claim is no longer accepted because Euclid's axioms and postulates are not considered basic truths which cannot be denied without contradiction. As is well known, the denial of some axioms, most notably the parallel postulate, merely leads to other bodies of geometric knowledge, namely non-Euclidean geometry. As well as the axioms, the proofs of Euclid's *Elements* are now also regarded as flawed and falling short of modern standards of rigor. For they smuggle in notions such as continuity, which is assumed for the accompanying diagrams, even though these have no formal justificatory role in the proofs.

Beyond Euclid, modern mathematical knowledge includes many branches which depend on the assumption of sets of axioms which cannot be claimed to be basic universal truths, for example, the axioms of group theory or of set theory. Maddy (1984) illustrates how modern set theorists add new axioms to Zermelo-Fraenkel set theory and then explore their consequences on a pragmatic basis, rather than regarding the additional axioms as intrinsically true. Henle (1991) also makes this point. However, my claim is that it is not just recondite axioms such as those of set theory that have no claim to be basic and unchallengeable universal truths, but that no such principles exist at all. Even the law of the excluded middle, regarded by philosophers since the time of Aristotle as one of the most basic of all logical principles (Kneale and Kneale 1962), is challenged by a significant group of modern mathematicians and philosophers (the intuitionists), indicating its dubitability and casting doubt on its self-evidence and incontrovertibility.

In what follows I shall be casting further doubt on the infallibility of mathematical knowledge and its foundation in mathematical proof.

THE PHILOSOPHY OF MATHEMATICS

According to Kitcher and Aspray (1988), Frege set the agenda and tone for the modern (i.e., twentieth-century) philosophy of mathematics. Frege ([1884] 1968) adopted the view that the central problem for the philosophy of mathematics is that of identifying the foundations of mathematical knowledge. Basing his analysis on Kant's distinction, Frege argued that mathematical knowledge consists of truths known *a priori*, and that reason alone, in the form of logical proof, provides certain and absolute foundations for it.

Consequently, until recently, twentieth century philosophy of mathematics has been dominated by the quest for absolute foundations for mathematical truth. Of course this can also be viewed as merely the latest expression of an epistemological quest since Plato made an attempt, renewed by Descartes, to find absolute foundations for knowledge in general and for its central pillar, mathematical knowledge.

The aim of this chapter is to offer a critique of this conception and its underlying assumptions. In particular, my main purpose is to expound and criticize the dominant view, for which I shall adopt the term *absolutist*, that mathematical truth is absolutely valid and thus infallible, and that mathematics (with logic) is the one and perhaps the only realm of incorrigible, indubitable, and objective knowledge. I will contrast this with the opposing view, for which I shall adopt the term *fallibilist*, that mathematical truth is fallible and corrigible and should never be regarded as being above revision and correction.

Fallibilism and Absolutism

The first philosopher of mathematics to explicitly state the importance of the absolutist-fallibilist dichotomy is Imre Lakatos (1978b), who relates it to the ancient controversy between dogmatists and skeptics. Lakatos introduced the term *fallibilism*, adapted from Popper's "critical fallibilism," into the philosophy of mathematics.

Lakatos is anticipated by C. S. Peirce's "principle of fallibilism" to the effect that we can know "only in an uncertain and inexact way" (Peirce 1931–58, 5:587) and "there are three things to which we can never hope to attain by reasoning, namely, absolute certainty, absolute exactitude, absolute universality" (1:141).

In philosophy there is some controversy as to what fallibilism means. Haack claims that "fallibilism is a thesis about [1] *our liability to error*, and not a thesis about [2] *the modal status* (possible falsity) *of what we believe*" (1979–80, 309, original emphasis). In contrast O'Hear (1992) suggests that fallibilism is the idea that any human opinions or judgements might turn out false, that is, thesis 2. Following Lakatos I take the view that fallibilism means—as the second of the two views expressed above—that it is theoretically possible that any accepted knowledge including mathematical knowledge may lose its modal status as true or necessary. Such knowledge may have its justificatory warrant rejected or withdrawn (losing its status as knowledge) and be rejected as unwarranted, invalid, or even false.[11]

Lakatos contrasts the term *fallibilism* both with its actual opposite of *infallibilism* (Lakatos 1961, 1976) and more often with an opposing set of perspectives in the philosophy of mathematics that he terms "Euclidean" (Lakatos 1978b, 1976). Infallibilism is synonymous with absolutism, since both mean that mathematical knowledge is indubitable, incorrigible, and infallible. There has been much discussion of the Absolute in the history of philosophy. It occurs metaphysically in the work of Hegel and the idealists Bosanquet, Bradley, and Royce. William James (1912) explicitly uses the term epistemologically when he contrasts absolutism with empiricism. Although the term has been in currency for some time, to the best of my knowledge Confrey (1981) is the first to apply the term in print to the philosophy of mathematics. Recently Harré and Krausz (1996) contrasted absolutism with relativism. Indeed they offer an analysis of different absolutisms and relativisms; this I discuss further in chapter 8.

The absolutist-fallibilist dichotomy distinguishes what in my view is the most important epistemological difference between competing accounts of the nature of mathematics and mathematical knowledge. Indeed, this distinction has pervasive effects through much broader realms than those of philosophy or mathematics alone (Ernest 1991). The distinction parallels that between apriorism and naturalism in the philosophy of mathematics of Kitcher (1984, 1988). Apriorism "is the doctrine that mathematical knowledge is *a priori*," and it "must be obtained from a source different from perceptual experience" (Kitcher 1984, 3). Naturalism opposes this doctrine, and it argues that there are empirical or quasi-empirical sources of justification of mathematical knowledge and that the role of the philosophy of mathematics is to accommodate this and offer a naturalistic account of mathematics. Evidently there is a very close parallel in the two dichotomies; and although there are definitional differences between them, they result in an identical partitioning of schools in the philosophy of mathematics.

Foundationalism in the Philosophy of Mathematics

The target of my critique is any attempt to establish absolutism by means of epistemological foundationalism. The term *foundationalism* is used to describe a number of different perspectives in which belief or knowledge is divided into two parts, foundation and superstructure, and in which the latter depends on the former for its justification, and not vice versa (Alston 1992). Alston points out that some of these senses concern the structure of an individual knower's system of beliefs. This accords with the fact that standard accounts of epistemology often begin discussions of knowledge by referring to individual acts of knowing (Chisholm 1966; Ryle 1949; Woozley 1949). In those acts that conform to Ryle's sense of "knowing that" what is known or grasped is a proposition, the informational content expressed by a sentence. Thus it is possible to consider the content of knowing in traditional epistemological accounts to be knowledge in the form of propositions or sentences. In general this assumption is unwarranted. However, in the case of mathematics (and science) epistemological discussions usually, but not always, refer to knowledge not knowing, that is, to the subject known instead of the knowing subject. Thus the form of knowledge may be taken as the sentence, or a logically organized structure of sentences, the theory. There is more to be said about individual acts of knowing in mathematics, but I shall defer the discussion to later.

Thus a widely adopted assumption in epistemology is that knowledge in any field is represented by a set of propositions, supported with a set of procedures for verifying them or providing a warrant for their assertion. This assumption is remarked upon by Harding (1986), among others, albeit critically. Viewed in this way, mathematical knowledge consists of a set of propositions warranted by proofs. Mathematical proofs are based on deductive reason, comprising chains of necessary inferences. Since it is warranted by reason alone, without recourse to empirical data, mathematical knowledge is understood to be the most infallible and certain of all knowledge, for it avoids the possibilities of error introduced by perception and other empirical sources of knowledge. Traditionally the philosophy of mathematics has seen its task as providing a foundation for this infallibility; that is, providing a system into which mathematical knowledge can be cast to systematically establish its truth. This depends on an assumption, which is widely adopted, implicitly if not explicitly.

The Foundationalist Assumption of the Philosophy of Mathematics: The primary concern of the philosophy of mathematics is establishing that there is, or can be, a systematic and absolutely secure foundation for mathematical knowledge and truth.

This assumption is the basis of foundationalism, the doctrine that the function of the philosophy of mathematics is to provide ultimate and infallible foundations for mathematical knowledge. Foundationalism is bound up with the absolutist view of mathematical knowledge, for it regards the justification of absolutism to be the central problem of the philosophy of mathematics.

Lakatos defines (and critiques) the position he terms "Euclideanism," which is a form of foundationalism modeled on the structure of Euclid's *Elements*. In that system a set of axioms, postulates, definitions, and rules is used to deduce a collection of theorems. Euclideanism similarly seeks to recast mathematical knowledge into a deductive structure based on a finite number of true axioms (or axiom schemes) analogous to Euclid's theory of geometry. This is very similar to, but less general than, the foundationalist assumption or position that I critique. The interpretation of foundationalism adopted here resembles that in Descartes's method. It entails the reconstruction of mathematical knowledge in terms of an absolute foundation and a superstructure infallibly derived from it. The strategy of my critique in this chapter is twofold, reflecting this structure. First, to attack the justificatory basis of the foundation of mathematical knowledge: I shall argue that no absolute foundation for mathematical knowledge can exist. Second, to attack the infallibility of the derivation of the superstructure from it: I shall argue that any such derivation is both fallible and incomplete. This second argument also addresses the position obtained by withdrawing the epistemological assumptions concerning the truth of the foundation. This derived position is a form of hypothetico-deductivism in which the axioms of mathematics are regarded as tentative as opposed to true assumptions. However this position still claims that the derivations of mathematical knowledge are infallible. As I shall show, this revised form remains a version of foundationalism, but one that is based on a different conception of truth.

Kitcher and Aspray (1988) attribute the epistemological and foundational tendency in the philosophy of mathematics to Frege, whom they regard as the founding father and "onlie begetter" of the modern philosophy of mathematics. Frege ([1884] 1968) undertook a thorough critical review of the range of philosophical positions possible, at least to his way of thinking, for arithmetic. This is still regarded as a classic expression of analytic reasoning, perhaps the first such application in the philosophy of mathematics. During the last quarter of the nineteenth century Frege took his main task to be the setting of arithmetic and arithmetical knowledge on a firm foundation. This, as Kitcher and Aspray point out, was a natural extension of the earlier enterprise of constructing firm foundations for analysis pursued by Dedekind, Weierstrass, Heine, and others.[12] Thus Frege installed the foundationalist program, which is essentially epistemological, at the heart of the philosophy of mathematics. He also severely weakened, at least temporarily, the claims of any other programs or approaches to the philosophy of mathematics.

According to Kitcher (1979) and Kitcher and Aspray (1988), Frege ([1884] 1968) analyzed the possible sources of support for the foundations of mathematics into three or four cases. He distinguished between justificatory procedures for mathematics that were *a priori* and *a posteriori*. He criticized and dismissed the possibility that the warrant for mathematical knowledge could be empirical or *a posteriori*.

Given that only two alternatives were admissible to Frege, this meant that the justificatory procedures for mathematics must be *a priori*. He reasoned that only two or three possibilities for justifying *a priori* knowledge are possible. These are, focusing on arithmetic only, as follows. First, that arithmetic is derivable from logic plus the definitions of a special arithmetical vocabulary. Second, that arithmetic is founded on some special *a priori* intuition. Third, a possibility he did not enumerate but treated incidentally, is that arithmetic is not a science with some definite content, but can be represented as a meaningless formal system. Thus, in the alternatives he considered, Frege distinguishes the well springs of empiricism, logicism, intuitionism, and formalism. These possibilities have dominated thinking in the philosophy of mathematics and continue to remain the main possibilities for justifying mathematical knowledge.

ABSOLUTIST VIEWS OF MATHEMATICAL KNOWLEDGE

The absolutist view of mathematical knowledge is that it consists of infallible and absolute truths and represents the unique realm of infallible knowledge (in addition to logic and analytic statements true by virtue of the meanings of terms, such as "All bachelors are unmarried"), which is necessarily true in all possible circumstances and contexts.

Many philosophers, both modern and traditional, hold absolutist views of mathematical knowledge. Thus according to Hempel, in his paper "on the nature of mathematical truth":

> the validity of mathematics derives from the stipulations which determine the meaning of the mathematical concepts, and that the propositions of mathematics are therefore essentially "true by definition." (Feigl and Sellars 1949, 225)

Another proponent of the infallibility of mathematical knowledge is Ayer, who is representative of logical positivism and logical empiricism when he claims that

> truths of mathematics and logic appear to everyone to be necessary and certain. (Ayer 1946, 72)

> The certainty of *a priori* propositions depends on the fact that they are tautologies. (Ayer 1946, 16)

The claim that mathematics (and logic) provide necessary knowledge—that is, truth—is based on the deductive method. Logical proof provides the warrant for the assertion of mathematical knowledge, as follows. First of all, the basic statements used in proofs are taken to be true. Mathematical axioms are assumed to be true, for the purposes of developing the system under consideration; mathematical definitions are true by fiat; and logical axioms are accepted as true. Second, the logical rules of inference preserve truth; that is, they allow nothing but truths to be deduced from truths. On the basis of these two facts, every statement in a deductive proof, including its conclusion, is true. Thus, since mathematical theorems are all established by means of deductive proofs, they are all necessary truths. This constitutes the basis of the claim of many philosophers that mathematical truths are infallible truths.

This absolutist view of mathematical knowledge is based on two types of assumptions: those of mathematics, concerning the assumption of axioms and definitions, and those of logic concerning the assumption of axioms, rules of inference, and the formal language and its syntax. These are local or micro-level assumptions. There is also the possibility of global or macro-level assumptions, such as whether logical deduction suffices to establish all mathematical truths, or whether it is always a safe method. I shall subsequently argue that each of these assumptions weakens the claim of infallibility for mathematical knowledge.

The absolutist view of mathematical knowledge encountered problems at the beginning of the twentieth century when a number of antinomies and contradictions were derived in mathematics (Kline 1980; Kneebone 1963; Wilder 1965).[13] In a series of publications Gottlob Frege ([1879] 1967, [1893] 1964) established by far the most rigorous formulation of mathematical logic known to that time, intended as a foundation for mathematical knowledge. Russell ([1902] 1967), however, was able to show that Frege's system was inconsistent. The problem lay in Frege's fifth basic law, which allows a set to be created from the extension of any concept, and for concepts or properties to be applied to this set (Furth 1964). Russell produced his well-known paradox by defining the property of "not being an element of itself." Frege's law allows the extension of this property to be regarded as a set. But then this set is an element of itself if, and only if, it is not; a contradiction. Frege's law could not be dropped without seriously weakening his system, and yet it could not be retained, on pain of contradiction.

Other paradoxes, antinomies, and contradictions emerged in the theories of sets and functions. Such findings have grave implications for the absolutist view of mathematical knowledge. For if mathematics is certain, and all its theorems are certain, how can contradictions (i.e., logical falsehoods) be among its theorems? Since there was no mistake about the appearance of these contradictions, something must be wrong in the foundations of mathematics. The outcome of this crisis was the development of a number of schools in the philosophy of mathematics whose aims were to account for the nature of mathematical knowledge and to reestablish its certainty. The three major schools are known as logicism, formalism, and constructivism (incorporating intuitionism). The tenets of these schools of thought were not fully developed until the twentieth century, but Körner (1960) shows that their philosophical roots can be traced back at least as far as Leibniz and Kant.[14]

Logicism

Logicism is the school of thought that regards pure mathematics as a part of logic. The major proponents of this view, following G. Leibniz's anticipation of it, are G. Frege ([1893] 1964), B. Russell (1919), A. N. Whitehead, and R. Carnap ([1931] 1964). The claims of logicism were most clearly and explicitly formulated by Russell. There are two claims.

1. All the concepts of mathematics can ultimately be reduced to logical concepts, provided that these are taken to include the concepts of set theory or some system of similar power, such as Russell's theory of types.

2. All mathematical truths can be proved from the axioms and rules of inference of logic alone.

The purpose of these claims is clear. If all of mathematics can be expressed in purely logical terms and proved from logical principles alone, then the necessity of mathematical knowledge can be reduced to that of logic. Logic was considered to provide a sure foundation for truth, apart from mistaken attempts, such as Frege's fifth law, that overextended logic. Thus if carried through, the logicist program would provide infallible logical foundations for mathematical knowledge, establishing the absolute validity of mathematics. As a youthful Russell expressed it, "I hoped sooner or later to arrive at a perfected mathematics which should leave no room for doubts" (Russell 1959, 28).

Extending the earlier work of Frege, Peano, and others, Whitehead and Russell (1910–13) were able to establish the first of the two claims by means of elaborate chains of definitions.[15] However logicism foundered on the second claim. Mathematics requires nonlogical rules of inference and axioms such as the principle of mathematical induction (Steiner 1975) and the axioms of infinity and choice.

> But although all logical (or mathematical) propositions can be expressed wholly in terms of logical constants together with variables, it is not the case that, conversely, all propositions that can be expressed in this way are logical. We have found so far a necessary but not a sufficient criterion of mathematical propositions. We have sufficiently defined the character of the primitive *ideas* in terms of which all the ideas of mathematics can be *defined*, but not of the primitive *propositions* from which all the propositions of mathematics can be *deduced*. This is a more difficult matter, as to which it is not yet known what the full answer is.
>
> We may take the axiom of infinity as an example of a proposition which, though it can be enunciated in logical terms, cannot be asserted by logic to be true. (Russell 1919, 202–3)

Russell's claim has been confirmed by subsequent developments. A number of important mathematical axioms are independent, and either the axiom or its negation can be adopted without inconsistency (Cohen 1966). This means that the axioms of mathematics are not eliminable in favor of those of logic. Mathematics is a science with a definite content, and mathematical theorems depend on an irreducible set of mathematical assumptions. Thus the second claim of logicism is refuted.

To overcome this problem Russell retreated to a weaker version of logicism, which has been called "if-thenism." This version obviates the need for mathematical axioms or assumptions by proving a mathematical theorem (T) as before, and then incorporating the conjunction of assumptions used in the proof (A) into an implication statement A→T as its antecedent (Carnap [1931] 1964). This artifice represents the view that mathematics is a hypothetico-deductive system, in which the consequences of assumed axiom sets are explored, without asserting their necessary truth.[16] So if-thenism represents a retreat from the absolutist position of logicism on mathematical knowledge. It is closer to conventionalism, which allows the assumptions of mathematics to be admitted as conventions, truths solely by fiat.

A problem with if-thenism is that many of the axiom sets used as the basis for modern mathematical theories are infinite, due to the use of axiom schemes and first-order logic. Thus both the induction axiom of Peano arithmetic and the axiom of separation of Zermelo-Fraenkel (ZF) set theory, for example, are such schemes (Bell and Machover 1977). Thus mathematical theorems in if-thenism are represented as logically proven implication statements with different finite subsets of axioms conjoined in their antecedents. This leads to misrepresentations such as equivalent results within an axiomatic theory no longer being equivalent, when their antecedents are of different logical power. This is not a refutation of if-thenism. It could be argued that the device is only for use in principle, not in practice, and so such difficulties are irrelevant.

However, the device employed still leads to failure on other grounds. For not all mathematical truths can be expressed in the above way as implication statements. Machover (1983) gives as an example the mathematical truth proved by Gentzen (1936), namely, "Peano Arithmetic is consistent," which is a proposition that cannot be expressed as an implication statement. Another counterexample is the Paris-Harrington proof of a version of Ramsey's theorem (Barwise 1977). This is true in the intended model of Peano arithmetic but not deducible from the axioms (see below). Hence it cannot be represented in the required if-then form. Thus the claim of if-thenism that it provides purely logical foundations for mathematical knowledge is refuted, just as it is with logicism.

A more general objection that holds irrespective of the validity of the two logicist claims also constitutes the major grounds for the rejection of formalism. This arises from Gödel's ([1931] 1967) first incompleteness theorem, which establishes that deductive proof is insufficient for demonstrating all mathematical truths. Hence the successful reduction of mathematical axioms to those of logic would still not suffice for the derivation of all mathematical truths. I shall return to this important result.

A further objection to the whole foundationalist enterprise of logicism, and not to its implementation, concerns the certainty and reliability of the underlying logical apparatus. This security depends on unexamined and, as will be argued, unjustified assumptions. Even if both of the logicist aims were met, the overall program could provide totally reliable foundations for mathematics only if logic were absolutely secure itself. This is assumed but not demonstrated by logicism.

The most important conclusion to be reached is that the logicist program of reducing the necessity of mathematical knowledge to that of logic failed in principle. Logic cannot provide a certain foundation for mathematical knowledge. Irrespective of the security of logic itself, the reliability of mathematical knowledge cannot be reduced to that of pure logic.

Of course, as a mathematical research program in the foundations of mathematics, logicism led to interesting and powerful theories and results. To fulfill the first of its claims alone was a major achievement for modern mathematics. Thus from a mathematical perspective, logicism was very fruitful and led to important successes. The logical definition of many mathematical concepts, Russell's theory of types, the explication of propositional and first-order logic, the early development of proof theory, all of these are among the successes of logicism. But as a philosophy of mathematics, and in particular, as an epistemology seeking to provide mathematical knowledge with an absolute foundation, logicism is without question a failure.

Formalism

In popular terms, formalism is the view that mathematics is a meaningless formal game played with marks on paper, following rules. Traces of a formalist view of mathematics can be found in the writings of Bishop Berkeley ([1710] 1962), but the major proponents of formalism are David Hilbert (1964), early J. von Neumann ([1931] 1964), and H. Curry (1951). Hilbert's formalist program aimed to translate mathematics into uninterpreted formal systems. These were to be shown to be adequate for representing all of mathematics by the creation of a restricted but meaningful ("finitary") metamathematics. Metamathematical proofs would show that the formal counterparts of all mathematical truths could be derived in formal mathematical systems.[17] They would also show, by means of consistency proofs, that the formal systems were safe for representing mathematics.

The goal of my theory is to establish once and for all the certitude of mathematical methods. (Hilbert 1964, 135)

The formalist thesis comprises two claims:

1. Pure mathematics can be expressed as uninterpreted formal systems in which the truths of mathematics are represented by formal theorems.

2. The safety of these formal systems can be demonstrated in terms of their freedom from inconsistency, by means of metamathematics.

These are very precise claims. However, Kurt Gödel's incompleteness theorems (Gödel [1931] 1967) showed that the program could not be fulfilled. His first theorem showed that not even all the truths of arithmetic can be derived from Peano's axioms (or any larger recursive axiom set). This proof-theoretic result has since been exemplified in mathematics by Paris and Harrington, whose version of Ramsey's theorem is true but not provable in Peano arithmetic (Barwise 1977). Thus the first claim of formalism is refuted in a profound way. It is not possible to translate nontrivial axiomatic theories into formal systems, so that the truths of mathematics are represented by formal theorems.

The second incompleteness theorem showed that in the desired cases consistency proofs require a metamathematics more powerful than the system to be safeguarded; thus there is no safeguard at all. For example, to prove the consistency of Peano arithmetic requires all the axioms of that system and further assumptions, such as the principle of transfinite induction over countable ordinals (Gentzen 1936). Thus it is not possible to prove the consistency of most formal systems of mathematics without, in effect, assuming it. In terms of fulfilling its program, formalism must be regarded as a failure.

The formalist program, had it been successful, would have provided support for an absolutist view of mathematical truth. For formal proof, based in consistent formal mathematical systems, would have provided a touchstone for mathematical truth. However, it can be seen that both the claims of formalism have been refuted. Not all the truths of mathematics can be represented as theorems in formal systems, and furthermore, the systems themselves cannot be guaranteed safe.

Since the refutation of Hilbert's formalist program by Gödel's results, formalists, like the logicists before them, have retreated to a number of weaker positions. Curry (1951), for example, relinquishes the second claim of formalism but maintains a version of the first claim to the effect that mathematics is the science of formal systems. But this position is insupportable as a philosophy of mathematics, for formal systems capture only a proper subset of mathematical knowledge, omitting constructive or recursive mathematics.

Although formalism has been refuted in this way, a number of mathematicians still regard themselves as formalists. For example A. Robinson and P. J. Cohen have written in this vein, as has Henle (1991) more recently. However, few if any try to maintain the refuted foundationalist or epistemological claims of formalism. More often it is the anti-realist ontological position of formalism that commands their support.

Quine (1953a) and Putnam (1972) point out the strong parallel between formalism and nominalism, which latter position originates in the medieval thought of the Schoolmen. Nominalism focuses on the symbolic function of language and, like formalism, denies that it denotes real universals or abstract entities. Thus although there is an illuminating analogy here, it is more relevant to ontological matters than those of epistemology.

Formalism, and related research in the foundations mathematics, can be judged from two perspectives, philosophical and mathematical. Philosophically, however interesting and important it might be historically, formalism is a failed attempt to provide mathematical knowledge with absolute foundations. Particularly in epistemological terms, the formalist program has been shown to be impossible.

In mathematical terms, the program has led to the development and clarification of axiomatic systems, especially set theory, proof theory, and metamathematics, and has contributed to the development of recursion theory, Turing machines, the lambda calculus, and other aspects of formal mathematics vital for the theory of computation. These indicate some of the powerful and important mathematical outcomes stemming at least in part from formalism. Thus mathematically, formalism was a very successful research program.

Constructivism

The constructivist strand in the philosophy of mathematics can be traced back at least as far as Kant and Kronecker (Körner 1960). Kant ([1781] 1961, [1783] 1950), developed an elaborate system of philosophy based on a number of universal mind-given categories of thought, including space and time. He regarded the knowledge of geometry and number as arising from the unfolding of our intuition within these two categories. This gives rise to what he termed the synthetic *a priori* truths of Euclidean geometry and number theory. After Kant's death, the advent of non-Euclidean geometries led many of his followers to abandon the notion that Euclidean geometry consists of synthetic *a priori* truths, derived from the pure intuition of space. However the modern intuitionists such as Brouwer still maintain the other plank of Kant's doctrine. That is, the truths of number are synthetic *a priori* and stem from our basic intuition of time. The attraction of this view is that it anchors mathematical knowledge, at least that of arithmetic, in intuition, guaranteeing its personally meaningful nature.

Against this background, the constructivist program is one of reconstructing mathematical knowledge (and reforming mathematical practice) in order to safeguard it from loss of meaning, and from contradiction. To this end, constructivists reject nonconstructive arguments such as Cantor's proof that the real numbers are uncountable, existence proofs by *reductio ad absurdum*, and the logical laws of double negation and the excluded middle.[18] For these results and modes of reasoning take mathematics beyond what can be constructed intuitively.

The best known constructivists are the intuitionists L. E. J. Brouwer ([1913] 1964) and A. Heyting ([1931] 1964, 1956). More recently the mathematician E. Bishop (1967) carried the constructivist program a long way forward by reconstructing a substantial portion of analysis by constructive means. Today various forms of constructivism still flourish, as in the work of the philosophical intuitionist M. Dummett (1973, 1977). Constructivism includes a whole range of different views, from the ultra-intuitionists (A. Yessenin-Volpin 1980), via what may be termed strict philosophical intuitionists (L. E. J. Brouwer), middle-of-the-road intuitionists (A. Heyting and early H. Weyl), modern logical intuitionists (A. Troelstra) to a range of more-or-less liberal constructivists including E. Bishop, L. Kalmar, G. Kreisel, P. Lorenzen, and P. Martin-Löf. Currently, "strict finitism," which may be classified as a constructivist position, still has a small but vocal body of supporters. Indeed Rotman (1993) recently offered a new version of "strict finitism" based on the limitations of the human body in coping with mathematical language and semiosis.

These mathematicians share the view that classical mathematics may be unsafe and that it needs to be rebuilt by "constructive" methods and reasoning. Constructivists claim that both mathematical truths and the existence of mathematical objects must be established by constructive methods alone. This means that what are needed to establish truth or existence are mathematical constructions, as opposed to indirect methods, particularly those relying on proof by contradiction. For constructivists, knowledge must be established through constructive proofs, based on restricted constructivist logic; and the meaning of mathematical terms and objects consists of the formal procedures by which they are constructed.

Although some constructivists maintain that mathematics is the study of constructive processes performed with pencil and paper, the stricter view of the Brouwerian intuitionists is that mathematics takes place primarily in the mind and that written mathematics is secondary. One consequence of this is that Brouwer regards all axiomatizations of intuitionistic logic to be incomplete. Reflection can always uncover further intuitively true axioms of intuitionistic logic, and so it can never be regarded as being in final form. Other more liberal intuitionists, such as Kalmar, may reject the notion that written mathematics is but a poor reflection of "real" intuitionist mathematics but nevertheless accept that intuition may give rise to further axioms. Because of this view that the basis and the body of mathematical knowledge both continue to develop through human creative activity intuitionism and related forms of constructivism may be called "progressive absolutism" (after Confrey 1981).

Intuitionism represents the most fully formulated constructivist philosophy of mathematics. It is possible to distinguish two separable claims of intuitionism, which Dummett terms the positive and the negative theses.

The positive one is to the effect that the intuitionistic way of construing mathematical notions and logical operations is a coherent and legitimate one, that intuitionistic mathematics forms an intelligible body of theory. The negative thesis is to the effect that the classical way of construing mathematical notions and logical operations is incoherent and illegitimate, that classical mathematics, while containing, in distorted form, much of value, is, nevertheless, as it stands unintelligible. (Dummett 1977, 360)

In the restricted areas where there are both classical and constructivist proofs of a result, the latter is often preferable as more informative. Whereas a classical existence proof may merely demonstrate the logical necessity of existence, a constructive existence proof shows how to construct the mathematical object whose existence is asserted. This lends strength to the positive thesis, from a mathematical point of view.

However, Dummett's version of the positive thesis of intuitionism does not capture its foundationalism, which is its most important epistemological feature. The intuitionist program of Brouwer, Heyting, and others explicitly aims to offer new and secure foundations to overcome logical antinomies and paradoxes in mathematics and to prevent their ever arising again in some new form. Thus the positive thesis of intuitionism as expressed by Brouwer and Heyting claims more than just coherence, legitimacy, and intelligibility. It also claims to provide security and certainty. This epistemological claim is flawed. The intuitionists claim to provide a certain foundation for their version of mathematical truth by deriving it from intuitively necessary axioms, using intuitively safe methods of proof. This view bases mathematical knowledge exclusively on subjective belief. But absolute truth (which the intuitionists claim to provide) cannot be based on subjective belief alone. Belief is necessary but far from sufficient to guarantee knowledge. Justification is also needed.

Intuitionism sacrificed large parts of mathematics in exchange for the soothing reassurance that what remained was justified by our "primordial intuition" (ur-intuition). But intuition is subjective, and not intersubjective enough to prevent intuitionists from differing about what their "primordial intuitions" should enshrine as the basis of mathematics. (Kalmar 1967, 190)

In intuitionism basic intuition is supposed to supply the self-evidently true axioms from which mathematical knowledge (or at least the intuitionistic version of it) is derived and on which its certainty rests. But, as Kalmar says, basic intuition does not give rise to a consensus as to what these axioms are. They are subjectively based and vary with the subject. This is a major weakness and represents a failure of the foundationalist program of intuitionism and, more generally, of constructivism.

Even if the intuitionists were unanimous about their intuitions, a case would still need to be made as to why those shared beliefs should be taken as necessary. Indeed, if they all did happen to be the same, all one could claim is coincidence. To claim that these shared intuitions coincided because the transcendental truth of mathematical knowledge standardizes intuition would be to smuggle in absolutism by the back door, not to establish it. Unjustified belief cannot constitute knowledge no matter how many share it. Some warrant, justification, or other public touchstone of truth is essential to turn belief into knowledge.

Thus the positive thesis of intuitionism does not provide a necessary foundation for even the restricted body of mathematical knowledge put forward by the intuitionists. This criticism extends to other forms of constructivism that also claim to base constructive mathematical truth on a foundation of self-evident constructivist assumptions. Intuitionism and, more generally, constructivism therefore fail to provide firm foundations for mathematical knowledge.

The negative thesis is also problematic, since intuitionism not only fails to account for the substantial body of nonconstructive classical mathematics, but also denies its legitimacy and intelligibility. But the constructivists have evidently *not* succeeded in demonstrating that there are inescapable problems facing classical mathematics, nor that it is incoherent and illegitimate, let alone unintelligible. The intelligibility of classical mathematics is demonstrated by its widespread acceptance and its near exponential growth this century, while coexisting with constructivism. Both pure and applied classical mathematics have gone from strength to strength since the constructivist program was proposed. Evidently, far from being unintelligible, it is intelligible to an increasing number of professional mathematicians.

Classical mathematics differs from constructivist mathematics in the assumptions on which it is based, so some of the results of intuitionistic mathematics are inconsistent with those of classical mathematics. Thus, for example, the intuitionistic real number continuum is countable. This contradicts the classical result, not because there is an inherent contradiction, but because the definition of real numbers is different. Constructivist notions often have a different meaning from the corresponding classical notions. Both types of mathematics are intelligible. Indeed, from a classical perspective, both are intertranslatable.[19]

Therefore the negative thesis of intuitionism cannot be sustained and is rejected for lack of justification. It leads to the unwarranted rejection of accepted mathematical knowledge, analogous to a type I error in statistics (the rejection of valid knowledge).

Constructivist mathematics may legitimately be regarded as a live and fruitful area of mathematics. Constructivist perspectives have contributed to proof theory, computation theory, and constructive set theory, among other branches of mathematics. The search for constructive formulations and proofs of classical results continues. Thus, in mathematical terms, constructivism is alive and well. Philosophers such as Dummett also continue to press the positive thesis of intuitionism, namely, that it offers a coherent and legitimate way of construing mathematical notions and logical operations. However as a philosophy of mathematics, and in particular as a foundationalist epistemology, constructivism has failed. The positing of subjective beliefs, both for the axiomatic basis of mathematics, and for logic itself, comes nowhere near providing the infallible foundation for mathematics required by absolutism. Like logicism and formalism before it, constructivism as an absolutist philosophy of mathematics has failed.

A CRITIQUE OF ABSOLUTISM

I have argued that a number of absolutist philosophies of mathematics have failed to establish the logical necessity of mathematical knowledge. Logicism, formalism, and intuitionism each attempt to provide a firm foundation for mathematical truth by deriving it by mathematical proof from a restricted but secure realm of truth. Each lays down what is intended to be a secure base of absolute truth: the axioms of logic; the intuitively certain principles of metamathematics; and intuitively self-evident axioms and rules, for the logicists, formalists, and intuitionists, respectively. Each of these foundations is assumed without demonstration, leaving them open to challenge and doubt. Each of the schools employs deductive logic to demonstrate the truth of the theorems of mathematics. Consequently these three schools of thought fail to establish the absolute validity of mathematical truth. For deductive logic can only transmit truth, not inject it, and the conclusion of a logical proof is no more certain than the weakest premise.

The fact that three schools of thought in the philosophy of mathematics have failed to establish the infallibility of mathematical knowledge does not settle the general issue. It might still be possible in principle for other as yet unconsidered grounds to be found for asserting the certainty of mathematical truth. The possibility of absolute truth in mathematics has not yet been closed off by the discussion presented to this point.[20] However I shall also deny this possibility.

The target of my critique is any attempt to establish absolutism by means of epistemological *foundationalism*. This term is used to describe a number of different perspectives in which belief or knowledge is divided into two parts, "foundation" and "superstructure," and in which the latter depends on the former for its justification, and not vice versa (Alston 1992). The interpretation of foundationalism I adopt resembles that of Descartes, namely, it entails the reconstruction of mathematical knowledge in terms of an absolute foundation and a superstructure infallibly derived from it. My critique is twofold. First, to attack the justificatory basis of the foundation of mathematical knowledge. Second, to attack the infallibility of the derivation of the superstructure from it. This second argument also addresses (critiques) the position derived by withdrawing the epistemological assumptions concerning the truth of the foundation.

First, there is the justificatory basis of the foundation of mathematical knowledge to consider. Lakatos (1978b), developing Popper's (1959, 1979) general epistemological argument, shows that the quest for certainty in mathematics leads inevitably to a vicious cycle. Any mathematical system depends on a set of assumptions, and trying to establish their certainty by proving them leads to infinite regression. There is no way of discharging the assumptions. Without proof, the assumptions remain fallible beliefs, not necessary knowledge. All that can be done is to minimize them, to get a reduced set of axioms, which have to be accepted without proof, thus breaking the vicious circle at the cost of forfeiting certainty. The only alternative is to replace one set of assumptions by another. But replacement merely starts off a further circuit of the vicious cycle. The reduced set of axioms can be dispensed with only by replacing it with assumptions of at least the same strength. Thus the certainty of mathematics cannot be established without making assumptions; this thereby fails to result in absolute certainty.

This argument must be directed at the whole body of mathematical knowledge, and it is not framed for a single formal system or language. Many attempts to provide a foundation for a restricted part of mathematics manage to reduce assumptions in that formal system or language. What is done in such a case is to push some or all of the basic assumptions into the metalanguage, as was the formalists' explicit strategy. Somewhere there must remain a kernel of assumptions that introduces truth into the system, which truth deduction transmits to the theorems of the system. As Lakatos says,

> we have to admit that *meta-mathematics does not stop the infinite regress in proofs which now reappears in the infinite hierarchy of ever richer meta-theories.* (Lakatos 1978c, 22, original emphasis).[21]

Mathematical truth ultimately depends on an irreducible set of assumptions, which are adopted without demonstration. But to qualify as true knowledge, the assumptions require a warrant for their assertion. I wish to claim that there is no valid warrant for mathematical knowledge other than demonstration or proof. Consider what other valid warrants there could be. They would have to provide other grounds for asserting that mathematical statements are true. The principal accounts of truth are the correspondence theory of truth, the coherence theory of truth (Woozley 1949), the pragmatic theory of truth (Dewey 1938), and truth as convention (Quine 1949; Quinton 1963).[22]

The coherence and pragmatic theories of truth do not claim that truth can be warranted absolutely, and so they need not be considered. The correspondence theory can be interpreted either empirically or nonempirically to say that basic mathematical truths describe true states of affairs either in the world or in some abstract realm. But then the truths of mathematics must be justified empirically or intuitively, given that proof is ruled out, and neither grounds serve as warrants for certain knowledge.

The conventional theory of truth asserts that basic mathematical statements are true by virtue of the meanings of the terms therein. But the fact that the axioms express what we want or believe terms to mean does not absolve us from having to assume them, even if we simply stipulate them by *fiat*. Rather it is an admission that we simply have to assume certain basic propositions. Beyond this, to say that complex axioms such as those of Zermelo-Fraenkel set theory are true by virtue of the meanings of the constituent terms is not supportable. Maddy (1984) gives an account of set-theoretic axioms in current use that by no stretch of the imagination are considered true. These axioms must be regarded instead as implicit definitions of their constituent terms, and it is evident that they must be assumed in order to proceed with set theory.

It is worth mentioning again the view that some mathematical assumptions are self-evident, that they are given by intuition or some form of immediate access to the (mathematical) objects known. In addition to the problems of subjectivity mentioned above in the context of intuitionism, there are also those of cultural relativism. Namely, those assumptions that the community of mathematicians regard as self-evident in one era often become the focus of intense scrutiny and doubt in another era (e.g., the axioms of geometry before and after Kant, and the axioms of arithmetic before and after Peano). Self-evidence does not seem to offer a viable basis for justifying the propositions involved, let alone the overall foundations of mathematical knowledge. I shall return to this issue in discussing Platonism.

Therefore, since there is no valid warrant for mathematical knowledge other than proof, mathematical knowledge must depend on assumptions. It follows that these assumptions have the status of beliefs, not knowledge; must remain open to challenge and doubt; and are eternally corrigible.

This is the central argument against the possibility of certain knowledge in mathematics. It directly contradicts the absolutist claims of the foundationalist schools of thought. It is considered to be an unanswerable refutation of absolutism by a number of authors, including the following.

[T]he absolute truth point of view must be discarded. The "facts" of any branch of pure mathematics must be recognised as being assumptions (postulates or axioms), or definitions or theorems . . . The most that can be claimed is that if the postulates are true and the definitions are accepted, and if the methods of reasoning are sound, then the theorems are true. In other words we arrive at a concept of relative truth (of theorems in relation to postulates, definitions, and logical reasoning) to replace the absolute truth point of view. (Stabler 1953, 24)

What we have called pure mathematics is therefore a hypothetico-deductive system. Its axioms serve as hypotheses or assumptions, which are entertained or considered for the propositions they imply. (Cohen and Nagel 1963, 133)

[W]e can only describe arithmetic, namely, find its rules, not give a basis for them. Such a basis could not satisfy us, for the very reason that it must end sometime and then refer to something which can no longer be founded. Only the convention is the ultimate. Anything that looks like a foundation is, strictly speaking, already adulterated and must not satisfy us. (Waismann 1951, 122)

Statements or propositions or theories may be formulated in assertions which may be true and their truth may be reduced, by way of derivations to that of primitive propositions. The attempt to establish (rather than reduce) by these means their truth leads to an infinite regress. (Popper 1979, 124, extract from table)

[A]ny foundation of . . . mathematics . . . is in a certain fashion circular. That is, there always remain presuppositions which must be accepted on faith or intuition without being themselves founded (Church 1962, 184).

I consider this to be a decisive criticism of the absolutist view of mathematics. However, it is possible to accept it without adopting a fallibilist philosophy of mathematics. For it is possible, indeed widespread, to accept a form of hypothetico-deductivism that acknowledges the tentative nature of the assumptions on which mathematics rests but that denies the corrigibility of mathematics and asserts the possibility of eliminating deep-seated error from it. Such a position views axioms simply as hypotheses from which the theorems of mathematics are logically deduced, and relative to which the theorems are certain. In other words, although the axioms of mathematics are tentative, logic and the use of logic to derive theorems from the axioms guarantee a secure development of mathematics, albeit from an assumed basis. This weakened form of the absolutist position resembles Russell's "if-thenism" in its strategy of adopting axioms without either proof or cost to the system's security. It should be acknowledged that it represents a weakened form of absolutism, one that no longer asserts the truth of mathematical knowledge (at least not its truth$_1$ or truth$_3$) but instead asserts the infallible correctness of its proofs.

The Fallibilist Critique of Absolutism

The hypothetico-deductive version of absolutism suffers from further major weaknesses. These leave it open to a fallibilist critique, leading, in my view, to a refutation of this weakened form of absolutism.

One central problem arises from the underlying logic on which mathematical proof rests. The establishment of mathematical theorems, that is, their deduction from axiom sets, requires further assumptions, namely, those of the axioms and rules of inference of logic itself. These are nontrivial and non-eliminable assumptions, and the above argument of the ultimate irreducibility of assumptions on pain of a vicious cycle applies equally to logic. Thus mathematical truth as represented by theorems depends on essential logical as well as mathematical assumptions. This dependence increases the set of assumptions on which mathematical knowledge rests, and these cannot be neutralized by the "if-thenist" strategy. Loading all logical and mathematical assumptions into the "hypothetico" part would leave no basis for the "deductive" part of the method, in which logic provides the canons of correct inference. The basis for deductive logic must simply be assumed. But any such assumptions without firm foundations are fallible.

A further presumption of an absolutist view is that mathematics is fundamentally free from error. For an inconsistency in a mathematical system immediately refutes any claims to truth and absolute knowledge. But consistency cannot be demonstrated. Mathematics consists of theories (e.g., group theory, category theory, and Zermelo-Fraenkel set theory) that are studied within mathematical systems, based on sets of assumptions (axioms). According to Gödel's ([1931] 1967) second incompleteness theorem, it is not possible to establish that such mathematical systems are safe (i.e., consistent). For any but trivial systems simpler than Peano arithmetic, a consistency proof requires additional assumptions beyond those of the system to be safeguarded itself. The consistency of a stronger system must be assumed in order to demonstrate that of a weaker. Therefore none but the most trivial mathematical systems can be known to be secure, and the possibility of error and inconsistency must always remain. Belief in the safety of mathematics must be based either on empirical grounds (no contradictions have yet been found in our current mathematical systems) or on faith, neither providing the certain basis or guaranteed safety that absolutism requires.

There are further problems attendant on the use of proof as a basis for certainty in mathematics. Nothing but a fully formal deductive proof can serve as a warrant for certainty in mathematics. But such proofs scarcely exist, and only for trivial results. Thus absolutism requires the recasting of informal mathematics into formal deductive systems, and recasting depends on the following further assumptions. Each of them, it is argued, is unwarranted.

Assumption A. All or the vast majority of mathematical proofs prove their results absolutely, beyond any real doubt.

Critique. The proofs that mathematicians publish are very commonly flawed and are by no means wholly reliable. Almost every mathematical text or monograph published contains errors and mistakes, some of substance (Davis 1972). Although in modern times there are more precise standards of rigor, mechanical aids to proof reading and other uses of computing in mathematics, the incidence of error is if anything increasing (De Millo, Lipton, and Perlis 1986). Furthermore, widespread acceptance and the passage of time by no means suffice to guarantee the reliability of mathematical knowledge. Even after twenty, thirty, forty, or more years, modern mathematical results are regularly found to be fundamentally flawed and rejected (Davis 1972; Tymoczko 1986b). The claim that all or most mathematical proofs prove their results absolutely, beyond any doubt, is simply false, empirically falsified.

If published proofs are unreliable, perhaps formalizing them would provide absolutely certain mathematical knowledge.

Assumption B. The proofs that mathematicians publish as warrants for asserting theorems can, in principle, be translated into fully rigorous formal proofs.

Critique. First of all, informal proofs are commonly flawed and are far from reliable or complete. Translating any one of them into fully rigorous formal proof is a major, nonmechanical task. It requires human ingenuity to bridge gaps and to remedy errors, and its success cannot be predicted.[23]

Second, the total formalization of mathematics is at best unlikely to be carried out and at worst, impossible. New mathematical results are being published faster than existing ones can ever be formalized, and there is no indication that any agency is planning such a program, which would dwarf the human genome project. Therefore the claim that informal proofs can be translated into formal proofs "in principle" has no basis beyond being an article of faith and is no grounds for certainty. For the whole of mathematics, total rigor is an unattained and unattainable ideal and not a practical reality.

Third, rigor is not a timeless ideal, because standards of rigor change historically, and it can be assumed that they will continue to evolve (as the contributors to Gillies 1992 illustrate). Therefore the achievement of full rigorization and hence total certainty could never be claimed for mathematical proofs, *even if the preceding criticisms were to be discounted.*

If today's standards of rigor were accepted as adequate, and today's body of knowledge was successfully formalized, would this provide a body of indubitable mathematical truth?

Assumption C. Rigorous formal proofs can be checked for correctness.

Critique. There now exist humanly uncheckable informal proofs of mathematical results, such as the Appel-Haken proof of the four-color theorem (Tymoczko 1979); the classification of finite simple groups (Davis and Hersh 1980); Lam, Thiel, and Swiercz's proof of the nonexistence of a projective plane of order 10 (Sangalli 1990); and so on. These informal proofs are already too long for any mathematician to check. Translated into fully rigorous formal proofs they would be much longer. If they cannot possibly be surveyed by a mathematician, they cannot be regarded as absolutely correct (Azzouni 1994). The existence of such proofs and their acceptance by the mathematical community further weakens the claims of absolutism.

If such proofs were to be checked by a computers, instead of humans, further problems would arise. No guarantees could be given that the software and hardware were designed absolutely flawlessly, nor that the software ran correctly. Given the complexity of computers and software these can no more be checked by a single person than can a large proof. Furthermore, such checks involve an irreducible empirical element (MacKenzie 1993). Consequently, any claim of absolute certainty must be relinquished (Tymoczko 1979).

If mathematical proofs can be improved by formalizing them, if not made absolutely safe, cannot the formalization of all mathematical theories remove *most* grounds for doubt?

Assumption D. Mathematical theories can be validly translated into formal axiom sets.

Critique. The formalization of intuitive mathematical theories in the past hundred years (e.g., mathematical logic, number theory, set theory, analysis) has led to unanticipated deep problems, as the concepts and proofs come under ever more piercing scrutiny, during attempts to explicate and reconstruct them. Even if these theories were regarded as adequately formalized, which they are not, the satisfactory formalization of the rest of mathematics cannot be assumed to be unproblematic. It is not possible to assert with certainty that it can be carried out validly. It is part of an ongoing and progressive research program.

If this formalization and rigorization of mathematical knowledge were carried out, would it justify an absolutist view if mathematics as absolutely certain?

Assumption E. The consistency of the representations of the bases of mathematical theories by formal axiom sets can be checked and guaranteed.

Critique. This assumption contradicts Gödel's second incompleteness theorem, for no recursive set of axioms with at least the power of Peano arithmetic can demonstrate its own consistency. Nor does any other finitistic argument exist to prove the consistency of such a system (Gödel 1967). Thus to assume the consistency of formal mathematical systems adds significantly to the burden of assumptions underpinning mathematical knowledge. Thus there are no *absolute* guarantees of safety.[24]

Is not this criticism nitpicking when mathematics is acknowledged to be the most certain knowledge known to humankind and which is all the while progressing and receiving stronger support amounting to practical or moral certainty?

Assumption F. Although the warrants of mathematical knowledge are not ultimate, they are all the while progressing in rigor toward certainty.

Critique. Mathematical knowledge may be growing and progressing, but any grounds for accepting that this progress is monotonic or converging to a limit is historical, that is, empirical. Thus even if it were wholly confirmatory, it would not guarantee certainty. However the historical data in fact contradict this. The history of mathematics exhibits unpredicted changes, reverses, ruptures, and revolutions just as complex as biological evolution and equally without teleology (Gillies 1992). A further problem is revealed by Popper's (1972) attempt to define the concept of verisimilitude in order to claim that scientific progress can be understood as increasing verisimilitude or closeness to the truth. The philosophy of science community's critique showed that this is an incoherent concept which cannot be made watertight or precise, and this critique applies equally to attempts to use it in mathematics (Anderson 1978).

The criticisms offered above indicate the problems in trying to transmit the assumed truth of mathematical assumptions to the rest of mathematical knowledge by means of deductive proof, and in establishing the reliability of the overall method. I have offered multiple arguments in criticism of absolutism in the philosophy of mathematics. I consider this to be a powerful and persistent doctrine, one which has remained alive for many years. Elsewhere I have speculated that this is due to its ideological rather than purely philosophical significance (Ernest 1991).

FALLIBILISM

To the extent that the above critique is persuasive, it leads to the acceptance of the opposing fallibilist view of mathematical knowledge. This is the view that mathematical truth is fallible and corrigible, and can never be regarded as beyond revision and correction. Support for the fallibilist viewpoint is broader than is sometimes supposed.

In his paper "A Renaissance of Empiricism in the Philosophy of Mathematics," Lakatos quotes from the later works of Russell, Fraenkel, Carnap, Weyl, von Neumann, Bernays, Church, Gödel, Quine, Rosser, Curry, Mostowski, and Kalmar (a list that includes many of the key logicians and researchers in the foundations of mathematics of the twentieth century) to demonstrate their common view concerning what Carnap terms "the impossibility of complete certainty" in mathematics (Lakatos 1978c, 25). Lakatos also indicates the widespread agreement that mathematical knowledge has some kind of an empirical basis, *contra* absolutism.

Although he expresses it pessimistically, Kline reaches a similar conclusion.

> It is now apparent that the concept of a universally accepted, infallible body of reasoning—the majestic mathematics of 1800 and the pride of man—is a grand illusion. Uncertainty and doubt concerning the future of mathematics have replaced the certainties and complacency of the past . . . The present state of mathematics is a mockery of the hitherto deep-rooted and widely reputed truth and logical perfection of mathematics. (Kline 1980, 6)

Popper promoted fallibilism in the philosophy of science for more than fifty years and is quite unequivocal in his epistemology.

> There are no authoritative sources of knowledge, and no "source" is particularly reliable. Everything is welcome as a source of inspiration, including "intuition" . . . But nothing is secure, and we are all fallible. (Popper 1979, 134)

An important philosopher who accepts the fallibility of mathematical knowledge is Wittgenstein.

> I should like to say that where surveyability is not present, i.e., where there is room for a doubt whether what we have really is the result of this substitution, the *proof* is destroyed. And not in some silly and unimportant way that has nothing to do with the *nature* of proof.
> Or: logic as the foundation of mathematics does not work, and to shew this it is enough that the cogency of logical proof stand and falls with its geometrical cogency . . .
> The logical certainty of proofs—I want to say—does not extend beyond their geometrical certainty. (Wittgenstein 1978, 174–75)

The philosopher of mathematics who has done the most to promote fallibilism is Imre Lakatos.

> A Euclidean theory may be claimed to be true; a Quasi-empirical theory—at best—to be well-corroborated, but always conjectural. Also, in a Euclidean theory the true basic statements at the "top" of the deductive system (usually called "axioms") *prove*, as it were, the rest of the system; in a Quasi-empirical theory the (true) basic statements are *explained* by the rest of the system (Lakatos 1978b, 28–29)
>
> Mathematics is Quasi-empirical (Lakatos 1978b, 30)

Polanyi has been concerned to bring the personal back into epistemology and the philosophy of science. He too concludes that mathematics is fallible.

> Tautologies are necessarily true, but mathematics is not. We cannot tell whether the axioms of arithmetic are consistent; and if they are not, any particular theorem of arithmetic may be false. Therefore these theorems are not tautologies. They are and must always remain tentative, while a tautology is an incontrovertible truism . . .
> . . . [T]he mathematician feels compelled to accept mathematics as true, even though he is today deprived of the belief in its logical necessity and doomed to admit forever the conceivable possibility that its whole fabric may suddenly collapse by revealing a decisive self-contradiction. (Polanyi 1958, 189)

Kitcher is part of a "maverick" tradition which rejects absolutism from the outset, and he proposes a quasi-empirical philosophy of mathematics instead.

> The doctrine that mathematical knowledge is *a priori, mathematical apriorism,* has been articulated many different ways during the course of reflection about mathematics . . . [I] offer a picture of mathematical knowledge which rejects mathematical apriorism . . . the alternative to mathematical apriorism—*mathematical empiricism*—has never been given a detailed articulation. (Kitcher 1984, 3–4)

The philosopher Hilary Putnam, also a practicing mathematician, is a critic of absolutism.

[M]athematical knowledge resembles *empirical* knowledge—that is, the criterion of truth in mathematics just as much as in physics is success of our ideas in practice, and that mathematical knowledge is corrigible and not absolute. (Putnam 1975, 51)

Reuben Hersh is a mathematician and philosopher of mathematics who has promoted fallibilism and led the calls for the reconceptualization of the philosophy of mathematics.

It is reasonable to propose a new task for mathematical philosophy: not to seek indubitable truth but to give an account of mathematical knowledge as it really is—fallible, corrigible, tentative and evolving, as is every other kind of human knowledge. (Hersh 1979, 43)

A final quotation is from Lakatos.

Why not honestly admit mathematical fallibility, and try to defend the dignity of fallible knowledge from cynical scepticism, rather than delude ourselves that we shall be able to mend invisibly the latest tear in the fabric of our "ultimate" intuitions. (Lakatos 1962, 184)

These quotations show that there is a widespread dissatisfaction with absolutism in the philosophy of mathematics, and an endorsement of fallibilism instead.

CONCLUSION

I have been concerned to criticize the absolutist view of mathematical knowledge and endorse fallibilism. A rejection of absolutism should not be seen as the banishment of mathematics from the "Garden of Eden,"[25] the realm of truth and certainty. This "loss of certainty" (Kline 1980) does not represent a loss of knowledge. In modern physics, general relativity theory requires relinquishing absolute, universal frames of reference in favor of a relativistic perspective. In quantum theory, Heisenberg's uncertainty principle means that the notions of precisely determined measurements of position and momentum for particles also has had to be given up.[26] But this does not represent the loss of knowledge of absolute frames and certainty. Instead it represents the growth of knowledge, bringing with it a realization of the limits of what can be known, given present theories. Relativity and uncertainty in physics represent major advances in knowledge which take humanity to the limits of what can be known (while the theories are retained).

Analogously in mathematics, with increased knowledge of the foundations of mathematics it appears to many that the absolutist view is an idealization, more a myth than a reality. To fallibilists, this represents an advance in knowledge, not a retreat from past certainty. According to this perspective, the absolutist Garden of Eden was nothing but a fool's paradise.

NOTES

1. Aleister Crowley ([1929] 1991), the celebrated black magician, even used the Euclidean form of definition—postulate—theorems for his work *Magick in Theory and Practice* to lend it a spurious authority.

2. Naturally more sophisticated accounts are available; such accounts include Goldman 1980, which is drawn upon by Kitcher (1984) in his philosophy of mathematics. Such accounts are motivated by the Gettier problem that in certain cases having justified true belief of a proposition does not amount to having knowledge of the proposition (Moser 1992; Everitt and Fisher 1995). This occurs when the proposition believed is true, but there is a mismatch in the justification supporting the proposition but not the belief in it. E.g., if a student correctly calculates and believes that 1000 × 1000 = 1,000,000 in base 2 arithmetic, but has no idea what base 2 arithmetic is and just regards the proposition and calculation as denary, then there is a correct justification of a true belief, since binary and denary arithmetic multiplications are identical for powers of the base; but the justification is misunderstood by the believer and does not warrant declaring the belief as knowledge.

3. Kant ([1783] 1950) also offers a second definition of analyticity: analytic statements are 'explicative' or tautologies, adding nothing to the content of knowledge. In such a statement the idea of the predicate is already contained in that of the subject. This is conceptually different from the first definition.

4. The discussion is restricted to finitary logics and proofs, since I regard these as having epistemological primacy. Infinitary logic presupposes a substantial part of mathematics for its very formulation.

5. The fact that virtually all proofs assume earlier theorems *does* have epistemological significance. It means that items of mathematical knowledge are contextually situated within mathematical theories that include a corpus of antecedent theorems and proofs, as well as axioms, definitions, and rules.

6. See below: Assumption B on page 29, and chapter 6 note 13.

7. For technical details see Ernest 1991, 5–6. The proof is: $x + sy = s(x + y)$, $1 + sy = s(1 + y)$, $1 + s0 = s(1 + 0)$, $x + 0 = x$, $1 + 0 = 1$, $1 + s0 = s1$, $s0 = 1$, $1 + 1 = s1$, $s1 = 2$, $1 + 1 = 2$. The first and fourth statements are axioms, the seventh and ninth are definitions, and the others are derived from one or more predecessors using logical rules of inference.

8. $1 + 1 = 2$ is true$_3$, provided attention is restricted to models of Peano arithmetic.

9. What I have shown is that given the assumptions of Peano arithmetic (and logic) $1 + 1 = 2$ is true. Consequently, by contradiction, $1 + 1 = 1$ and $1 + 1 = 0$ are false. But this only holds in Peano arithmetic and comparable systems. In Boolean algebra, which does not include equivalent assumptions, using the usual conventions of that system $1 + 1 = 1$ is true. In base 2 modular arithmetic $1 + 1 = 0$ is true. Thus the truth of the most elementary arithmetical statement depends on contextual assumptions. The informal number assumptions embedded in natural language make $1 + 1 = 2$ true$_1$, and $1 + 1 = 1$ and $1 + 1 = 0$ false$_1$ (i.e., not true$_1$). College-level mathematics subsequently detaches the signifiers of arithmetic from the received ("default") set of signified meanings, shifting to truth$_2$ or truth$_3$. Consequently we have both $1 + 1 = 1$ and $1 + 1 = 0$ are true$_2$.

10. Scholars believe that Euclid's fifth postulate was not considered to be as self-evident as the others. It is less terse, and more like a theorem than a postulate (it is the converse of proposition I 17). Euclid does not use it until proposition I 29. For this reason, over the ages, many attempts to prove the postulate were made, including Sacchieri's attempt to prove it by *reductio ad absurdum* based on its denial (Eves 1964).

11. Two different interpretations of fallibilism should be distinguished (ignoring the trivially true view that humans make mistakes in their attempts to know). The first is the doctrine that mathematical knowledge is or may be false. This implies that absolute true/false judgements about mathematical knowledge claims can be made, that is, there is absolute truth, but mathematics may fail to attain it. The second version rejects the assumption that absolute judgements regarding truth/falsity and correctness/incorrectness can be made, on the grounds that the relevant criteria and definitions, including the rules of truth and proof, change and will never attain a final state. This version of fallibilism, which is the position adopted here, leads to the view that mathematical knowledge is a relative, contingent, historical construct.

12. Like Dedekind ([1888] 1901), Frege believed that arithmetic is a branch of logic.

13. Many factors, including the new abstract content, contributed historically to this "crisis" in the foundations of mathematics. Perhaps most notable was the shift in orientation with regard to the foundations of mathematics and the associated notions of truth, validity, and proof (Richards 1980, 1989). This could be termed a metalevel revolution in mathematics (Dunmore 1992). Mathematics was no longer the natural history of intuitively given domains such as the natural numbers, the real line, or geometry. Mathematics became abstracted from these roots and increasingly generalized. A key example is Cantor's set theory, which began as a tool for proving the uniqueness of trigonometric series expansions of functions by collecting accumulation points into sets. Thus Cantor began with functions defined on the real line and ended up with set theory, a treatment of infinity, and the associated paradoxes (Hallett 1984).

14. Quine (1953a) goes further back, remarking on the strong parallel between logicism, formalism, and intuitionism and the medieval positions of realism, nominalism, and conceptualism, respectively. Mathematical realism, of course, originates with the ancient Greeks, most notably Plato.

15. It is interesting to note that the example $1 + 1 = 2$ discussed above is first implied in *54.43 of Whitehead and Russell (1910–13), barring the definition of arithmetical addition, which is given later. This section is on page 360 of Whitehead and Russell 1962, the abridgment of the 1927 second edition of *Principia Mathematica*, illustrating the complexity of proving even the most trivial mathematical truth rigorously.

16. This ploy would doubtless be unacceptable to Frege ([1903] 1968), who viewed axioms as self-evident truths, not tentative assumptions.

17. These would include symbols for infinite cardinals and ordinals, treated analogously to 'ideal points' in projective geometry.

18. The law of the excluded middle is accepted only for finite cases.

19. The classical predicate calculus is translatable into intuitionist logic in a constructive way that preserves deducibility (see Bell and Machover 1977). This means that all the theorems of classical mathematics expressible in the predicate calculus can be represented as intuitionistic theorems. Thus classical mathematics cannot easily be claimed to be intuitionistically unintelligible. It can be rejoined, of course, that there is a shift in the meaning during the translation, as far as the intuitionists are concerned. The reverse translation procedure, however, is intuitionistically unacceptable, since it replaces $\neg\neg P$ by P, and $\neg\forall x\neg P$ by $\exists xP$.

20. *Ab initio* this is a very slim possibility if Frege's classification of justifications of mathematical knowledge are accepted, for this offers a choice between empiricism, logicism, constructivism, and formalism. Empiricism is not absolutist. So one of these programs must be radically changed to circumvent the above critique.

21. The argument is an instance of the infinite regress argument known since the time of Aristotle, namely, that in foundationalism a set of basic truths must be assumed (Post 1992).

22. Other theories of truth (as, e.g., in Haack 1978), do not help here.

23. As is indicated in chapter 6 note 13 it follows from the Craig interpolation lemma that there is no ultimate basic logical form into which even a correct mathematical proof can be translated.

24. An absolutist might object that although Gödel's results are valid, I am disallowed from using them, since I claim all mathematical knowledge is fallible. My answer is: (*a*) I use accepted mathematical knowledge as correct but corrigible working knowledge, until it is rejected by the mathematical community; (*b*) my arguments are fallible (much more so than most mathematics), so using fallible theorems does not

weaken them further; (c) an absolutist who accepts Gödel's results must concede the limitations of the axiomatic method; (d) Gödel's theorems are proved constructively, so accepting them does not mean accepting all of mathematical knowledge.

25. Hilbert called it "Cantor's Paradise."

26. Likewise, the emerging science of chaos shows us that infinitesimal perturbations within models of the world lead to globally different outcomes, confirming that we can never hope to predict or control the future (Prigogine and Stengers 1984).

CHAPTER 2

RECONCEPTUALIZING THE PHILOSOPHY OF MATHEMATICS

WHAT IS THE PHILOSOPHY OF MATHEMATICS?

The Relationship between Mathematics and the Philosophy of Mathematics

The philosophy of mathematics is neither mathematics nor a subset of mathematics. It is a field of study which reflects on mathematics from the outside. It is one of a number of metatheories of mathematics, which also include the sociology, history, psychology, and anthropology of mathematics as well as mathematics education. Mathematics is variously classified as an art and a science, it is the "queen and servant of science" according to Bell (1952), whereas the metatheories are all humanities or social sciences. So these metatheories not only are distinct from their subject matter, they occur in a different category of human intellectual endeavor. In particular, to philosophize about mathematics, which I take to be the business of the philosophy of mathematics, is to do philosophy, albeit informed by mathematics, and not to do mathematics. Obvious as this point is, there are pulls to bridge the gap.

The language that textual critics, for example, use to talk about criticism will be permeated by precisely those features—figures of ambiguity, polysemy, compression of meaning, subtlety and plurality of interpretation, rhetorical tropes, and so on—which these critics value in the texts they study; likewise mathematicians will create and respond to just those discussions of mathematics that ape what attracts them to their subject matter. Where textual critics literalise their metalanguage, mathematicians mathematise theirs. And since for mathematicians the principal activity is proving new theorems, what will they ask of any description of their subject is: can it be the source of new mathematical material? Does it suggest new notational systems, definitions, assertions, proofs . . . ? (Rotman 1988, 1–2)

Rotman offers a provocative thesis about the relationship between a subject and its theories; how there is a pull to apply the values, methods, and conceptual tools of the subject in its metatheory. He continues by arguing that the traditional philosophies of mathematics can all be interpreted in this way.

Now it is certainly the case that the accounts offered by Frege, Brouwer and Hilbert all satisfied this requirement: each put forward a programme that engendered new mathematics; each acted in and wrote the play, and in doing so, gave a necessarily truncated and misleading account of mathematics (Rotman 1988, 2)

This suggests a gloss on the activities of the foundationalist schools discussed in chapter 1, namely, that the philosophers of mathematics were trying to apply to the philosophy of mathematics what is the legitimate business of mathematics itself; the formalization of theories followed by the derivation of new theorems and the rigorous proof of theorems in such theories. As I suggested, mathematically these programs were very successful. However the reduction of philosophy to mathematics was less successful, as one might expect, given the distinction between the two fields. Körner expresses this difference as follows:

As the philosophy of law does not legislate, or the philosophy of science devise or test scientific hypotheses—the philosophy of mathematics does not add to the number of mathematical theorems and theories. It is not mathematics. It is reflection upon mathematics, giving rise to its own particular questions and answers. (Körner 1960, 9)

The distinction between mathematics and the philosophy of mathematics is *now* an obvious one. Nevertheless, during the first half of the twentieth century, there was very little work in the philosophy of mathematics that was not foundational or mathematical in character. The absolutist schools of logicism, formalism, and intuitionism dominated the field, and they were primarily research programs in the foundations of mathematics, albeit philosophically motivated. Thus absolutism and the associated foundationalism represented a mathematical tendency in the philosophy of mathematics, one which shaped the whole field of study. This resulted in a distortion in the nature of the enterprise, in my view, toward mathematical solutions to narrowly epistemological problems.

Only since the Second World War, and especially in the past three decades, has a more genuinely philosophical (as opposed to mathematical) philosophy of mathematics emerged, as Kitcher and Aspray (1988) point out. This includes more emphasis on ontological questions, as well as including a "maverick" tradition concerned with mathematical practice and its methodology. Thus it is only recently that the philosophy of mathematics has ceased to be defined by mathematical questions concerning foundations. But given that this domination is diminishing, it is appropriate to reconsider the issue of the nature and scope of the philosophy of mathematics.

The Analogy with the Philosophy of Science

Just as there are a number of metatheories of mathematics, so too are there of science. In fact, there is a direct analogy in terms of metatheories with empirical science. For in addition to the philosophy of science there are also the sociology, history, psychology, and anthropology of science and science education. Losee (1987) considers the relationship between two of these, the history of science and the philosophy of science, which he describes as second-order interpretations of a first-order subject matter. He considers the various relations of dependency and independence that might hold between the history and the philosophy of science, distinguishing strong and weak forms of interdependence. The strong sense of interdependence would mean that no philosophy of science may be undertaken without historical inquiry (and vice versa). In the weak sense there are at least some aspects of the philosophy of science that require historical enquiry (and vice versa). Losee claims that this latter relationship of weak interdependence is what holds between the history and the philosophy of science.

Losee also argues that the distinction between these two fields of enquiry depends largely on their distinct methodological standards, which are those of explanatory historical narrative and theory evaluation. The history of science is concerned to provide historical narratives and explanations of science, which, according to Kuhn (1977) involves puzzle-solving in order to provide historical interpretations and reconstructions. This requires judgements as to the significance of developments in the history of science, including the confirmation and appraisal of theories, which brings in matters pertaining to the philosophy of science.

The main concern of the philosophy of science, according to Losee, is with the evaluative standards and norms of science. Within this focus he distinguishes prescriptive and descriptive approaches to the philosophy of science. The former is concerned to legislate evaluative standards for "good science," whereas the latter formulates evaluative standards which have implicitly or explicitly informed actual historical scientific developments. Although

Losee himself favors the prescriptive approach to the philosophy of science, he defends the legitimacy of a descriptive philosophy of science. He argues, with Kuhn (1977), that such a perspective is interested not in narration *per se* but in uncovering the standards which underlie individual evaluative judgements.

The prescriptive-descriptive dichotomy parallels other distinctions in the philosophy of science such as that between internalist and externalist views of the philosophy of science and that between the context of discovery and the context of justification in science. Indeed, it is possible to link prescriptive and internalist accounts and a focus on the context of justification. But these are loose links, and as Losee argues, it is incorrect to identify the focus of a descriptive philosophy of science with context of discovery, as internalist philosophers of science, such as the logical empiricists and Popper, do. Many philosophers of science, whose views are legitimately philosophical, espouse an externalist view. The latter include many of the most influential recent philosophers of science, such as Feyerabend, Hanson, Kuhn, Lakatos, Laudan, and Toulmin. The contributions of these authors to the philosophy of science is a powerful testimony to the necessity of considering "external" questions in the philosophy of the sciences. However, it must be said, in the philosophy of science, even philosophers espousing an internalist position, such as Popper, admit the importance of considering the *development* of scientific knowledge for epistemology.

Before drawing parallels for the philosophy of mathematics, it is worth remarking that Losee's focus on the evaluation of theories as the principal concern of the philosophy of science is rather restrictive. Other issues also have a legitimate claim for attention; these include the existence of theoretical entities, realism, the relation between the external world and scientific descriptions, explanatory metaphors and scientific models, the language and rhetoric of science, the overall nature and purpose of science, and its relation to other areas of knowledge and value. Thus Losee's concentration on the evaluation of theories offers a parallel to the foundationalist concerns of the absolutist philosophies considered in chapter 1, the major difference being that he admits as legitimate alternative conceptions, such as descriptive or externalist philosophy of science.

What this analogy suggests for the philosophy of mathematics is that a broader perspective than that allowed by the absolutist philosophies of mathematics could be valuable and should be considered for admittance as legitimate. Although the justificatory basis of mathematical knowledge is undeniably a central concern of the philosophy of mathematics, it is possible to conceive of this descriptively as well as prescriptively. This would entail considering the history and practice of mathematics. It would necessitate accounting for the standards of proof actually employed in mathematics, as well as the idealized canons of rigorous proof which are rarely, if ever, realized (as argued in chap. 1). With humanly uncheckable computer generated proofs now accepted, it is hard to see how the philosophy of mathematics can avoid considering such issues. In practice it cannot, and issues of proof are central to the current interests of a growing number of philosophers of mathematics, including Davis and Hersh (1980); De Millo, Lipton, and Perlis (1986); and Tymoczko (1979).

The controversy between internalist, foundationalist philosophies of mathematics and the "maverick" tradition of fallibilism and quasi-empiricism[1] finds a parallel in the debate over the internalist-externalist dichotomy in the philosophy of science (Losee 1987). However, the difference is that there is strong support for the necessity of considering "external" questions in the philosophy of the sciences, and even philosophers such as Popper espousing an internalist position admit the importance of considering the development of scientific knowledge for epistemology, albeit in a stylized, logically reconstructed form. In contrast, supporters of absolutist philosophies of mathematics remain resistant to the admission of even such reconstructed traces of human agency. However, the case for reconceptualizing the philosophy of mathematics has been growing stronger, and many absolutist philosophers of mathematics admit that more acknowledgment of human activity and experience needs to be conceded than hitherto (Lakatos 1978c).

By analogy with Losee (1987), I wish to suggest that the relationship between the history of mathematics and philosophy of mathematics is something that needs to be considered, and I shall argue that a weak relation of interdependence exists between the two fields. That is, there are at least some aspects of the philosophy of mathematics that require historical enquiry (and vice versa).

PHILOSOPHICAL CONFLICTS ABOUT MATHEMATICS

The conflict between absolutism and fallibilism in the philosophy of mathematics also represents a conflict between externalist and internalist conceptions of the philosophy of mathematics. Below, the opposing positions of fallibilism and absolutism are contrasted on a number controversial issues. The special feature of these issues is that the traditional internalist conception of the philosophy of mathematics attempts to exclude them. But since they concern important issues about the nature of mathematical knowledge, their exclusion suggests that a reconceptualization of the philosophy of mathematics might be called for.

The Context of Discovery versus the Context of Justification

A central area of controversy between absolutist and fallibilist philosophies of mathematics concerns the distinction between the contexts of discovery and justification, and the legitimacy of considering the context of discovery within philosophy. The traditional absolutist position is that a clear-cut categorical distinction can be drawn between these two contexts in considering mathematical knowledge, permitting the exclusion of the context of discovery as illegitimate.

According to Losee the acceptance of the separation of the contexts of discovery and justification in the philosophy of science community was inspired by the foundationalist domination of the philosophy of mathematics early this century.

Philosophers of science who sought to develop their discipline as an analogue of foundation studies in mathematics accepted Reichenbach's distinction between the context of scientific discovery and the context of justification. They agreed the proper domain of the philosophy of science is the context of justification. In addition, they sought to reformulate scientific laws and theories in the patterns of formal logic, so that questions about explanation and confirmation could be dealt with as problem of applied logic. (Losee 1980, 174)

This "logical reconstructionist philosophy of science," as Losee terms it (1980, 173, chapter heading), was concerned with *prescription*; just as were the foundationist schools in the philosophy of mathematics. Thus it is ironic that this conceptual distinction should be reapplied to the philosophy of mathematics in attempts to invalidate naturalistic, descriptive approaches.

Although fallibilism acknowledges that this distinction is based on a valid conceptual and theoretical analysis, it argues on naturalistic grounds that it is not possible to separate these contexts completely within mathematics. Both the creation and justification of mathematical knowledge, including the scrutiny of mathematical warrants or proofs, are bound to their human and historical context (Lakatos 1976).

The absolutist criticism of this position, following Popper (1959) and Reichenbach (1951), is that it conflates the context of discovery with the context of justification and that only the latter is the proper business of philosophy. In considering items of mathematical knowledge it is both possible in principle and necessary in practice to separate these two contexts completely, because the domains of knowledge that deal with them are distinct. The context of justification is concerned with the objective and logical conditions of knowledge, the rational business of knowledge appraisal, and hence is the business of epistemology and the philosophy of mathematics. The context of discovery concerns the contingent circumstances of human or historical invention, which is not a rational process, cannot be treated objectively and logically, and therefore is the business of the psychology or history of mathematics.

A fallibilist answer to this criticism might note, first of all, that it is applied inconsistently. Traditional epistemology, from the British empiricists to the present, take the sense data that present themselves to the individual knowing subject as the basis of empirical knowledge, both in terms of genesis and justification. It is therefore inconsistent to absolutely exclude human and genetic considerations in epistemology as invalid, since these figure so significantly in its history up to the present day.

Second, in the practice of mathematics, it is not possible to separate out those aspects related to the context of discovery from those pertaining to the context of justification. The actual standards of knowledge appraisal and acceptance employed in mathematics cannot be isolated from the context of discovery even though they are central to the context of justification. These contexts interpenetrate and overlap, and the acceptance of a theorem or theory (part of the context of justification) often requires the reworking of details of its exposition or proof (part of the context of discovery). Although a prescriptive approach to the philosophy of mathematics may notionally separate these contexts out by fiat, if a descriptive philosophy of mathematics is to accommodate practice without distortion, it cannot so neatly divide them. This is a central thesis of Lakatos's philosophy of mathematics, which is the subject of chapter 4, below.[2]

Third, there is a growing trend in the philosophy of mathematics to consider the history of mathematics and philosophy of mathematics, at least in part, together. This is one of the central planks of the "maverick" tradition, identified by Kitcher and Asprey (1988). A descriptive philosophy of mathematics must be able to account for the justification of mathematical knowledge and theories in practice, to satisfy its epithet, and this introduces the history of mathematics. But the history of mathematics necessarily concerns the growth and development of mathematical knowledge, and this is part of the context of discovery. This does not amount to admitting psychologism by the back door, as some absolutists might fear. For the history of mathematics concerns the public development of mathematics, and this includes many logical elements and is, at least partly, open to rational reconstruction. Likewise, as I shall argue below, justification in mathematics is not wholly explicable in terms of logic or explicit rule-governed rational behavior. Thus the separation of contexts of discovery and justification on the grounds that they treat psychology and logic, respectively, cannot be sustained, at least from some significant points of view.

Internal versus External Views of Mathematical Proof

The absolutist view of mathematical proof is that it provides an objective warrant for mathematical knowledge, for the theorem proved. The warrant depends solely on the logical correctness of the proof. Humans may play a part in the genesis of knowledge, but once warranted mathematical knowledge is objective and final. If errors in knowledge or proof are detected they show that the so-called theorem was mistakenly labeled and lacking an objective warrant and that it was mistakenly identified as a part of the body of knowledge. Humans may mistakenly identify something as having an objective warrant, but true knowledge is incorrigible and final.

Typically, the fallibilist view is that the justification of mathematical knowledge centrally involves human agency and cannot be reduced to the objective conditions of knowledge. Standards of proof are never objective and ultimate, but "sufficient unto the day," and they are perpetually open to revision (Kitcher 1984). Mathematical proofs are accepted because they satisfy individuals (especially the appropriate representatives of the mathematical community) that they are adequate warrants, not because they satisfy explicit, objective logical rules of proof (Manin 1977). Thus mathematical knowledge and the standards of proof that support it depend what the mathematicians of the day accept. This metaknowledge varies according to its location in history; and the present is not, and can never be, in a privileged position with regard to the truth or ultimate standards of proof.

However this is not to say that mathematical knowledge (or the standards of proof) are arbitrary, irrational, or illogical. On the contrary, mathematicians accept as mathematical knowledge only that which stands up to rational public criticism and scrutiny, based on their best professional judgement and some explicitly stated rules. Furthermore, there is a continuity between the application of professional judgement (and the rules employed) from one generation to the next, and any changes are themselves publicly debated and justified. Mathematical concepts, definitions, theorems, proofs, theories, and proof-standards grow, change, and are sometimes abandoned with the passage of time, as standards of rigor and proof change. Thus their "objectivity" is actually intersubjectivity, is time and community dependent, and is rooted in historical continuity and tradition.

An absolutist response is to deny that rationality and logic depend on humanity and to rule out as illegitimate to philosophy the empirical fact that the standards of rationality and logic do change, and have changed. The standard way to do this is to argue that logic and proof alone are relevant to the context of justification. This position can be maintained consistently, but as I have already argued, it fails to accommodate the justification of mathematical knowledge naturalistically.

Another absolutist position is that the knowledge vouchsafed by human logic and rationality is always a potentially fallible representation of the truth, which is gradually uncovered by human endeavor but exists independently of us. But then a fallibilist rejoinder is to ask how we could ever know when we attained the truth. No guarantee or proof could be given that we had attained the truth, for it would be circular and would either fail or lead us into infinite regress.

A third absolutist position might be that proof remains purely objective, even though complete rigor has not yet been attained. But the problem with this claim is that if proofs are not reducible to explicit and rigorous rules, then judgement is required to decide which proofs are acceptable. This admits the external human dimension, undercutting the claim to objectivity.

The role of mathematical proof is discussed at greater length in chapters 1 and 6. Here it suffices to say that an increasing number of philosophers concerned with epistemology (Bernstein 1983; Everitt and Fisher 1995; Rorty 1979) and mathematics (Kitcher 1984; Tymoczko 1986b) no longer accept it as providing a human-independent warrant for mathematical knowledge.

Mathematics as Discrete versus Mathematics as Connected with Other Knowledge

The traditional distinction between *a priori* and empirical knowledge serves as a basis for a categorical dichotomy which separates mathematics from other realms of knowledge, according to the means of justification employed. It follows therefore from absolutist positions that mathematics is separate and disconnected from other realms of knowledge (although parts of it can be empirically interpreted and applied).

Fallibilism[3] rejects the absolute separation of mathematics from other areas of knowledge for two reasons. First, following the critique of absolutism, the aprioristic view of mathematical knowledge as a body of truths derived by truth-preserving inferences from true premises is rejected. Instead, mathematical knowledge is seen as quasi-empirical. According to Lakatos (1976, 1978c) consequences are deduced from hypothetical sets of mathematical assumptions; and if falsified by contradictions, or by informal theories, the assumptions are rejected or modified. Thus the appraisal of putative mathematical knowledge includes a quasi-empirical element depending on human experience (chap. 4 treats this issue more extensively). Kitcher (1984) also regards mathematics as empirical, because particular experiences are needed to warrant knowledge. Neither of these two types of experience consists of observations of the external world, but since mathematics is seen as quasi-empirical, it cannot be categorically divorced from the knowledge of the physical and other sciences.

Second, fallibilists include human knowing as a legitimate concern of the philosophy of mathematics. As the outcome of one of the cognitive activities of humans, mathematics is connected with, and is indissolubly a part of, the whole fabric of human knowledge. Mathematical knowledge is the result

of one of the forms of human knowing, forms that are all founded on the powers of understanding of the human subject, thus connecting all realms of
knowledge.

The various forms of knowledge can be seen in low-level developments
within the common area of our knowledge of the everyday world. From
this there branch out the developed forms which, taking certain elements in our common knowledge as a basis, have grown in distinctive
ways. (Hirst in Brown, Fauvel, and Finnegan 1981, 230)

The claim is therefore that all knowledge is rooted in basic human knowledge
and is thus connected by a shared foundation. The social form of fallibilism
that I shall be developing in this book (social constructivism) also posits that
human agreement is the ultimate arbiter of what counts as justified knowledge. In other words, the justification of all knowledge also rests on a shared
foundation, namely, human agreement. Thus both in terms of its origins and
its justificatory foundations, human knowledge has a fundamental unity; and
all fields of human knowledge are thereby interconnected.

In its modern form, the *a priori* versus empirical distinction in knowledge finds its roots in Descartes's ([1637] 1955) mind-body dualism. *A priori*
knowledge derives from the exercise of reason and logic in the realm of mind,
while empirical knowledge is derived *a posteriori* from sensory experience in
the material realm of body. However many modern philosophers reject this as
an untenable dualism, arguing that mind and thought are not immaterial (e.g.,
Merleau-Ponty [1945] 1964; Ryle 1949; Johnson 1987; Dennett 1992).
According to Rorty (1979), mind-body dualism underpins the separation of
universals from particulars, of representations from reality, and of *a priori*
from empirical knowledge. He and others argue instead that reasoning is
embodied, and cognition essentially involves experiences with material representations. Thus, according to this argument, and the fallibilist position,
mathematical and other forms of knowledge traditionally categorized as *a
priori* cannot be wholly separated from *a posteriori* knowledge. Mathematical knowing, according to this view, is just as materially embodied as scientific or empirical knowing, and the nature of the knower cannot simply be factored out of considerations of knowledge.

RECONCEPTUALIZING THE PHILOSOPHY OF MATHEMATICS

The central goal of this chapter is to consider afresh the nature of the
philosophy of mathematics in the light of the growth of fallibilism and the critique of absolutism. In addition, the significant if controversial issues con-

cerning the character of mathematical knowledge discussed above are excluded by the traditional view of the field. Irrespective of whether the arguments offered above are accepted, it is clear that matters of philosophical import are raised by them, and the possibility of hearing, supporting, strengthening, or refuting them should be admitted by the philosophy of mathematics. So the following questions arise. What are the legitimate concerns of the philosophy of mathematics? What should be the nature and extent of this field of study? Should the philosophy of mathematics be reconceptualized so that issues of conflict, including the above, can be legitimately discussed within the field?

What Is the Philosophy of Mathematics?

Some preliminary answers are provided by the following authors. Maddy, first of all, reaffirms the descriptive function of the philosophy of mathematics.

I assume that the job of the philosopher of mathematics is to *describe* and *explain* mathematics, not to reform it. (Maddy 1990, 28, emphasis added)

The themes of description and explanation are further elaborated by Tymoczko.

The philosophy of mathematics begins when we ask for a general account of mathematics, a synoptic vision of the discipline that reveals its essential features and explains just how it is that human beings are able to do mathematics. (Tymoczko 1986b, viii)

In proposing the tasks of description and explanation these authors provide a necessary but not sufficient starting point, for they do not yet indicate the specific concerns of the philosophy of mathematics as opposed to those of the history and sociology of mathematics. For this the philosophical aspects of the task of the philosophy of mathematics need to be distinguished. Priest (1973) offers a personal view of this task and describes some of the uniquely philosophical and mathematical features involved.

All the problems concerning the philosophy of mathematics can neatly be summarized by the question:
Question 0 What is (pure) mathematics? . . .
Firstly, what is meant by "mathematics"? The only answer we can give without begging the question is "That which is done and has been

done for the last four thousand years by mathematicians" . . . Knowledge of the nature of mathematics lies in an ability to do it . . . Now, what is it that mathematicians do? They are interested in establishing the truth or otherwise of certain statements.

Question 1 Why are the truths of mathematics true?

Any reasonable answer must also permit reasonable answers to the following questions.

Question 1(a) Why is it that such truths appear necessary and inviolable, and why we are unable to conceive of them being false?

Question 1(b) How is it we come to know such truths?

Question 1(c) Why is it that the truths of mathematics can be applied in practical matters, e.g., surveying, building bridges, sending rockets to the moon, etc. In short, why are they useful? . . .

Now the naive answer to question 1 is that mathematical truths are so because they are true of certain objects such as numbers, functions, propositions, points, groups, models etc., i.e., these are what mathematics is about.

Hence we must be able to answer:

Question 2 What exactly are the above objects, and in what sense do they exist? . . .

Question 2 (cont.) And if they don't exist, why is it we have such a strong impression that they do? (Priest 1973, 115–17)

Priest regards the major concerns of the philosophy of mathematics to be epistemological (concerning the nature and status of mathematical knowledge), and ontological (concerning the nature and status of mathematical objects and their existence). This much is traditional. But Priest insists that these matters are considered in a broader context than is traditionally done. He asks that human activity and social uses not be left out of matters epistemological and ontological. He includes philosophical questions about its sources, history, and uses. This represents a radical broadening of the traditional limits of enquiry in the philosophy of mathematics.

Thus the role of the philosophy of mathematics is to reflect on, and give an account of, the nature of mathematics. From a philosophical perspective, the nature of mathematical knowledge is perhaps the central feature which the philosophy of mathematics needs to account for and reflect on. However, the key issue concerns how "giving an account of" mathematics and mathematical knowledge is conceived. Here the prescriptive-descriptive distinction of the philosophy of science serves as a valuable conceptual tool. Absolutist philosophies of mathematics such as logicism, formalism, and intuitionism attempt to provide *prescriptive* accounts of the nature of mathematics. Such accounts are programmatic, legislating how mathematics should be understood, rather than providing accurately *descriptive* accounts of the nature of mathematics. Thus they are failing to account for mathematics as it is, in the hope of fulfilling their vision of how it should be. Körner argues that this is a mistaken approach.

> To confuse description and programme—to confuse "is" with "ought to be" or "should be"—is just as harmful in the philosophy of mathematics as elsewhere. (Körner 1960, 12)

Elsewhere, this confusion is recognized as a lapse in reasoning known as the *naturalistic fallacy*. In recognizing that the task of the philosophy of mathematics is to reflect on and to give an account of the nature of mathematics, there is no need to make the foundationalist assumption of absolutism. This prejudges and narrows down the scope of the philosophy of mathematics, in what appears to be a vain quest for certainty. The inquiry can still begin with the traditional questions of epistemology and ontology. What is the nature and basis of mathematical knowledge? What is the nature of and how to account for the existence of mathematical objects (numbers, functions, sets, etc.)?

However, the answers to these questions will not provide a descriptive account of the nature of mathematics. For the narrow focus of these "internal" questions fails to locate mathematics within the broader context of human thought and history. Without such a context, according to Lakatos, the philosophy of mathematics loses its content.

> Under the present dominance of formalism [i.e., foundationalism], one is tempted to paraphrase Kant: the history of mathematics, lacking the guidance of philosophy has become *blind*, while the philosophy of mathematics turning its back on the most intriguing phenomena in the history of mathematics, has become *empty*. (Lakatos 1976, 2)

Following this line of argument, much more should fall within the scope of the philosophy of mathematics than just the justification of mathematical knowledge and ontology. Mathematics is multifaceted, and as well as a body of propositional knowledge, it can be described in terms of its concepts, characteristics, theories, history, and practices. The philosophy of mathematics should account for this complexity, which Wittgenstein describes as the "motley of mathematics." A descriptive philosophy of mathematics needs to extend the concerns it addresses to include questions such as the following:

1. What account can be given of the justification of mathematical knowledge which does not necessarily presuppose absolutism?
2. What account can be given of the character and ontological status of the objects of mathematics?

3. Why is Platonism or mathematical realism so plausible and successful a perspective?
4. How are the practices of mathematicians and the character of mathematics interrelated?
5. What is the relationship between the subjective mathematical knowledge of individuals and accepted mathematical knowledge?
6. How do individuals learn mathematics and thus come to know extant mathematical knowledge?
7. How do individuals creatively transmute their knowledge of mathematics into new mathematical knowledge?
8. How does mathematical knowledge evolve? How do the underlying proof and definition standards, and the metaknowledge of mathematics evolve?
9. What is the interrelationship among mathematics, language, and information technology (from clay tablets to computers)?
10. How does history illuminate the philosophy of mathematics?
11. What is the relationship between mathematics and the other areas of human knowledge, values, culture, and experience?
12. Why have the theories of pure mathematics proved to be so powerful and useful in their applications to science and to practical problems?
13. How can mathematical theories be evaluated and appraised? Can there be criteria for such purposes, and if so what values are involved?

These questions are not all uniquely philosophical, for answers to several of them might also be found in the history, sociology, and psychology of mathematics, and elsewhere. My claim is that each question potentially offers a legitimate task and challenge to the philosophy of mathematics. Ultimately, it may turn out that some of these questions are most usefully addressed by some other metatheory of mathematics. But *ab initio* this is far from clear, and whether it is the case will depend on the nature of the enquiry and account of mathematics that results.

If accepted as potentially legitimate, these questions represent a substantial broadening of the scope of the philosophy of mathematics from the internal concerns of foundationalist approaches. This suggests the need for a reconceptualization to admit a human presence including the domain of the social into the philosophy of mathematics. Traditionally, in its prescriptive form, the philosophy of mathematics following the practice of mathematics itself treats only impersonal objective concepts and issues of logic, with no reference to human beings. This led the mathematician Hammer to remark on the absence of the human presence from mathematics: "The most neglected existence theorem in mathematics is the existence of people" (Hammer 1964, 514) .

The challenge to tradition posed by the reconceptualization that I am proposing means that the following objection must be anticipated. This objection, in brief, is that human beings have no business in the domain of discourse addressed by the philosophy of mathematics. The *philosophical* nature of such an enquiry precludes reference to the practices and roles of human beings with regard to mathematics; these are legitimately accommodated elsewhere, in the history, sociology, or psychology of mathematics.

This objection reflects the fact that none of the traditional philosophers of mathematics make reference to human beings in any essential way—with the exception of Brouwer and the intuitionists who locates intuition in the individual's mind (a position which has consequently been criticized for psychologism, with some legitimacy). However, this argument is not valid. There is nothing fundamentally *unphilosophical* in considering human beings. What matters is the character of the inquiry, its scope, and the concepts and methods employed.

There is a time-honored tradition in epistemology which addresses the basis of an individual knower's experience, belief, and knowledge. Likewise, the philosophy of mind considers the nature of the human mind. Naturalized epistemology explores the grounds for individuals' knowledge which are found in their experiences and environment and in scientific theories and explanations of knowing (Quine 1969). What makes these different inquiries into the nature and capacity of human beings legitimately philosophical is a focus on the possibilities of, and the conceptual boundaries of, the individual mind, experience, belief, or knowledge. Such inquiries are general, based on reasoning and conceptual analysis within the philosophical genre, albeit informed by the theories and empirical data of other fields of knowledge. Despite current practice in the philosophy of mathematics there is no *a priori* reason to rule out the consideration of persons on philosophical grounds.[4]

Developments in Modern Philosophy of Mathematics

A sketch of the recent development of the philosophy of mathematics, painted in broad brush strokes, suggests that it has passed through two main phases. First of all, in the earlier part of this century, the field was dominated by philosophically inclined professional *mathematicians*, who with their foundationalist programs focused the philosophy of mathematics on *mathematical* concerns and problems (albeit of philosophical significance). The dominance of the philosophy of mathematics by mathematicians and their mathematical concerns has been argued and illustrated above. As Rotman (1988) points out, it is that which mathematicians value in their own work which was sought in the philosophy of mathematics, namely, definitions, theorems, proofs, and so on.

The second phase overlaps the first but has gained prominence in the second half of the century. It represents a switch, for in this phase the field has been dominated by mathematically informed or inclined professional *philosophers*, who have refocused the philosophy of mathematics on *philosophical* concerns and problems (albeit of mathematical significance). Thus much of recent discussion has been of Platonism, mathematical realism, and ontology (Quine 1969; Field 1989; Maddy 1990); and epistemology, modality, and necessity in mathematics (Kripke 1980); or a combination of these concerns (Steiner 1975; Benacerraf and Putnam 1983). In this phase, work in the philosophy of mathematics has shown the style and concerns of professional philosophers, namely, subtle conceptual analyses, sustained carefully formulated arguments directed at tightly focused concerns, in-depth responses to other philosophers' analyses comprising detailed cases and refutations, and, in general, an inward professional focus on narrow philosophical problems.

My claim is that during these two phases the philosophy of mathematics has been dominated by the internal professional concerns of mathematicians and philosophers, respectively, and that this is reflected in the concerns, focuses, problems, and professional styles of thought, discourse, and argument deployed. In each case, the result has been a concentration on internal issues and concerns; internal to mathematics, first of all, and internal to philosophy, later, to somewhat caricature recent history. In neither case has the concern been to give a descriptive account of mathematics or to address the philosophical questions listed above.

In addition, a fallibilist "maverick" tradition with an externalist tendency has been emerging (Kitcher and Aspray 1988). This represents an alternative to the mainstream developments described above, and it is perhaps the beginning of a third phase in the philosophy of mathematics. However, it seems to be emerging as the result of inter- and intradisciplinary developments. These include, first of all, general developments in philosophy and in the history of thought. Positivism, which dominated much of philosophy for the first part of this century (as behaviorism dominated psychology), and which helped to buttress absolutism, has retreated before an increasing number of attacks (Kolakowski 1972). Following the later Wittgenstein, Anglo-American analytical philosophy took on a linguistic turn, heralding a new naturalism; a move toward descriptive and away from prescriptive approaches to philosophy. Continental (i.e., mainland European) and Hegelian/Marxist philosophy has brought an emphasis on social and historical dimensions of knowledge (Bachelard, Enriques, Foucault, M. Serres), and this has been increasingly influential on Anglo-American analytic philosophy (Rorty 1979), including the philosophy of mathematics (Lakatos 1963–64; Tiles 1991).

Second, there have been developments in the philosophies and metatheories of the sciences. Over the past thirty years, the philosophy of science has accepted as legitimate a consideration of external and historical issues, particularly after Hanson (1958) and Kuhn (1962). The philosophy of mathematics lagged behind in this development, and Lakatos (1963–64) did not have the same impact as, for example, his contemporary Kuhn did. However these developments in the philosophy of science, and the current of ideas that led to them, might be expected to have a delayed impact on the philosophy of mathematics. At the same time there has been a great increase in interdisciplinary thought in the sociology and social studies of science and mathematics, in which fallibilist positions are now the norm (Bloor 1976; Fuller 1988; Restivo 1985; Wilder 1974, 1981). Likewise, there has been a shift in the history of mathematics toward naturalistic description and away from a received absolutist doctrine (Kline 1980; Richards 1989; Gillies 1992). The influence of the failure of the foundationalist programs for the philosophy of mathematics should not be discounted. This probably led to disillusionment with prescriptive philosophies among some mathematicians. Coupled with the desire for philosophical recognition of their actual practices, this has encouraged some mathematicians to question the traditional boundaries of the philosophy of mathematics (Hersh 1979; McCleary and McKinney 1986).

Third, there have been significant social changes with a direct impact on mathematics. Over the course of the century, mathematicians have been increasingly affected by technological changes and social pressures and demands. Even pure mathematicians have become increasingly aware of the potential utility of their research and have felt the impact of social and technological change (Steen 1988), unlike the mathematics of Hardy's (1941) day. The great expansion of public schooling in line with the aims of social and technological development has led to an increased emphasis on mathematical education during this period. This has brought a great number of mathematicians into contact with educational developments and teaching, and the humanizing influence of such practices on thought should not be underestimated. They bring human issues into the otherwise impersonal domain of mathematics, through the back door (Cooper 1985, Ernest 1991).

Possibly as a consequence of these interrelated intellectual forces, both academics within mathematics and those working in its penumbra of meta-theories have become aware of the possibility of challenging the focus on exclusively internal concerns in the philosophy of mathematics. The existence of a powerful external current of ideas centering on naturalistic, fallibilist, and social views of knowledge provides an important stimulus for this. Thus the proposed reconceptualizing of the philosophy of mathematics to legitimate the concerns of the "maverick" tradition represents a response to powerful intellectual forces at work in Western culture, even though it represents a minority perspective within the philosophy of mathematics itself.

Adequacy Criteria for the
Philosophy of Mathematics Reconceptualized

I have argued that external questions as to the historical origins and social context of mathematics should, in principle, be admissible as proper concerns of the philosophy of mathematics. Their traditional exclusion is based on prior assumptions about the philosophy of mathematics—namely, the influence of absolutism—and not on the limits of philosophical enquiry. To restrict the scope of the philosophy of mathematics to the issues raised by absolutism alone cannot be right, now that alternative positions exist. For this would be to mistakenly impute the characteristics of absolutism to the whole field of inquiry.

Fallibilist views are now sufficiently widespread to justify reconceptualizing the scope of the philosophy of mathematics to include the broader external issues raised (Aspray and Kitcher 1988; Davis and Hersh 1980; Hersh 1979; Kitcher 1984; Lakatos 1976, 1978c; Tymoczko 1986b; Van Bendegem 1988–89; Wittgenstein 1953, 1956). My argument is *not* that the correctness of fallibilism necessitates an extension of the philosophy of mathematics. It would be foolish and inconsistent to assert the correctness of fallibilism and to discount the support that absolutism continues to command. Instead, my argument is that fallibilist views are admissible for critical consideration and discussion alongside absolutist views, as a growing literature attests. Indeed, the conflict between absolutist philosophies and the "maverick" tradition of fallibilism is itself a central issue for the philosophy of mathematics and should be accommodated within it. A reconceptualization of the philosophy of mathematics which admits this controversy, and hence the concerns of both types of perspective, is what is called for.

Overall, I have argued that the role of the philosophy of mathematics is to account for mathematics, where this task is conceived broadly to include "external" issues, such as the history, genesis, and practice of mathematics, as well as "internal" epistemological and ontological issues, such as the justification of mathematical knowledge. These issues are expressed in an explicit set of adequacy criteria:

An adequate philosophy of mathematics should account for the following:

1. Mathematical knowledge: its character, genesis and justification, with special attention to the role of proof
2. Mathematical theories, both constructive and structural: their character and development, and the issues in their appraisal and evaluation
3. The objects of mathematics: their character, origins, and relationship with the language of mathematics

4. The applications of mathematics: its effectiveness in science, technology, and other realms and, more generally, the relationship of mathematics with other areas of knowledge and values
5. Mathematical practice: its character, and the mathematical activities of mathematicians, in the present and past
6. The learning of mathematics: its character, and its role in the onward transmission of mathematical knowledge and in the creativity of individual mathematicians.

Criteria 1 and 3 include the traditional epistemological and ontological focuses of the philosophy of mathematics but add a concern with the genesis of both mathematical knowledge and the objects of mathematics, as well as with the language in which mathematical knowledge is expressed and mathematical objects named. Criterion 2 adds a concern with the form that mathematical knowledge usually takes: that is in mathematical theories. It allows as admissible the notion that theories evolve over time and can be appraised. The discussion of standards and theory appraisal is evidently a matter for the philosophy of mathematics, even if theory choice is not the same kind of issue as it is in philosophy of science. This criterion also indicates the dual nature of mathematical theories and concepts, which can be either constructive or structural, and this is a philosophically significant distinction. Criteria 4 and 5 go beyond the traditional boundaries of the philosophy of mathematics by admitting the application of mathematics and human mathematical practice as legitimate philosophical concerns, as well as its relations with other areas of human knowledge. They unambiguously admit social aspects of mathematics as legitimate areas of philosophical enquiry. Criterion 6 adds a concern with how mathematics is transmitted onward from one generation to the next and, in particular, how it is learnt by individuals and the dialectical relation between individuals and existing knowledge in creativity.

The legitimacy of all of these extended concerns arises from the possibility of considering the relationship between mathematics and its corporeal agents, that is, human beings, as I have argued. The above are proposed as adequacy criteria for evaluating extant or putative philosophies of mathematics. They frankly represent a reconceptualization of the role of the philosophy of mathematics. However, as I have argued, they are needed to accommodate what on the face of it is the simple and clear task of the philosophy of mathematics, namely, to give an account of mathematics, descriptively or otherwise.

In addition there is an unstated further criterion, namely, that an adequate philosophy of mathematics must give an account of mathematics in philosophically acceptable terms, understood broadly, employing types of explanation and justification that can broadly be regarded as appropriate. This addendum is necessary, or else the reconceptualization has no chance of being accepted as such by philosophers of mathematics, and hence can have no impact on the field. In addition, some histories of mathematics might satisfy the criteria better than some traditional philosophical accounts, such as that classic of logicism, Russell's *Introduction to Mathematical Philosophy*, but the aim is to characterize new contributions to the *philosophy* of mathematics.

A CRITICAL EXAMINATION OF PHILOSOPHICAL POSITIONS

The new criteria provide a means to assess the adequacy of various schools of thought in the philosophy of mathematics. Elsewhere I have applied something more or less equivalent to them to conventionalism and (naive) empiricism (Ernest 1991).

Progressive Absolutism

Different forms of absolutism in mathematics—including a weaker form—can be distinguished. Drawing a parallel with the philosophy of science, Confrey 1981 distinguishes *progressive absolutism* in the philosophy of mathematics; this, while absolutist, regards mathematics as resulting from human striving for truth, rather than its attainment. According to this view

> progress is a process of replacement of previous theories by superior theories which account for all the previous data and more. Each progressive theory approximates truth more and more precisely . . . progress consists of discovering mathematical truths which are not consistent with a theory or not accounted for in the theory, and then extending the theory to account for this larger realm of mathematical phenomenon. (Confrey 1981, 247–48)

Progressive absolutism is modeled on Popper's philosophy of science, in which he acknowledges that all scientific theories are fallible and liable to refutation, but that over the course of history scientific approaches the truth more closely (a thesis of increasing verisimilitude). Thus the key distinction made by Confrey is that between static and dynamic absolutist conceptions of mathematical knowledge and theories, with human activity contributing the dynamic in progressive absolutism. Formalism and logicism are straightforwardly absolutist. They are concerned only with finished mathematical knowledge and do not treat the creation or change of mathematical theories nor informal mathematics, let alone human agency. Such views treat nothing other than fixed, formal mathematical theories, and hence, by implication, regard the philosophy of mathematics as concerned only with such.

In contrast, progressive absolutist philosophies: (*a*) accommodate the creation and change of axiomatic theories; (*b*) acknowledge that more than purely formal mathematics exists, for mathematical intuition is needed as the basis for theory creation; and hence (*c*) acknowledge human activity and its outcomes, in the creation of new knowledge and theories. However, they also (*d*) view the replacement of old mathematical theories by new ones as progressive steps toward ultimate mathematical truth.

Intuitionism (and constructivism, more generally) fits this description. Intuitionism is foundationalist and absolutist, seeking secure foundations for mathematical knowledge through intuitionistic proofs and "ur-intuition" (Kalmar 1967). However, intuitionism acknowledges (*a*) that human mathematical activity is fundamental in the construction of proofs, mathematical objects, and in the creation of new mathematical knowledge and (*b*) that the axioms of intuitionistic mathematical theory (and logic) are fundamentally incomplete and need to be added to as more mathematical truth is revealed informally or by intuition (Brouwer [1927] 1967; Dummett 1977). Thus intuitionists embrace the possibility of the continued development of the basis of intuitionist mathematics, as it progresses toward mathematical truth.[5]

A consequence of this is that intuitionism and progressive absolutist philosophies in general satisfy more of the adequacy criteria than formal absolutist philosophies, while nevertheless remaining refuted overall. For they give some place, although restricted, to the activities of mathematicians (criterion 5). They acknowledge human agency, albeit in stylized form, in the domain of informal mathematics. This partial fulfillment of the criteria deserves acknowledgment, for it means that not all absolutist philosophies are on a par, in evaluative terms. However the admission of the cognizing subject into intuitionism, although it constitutes the shadow of a human presence, falls a long way short of seeing mathematics as embedded in human mathematical practice and history, as criterion 5 requires.

Platonism

Platonism is the view that the objects of mathematics have a real, objective existence in some ideal realm. Naturally Platonism originates with Plato, but more recently it can be discerned in the writings of the logicists Frege and Russell, and includes Cantor, Bernays (1934), Hardy (1941) and Gödel (1964) among its distinguished supporters. Platonists maintain that the objects and structures of mathematics have a real existence independent of humanity, and that doing mathematics is the process of discovering their preexisting relationships. According to Platonism, mathematical knowledge consists of descriptions of the objects and structures of mathematics and the relationships between them.

A distinction has been drawn between mathematical realism and mathematical Platonism.

> "Realism" as applied to the subject matter of mathematics [asserts that] mathematics is the scientific study of objectively existing mathematical entities just as science is the study of physical entities. The statements of mathematics are true or false depending on the properties of those entities, independent of our ability, or lack thereof, to determine which. Traditionally Platonism in the philosophy of mathematics has been taken to involve somewhat more than this. Following some of what Plato had to say about his Forms, many thinkers have characterized mathematical entities as abstract—outside of physical space, eternal and unchanging—and as existing necessarily—regardless of the details of the contingent make-up of the physical world. Knowledge of such entities is often thought to be *a priori*—sense experience can tell us about how things are, not how they must be—and certain—as distinguished from fallible scientific knowledge. (Maddy 1990, 21)

Platonism evidently provides a solution to the problem of explaining the objectivity of mathematics. It accounts both for its truths and for the existence of its objects, as well as for the apparent autonomy of mathematics, which obeys its own inner laws and logic.

Platonism is primarily an ontological position, as opposed to an epistemology, although in this case these cannot be entirely separated. For although it follows from Platonism as described by Maddy that the truths of mathematics are the states of affairs that hold in the realm of Platonic mathematical entities, it is the ontological assumptions that give rise to this. Thus Platonism is not foundationalist. Its various forms have not been based on an attempt to provide mathematical knowledge with a secure foundation.

The problem of Platonism, unlike that of the absolutist schools, is therefore not entirely one of failure. For Platonism offers no foundationalist program to reconstruct and safeguard mathematics that has failed. What is of more interest is to account for the fact that such an implausible philosophy provides aid and comfort to successful mathematicians with the stature of Cantor and Gödel.

Rotman (1988) offers an enlightening semiotic analysis of philosophies of mathematics, considered as sign systems. Following Saussure and Peirce, he adopts the standard semiotic analysis of the sign as a an ordered pair of "signifier" and "signified." One of the major developments in nineteenth-century mathematics was the detachment of signifier systems (formal systems) from the accompanying class of signifieds. This lay behind the shift in the meaning of truth, described in chapter 1. Two absolutist philosophies of mathematics capitalized on this development and tried to recast mathematical theories into systems of detached signifiers. These are formalism and logicism, although in this context Rotman explicitly mentions only formalism, which resembles the nominalism of the medieval Schoolmen.

Another philosophy of mathematics adopted the complementary position of viewing mathematics as a system of detached signifieds. Intuitionism, at least in Brouwer's presentation, regards mathematics as a set of subjective meanings, signifieds initially without signifiers. Brouwer might deny the subjective label, but I apply it since he arrogates universality to his own intuition, which evidently does not always coincide with that of others. I have shown above that this weakness, together with others, is ultimately *philosophically* fatal. Nevertheless, intuitionism and constructivism still flourish, because they admit the human signifying activities essential for mathematical practice, as well as restricting signifieds to a realm of privileged constructive meaning. Rotman compares this position to that of the conceptualist Schoolmen (as does Quine 1953c).

In contrast, Rotman claims that Platonism is a view of mathematics as a full sign system, comprising both signifiers and signifieds. Unlike intuitionism, the signifieds are a set of objective meanings, external to any or all individual human consciousness. In order to practice, mathematicians need to work in a realm of meanings, and indeed the language they work in supplies the signifiers to complete the sign system. Beyond this, since mathematics is a social practice, the need for a shared set of meanings, in the extreme an objective set of meanings, is also evident. Platonism may not accommodate the human subject, but it accommodates human signifying activities, and these are essential for mathematical practice. Thus Rotman's semiotic analysis begins to show why certain philosophies of mathematics are preferred to others by mathematicians. They allow the new criteria for the philosophy of mathematics—especially criterion 5—to be fulfilled informally, by leaving space for human signifying activity, even if this is independent of the stated philosophy. Thus the success of Platonism, and hence its interest, is not its strength as an ontology or, still less, as an epistemology. Rather it lies in the illusory way it allows mathematicians to satisfy the new adequacy criteria privately, to their own satisfaction, while falling short of them in public accountability terms.

This interest notwithstanding, judged as a philosophy of mathematics Platonism suffers from at least two major weaknesses. First of all, it is not able to offer an adequate account of how mathematicians gain access to knowledge of the Platonic realm. Platonism accounts for mathematical knowledge in the same way as a naive inductivist view of science; that is, as being based on observations of the real world (an ideal world, in the case of Platonism), subsequently generalized. But if mathematics is the natural history of the crystalline Platonic universe, how is it that mathematicians gain knowledge of it? It must surely be through intuition, or some such special mental faculty, and no convincing account of this is given by Platonists. If access is through intuition, then a reconciliation is needed between the facts that (1) different mathematicians' intuitions vary, in keeping with the subjectivity of intuition, and (2) Platonist intuition must be objective, or intersubjective at least, and lead to agreement. Thus the Platonist view is inadequate without an account of human access to the realm of Platonic objects which overcomes these difficulties.

If, on the other hand, the Platonist's access to the world of mathematical objects is not through intuition but through reason and logic, then further problems arise. How does the Platonist know that his or her reasoning is correct? Either another form of intuition is needed, one that allows the Platonist to see which proofs correctly describe mathematical reality, or the Platonist is in the same boat as everybody else with regard to proof. But in this second case, what is Platonism but empty faith, since it provides no insight into truth or existence?

The second flaw in the Platonist account is that it is not able to offer an adequate account of mathematics, either internally or externally. Internally, an important part of mathematics is its constructive, computational side (part of criterion 2). This depends vitally on the representation of dynamic mathematical processes, such as iteration, recursive functions, proof theory, and so on. Platonism accounts primarily for the static set-theoretic and structural aspects of mathematics. Thus it omits a central area of mathematics from its account. Externally, Platonism fails to account adequately for the utility of mathematics, its relations with science, human activity or culture, and the genesis of knowledge (criteria 1 and 4). For Platonists to say that knowledge of mathematics advances as it is progressively uncovered, just as geography advanced with the voyages of the explorers, is not enough. Nor does it suffice to say its utility stems from the fact that mathematics describes the necessary structure of observable reality. For these explanations beg the very questions they are meant to settle.

Since it fails on the above counts, Platonism must be rejected as a philosophy of mathematics. I have suggested that it may satisfy some mathematicians because of its heuristic value, when accepted as an article of faith. But as in the case of many other worldviews, ideologies, and religions accepted likewise on faith, having such a basis does not constitute philosophical adequacy. However, Platonism does offer an explanation of certain aspects of mathematics that a philosophy of mathematics needs to accommodate.

NOTES

1. This is Lakatos's term for his philosophy of mathematics and is fully explained in chapter 4.

2. Lakatos himself approaches the issue through the rational reconstruction of history, to show that discovery is based on logic and not subjective whim.

3. This should be read as Lakatosian (and later social constructivist) fallibilism, since there is some ambiguity in the term.

4. Of course there were good historical reasons for avoiding the mention of persons and their beliefs, because of the quest for objectivity in mathematics, and because of historical lapses into psychologism such those critiqued by Frege (1884).

5. There is an apparent contradiction in intuitionism which both asserts the intuitively certain basis for mathematics and the revisable nature of mathematics. Thus, on the one hand, the logical and mathematical axioms and rules of inference are given directly and incontrovertibly by the knowing subject's intuition. Hence assuming that this intuition is universal (as Brouwer does), mathematics is certain, although it can of course grow by the discovery and addition of new basic principles or axioms. On the other hand, the intuitive basis of mathematics, including its logical and mathematical foundations, is open to revision to reflect the discovery or refinement of intuitive principles by the subject. But this entails the rejection or the revision of the basic axioms and principles, held to be given directly by intuition to the knowing subject. The strongest commitments of the intuitionist seem to be to the former, absolutist view. As Heyting says: "intuitionism contains no arbitrary assumptions . . . intuitionism is the only possible way to construct mathematics." (Benacerraf and Putnam 1964, 49). The apparent contradiction may be accounted for in terms of the principle that intuitionist mathematics is at base prior to logic and linguistic formulations, which are pale and possibly flawed reflections of the basal "ur-intuition." Thus the axioms and other linguistic principles of mathematics are corrigible and open to revision, since they are secondary, and might prove to be unfaithful representations of "ur-intuition."

CHAPTER 3

WITTGENSTEIN'S PHILOSOPHY
OF MATHEMATICS

WITTGENSTEIN'S PHILOSOPHICAL THOUGHT AND BACKGROUND

Introduction and Biographical Sketch

This chapter is about Wittgenstein's philosophy of mathematics. Over his lifetime he contributed to two related but distinct philosophies of mathematics. The first of these is conventionalism, and he suggested the notion that all mathematical theorems or truths follow from the syntax of the language in which they are expressed. This was interpreted as saying that mathematical theorems are tautologies that tell us about the nature of language, not the world and are true by virtue of the meanings of their constituent terms. Shanker (1987) argues that the attribution of this view to Wittgenstein by members of the Vienna Circle and others is based on a misconception.

However, Wittgenstein's second, more extensive, and in my view far more profound contribution to the philosophy of mathematics is in his later work in which he developed a unique social philosophy of mathematics. This chapter is devoted to an exposition of this second philosophy of mathematics, based on my interpretation of his work.

Ludwig Wittgenstein (1889–1951) was born in Vienna to an artistic family of Jewish descent. His father was an engineer whose wealth was based in the steel industry. Wittgenstein studied engineering in Berlin and then in 1908 registered as a research student in aeronautical engineering at Manchester. While he was working on problems of propeller design his interests shifted toward mathematics, and this ultimately led him to the foundations and philosophy of mathematics. In 1911 he visited Frege at Jena, and Frege advised him to study with Russell at Cambridge, which he did for five terms during 1912–13. This was the first of four periods spent there; these included 1929–35 and 1937–39 as fellow and 1945–47 as professor. This intermittent residence is characteristic of his life of asceticism, self-sacrifice, integrity (he gave away his inherited fortune), and perhaps instability. He spent the First World War as a volunteer in the Austrian army and wrote the *Tractatus* during this period. He spent the Second World War serving as a medical orderly in London and Newcastle, although he had just been given a chair at Cambridge. He never settled for long into a fixed pattern of life. Nevertheless, philosophy dominated his thinking except after finishing the *Tractatus*, when he thought he had solved the problems of philosophy. Then he trained as a elementary teacher and taught in Austrian village schools from 1919 to 1926. Afterwards, living in Vienna (designing a house), he had philosophical discussions with members of the Vienna Circle. His reviving interest in philosophy was given a further impetus by hearing Brouwer lecture in 1928. The early 1930s at Cambridge are regarded as his most productive period, but he continued working at a variety of aspects of philosophy including the philosophy of mathematics until his death from cancer in 1951 (Malcolm 1958; Peursen 1969; Kenny 1973; Monk 1990).

Wittgenstein's Philosophy: Preliminary Considerations

Wittgenstein was one of this century's most original and creative philosophers. Although he published little in his lifetime, ever since his death a stream of books composed of collections of his writings and lecture courses reconstructed from notes taken by his students have been published. By now these books probably number more than twenty. Large as the scale of Wittgenstein's posthumous publications might be, it is dwarfed by the stream of commentaries on Wittgenstein's thought and life. In this torrent, a significant number of books treat Wittgenstein's philosophy of mathematics, as did an international conference at Kirchberg in 1992. Indeed it is hard for any book on Wittgenstein's thought to avoid this area, because of his lifelong central preoccupation with the interconnected triad of logic, language, and mathematics, and their philosophical problems or puzzles, as he put it.

Wittgenstein's writings, largely unfinished and posthumous as they are, offer the interpreter a particular problem. Throughout his life, Wittgenstein eschewed the narrative style of connected discursive prose. Instead he wrote a series of usually short, disconnected paragraphs, comprising individual thoughts, thought-experiments, remarks, problems, epigrams, or vignettes. This style makes the understanding of Wittgenstein's philosophy a difficult task. Indeed, "understanding" Wittgenstein probably involves a more extensive act of construal and meaning construction than required by most other philosophers. There is no universally accepted interpretation of Wittgenstein, and the literature abounds with variant readings of his philosophy and dramatically differing assessments of the significance of his philosophy of mathematics.

The difficulty of Wittgenstein's writing raises the issue of the relationship between his style and his overall approach to philosophy. Wittgenstein held strong views about the nature of philosophy, and he regarded its task as the dissolution of puzzles and the resolution of paradoxes. Above all, he regarded philosophy as a process of clarifying thought, rather than as a body of knowledge and answers (Kenny 1973). Seen in this light, his writing style is legitimated. His aim is to provoke thought and to share with the reader his questions and problems, not any answers he might have. "In philosophy it is always good to put a *question* instead of an answer to a question." (Wittgenstein 1978, 147) Wittgenstein's style thus epitomizes and reflects his philosophical position.

Wittgenstein's "style" is closely bound up with his philosophic outlook and characteristic manner of thought. Like Nietzsche, although with very different ends in view, he adopted a cryptic, aphoristic style of address, a mode of perpetual self-interrogation which went along with his rejection of large-scale systematizing philosophy. "The best that I could write would never be more than philosophical remarks; my thoughts were soon crippled if I tried to force them on in any one direction against their natural inclination" (Wittgenstein 1953, vii). To this extent as the commentators agree: Wittgenstein's thought can scarcely be grasped without taking account of his style (Norris 1983, 35).

In addition, virtually all of Wittgenstein's writings were published posthumously, and he did not consider them ready for publication. His manuscripts show very extensive reworking of themes over many years. Only the *Tractatus* was published in his lifetime, and even the *Philosophical Investigations* was left only partly complete. Both of these texts have more finish and continuity of subject-matter and thought in their presentation than do his other writings, which are often arranged and selected by his editors. It must also be stressed that Wittgenstein wrote in German, so his English works are translations.

A further complication arises from the fact that Wittgenstein's philosophy in general, and philosophy of mathematics in particular, changed and developed greatly over his lifetime. The myth of the two philosophers who might be called Early-Wittgenstein and Late-Wittgenstein is no longer widely accepted, as the development and continuity in his thought can be shown (Kenny 1973; Shanker 1987). But the fact remains that on central themes such as the nature of meaning, language, logic, necessity, and mathematics Wittgenstein's thought underwent major changes. Furthermore, many of his later views took him into the relatively uncharted waters of philosophy with a naturalistic and social perspective, whereas his early philosophy was pre-scriptive, objectivist, and certainly not social.

My own attitude to Wittgenstein's writings has varied over the years, too. Starting with respectful incomprehension, I developed a sense of under-standing but disagreement with the meaning theory of the *Tractatus*. My views continued to develop, via a dismissal of his philosophy of mathematics as obscurantist and irrelevant, to a dawning recognition that he has something profound and revolutionary to say about mathematics. I now con-sider him to have been one of the two most important and original thinkers in the philosophy of mathematics in the last two-thirds of the twentieth cen-tury—the other being Lakatos. Of the two, Wittgenstein is the more pro-found thinker, in my estimation, his philosophy of mathematics being an integral part of a radically new approach to many of the central problems in philosophy. My changing attitude to Wittgenstein has to a large part been a function of my own evolving philosophical position. Starting from a fixed logical empiricist stance, I have gradually softened and humanized my views of meaning, knowledge, science, and mathematics to my current fal-libilist position. Only when my personal theories had developed so that they resonated with Wittgenstein's philosophy was I able to look beneath the sur-face of his writings and comprehend (or so I think) his philosophy of math-ematics.

I offer this personal account as testimony to the difficulty and complex-ity in understanding Wittgenstein. My own intellectual journey also happens to reflect aspects of the changing way in which Wittgenstein's philosophy of mathematics has been received by some (but far from all) of those interested in this area.

A problem for anyone giving an account of Wittgenstein's philosophy of mathematics arises from the extensive and varied literature on Wittgen-stein's thought—representing a veritable "Wittgenstein industry." In particu-lar, there is a range of differing interpretations of Wittgenstein's philosophy of mathematics. He has been called a "strict finitist" (Kreisel 1958; Kielkopf 1970), "anthropologistic" (Hao Wang), a "full blooded conventionalist" (Dummett 1964), and the promoter of an "anti-philosophy of mathematics" (Maddy 1992). A number of distinguished thinkers have claimed that he was simply wrong and misunderstood important aspects of the foundations of mathematics, such as Gödel's theorem (Anderson 1964; Bernays 1959; Kreisel 1964). Others have dismissed or ignored this criticism (Bloor 1983; Tymoczko 1985; Shanker 1987).

Despite almost fifty years having elapsed since Wittgenstein's death, the import of his work for the philosophy of mathematics is in my view still widely underrated and misunderstood. For example, the usually acute Kreisel characterized his philosophy of mathematics as "the surprisingly insignificant product of a sparkling mind" (1958, 158). A more recent appraisal can be inferred from the fact that a second edition of the best-known collection of readings in the philosophy of mathematics has omitted all discussion of Wittgenstein's contribution, although this once occupied the entire fourth part of the book (Benacerraf and Putnam 1983, 1964). While the editors justify this move in their revised introduction, the omission is nevertheless indicative. Again, a highly regarded contributor to the philosophy of logic has put forward a reading of Wittgenstein of some importance for the philosophy of mathematics (Kripke 1982) which has been strongly criticized for misinterpreting him (Shanker 1987). Likewise, Shanker is critical of Wright (1980) for what he regards as a sympathetic misinterpretation of Wittgenstein's philosophy of mathematics and, in particular, of his views on the objectivity of mathematical knowledge.

More recently, a number of scholars including Bloor (1983), Tymoczko (1985), and Shanker (1987) have interpreted Wittgenstein as putting forward a social philosophy of mathematics. But Hacking's (1984) review of Bloor (1983) castigates him for infidelity to Wittgenstein's thought, in what I view as a sensible interpretation and development of his philosophy for sociology. Of course part of my sympathy with Bloor lies in the proximity of my interpretation of Wittgenstein to his, and indeed my debt to Bloor will become apparent, here and in later chapters.

Thus, given the disagreement and controversy that continues to this day, offering further reinterpretations of Wittgenstein, as I do here, is legitimate. However, I should make it clear at the outset that my exposition is not an exercise in Wittgenstein scholarship, not a faithful exegesis of his canon. It is instead a personal interpretation which will undoubtedly be rejected by some as subjective and inaccurate. To maximize its fidelity I will build my account of Wittgenstein's philosophy of mathematics around an extensive set of quotations from his writings. But ultimately, although my aim is to reflect Wittgenstein's ideas (as I understand them) without too much distortion, my purpose is to put forward his position as a platform on which to develop a social constructivist philosophy of mathematics.

The Social Basis of Wittgenstein's Philosophy

Preliminary to considering Wittgenstein's position on the philosophy of mathematics, it is important to sketch his approach to a number of critical areas in philosophy. His radical social views on the philosophy of language, meaning, and necessity in particular provide the foundation for his philosophy of mathematics. Although, as I said above, the continuity in Wittgenstein's philosophical though is undeniable, so too are the radical changes in his position. It is the later flowering of his thought that introduces the social element as central. Consequently I am here and below focusing on the later philosophy of Wittgenstein, primarily that given in *Philosophical Investigations* and *Remarks on the Foundations of Mathematics*, which reflect his thought in the late 1930s and the 1940s (although some of it is anticipated in his work of the early and mid-1930s).

Meaning as use. A major innovation in meaning theory is Wittgenstein's introduction of the notion that the meaning of a word or proposition is given by its use.[1]

> For a large class of statements—though not all—in which we employ the word "meaning" it can be defined thus: the meaning of a word is its use in the language. (Wittgenstein 1953, 20)

> Only in the practice of a language can a word have meaning. (Wittgenstein 1978, 344)

In particular, Wittgenstein claims that the sense of a mathematical proposition or theorem is given by its proof (and that a new proof of a theorem changes its sense) (Kenny 1973, 130). As Dummett (1973) argues, Wittgenstein is here fixing on one central aspect of use as the indication of meaning.

"Language games." In his later philosophy, typified by the *Philosophical Investigations* (Wittgenstein 1953), his notion of meaning as use was part of a more encompassing theory of language. This philosophy of language, which was largely expounded in concrete as opposed to theoretical terms, identified "language games" (*Sprachspiele*) as the contexts in which meanings are deployed. In fact, for Wittgenstein, it is the language game which has priority—the language game as embodied in social practice. Reflecting on one or two examples of social practice incorporating a pattern of language use he says:

> I shall call the whole, consisting of language and the actions into which it is woven the "language-game." (Wittgenstein 1953, 5)

> Here the term "language-*game* is meant to bring into prominence the fact that *speaking* of language is part of an activity, or of a form of life. (11)

"Forms of life." "Form of life" is the second of the characteristic and novel concepts introduced by Wittgenstein as the basis for his philosophy. A form of life as I understand it is an established and lived human social practice, with its own purposes, implicit rules, behavioral patterns, and linguistic usages or language games.[2]

Language, I should like to say, relates to a *way* of living.
In order to describe the phenomenon of language, one must describe a practice, not something that happens once, *no matter of what kind*. (Wittgenstein 1978, 335)

Some of the more important features of Wittgenstein's theory of meaning and language games are brought out by the following quotation from an authoritative commentator.

This [family-likeness] feature of "game" is one which Wittgenstein believed it shared with "language," and this made it particularly appropriate to call particular mini-languages "language-games." There were others. Most importantly, even though not all games have rules, the function of rules in many games has similarities with the function of rules in language (Wittgenstein 1969). Language games, like games, need have no external goal; they can be autonomous activities (Wittgenstein 1953, 1969). But the comparison of language to a game was not meant to suggest that language was a pastime, or something trivial: on the contrary it was meant to bring out the connection between the speaking of a language and non-linguistic activities. Indeed the speaking of a language is part of a communal activity, a way of living in society which Wittgenstein calls a "form of life" (Wittgenstein 1953). It is through sharing in the playing of language-games that language is connected with our life (Wittgenstein 1969). (Kenny 1973, 163, original citations, modified for consistency)

Philosophy of language. The following is an explicit summary of (my interpretation of) Wittgenstein's theory of meaning and language games—which might be termed his philosophy of language.

1. Terms and sentences do not in general have distinct individual references or meanings.
2. Instead, their meaning(s) are identical with their roles and uses in language games.
3. Language games are the patterns of linguistic behavior embodied in types of social activity: "forms of life."
4. Language games are based on rules. These may be implicit, but are the invariants or norms underpinning patterns of linguistic behavior anchored in forms of life.
5. Forms of life have priority; they are the socially given. They are the identifiable clusters of social behavior, social practices, which can only be given extensionally, because their existence alone is what legitimates them.

6. There are many forms of life and many language games, and any particular word or expression may be involved in several of them.
7. Forms of life may develop and change. Similarly language games have an open texture and may grow, change, and lead in unanticipated directions.
8. Language games are largely learned by participating in them. Nevertheless, explanation is undeniably a part of many language games.
9. Just as games do not share a set of essential properties but a "family resemblance," so too language games are of varying and different types.

Wittgenstein's philosophy of language is a revolutionary theory, and its radical nature is not yet fully appreciated, especially in scientific circles, although it has permeated many aspects of modern intellectual life beyond the Anglo-American tradition in philosophy (see, for example, Bhaskar 1991; Bloor 1983; Lyotard 1984; Rorty 1979). In his theory, meaning is no longer perceived as a relationship between language and the world, as it is in the correspondence theory of meaning (e.g., Russell 1940). Meaning resides instead in social patterns of use, which are themselves irrevocably woven into other aspects of social life.

Necessity and following a rule. Out of his theory of language games comes Wittgenstein's view of logical and mathematical necessity. His view is that necessity, such as that of an inference following the laws of deductive logic, arises from the human agreement in following a rule that is stipulated by (and presupposed by and embedded in) a language game.

> The word "agreement" and the word "rule" are related to one another, they are cousins. If I teach anyone the use of the one word, he learns the use of the other word with it. (Wittgenstein 1953, 86)

Thus there is no extrahuman or objective force that compels anyone to follow a logical rule or to accept the conclusion of a logical deduction. It is, rather, that participating in certain language games entails accepting certain rules. If one rejects the rule one is repudiating the game as it is understood and played by others. "To obey a rule, to make a report, to give an order, to play a game of chess, are *customs* (uses, institutions)" (81).

Of course the traditional view that logical necessity underpins deduction and rational thought is very firmly entrenched. Wittgenstein anticipates the obvious philosophical objection that rule following in logic and elsewhere stems not from human agreement and but from logical necessity. But even to communicate disagreements about truth, falsity, or necessity presupposes that we agree to use the terms comparably in social discourse and life.

"So you are saying that human agreement decides what is true and what is false?"—It is what human beings *say* that is true and false; they agree in the *language* they use. That is not agreement in opinions but in forms of life. (Wittgenstein 1953, 88).

Agreement in Wittgenstein's sense arises from our participating in shared language games (woven into our forms of life) and does not consist of arbitrarily adopting conventions. This gives us the shared constraints on the meanings of our language and ultimately leads us to decide what counts as truth and falsehood. Thus the relation among agreement, convention, and truth is far more subtle and complex in Wittgenstein's philosophy than in naive conventionalism.

This point is so central that it is worth illustrating it with an example (not from Wittgenstein). The traditional view of philosophy and logic is that the following logical inference is necessary without qualification: given A and A→B, then B. My understanding of Wittgenstein's position on this is as follows. Agreeing that this inference is necessary depends on many prior implicit agreements. First of all, the parties to the agreement must all share an understanding of a sophisticated language, written English in this case. This in turn presupposes that the parties are part of a linguistic community and routinely communicate, interact with others, and take part in shared social activities. Second, the parties (to the agreement) must agree that "A" and "B" are metalinguistic symbols denoting fixed but arbitrary English propositions, and that every instance of one of them has the same denotation (within an assumed but delimited meaning context). Third, the parties accept the rule of inference *modus ponens* as valid (i.e., whenever its premises have the truth as their value, they agree that invariably the conclusion does too.)

Although not an exhaustive analysis, these assumptions show that the logical necessity of the inference depends on shared forms of life (assumption 1) and participation in language games (assumptions 1, 2, and 3). Once these assumptions are made (and most of them you, the reader, and I, the writer, as participating members of modern literary society have no option but to make) then the conclusion is necessary. Likewise, given another, simpler set of assumptions about the game of chess, and a particular board configuration, checkmate in two moves is similarly necessary.

Private languages. One of the key features of Wittgenstein's theory of language is the view that language is something that is essentially public. Since our understanding of language arises from our shared language games and mutual participation in social forms of life, there can be no such thing as a "private language." The private language argument, as it is called, is an area of widespread discussion and dispute in philosophy (see Ayer 1956; Kenny

1973; Kripke 1982; Shanker 1987). A private language would simply refer to one person's private experiences. Wittgenstein's view is that language concerns language games, which are regulated by agreement and rules and—by their very nature—are public. Therefore it makes no sense to talk of a private language.

And hence "obeying a rule" is a practice. And to *think* one is obeying a rule is not to obey a rule. Hence it is not possible to obey a rule "privately." (Wittgenstein 1953, 81)

Wittgenstein makes this point explicitly for arithmetical rules, a particular linguistic context which is most apposite for this chapter, given its subject matter.

Could there be arithmetic without agreement on the part of the calculators?
Could there be only one human being that calculated?
It only makes sense to say "and so on" when "and so on" is *understood*. I.e., when the other is as capable of going on as I am, i.e., does go on just as I do. (Wittgenstein 1978, 349)

Wittgenstein's Approach to Philosophy and His Impact

From the above exposition it is clear that Wittgenstein proposes revolutionary accounts of meaning, language, and knowledge. I shall show that the same is true of his approach to the philosophy of mathematics. Since Wittgenstein is far from neglected, being probably the most influential philosopher in the Anglo-Saxon world in the second half of the twentieth century, what is surprising is how little impact these innovations have made. Thus Passmore (1957), Sheffler (1965), and Chisholm (1966), for example, do not comment on the implications of Wittgenstein's thought for epistemology.

Wittgenstein strongly believed that there are no philosophical problems, only philosophical puzzles, which can be sorted out by logical or linguistic analysis. ("The philosopher's treatment of a question is like the treatment of an illness" [Wittgenstein 1953, 91].) This view became the cornerstone of linguistic philosophy, associated with Oxford in the 1950s and 1960s, and representing the inheritors of Wittgenstein's approach. But if there are no philosophical problems, neither is there any need for philosophical theories. Wittgenstein's immediate impact resulted in an influential school of philosophical method, but not a body of explicit theory.[3] Thus the practitioners of Wittgenstein's method eschewed theory building, focusing instead on the uses of natural language, and theory builders such as epistemologists carried on regardless. To have developed a theory from Wittgenstein's work would have apparently been contrary to the spirit of his philosophy, which ruled it out for the linguistic philosophers.

Only now, with the benefit of hindsight (and the publication of the Wittgenstein oeuvre), is it possible to question Wittgenstein's self-characterization and dicta and realize that he did in fact offer radical theories of meaning, language, knowledge, necessity, and mathematics. Both Bloor (1983) and Specht (1969) argue that Wittgenstein's work contains an implicit but powerful and general theory. My contention is that Wittgenstein's philosophical *method* may have prevented or retarded the development of the consequences of his philosophical *theories*.

There is some evidence to corroborate this interpretation. Wittgenstein's own writings are quite clear that philosophy is a therapeutic method for dispelling confusion, and does not give rise to enduring theories or knowledge. Gellner, in his celebrated attack on linguistic philosophy, characterizes it as claiming that philosophy is activity, not doctrine, and that "past philosophy has been mainly abuse of language, future good philosophy will be the diagnosis and elimination of such abuse" (1959, 20). Popper (1976) reports conflicts with Wittgenstein on the issue of whether any philosophical problems exist. Passmore (1957) also suggests that in pursuing his method, Wittgenstein's failure to engage with the writings or problems of traditional philosophy rendered him inaccessible to many. Whatever the reason, ultimately my claim is that until recently the important implications of Wittgenstein's thought for the philosophy of mathematics have been both neglected and misunderstood. Only in the past decade or two have thinkers such as Toulmin (1972), Bloor (1983), Tymoczko (1985), and Shanker (1987) been reinterpreting Wittgenstein as putting forward a radical new social philosophy of mathematics.[4] This is my contention, too.

WITTGENSTEIN'S PHILOSOPHY OF MATHEMATICS

Wittgenstein's Philosophy of Mathematics: An Interpretation

Giving an explicit account of Wittgenstein's philosophy of mathematics is problematic for a number of reasons, including the fact that he might have denied having one. However, publications are appearing which elucidate parts of the philosophy of mathematics that is implicit in Wittgenstein's writings (e.g., Klenk 1976; Shanker 1987; Tymoczko 1985).

Wittgenstein has been described as a conventionalist, although usually with caution and disclaimers (Klenk 1976). Shanker (1987) makes it clear that Wittgenstein's position differs from all of those previously described as conventionalist, while conceding that there are elements of his thought that can legitimately be so described. Dummett (1964) refers to Wittgenstein's position as "full blooded" conventionalism, because he interprets it to mean that every mathematical theorem is adopted (or rejected) freely by convention. I shall argue that this account is a parody, based on a misunderstanding.

My interpretation is that Wittgenstein proposed a naturalistic and fallibilist social philosophy of mathematics. The naturalism relates to his attachment to descriptive philosophy, which gives priority to mathematical practice (Maddy 1992). This latter is social, since it comprises one or more forms of life (Bloor 1983). His philosophy is fallibilist, because he grounds certainty in the accepted (but always revisable) rules of language games (Rorty 1979).

Wittgenstein on the foundations of mathematics. Wittgenstein repudiates the notion that mathematics needs or derives any security from its "foundations."

What does mathematics need a foundation for? It no more needs one, I believe, than propositions about physical objects—or about sense impressions, need an *analysis*. What mathematical propositions do stand in need of is a clarification of their grammar, just as do those other propositions.

The *mathematical* problems of what is called foundations are no more the foundation of mathematics for us than the painted rock is the support of a painted tower.

"But didn't the contradiction make Frege's logic useless for giving a foundation for arithmetic?" Yes, it did. But then who said that it had to be useful for this purpose? (Wittgenstein 1978, 378)

As this indicates, Wittgenstein rejects foundationalism and the foundationalist programs of logicism, formalism, and intuitionism (Klenk 1976). Not only does he repudiate absolutism and apriorism, he also asserts that mathematical knowledge is synthetic a priori.

The distribution of primes would be an ideal example of what could be called synthetic *a priori*, for one can say that it is at any rate not discoverable by an analysis of the concept of a prime number. (Wittgenstein 1978, 246)

Wittgenstein on Platonism and ontology. The view that mathematical knowledge is synthetic *a priori* arises from Wittgenstein's conviction that mathematics is constructed by the mathematician and is not a preexisting realm that is discovered. ("The mathematician is an inventor, not a discoverer," Wittgenstein 1978, 99). As this suggests, Wittgenstein also rejects Platonistic conceptions of mathematical existence.

Is it already mathematical alchemy, that mathematical propositions are regarded as statements about mathematical objects—and mathematics as the exploration of these objects?

In a certain sense it is not possible to appeal to the meaning of the signs in mathematics, just because it is only mathematics that give them their meaning.

What is typical of the phenomenon I am talking about is that a mysteriousness about some mathematical concept is not straight away interpreted as an erroneous conception, as a mistake of ideas; but rather as something that is at any rate not to be despised, is perhaps even rather to be respected.

All that I can do, is to show an easy escape from this obscurity and this glitter of concepts . . . which only looks like a gleam without a corporeal substrate when seen from . . . [an]other direction. (Wittgenstein 1978, 274–75)

This quotation indicates Wittgenstein's rejection of Platonistic conceptions of the independent existence of mathematical objects—which is well known in the literature (Bernays 1964; Klenk 1976; Maddy 1992; Shanker 1987). It also hints at Wittgenstein's position on ontology, which arises from his adoption of his "use" and "language game" theory of meaning in place of a correspondence theory. Instead of mathematical names indicating mathematical objects, according to Wittgenstein's theory, the names' meaning is given by their use in a mathematical language game. Thus mathematical names need not in general have any independent or extra-human reference.[5]

Wittgenstein's philosophy of mathematics. Wittgenstein claims that mathematics comprises a language game, or rather a cluster of language games. "Mathematics—I want to say—teaches you, not just the answer to a question, but a whole language-game with questions and answers" (Wittgenstein 1978, 381). This quotation refers to a particular arithmetical language game involving counting and calculating. However it is clear that Wittgenstein views mathematics as a complex set of overlapping activities and language games. Thus Wittgenstein refers to the "motley of mathematics" and asks, "Why should I not say that what we call mathematics is a family of activities with a family of purposes?" (275). Pole (1958) identifies Euclidean geometry as a language game according to Wittgenstein's conception. Wittgenstein draws further examples from mathematical sequences, formal logic, metamathematics, combinatorics, and other topics, suggesting that mathematics is made up of a motley of language games and that new ones can be invented and added.

Waismann (1951) interprets Wittgenstein's position as meaning that mathematics is made up of a number of deductive systems, and no one of them, such as formal logic, is privileged over the others. Although this is partially correct, it is clear from Wittgenstein's writings that the language games of mathematics are by no means all formal mathematical systems and that, based on the examples he uses, a number of informal mathematical practices also constitute language games. As elsewhere, language games in mathematics are founded in forms of life and cannot be reduced to purely linguistic activities. The "understanding of a mathematical proposition is not guaranteed by its verbal form . . . the words don't determine the *language-game* in which the proposition functions" (Wittgenstein 1978, 284).

Mathematics is a game. Wittgenstein not only develops a theory of mathematics as a motley of language games, but also pursues the direct analogy between mathematics and games such as chess (Wittgenstein 1969). In fact, according to Kenny (1973) and Waismann (1967), Wittgenstein first used the metaphor of a game to illuminate mathematics and mathematical formalism as early as 1930, some time before he developed his general language-game theory.

Formalism contains both truth and falsehood. The truth in formalism is that every syntax can be regarded as a system of rules for a game. I have been reflecting on what Weyl can mean when he says that a formalist regards the axioms of mathematics as similar to the rules of chess. I would like to say: not only the axioms, but the whole of syntax is arbitrary.

I was asked in Cambridge whether I think that mathematics concerns ink marks on paper. I reply, in just the same sense in which chess concerns wooden figures . . . It does not matter what a pawn looks like. What is much rather the case is that the totality of rules of the game determines the logical place of a pawn. A pawn is a variable, like the "x" in logic. (Waismann 1967, 104)

The early notion that mathematics "is a game with signs according to rules" (Wittgenstein 1978, 265), as well as the analogy with the game of chess persisted in the later publications and thought of Wittgenstein (1953, 1976, 1978). However the basis for the rules was deepened, and founded on the later notion of a "form of life." This represented a shift away from Wittgenstein's earlier position, which was close to conventionalism.

Wittgenstein's social philosophy of mathematics. Wittgenstein's conception of mathematics developed so that in his mature philosophy rules in mathematics are not simply something assented to or rejected by mathematicians. This would give rise to a shallow form of conventionalism in which logical necessity prevails, unchanged, or in which anything goes, as Dummett (1964) argues. Instead, the rules in mathematics, according to Wittgenstein's conception, penetrate deep to the heart of human social activity and "forms of life." In following a rule, although it is based on a nexus of decisions, each step does not require an independent decision. "You don't make a decision: you simply do a certain thing. It is a question of a certain practice" (Wittgenstein 1976, 237). The rules are not arbitrary in the sense that they are not adopted willy-nilly in a series of disconnected decisions. Instead their form and acceptance have evolved with context-related linguistic and social practices. Consequently Wittgenstein sees mathematics in large part as an activity based on language games and their associated deeply entrenched rules.

> Of course, in one sense mathematics is a branch of knowledge,—but still it is also an *activity*. And "false moves" can only exist as the exception. For if what we now call by that name became the rule, the game in which they were false moves would have been abrogated. (Wittgenstein 1953, 227)

As Shanker (1987) makes clear, Wittgenstein does not repudiate the notions of objectivity or certainty for mathematical knowledge. Instead he reinterprets these notions to mean that mathematical knowledge rests without the need for doubt on our language games and forms of life. Their assumption provides an agreed basis for mathematical knowledge, which makes it public and thus objective, and puts it above doubt, which would be inappropriate. But this agreed basis for mathematical knowledge does not put it above change.

It is clear that Wittgenstein's notions of truth, falsity, logical necessity, and inconsistency are very different from the traditional absolutist versions. Instead, the central concept is that of agreement with a rule. "The words 'right' and 'wrong' are used when giving instruction in proceeding according to a rule. The word 'right' makes the pupil go on, the word 'wrong' holds him back" (Wittgenstein 1978, 405).

A consequence is that Wittgenstein's view of proofs and what is proven takes on a new significance too.

> *What* is unshakably certain about what is proved? To accept a proposition as unshakably certain—I want to say—means to use it as a grammatical rule: this removes uncertainty from it. (Wittgenstein 1978, 170)

More on truth and necessity. This reveals an underpinning and characteristic theme in Wittgenstein's philosophy of mathematics, namely, his treatment of logical or mathematical necessity based on the notion of following a rule. Wittgenstein's view is that the uses of language (in various language games or meaning contexts) involves the acceptance of rules, which are a precondition, a *sine qua non*, for linguistic communication. The agreement he refers to is the sharing of form of life, a group sociolinguistic practice based on the common following of rules, which is essential for any meaningful language use. Such agreement is not merely the voluntary assent to a practice, such as with the conventions of the game of bridge. Rather, it is built into our communicative behavior, which presupposes a common underlying language usage and rule following (Bloor 1983).

Thus according to Wittgenstein's philosophy of mathematics the "truths" of mathematics and logic depend for their acceptance on the linguistic rules of use of terms and grammar, as well on the rules governing proofs. These underlying rules confer certainty on the "truths," for they cannot be false without breaking the rules, which would be flying in the face of accepted use. Thus it is the linguistic rules underlying the "truths" of mathematics and logic that ensure that they cannot be falsified.

> I have not yet made the role of miscalculating clear. The role of the proposition: "I must have miscalculated." It is really the key to an understanding of the "foundations" of mathematics. (Wittgenstein 1978, 221)

What Wittgenstein is saying here is that if our results contradict the underlying rules of use, then we reject the results: we do not question the underlying rules (unless for some reason we want to change the game).

Wittgenstein proposes that the logical necessity of mathematical (and logical) knowledge rests on linguistic conventions or norms embedded in our sociolinguistic practices. "What I am saying comes to this, that mathematics is *normative*. But 'norm' does not mean the same thing as 'ideal'" (Wittgenstein 1978, 425).

The role of contradiction. A special case of a logical rule whose necessity rests on our assumption of linguistic convention is the law of contradiction (the principle of noncontradiction). First of all, he argues that despite its traditionally privileged status this is like any other convention. Under ordinary circumstances, a contradictory proposition can be harmless (but useless).

> Is there harm in the contradiction that arises when someone says: "I am lying.—So I am not lying.—So I am lying.—etc."? I mean: does it make our language less usable if in this case, according to the ordinary rules, a proposition yields its contradictory, and vice versa?—The proposition *itself* is unusable, and these inferences equally; but why should they not

be made?—It is a profitless performance!—It is a language-game with some similarity to the game of thumb-catching. (Wittgenstein 1978, 120)

In itself, Wittgenstein considers the power to formulate a contradiction to be harmless, if the statement merely invalidates itself. However, the law of contradiction, like many of the assumptions of truth functional logic, is woven into the accepted fabric of our language games, especially mathematical ones, and to abrogate it would be to significantly change their nature. For Wittgenstein the key question is whether the rules of the language game are inconsistent, for then following them all simultaneously would be impossible.

Not letting a contradiction stand is something that characterizes the technique of our employment of our truth-functions. If we do let the contradiction stand in our language games, we alter that technique—as, if we departed from regarding a double negative as an affirmative. And this alteration would be significant, because the technique of our logic is connected in its character with the conception of the truth functions.

. . . And it is something like this, when I discover that the rules lead to a contradiction. I am now compelled to acknowledge that this is not a proper game. (Wittgenstein 1978, 394)

Thus Wittgenstein is according a privileged role to noncontradiction in a special metatheoretical context, namely, to the rules (and their consequences) within a language game. This is because such an outcome would lead to ambiguities and contradictions about what it is to follow a rule, to engage in that particular language game. "Now a language-game can lose its sense through a contradiction, can lose the character of a language-game" (Wittgenstein 1978, 208).

Following a rule. A central part of Wittgenstein's critical revaluation of logical (and mathematical) necessity hinges on his discussion of the notion of following a rule. Rules are woven into language games and forms of life, including mathematics, supplying its *normative* basis. Wittgenstein argues that logical necessity—be it computing an algorithm, proving a theorem, drawing a deductive inference, or whatever—concerns the following of a rule. Rule following raises the issue of the compulsion to reach a conclusion that is fixed and, if not predetermined, then at least unique and determinate.

By translating the issue of logical necessity into the compulsion to follow a rule, Wittgenstein is implicitly denying the validity of considering necessity solely in traditionally objectified and depersonalized terms. This is essential and inescapable, given his philosophy of language, since logic, rules, and language are at root located in human forms of life.

We say: "If you really follow the rule in multiplying, you *must* all get the same result" . . . The emphasis of the *must* corresponds only to the inexorableness of [our] attitude both to the technique of calculating and to a host of related techniques.

The mathematical Must is only another expression of the fact that mathematics forms concepts.

And concepts help us to comprehend things. They correspond to a particular way of dealing with situations.

Mathematics forms a network of norms. (Wittgenstein 1978, 430–41)

Wittgenstein devoted a great deal of thought to the issue of necessity, compulsion, and the nature of rule following. A very substantial part of Wittgenstein (1953, 1976, 1978), which includes the bulk of his late writings on the philosophy of mathematics, treat this and related notions. He was concerned to elucidate the relationship between logical necessity and rule following, and how one could know if the next application of a rule was lawlike. In his view, no initial sequence of rule applications can uniquely determine the next application, let alone the underlying rule. He was also very concerned with the related problem of how one could tell if someone had grasped a rule, and what behavioral evidence would provide proof. He concluded that no finite number of applications could satisfactorily demonstrate that someone had grasped the intended sense of a rule.[6]

If a rule does not compel you, then you aren't *following* a rule.

But how am I supposed to be following it; if I can after all follow it as I like? . . . that everything can be interpreted as following doesn't mean that everything is following.

But how then does the teacher interpret the rule for the pupil? (For he is certainly supposed to give it a particular interpretation.)—Well, how but by means of words and by training?

And if the pupil reacts to it thus and thus; he possesses the rule inwardly.

But *this* is important, namely that this reaction, which is our guarantee of understanding, presupposes as a surrounding particular circumstances, particular forms of life and speech.

Suppose someone follows the series "1, 3, 5, 7, . . ." in writing the series $2x + 1$; and he asked himself "But am I always doing the same thing, or something different every time?"

How is it to be decided whether he always does the same, when the line intimates to him how he is to go? (Wittgenstein 1978, 413–15)[7]

A further quotation makes clear that following a rule is not predetermined by past performance, as Kripke (1982) points out, and that continuing to follow a rule requires what is tantamount to a decision, rather than an imposed logical compulsion.[8]

> Now we get the pupil to continue a series (say +2) beyond 1000—and he writes 1000, 1004, 1008, 1012.
> We say to him: "Look what you've done!"—He doesn't understand. We say: "You were meant to add *two*: look at how you began the series!"—He answers: "Yes, isn't it right? I though that was how I was *meant* to do it . . . Add 2 up to 1000, 4 up to 2000, 6 up to 3000, and so on" . . .
> "What you are saying, then, comes to this: a new insight—intuition—is needed at every step to carry out the order '+n' correctly!" . . . It would almost be more correct to say, not that an intuition was needed at every stage, but that a new decision was needed at every stage (Wittgenstein 1953, 75)

Mathematical proof. In Wittgenstein's philosophy, necessity is founded in following socially accepted rules (i.e., those that are standard usage in mathematical practice). It follows that neither the individual's personal interpretation of rule following, nor the logical necessity of a mathematical proof, in particular, has the absolute and extrahuman basis of certainty presumed by absolutism. "Proof must be a procedure of which I say: Yes this is how it has to be; this must come out if I proceed according to the rule" (Wittgenstein 1978, 160). Thus mathematical knowledge, like any other form of knowledge, has its justification in certain rules, language games, and forms of life. In the case of mathematics, a particular form of justification, namely, mathematical proof, is employed. But this too rests on the basis of social conventions.

> I am trying to say something like this: even if the proved mathematical proposition seems to point to a reality outside itself, still it is only the expression of acceptance of a new measure (of reality)
> We have won through to a new piece of knowledge in the proof?
> Why should I not say: in the proof I have won through to a *decision*?
> The proof places this decision in a system of decisions. (Wittgenstein 1978, 162–63)

Although Wittgenstein characterizes the acceptance of a new mathematical theorem as a decision, it does not constitute a frivolous decision or an arbitrary addition to the body of mathematical knowledge. It has a justification, but constitutes a decision for the following reasons. First, we have chosen to accept the basis of a mathematical system (a language game) by participating in a form of life and thus concurring with "how things are done" in it. Second, we agree to follow the deductive reasoning in a proof because we choose to assent to the rules of inference *and* the particular applications in question, not because we are compelled to do so. Consequently, in effect, we have decided to accept the theorem as a new piece of mathematical knowledge.

> I go through the proof and say: "Yes, this is how it *has* to be; I must fix the use of my language in *this* way."
>
> I want to say that the *must* corresponds to a track which I lay down in language. (Wittgenstein 1978, 165–66)

The decision is neither arbitrary nor preordained. It is a composite decision that is built up from a number of overarching earlier choices, and from choosing to follow and to maintain our assent to a particular line of reasoning. We need not be aware of all of these decisions in deciding to accept the theorem as a new item of mathematical knowledge. But epistemologically, in establishing what constitutes the basis of the theorem, we need to acknowledge their role.

The role of assent in the acceptance of mathematical proof contrasts importantly with the traditional view of proof in which logical necessity is preeminent. Wittgenstein's view is that a mathematical proof serves to justify an item of mathematical knowledge by its persuasiveness, not by its inherent logical necessity. ("*In* a demonstration we *get agreement* with someone" [Wittgenstein 1978, 62].) Of course a proof's logical structure and reference to the rules and norms of accepted language games are an essential part of its persuasive power.

> "A mathematical proof must be perspicuous" . . .
>
> I want to say: if you have a proof-pattern which cannot be taken in, and by a change in notation you change it into one that can, then you are producing a proof, where there was none before. (Wittgenstein 1978, 143)

Ultimately, a proof is a narrative for human consumption, a "procedure that is *plain to view*" (Wittgenstein 1978, 173), not a superhuman objective structure. For the primary function of a proof is to convince, and logical structure is just a means to that end. Thus mathematical knowledge is founded on human persuasion and acceptance.

The mathematician is an inventor. Wittgenstein's philosophy of mathematics undermines the often unacknowledged Platonism which leads mathematicians to believe that the discovery of mathematical propositions and objects is predetermined, once a mathematical system is specified. This view suggests that the conclusions of mathematical proofs, the terms of mathematical sequences, and so on, force themselves on us as soon as the initial conditions are laid down. Wittgenstein refutes this by demonstrating that no such compulsion exists, as I described above. But beyond this, Wittgenstein's view is that all such consequences, sequences, and so on, have to be created by mathematicians, and cannot be said to exist until they are created. As he says "the mathematician is not a discoverer: he is an inventor" (Wittgenstein 1978, 111). Even after listing untold millions of terms in a sequence given by a rule, the continuation "has to be invented just as much as any mathematics" (270)

The mathematician who constructs a new proof always creates a new concept (or changes the meaning of an existing one).

> When I said that a proof introduces a new concept, I meant something like: the proof puts a new paradigm among the paradigms of the language . . .
> One would like to say: the proof changes the grammar of our language, changes our concepts. It makes new connexions, and it creates the concept of these connexions. (It does not establish that they are there; they do not exist until it makes them.) (Wittgenstein 1978, 166)

Thus Wittgenstein not only views mathematical propositions and theorems as the invention of the mathematician, but also sees the concepts of mathematics and senses of mathematical expressions as being such invention.

"Strict finitism" and the role of the philosophy of mathematics. Because of this view, which appears to make him even more constructively rigorous than the intuitionists, Wittgenstein has been called a "strict finitist" (Kielkopf 1970; Kreisel 1958). I maintain that this is based on a fundamental misunderstanding. Wittgenstein is undoubtedly attacking Platonistic assumptions and modes of speech in his assertion that all mathematics has to be invented and that human decision making is central in this process. But this does not make him a strict finitist in the sense that Brouwer is an intuitionist, let alone in the sense in which Yessenin-Volpin (1980) is an ultra-intuitionist. For Wittgenstein's remarks are philosophical reflections on mathematical practice, quite consistent with the acceptance of mathematical practice. He does not assert that nonfinitary mathematics is meaningless or in need of reform (Klenk 1976; Shanker 1987). "I am *not* saying transfinite propositions are false (Wittgenstein 1976, 141). Elsewhere he discusses completed infinities, set theory, and Cantor's proof of the

uncountability of the real numbers without any qualms or strictures about the nonfinitistic reasoning or subject matter involved (Wittgenstein 1978). Further evidence that Wittgenstein did not adopt a strongly constructivist position is to be found in his treatment of double negation.

> . . . if we departed from regarding a double negative as an affirmative . . . this alteration would be significant, because the technique of our logic is connected in its character with the conception of the truth-functions. (Wittgenstein 1978, 394)

Thus Wittgenstein acknowledges the law of double negation as part of "our logic" and argues that to drop it involves changing (classical) logic. But intuitionists and other constructivists strongly reject this law. Elsewhere, in his *Philosophical Grammar* and *Philosophical Remarks*, Wittgenstein also affirms the centrality of the law of the excluded middle in the practice of logic and mathematics as well as of nonconstructive existence proofs, *contra* the intuitionists, as Maddy (1992) and Lear (1982) emphasize.

Wittgenstein argues that the role of the philosopher of mathematics is not to solve mathematical problems or to reform mathematics.

> His labour in philosophy is as it were an idleness in mathematics.
> It is not that a new building has to be erected, or that a new bridge has to be built, but that the geography, *as it is now*, has to be described . . .
> This is why it is no use in the philosophy of mathematics to recast proofs in new forms . . .
> Even 500 years ago a philosophy of mathematics was possible, a philosophy of what of mathematics was then. (Wittgenstein 1978, 302).

This is an unambiguous rejection of the foundationalist assumption of the various constructivist and intuitionist philosophies, that mathematics needs to be reformed. According to Wittgenstein, to do that would be to do mathematics. In contrast, the role of the philosophy of mathematics is naturalistic: to describe mathematical practice, not to practice mathematics, let alone reform it. Thus the claim that Wittgenstein is a "strict finitist" is refuted.

Finally, the above quotation shows that Wittgenstein acknowledges the legitimacy of the philosophy of mathematics, despite his antitheoretical stance in philosophy. Indeed, this stance is manifested in his call for a descriptive (as opposed to prescriptive or reforming) philosophy of mathematics.

> It is the business of philosophy . . . to make it possible for us to get a clear view of the state of mathematics . . .

Philosophy simply puts everything before us, and neither explains nor deduces anything. (Wittgenstein 1953, 50)

This concludes my simplified and selective account of Wittgenstein's philosophy of mathematics. It is a complex and sophisticated perspective that challenges many of the presuppositions and analyses of the traditional approaches to the philosophy of mathematics, as well as their tenets. In view of the way Wittgenstein reconceptualizes some of the central notions such as truth, rule, necessity, proof, and philosophy of mathematics itself, it is not surprising that it is misunderstood.

CRITICAL APPRAISAL OF WITTGENSTEIN'S PHILOSOPHY OF MATHEMATICS

Criticism of Wittgenstein's Philosophy of Mathematics

The denial of philosophy. I have presented my interpretation as an account of Wittgenstein's philosophy of mathematics. This raises the question of its fidelity. Can my account be regarded as an accurate reflection of Wittgenstein's philosophy of mathematics? The assumption that Wittgenstein had an articulated philosophy of mathematics might be criticized as a misrepresentation. Wittgenstein claimed that the sole role of philosophy is to dissolve logical and linguistic puzzles or antinomies. He believed that there are no genuine problems in philosophy, only pseudoproblems. According to Wittgenstein philosophy is a form of therapy, and when it has done its work it is obsolete. In keeping with these claims, Maddy interprets Wittgenstein as proposing an "anti-philosophy of mathematics," which "makes no attempt at explanations or true theories" (Maddy 1992, 9). Wittgenstein's style of philosophizing can be used in support of this view. For throughout his later work he offers concrete examples and discusses particulars, not generalities, in an attempt to avoid constructing a theory or metaphysics. This contradicts my interpretation.

In contrast, Popper (1972, 1976) argues unambiguously that there *are* philosophical problems and that it is the job of philosophy to address them; although *"Genuine philosophical problems are always rooted in urgent problems outside philosophy,"* he argues, "in mathematics, for example" (Popper 1972, 72, original emphasis). Like Popper and others I reject Wittgenstein's antiphilosophical stance, which led to the rather stultifying ordinary language philosophy that Gellner (1959) powerfully critiques.

However my contention here is that Wittgenstein's claims on this matter are inconsistent with his own philosophical practice. He spent years developing a philosophical framework with its characteristic and novel theoretical constructs such as 'language game', 'form of life', and so on. This is both philosophy and theory (although the purpose is to accommodate practice in philosophy). These constructs are directed, it seems to me, at explaining practice and solving philosophical problems, in direct contradiction to his claims.

What I have termed his philosophy of mathematics is his overall, albeit somewhat implicit, approach to philosophical problems concerning mathematics, and the body of reflection and theory that results. It is undeniable that he was addressing such problems as the nature of mathematical and logical necessity, the problems of Platonism, foundationalism, and so on and that he was building a substantial body of philosophy. Therefore I ignore his dictum, on the grounds that it was contradicted by his practice. I am therefore also circumventing the Popperian criticism, namely, that by denying the existence of philosophical problems Wittgenstein is denying philosophy.

Rorty's (1979) view of Wittgenstein is consistent with my interpretation. He terms Wittgenstein's anti-philosophical stance as "edifying" (as opposed to "systematic"). Rorty claims that, like Dewey and Heidegger, Wittgenstein gives up an earlier systematic approach (the *Tractatus*) and is subsequently concerned to guard against the pitfalls of prescriptive theorizing: the error he perceives himself to have committed.

My interpretation of Wittgenstein's view of the philosophy of mathematics hinges on the domination of the field, during his lifetime, by the *prescriptive* philosophies of logicism, intuitionism, and formalism. The field itself was largely defined by the presuppositions and concerns of absolutism and foundationalism. In my view it is these assumptions and the reformist philosophies of mathematics, not the philosophy of mathematics itself, that Wittgenstein is opposed to. He explicitly admits the possibility of a *descriptive* or naturalistic philosophy of mathematics (which did not then exist) but denies the possibility of any other kind (the only kind, at the time). Thus he says:

"Mathematical logic" has completely deformed the thinking of mathematicians and philosophers . . . (Wittgenstein 1978, 300)

We must do away with *explanation*, and description alone must take its place. (Wittgenstein 1953, 47)

What he is rejecting, in my view, is the traditional foundationalist enterprise of the philosophy of mathematics. For instead of systematic logical foundations, he substitutes the preexisting actual social practices, including their patterns of language usage, as the basis of mathematics and language. This is a radical departure that may have led him to think that he is sweeping away all of philosophical tradition, especially in the philosophy of mathematics. He is, after all, rejecting all schools of thought in the philosophy of mathematics as misconceived; and no alternative to foundationalism existed then, whereas today there is the "maverick" tradition. So Wittgenstein is fighting this battle in isolation and developing a completely new naturalistic philosophy of mathematics. Thus his strong antiphilosophical claims might be expected. He might also be expected to underestimate the explanatory and theoretical nature of his own novel approach to the philosophy of mathematics. Although he keeps his philosophical dicta as concrete and particular as possible, his use of metaphor and imagery (and novel constructs) admits a theoretical dimension to his philosophy. On this interpretation, my account may not so greatly misrepresent Wittgenstein. Instead it may be that he misrepresents or even contradicts himself.

"Full blooded conventionalism" and logical necessity. Dummett (1964) accuses Wittgenstein of a "full blooded conventionalism" that regards all "truths" of mathematics and logic as direct expressions of linguistic conventions, arbitrarily adopted by fiat. His own view is that "mathematical proof drives us along willy-nilly until we arrive at the theorem" (Dummett 1964, 495). Hence whatever the status of the axioms or premises, once accepted they lead irresistibly via mathematical proof to theorems. Thus not all of mathematical knowledge is based on decisions or convention; some of it follows necessarily from the assumed part.

In my view, this critique of Wittgenstein is based on a number of misunderstandings concerning, first, the conventional basis of mathematics and, second, the nature of necessity and following a rule. First of all, Wittgenstein makes it clear that the decisional basis of mathematics is not a matter of free or arbitrary choice, but a function of what is accepted in practice. Not all accepted propositions of mathematics are individually and directly stipulated conventions. Rather, it is when a proposition of mathematics is accepted as *unshakeably certain* that the status of grammatical rule or convention must be accorded to it.

Second, Wittgenstein questions the necessity of following a logical or mathematical rule. Our following it at best reflects an earlier "choice" to participate in certain socially shared activities, meanings, language games, and forms of life. Entering into the practices of research mathematicians means agreeing to accept certain forms of mathematical argument, to avoid inconsistency, even to act *as if* logical necessity underpins mathematical proofs. But accepting a mathematical proof or theorem is not simply a mechanical matter of following a rule and agreeing (perhaps implicitly) to its conventional underpinnings. It also involves a decision that the new application can be legitimately be subsumed under existing rules, for rules underdetermine their applications. Such a decision may, in effect, add further rules to what is accepted in the community. In short, the decisions and conventions described underpin logical rule following and give it the semblance of necessity. It is not that human beings struggle to follow and apply absolute rules and logic. Rather, the latter are idealizations of the rules evidenced in human linguistic behavior.

This argument and conclusion would be unpalatable to many, including Dummett. To concede it is to concede the cornerstone of absolutism, if not the whole edifice. It means that Wittgenstein is giving up logical necessity as it is traditionally understood. In its place he offers a rich, naturalistic social account of following a rule and related ideas, including logic, meaning, language, and mathematics.

Failure to distinguish degrees of certainty. The subsumption of logical and mathematical necessity to the social leads to a problem; that is, the lack of discrimination among different levels of convention and social acceptance. Mathematicians and others attach differing degrees of certainty to (1) a mathematical conjecture for which a tentative proof has just been constructed, (2) a well-established and much used (and proved) mathematical theorem, and (3) a law of logic. As I showed above, Wittgenstein gives a privileged role to certain logic principles, such as the law of contradiction, in certain contexts. However, beyond this exception no account is given of the differential certainty that is accorded to the different types of mathematical knowledge. No distinction is drawn between more tentative "peripheral" items of mathematical knowledge and very firmly held "core" items, to use a spatial metaphor. A partial account could be constructed in terms of certain language games and rules being more central, more richly and rigidly interlocking, and more deeply embedded in our forms of life than others. Consequently the items of mathematical knowledge associated with the former language games would have a greater degree of certainty than the latter. But such account would require further elaboration, and no such account is given by Wittgenstein.

Lack of historicism. One of Gellner's (1959) criticisms of linguistic philosophy is its lack of historicism. Of course his vantage point is that of one who is primarily interested in the social sciences, and hence requires an historical perspective as a sine qua non. In philosophy and in the philosophy of mathematics the need for an historical dimension is not widely felt, although it is a central plank of the "maverick" tradition. Wittgenstein does not treat the history of thought or of mathematics at all; this is, as I have argued above, a weakness for a philosophy of mathematics, especially one which attends so closely to mathematical practice. The lack of any historical dimension to Wittgenstein's philosophy of mathematics is a weakness. There is no account or mechanism given for changes in the body of mathematical knowledge, logic, notions of proof, truth, and so on.

However, there is room for a historical dimension in an extension of Wittgenstein's philosophy, in the social practice of mathematicians (with its language games and forms of life). For a social practice embodies its own history. It can only be understood fully as the endpoint of an evolutionary pattern of development. Wittgenstein prefers to chart the elaboration of a language game from a simple one to a more complex one by means of fictional thought-experiments. But to account for the actual concepts of mathematics as they exist it is not enough to conjure thought-experiments out of thin air. Attention needs to be paid to the actual concepts and language games in use, their inter-relationships, and their evolution. Of course, out of Wittgenstein's philosophy came ordinary language philosophy which tried to attend to actual patterns of use in the present. Analogously, I am arguing that the actual use of mathematical concepts and language needs to be explored—but in their past as well as in their present use.

Lack of theory of genesis of mathematical knowledge. Continuing in the same vein, one of the major weaknesses of Wittgenstein's philosophy of mathematics in my eyes is its lack of real engagement with the concepts and methods of mathematics in a way that allows for the treatment of mathematical invention and creation. Wittgenstein offers a revolutionary account of the justificatory basis of mathematical knowledge. Philosophically, this must needs take priority, for the problems of necessity and objectivity are pressing. But a full accounting for the nature of mathematics also requires a theory of mathematical invention.

Bloor (1983) offers the general criticism that Wittgenstein does not account for the genesis of new language games or explain why old ones are modified. Likewise, in the more specific context of the language games that constitute mathematics, it can be said that Wittgenstein fails to offer an account of the growth or development of mathematical knowledge, theories, or language games. Wittgenstein does acknowledge that mathematics is created and that new proofs change the meanings of language games. But he does not provide an adequate account of the genesis of mathematical knowledge.

Applying the Adequacy Criteria

Mathematical knowledge. Wittgenstein's philosophy of mathematics provides an implicit but relatively complete account of the nature and justification of mathematical knowledge, albeit from a new, social perspective. According to this account, mathematical knowledge is the product of mathematical activity by mathematicians (and others) engaging in a growing range of language games. The assumptions and logic of mathematics are anchored in social forms of life, including the generally accepted law of contradiction, which underpins the coherence (and possibility) of language games in mathematics. Mathematical language games are particular and specialized, but most if not all interconnect and overlap with others in a regular way reflecting this law.

Mathematical knowledge is created by mathematicians engaged and engaging in language games, and a mathematical rule adhered to by them is that such knowledge is justified by means of mathematical proofs. Wittgenstein gives a detailed account of the role and nature of proofs in mathematics. Of particular importance is the account it provides of the certainty of mathematical proofs without presupposing its necessity, absolute basis, or incorrigibility (in fact it allows for the opposites). By *not* accepting the preexistence of mathematical knowledge until it is created, Wittgenstein also allows for, but does not account for, its genesis. For even though it is asserted that mathematical knowledge is invented, no mechanism or even purpose for its creation figures in Wittgenstein's account. In this area, his philosophy of mathematics is weak or underdeveloped.

Mathematical theories. With regard to the appraisal of mathematical theories, according to Maddy (1992, 29), Wittgenstein's view is that "the parts of mathematics without application are just empty games with meaningless signs" and that pure mathematics is

> a piece of mathematical architecture which hangs in the air, and looks as if it were, let us say, an architrave, but not supported by anything and supporting nothing. (Wittgenstein 1978, 135)

Maddy's reading is that Wittgenstein regards pure mathematical theories as needing to be pruned away. This suggests a very strong position on theory evaluation, namely, the rejection of pure mathematical theories in favor of applied.

However, my reading is that Wittgenstein opposes only uninterpreted formal theories, not pure theories in general. The above quotation concerns the statement of Cantor's theorem ($2^{\aleph_0} > \aleph_0$), and Wittgenstein carries on to say: "The proposition is worth as much as its grounds are. It supports as much as the grounds that support it do." This can be interpreted as saying that formal theorems are worth no more epistemologically or semantically than the informal mathematical theories that support them. This reading is consistent with Wittgenstein's frequent assertions that the philosopher has no business attempting to reform mathematics, such as via its replacement by formal theories, but should stick to describing it.

> Philosophy . . . can in the end only describe . . . it cannot give any foundation . . . [it] leaves mathematics as it is . . . (Wittgenstein 1953, 49)

Rejecting a large part of pure mathematics would not be consistent with this view. In my view, Wittgenstein's philosophy of mathematics is naturalistic and pragmatic when it comes to mathematical theory evaluation, appraisal, and choice. It is a descriptive philosophy of mathematics rather than a normative one, and whatever is sanctioned by mathematical practice is acceptable to Wittgenstein. This has the outcome of not preferring and valuing formal mathematical theories over informal ones, which, as I have argued, is an important and desirable characteristic of a philosophy of mathematics. Indeed, uninterpreted formal theories are perceived not as the acme of mathematical knowledge but as meaningless.

The objects of mathematics. Wittgenstein is antirealist: strongly critical of Platonistic conceptions of the extrahuman existence of the objects of mathematics. What is primary is not the objects themselves, but the language games which provide the meaning contexts for a discussion of mathematical objects. Thus this account of mathematical objects is almost nominalistic: they are linguistic entities whose existence follows from (and is limited to) the language games of mathematics. To paraphrase a dictum of Kreisel: the essential issue has more to with the objectivity of mathematical knowledge than with the existence of mathematical objects (Shanker 1987). Thus Wittgenstein offers an approach to the problem of the nature and existence of mathematical objects; only it does not answer the usual question by saying where they exist. As to the origins of mathematical objects, although Wittgenstein does not say enough explicitly, it is clear that they are human linguistic creations, brought into being by new or extended language games.

Such answers may be less than satisfactory from a traditional philosophical perspective. Many questions and puzzles remain unanswered. In particular there is a resurgence of interest in the philosophy of mathematics in mathematical realism, and its proponents are less than happy with Wittgenstein's treatment of the issue (Maddy 1990; Chihara 1990).

The applications of mathematics. Wittgenstein's philosophy of mathematics offers much more of an account of the applications of mathematics than traditional absolutist philosophies of mathematics, because it locates mathematics in language games and forms of life. Thus mathematics is anchored in human practice, alongside science, technology, and other realms of knowledge. The particular language games of mathematics may differ from those in these other areas, but epistemologically they are commensurable, because of this shared basis (in language games and forms of life). This means that the applicability of mathematics is far from mysterious, and potentially there is room for very persuasive arguments to be mounted. But these are far from completely or satisfactorily stated, which is not surprising, given Wittgenstein's philosophical and methodological stance.

It should be made clear however, that Wittgenstein drew a sharp distinction between mathematics and empirical science. Although he admits important connections between proofs or calculations in mathematics and experiments in science, he regards the two processes as fundamentally different (Tymoczko 1985). Thus he said, "I can *calculate* in the medium of imagination, but not experiment" (Wittgenstein 1978, 73).

Mathematical practice, learning, and creativity. Wittgenstein accounts for mathematical practice in general, or at least for the activities of mathematicians in the present, through the role he accords to forms of life. Thus the actual practices of mathematicians, their language games and interactions— not abstract mathematical knowledge or mathematical objects—are the given for this perspective. In this respect, Wittgenstein's view has a major advantage over absolutist philosophies of mathematics. However, Wittgenstein does not identify anything uniquely or characteristically mathematical. Forms of life and language games describe and underpin all social activities. In what way do the activities of mathematicians differ from all other practices? Except for a concern with calculating and proving, Wittgenstein does not offer a satisfactory answer to this question.

Wittgenstein's philosophy of mathematics may potentially account for the genesis of mathematical knowledge in the mind of the individual. First, his account of mind and coming to know in mathematics acknowledges the idiosyncratic nature of each individual's construction of meanings. His approach accounts for the uniqueness and indeterminacy of individually constructed concepts and meanings of mathematics while avoiding the pitfalls of subjectivism. In this, he anticipates the current widely accepted constructivist and social accounts of learning in mathematics (Ernest 1994b; Glasersfeld 1995). He also anticipates some of the problems in teaching concepts and rules, and in assessing competence through performance. Second, a social view of learning is also implicit in Wittgenstein. For an immersion in shared forms of life followed by an induction into a sequence of increasingly inclusive mathematical language games suggests, schematically at least, how mathematics may be learned socially. Schematic as what he says is, a growing number of theorists offer parallel or consonant accounts of learning (Vygotsky 1978; Lave and Wenger 1991).

Finally, it may be remarked that Wittgenstein accommodates the creativity of mathematicians in principle. Since he regards mathematical knowledge as invented and not discovered, his account creates a space within the constraints of existing rules, concepts, and conventions where the mathematician can be creative. In this space, a mathematician may explore new consequences of assumptions, or even vary the latter in an attempt to modify the practice. Such innovations may be incoherent or unacceptable to others, but they can also result in new language games or mathematical theories. In either case, the outcome can be mathematical invention. Thus in principle Wittgenstein can accommodate both learning and creativity in mathematics. However, he does not account for these as much as open up the possibility of accounting for them in one or another elaboration of his philosophy of mathematics.

Wittgenstein's Achievement

In conclusion, I wish to emphasize the greatness of Wittgenstein's achievement in putting forward a revolutionary social constructivist approach to the philosophy of mathematics. First of all, Wittgenstein challenges foundationalism and the traditional approach to the philosophy of mathematics. He rejects the universally adopted *prescriptive* approach of his day and, instead, demands the reconceptualization of the philosophy of mathematics so as to be *descriptive*. This was, and still is, a revolutionary project: to account for mathematics, and mathematical practice as it is, rather than focusing on a reductive formula. It involves recognizing the multiplicity ("motley") of interlocking practices, both formal and informal, that make up mathematics. It means abandoning the notion that philosophy or logic precede mathematics and validate its knowledge claims. Instead of providing an overarching metanarrative which legitimated mathematical knowledge, Wittgenstein repositioned the philosophy of mathematics on the sidelines, concerned to observe, to describe, not to validate mathematics.[9]

Second, Wittgenstein questions absolutism in the philosophy of mathematics and in philosophy in general. Wittgenstein agonized over the notions of logical and mathematical necessity, and the logical compulsion to follow a rule, which lie at the heart of absolutism and apriorism. He was able to wrest himself free from the traditional accounts of logical necessity and build instead a novel social theory of necessity and rule-following.

Third, Wittgenstein's philosophy made a revolutionary break in ceasing to discuss knowledge, mathematical knowledge in particular, in realist or idealist terms. He inverts the Platonistic hierarchy and, instead of founding his theory on abstract idealizations, he takes human and social practice as the given. Wittgenstein develops a sophisticated and thoroughgoing social epistemology founded on concrete forms of life, language games, and meaning-as-use. He foregrounds the vital role played by human language in knowing and is the first philosopher of mathematics to recognize the essential interdependence between language and mathematical knowledge, and to build a systematic account around this relationship. The outcome is a naturalistic philosophy of mathematics which is grounded in key elements of concrete mathematical practice instead of abstract idealizations, be they subjective or Platonistic.

This brief listing begins to indicate the novelty of Wittgenstein's ideas for the philosophy of mathematics. But it does not reveal the difficulties he had to face in overcoming entrenched philosophical positions, as deeply a part of himself as of the rest of the philosophical community. However, the magnitude of the obstacles he faced throws some light on why he felt it necessary to reject the traditional approach of philosophy, especially the philosophy of mathematics. His approach involved changing the questions to be addressed, not just changing the answers to the old questions. This was a revolutionary break with tradition, a reconceptualizing of the field. So perhaps he felt he had wiped the slate clean, throwing off all past philosophy and philosophy of mathematics.

With hindsight, it can be seen that the philosophy Wittgenstein practiced, while revolutionary, did not make as complete a break with tradition as he thought. He did not invalidate all philosophy that went before him and replace it with a pure new method of inquiry. Wittgenstein does offer a radical new approach to the philosophy of mathematics, but at the heart of it, despite his denials, lies a new set of problems, analyses, concepts, and theories. However, his philosophy of mathematics is sufficiently revolutionary for several decades to have passed before it has begun to be understood and appreciated. But it can now be seen as a prescient offering in the "maverick" tradition (although Kitcher and Aspray 1988 does not mention Wittgenstein). This tradition can be characterized as descriptive and fallibilist, and Wittgenstein's approach to the philosophy of mathematics is certainly both of these.

NOTES

1. This notion is already foreshadowed in the *Tractatus*: "In philosophy the question, 'What do we actually *use* this word or this proposition for?' repeatedly leads to valuable insights" (Wittgenstein 1922, 65, emphasis added). This quotation occurs half a page down from a discussion of Frege, who in his influential paper on meaning wrote, "one must be content if the same word has the same sense in the same context" (Frege [1892] 1966, 58). It has been suggested that the meaning-as-use theory is an elaboration of Frege's "context principle" (Thomas 1996).

2. The notion of a "form of life" is at least partly anticipated by Husserl's "life-world" (*lebenswelt*), the empirical world of daily life and common sense, and Heidegger's "being in the world" (*Dasein*) (Anderson *et al.* 1986). Heidegger argues that the different social practices of a culture make up the "worlds" inhabited by (and constitutive of) human beings and that "language is the house of Being" (Lemay and Pitts 1994, 93). This raises the question of how much these ideas influenced Wittgenstein. Wittgenstein certainly knew Husserl's work and adopted his term *intentionality* in the early 1930s (Kenny 1973).

There is a well-known parallel (Dreyfus and Rabinow 1982) between Wittgenstein's notion of "form of life," with its embedded language games, and Foucault's

(1972) notion of a "discursive practice." Like the former, a discursive practice includes a social practice, an associated discourse or set of language-games, and an associated body of knowledge. A further parallel is that both the terms *form of life* and *discursive practice* are accorded epistemological priority by their coiners, that is, they provide both the source and the justificatory basis for knowledge, in their respective theories. But a discursive practice goes beyond a form of life because it also explicitly includes the roles and positionings of human subjects, something that Wittgenstein never discusses.

3. One area in which Wittgenstein was very influential is in the philosophy of the social sciences (Winch 1958; Bloor 1983).

4. Lakatos (1978c) describes Wittgenstein's epistemology and possibly his philosophy of mathematics as pragmatic, relating him to the American tradition of Peirce, James, and Dewey. This is quite apt, as Rorty (1979) agrees, because of the fallibilist strand in that tradition, and because the pragmatic theory of truth can ultimately be construed as social. However, in view of the context in which he was writing (criticizing Toulmin), it can be said that Lakatos was not intending to be flattering.

5. This view shares some points of contact with the views of a number of philosophers. Carnap (1956) argues that any talk of the existence of mathematical entities outside of the context of a mathematical system in which they are defined is meaningless. Bar-Hillel (see his comments reported in Lakatos 1967) follows the same line, and Ajdukiewicz reached a similar conclusion. Quine (1953c, 1970) takes a less stringent line but argues nonetheless for "ontological parsimony."

A significant difference is that Wittgenstein wants mathematical signs to have uses in practices beyond mathematics: "it is essential to mathematics that its signs are also employed in *mufti*. It is the use outside mathematics, and so the *meaning* of the signs, that makes the sign-game into mathematics" (Wittgenstein 1978, 257).

6. There is an obvious analogy here with tests of a scientific generalization. No finite number of tests can confirm it.

7. Here and elsewhere the term *series* is mistakenly used for *sequence*. The term is the translator's, since Wittgenstein wrote in German and consistently used the word *Reihe* which also means "row," i.e., ordered arrangement.

8. But many of these decisions are implicit in participation in a given language game and form of life, and require no conscious attention, as Wittgenstein (1976, 237) points out in a quotation given above.

9. Based on Lyotard's definition of the postmodern as "incredulity toward metanarratives" (1984, xxiv), Wittgenstein might be termed the first postmodern philosopher of mathematics.

CHAPTER 4

LAKATOS'S PHILOSOPHY
OF MATHEMATICS

THE BACKGROUND TO LAKATOS'S PHILOSOPHICAL POSITION

Biographical Sketch of Lakatos

Imre Lakatos's (1922–74) short career as a philosopher lasted from around 1957 until his untimely death in 1974.[1] He graduated in mathematics, physics, and philosophy from the University of Debrecen in 1944. In the late 1940s he was an active Communist, published several papers and reviews, and became a high official in the Hungarian ministry of education. However in 1950, because of "revisionist tendencies" he was arrested and served two or three years in prison. Two years after his release, with the help of the mathematician A. Renyi, he found employment as a translator of mathematical works into Hungarian, including Polya's (1945) *How to Solve It*.

After the Hungarian uprising of 1956 Lakatos was warned of the likelihood of rearrest. He fled to Vienna, and eventually made his way to Cambridge. There at King's College, in 1958–59, supported by the Rockefeller Foundation, he began his research into the philosophy of mathematics, supervised by R. B. Braithewaite. This work resulted in his Cambridge Ph.D. thesis, "Essays in the Logic of Mathematical Discovery." However most of chapters 2–4 were written at the London School of Economics (LSE) during 1960–61. Lakatos continued to devote much of his time up to 1963–64 to this, his major work in the philosophy of mathematics. He submitted part of it for publication in December 1960, but its four parts did not begin to appear in print until May 1963, following further revision. Even then the published list of contents given in part 1 is inaccurate, and parts 3 and 4 have a more extended sequence of sections than advertised, indicating that further revisions took place near the end of this period (Lakatos 1963–64).

Lakatos began teaching in the philosophy department at LSE in 1960 as a junior colleague of Karl Popper. He remained there until his death in 1974, having meanwhile been promoted to professor of logic with special reference to the philosophy of mathematics. This department is said to have followed an orthodox Popperian "party line" (Berkson 1976), which was partly Lakatos's position. However he was an original philosopher in his own right, and he combined admiration and acceptance of Popper's assumptions about philosophy with an increasingly critical stance towards certain aspects of Popper's philosophy.

From the mid-1960s on, Lakatos increasingly turned his attention to the philosophy of science. There he made a name for himself a major contributor with his "methodology of scientific research programmes" (Lakatos 1978d). The shift of interest may have begun in July 1965 (as Toulmin 1976 says), when Lakatos served as honorary secretary to the International Colloquium in the Philosophy of Science at Bedford College, London. The participants included Bar-Hillel, Bernays, Feyerabend, Kalmar, Körner, Kneale, Kuhn, Popper, Szabo, and Toulmin; and four important volumes of proceedings resulted. The first deals with problems in the philosophy of mathematics (Lakatos 1967). The remaining three treat issues in the philosophy of science (Lakatos 1968), the problem of inductive logic (Lakatos and Musgrave 1968), and Kuhn's philosophy of science (Lakatos and Musgrave 1970). Each volume embodies a dialogical style, with the presentation of philosophical positions followed by critical discussion and replies. Editing these volumes and writing his own substantial contributions (which involved developing his methodology of scientific research programs) seems to have taken up most of Lakatos's creative energy in the period 1965–69.

Lakatos was apparently active in the philosophy of mathematics only from the late 1950s to 1967, with some renewed work around 1973. His major work in the philosophy of mathematics, "Proofs and Refutations" (1963–64), was posthumously republished in 1976 with further selections from the Ph.D. thesis as *Proofs and Refutations: The Logic of Mathematical Discovery*. Apart from this, only five papers on the philosophy of mathematics are known to have been written by him. Using the chapter numbering of Lakatos 1978c, these are as follows:

1. Infinite regress and foundations of knowledge (first published in 1962)
2. A renaissance of empiricism in the recent philosophy of mathematics? (originated in brief conference remarks made in 1965, with the final version completed in 1967)
3. Cauchy and the continuum: the significance of non-standard analysis for the history and philosophy of mathematics (written and presented in 1966)

4. What does a mathematical proof prove? (written in the period 1959–61)
5. The method of analysis-synthesis (section 1 being the final chapter of his Ph.D. thesis, probably from 1960–61, and section 2 prepared for presentation in Finland in 1973)

Some of the other chapters in his collected papers (Lakatos 1978d, 1978c) touch on the philosophy of mathematics, but only tangentially. Thus his overall output in this field is small.

The Roots of Lakatos's Philosophy of Mathematics

The influence of Popper. Popper's work may have been known to Lakatos before he left Hungary (Hersh 1978b). Lakatos had certainly encountered it by the late 1950s, and it was one of the major influences on his thought. Popper's influence is immediately obvious in the parallel names used by Lakatos. Just as Popper's methodology is termed the "logic of scientific discovery" (LSD), as is his best known work (Popper 1959), Lakatos called his method the "logic of mathematical discovery" (LMD), the direct transposition of Popper's title to mathematics (Lakatos 1961). Likewise, the name of Lakatos's major work, *Proofs and Refutations* (1963–64) is a direct play on Popper's 1963 *Conjectures and Refutations*, and first appeared in the same year. Evidently Lakatos is paying homage to his mentor with his choice of titles.

A central idea of Popper's that greatly influenced Lakatos is his antifoundationalist fallibilism. Popper 1960 argues that any attempt to establish the truth of propositions or theories on the basis of a set of primitive propositions leads irrevocably to an infinite regress. Lakatos translated this insight to mathematics in an early philosophical paper (Lakatos 1978b), where he argues that any attempt to provide mathematics with an ultimate foundation results in an infinite regress, or founders in the attempt to avoid it.

Beyond the mere titles, there is, as Yuxin (1990) has shown, a deep analogy between Lakatos's LMD and Popper's LSD (table 4.1). This illustrates how both methods share a similar cycle of conjecture—refutation—new conjecture. Each begins with a conjecture, which is then open to criticism and refutation. After refutation, a new conjecture is formulated, completing the cycle. The analogy is striking, but there is also an important difference. For Popper, there is no necessary connection between the new problem and conjecture, and the original (refuted) conjecture. Popper (1959) explicitly states that in his methodology nothing can be said about the genesis of conjectures, and that this belongs to the context of discovery, not the philosophy of science. In contrast, for Lakatos there is an essential continuity between the primitive conjecture and the improved conjecture. The link

TABLE 4.1
A COMPARISON OF POPPER'S LSD AND LAKATOS'S LMD
(ADAPTED FROM YUXIN 1990)

	Stage of Cycle		
Methodology	Beginning	Mid-Cycle	New Beginning
LMD (Lakatos)	Primitive Conjecture	Proofs and Refutations	Improved Conjecture
LSD (Popper)	Problem and Conjecture	Refutation	New Problem and New Conjecture

is that the criticism, analysis, and strengthening of the proof of the primitive conjecture is what leads to the new conjecture. In this, Lakatos brings together the context of discovery and that of justification, which Popper carefully keeps apart.

Another parallel is between Popper's logic of falsification (basically *modus tollens*) and Lakatos's quasi-empiricism. Lakatos's analysis of mathematical proofs involves not the usual forward transmission of truth, but the "retransmission" (i.e., backward or retro-transmission) of falsity, as in Popper's "logic."

Lakatos regarded what he was attempting to do for mathematics as a direct parallel to what Popper had done for science.

> Now while Popper showed that those who claim that induction is the logic of scientific discovery are wrong, these essays intend to show that those who claim that deduction is the logic of mathematical discovery are wrong. While Popper criticized inductivist style . . . these essays try to criticize deductivist style. (Lakatos 1961, 173)

Finally, Lakatos shared, and was probably influenced by, Popper's view that philosophy need only concern itself with internalist history. This concerns the logical relations between scientific and mathematical concepts and their appraisal, and it excludes external social or contextual factors. Lakatos goes beyond Popper in seeing that his LMD was essentially historical, whereas Popper uses history only to illustrate the LSD—but all of Lakatos's work is bounded to a greater or lesser extent by an internalist view of scientific and mathematical history.

Thus, the powerful and formative influence of Popper's critical fallibilist philosophy of science on Lakatos's philosophy of mathematics is very clear. However, as the above indicates, there is an important divergence. This arises from Lakatos's introduction of the logic and context of discovery and its methodology into the philosophy of mathematics, and his related claim of the relevance of the history of mathematics to its philosophy. To Popper, this is anathema.

The influence of Polya. A second source of Lakatos's philosophy of mathematics is Polya's account of mathematical heuristics. Polya (1945) proposes a four-stage heuristic method for solving mathematical problems. The stages are as follows:

1. Understanding the problem
2. Devising a plan
3. Carrying out the plan
4. Looking back

This is elaborated in great detail by Polya, who also offers examples from history (Polya 1945, 1954). However, this is a general mathematical problem-solving method, and not just a proof-generating method. Polya regards the provision of a proof for a conjecture to be one of a broad range of mathematical problem-solving activities. But then Polya's heuristic is largely developed as a pedagogical aid; to make the learning of mathematics more active by inducting learners into the activity of mathematicians, but at their own level. Thus it understresses the activity that absorbs almost all of the pure mathematician's time, the refinement of conjectures and their proofs.[2]

Perhaps because it is widely subsumed into mathematics education, the philosophical significance of Polya's work for the methodology of mathematics is often overlooked. His claim is that there are rational elements in the process, which underpins mathematical discovery and problem solving. This is contrary to a widespread tradition in modern thought, which tends to mystify and psychologize creation and discovery, confirming Popper's view. Thus Hadamard (1954) characterizes mathematical invention as following the four-stage sequence: preparation, incubation, illumination, and later conscious work. He suggests that much of mathematical invention is driven by the unconscious mind, from whence flashes of insight are granted to geniuses. In contrast to this essentially mysterious and individualistic approach, Polya stresses the rational, publicly observable aspects of mathematical creation. Following Polya's approach (and that of Gestalt psychology, e.g., Wertheimer 1945) in examining the rational strategies employed, real progress been made in the study of mathematical problem solving. However, beyond the realms of psychology, cognitive science, and education, Lakatos is one of the few philosophers to have taken Polya's work seriously.[3] "Not all mathematicians claim that the logic of mathematical discovery is deduction; most of them realise that it is not. But they claim that it is totally irrational" (Lakatos 1961, 173–74). Polya provided the starting point of the famous classroom dialogue in Lakatos 1976 and, indeed, suggested it to Lakatos.[4]

Polya (1954, 35–43) offers a discussion, almost in dialogue form, that explores the inductive genesis of the Euler conjecture, its testing, the production of a counterexample,[5] and its barring. Polya rhetorically poses questions and answers them in the first-person plural. However, this is not true dialogue but a rhetorical question and answer style (Pimm 1987). Lakatos's dialogue begins where Polya's account ends: "In our last lesson we arrived at a conjecture concerning polyhedra . . ." (Lakatos 1976, 7).

Thus Polya provided the subject matter but not the dialogical format of Lakatos's work, although it is implicitly suggested. However there is direct evidence that Lakatos was influenced by Renyi and Galileo, both of whom published philosophical or mathematical dialogues.[6]

Finally, with regard to the structure of Polya's heuristics, it can be said that although there is the suggestion that the result or method developed in the solving of a problem might be applied to some other problem, there is no built-in cyclical pattern, as there is in Lakatos's model of knowledge growth. For this idea, another source is needed.

The influence of Hegel. There was another source and motive for adopting a dialogical form, one that has been largely neglected in standard accounts of Lakatos's thought, although it is evident in Lakatos's writings. "The dialogue form should reflect the dialectic of the story" (Lakatos 1976, 5). This refers to Hegel's philosophy and dialectic. A few scholars such as Feyerabend (1975), Hacking (1979), and Wartofsky (1976) acknowledge the influence of Hegel on Lakatos, but they hardly go further than mention it in passing. Most commentators ignore it or mention it only disparagingly, as a youthful folly which Lakatos had put behind him (e.g., Currie 1979). Virtually the only scholar known to me to acknowledge the seminal part played by Hegel's ideas in Lakatos's philosophy of mathematics is Kadvany, writing for an audience of historians.

> For what Lakatos has done is to embed, within a heretofore completely separate and self-contained domain—almost the exclusive concern of Anglo-American philosophers of science and method—an entire network of ideas of history drawn from Hegel and, to a lesser extent, Hegelian-Marxism. (Kadvany 1989, 26)

There is incontestable evidence of this influence throughout his earlier writings, although he systematically eliminated references to Hegel and Engels in later revisions.

The three major—apparently quite incompatible—"ideological" sources of the thesis are Polya's mathematical heuristic, Hegel's dialectic and Popper's critical philosophy. (Lakatos 1961, 5)

By the time of the publication of the revised selection from the Ph.D. thesis, the reference to Hegel is omitted from the footnote containing his acknowledgments.

The paper should be seen against the background of Polya's revival of mathematical heuristic, and Popper's critical philosophy. (Lakatos 1963–64, 1)

As the suppression of the reference to Hegel shows, Lakatos's attitude to Hegel changes and is ambivalent, to say the least. Nevertheless, Hegel's philosophy is central to Lakatos's philosophy of mathematics, even if he tries to conceal the evidence later.

Hegel's fallibilism. First of all, Hegel's fallibilism greatly influenced Lakatos.

It is no coincidence that the discovery of the proof-procedure occurred in the forties of the nineteenth century, when the breakdown of Newtonian optics . . . and the discovery of non-Euclidean geometries . . . shattered infallibilist conceit. These same forties saw Hegelian dialectic win over some of the most progressive minds of the period. Hegel offered both a radical break with its infallibilist predecessors and a powerful start for a thoroughly novel approach to knowledge. His inimicality and lack of understanding towards mathematics may have been due to his rash anticipation that infallibilist Euclideanism and mathematics are inseparable. But this mistake has been repeated by K. R. Popper, who a hundred years later tried to build up a new fallibilist philosophy which is not bound to fall back—like the Hegelian—to infallibilism.

In fact the only two philosophies yet which can embrace the proof procedure—and in general, mathematical heuristic—are the Hegelian and the Popperian. (Lakatos 1961, 166–67)[7]

This quotation suggests a motive for bringing together elements of the apparently disparate philosophies of Popper and Hegel. They are both fallibilist (although neither goes so far as to apply this to mathematics) and can accommodate mathematical knowledge growth.

In a 1960 paper Lakatos criticizes Popper for being "a rigid infallibilist . . . about mathematical and logical knowledge." He says, "I tried to correct it in a true Marxist spirit" (Lakatos 1978c, 124, 126). He also quotes

Engels on fallibilism and the nonattainability of ultimate, true knowledge. Clearly Lakatos was influenced not only by Hegel's philosophy but also as an ex-Communist, by Marx and Engels's development of it.

Hegel's dialectic. The second key idea from Hegel which influenced Lakatos is his "logic" or dialectic.

> According to Hegel, dialectical opposition is characteristic of all valid thinking about reality. Every "thesis," as Kant saw, generates it own contradictory antithesis. What Kant did not see is that the thesis and its antithesis may both be regarded as true if both are understood, in a new light, as imperfect expressions of a higher, more inclusive proposition which includes what is significant in both of them. Such a proposition Hegel calls a 'synthesis'. (Aiken 1956, 74)

Hegel's dialectical triad is a cyclical process that involves a proposition (the thesis) inevitably generating its contradiction (the antithesis), which are both subsumed in a new, more encompassing proposition (the synthesis) completing the cycle. Lakatos explicitly bases his LMD on Hegel's dialectic in his earlier work.

> The proof procedure seems to me to be a remarkable example of the dialectic triad of thesis, antithesis and synthesis. The progress of mathematical thought—in this case—starts with the primitive conjecture. This is the thesis. This thesis produces its antithesis which consists of the tension and struggle of the proof and refutations.
>
> In the antithesis we have on the one hand the proof which is the positive pole of the antithesis and supports the thesis, lifts it onto a higher level; and we have on the other hand the negative pole of the antithesis, the counterexamples, which tend to destroy the positive pole. It is very much in keeping with this dialectic that by strengthening the negative pole (finding ever more counterexamples) the positive pole will also be stronger (the proof will be ever more improved by the better specification of the lemmas corresponding to the counterexamples), and vice versa by strengthening the positive pole (building up a better proof-analysis) the negative pole will also be stronger (new counterexamples being suggested by the clearly stated lemmas). Of course the whole of the antithesis—both proof and counterexamples—is produced by the thesis which contains it in embryo. Now the synthesis is the theorem which embodies the respective values of both poles of the antithesis—proof and refutations—on a higher level, without the limitations of both. The theorem negates and preserves both the proof and the coun-

terexamples. And I shall not be surprised, if the synthesis turns into a new thesis and the dialectical process starts again. (Lakatos 1961, 51)

Hegel's historicism. Hegel's dialectic is closely linked with his philosophy of history.

Briefly put, Hegel regards all change as historical, and history itself as the dialectic deployed in time. As such, it is, in effect, a great waltz-like movement, from thesis through antithesis to synthesis, with each step representing a still higher stage in the self-development of the Absolute. (Aiken 1956, 76)

Thus Hegel not only locates his dialectic in history, but sees dialectic as the essential structure of historical development. This historicism, I suggest, supplies the final source for Lakatos's philosophy—the re-embedding of the methodology and philosophical development of mathematical knowledge in history. Contrary to the prevailing orthodoxy in the philosophy of mathematics and science at the time, a position endorsed by Popper, Lakatos (1963–64) claims that the philosophy of mathematics is empty of content without a deep and essential consideration of the history of mathematics. Beyond this, the inevitability of the unfolding of history according to Hegel's dialectic provides the source for the autonomy that Lakatos attributes to the development of mathematical ideas.

The Hegelian language gives a global vision of the movement of mathematical thought and has both its attractions and its dangers. The underlying Hegelian conception of heuristic is roughly this. Mathematical activity is human activity. Certain aspects of this activity—as of any human activity—can be studied by psychology, others by history. Heuristic is not primarily interested in these aspects. But mathematical activity produces mathematics. Mathematics, this product of human activity, alienates itself from the human activity which has been producing it. It becomes a living, growing organism, that acquires a certain autonomy from the activity which has produced it, that develops its own autonomous laws of growth, its own dialectic. The genuine creative mathematician is just a personification, an incarnation of these laws which can only realise themselves in human action. Their incarnation, however, is rarely perfect. The activity of human mathematicians, as it appears in history, is only a fumbling realisation of the superb dialectic of mathematical ideas. But any worthwhile mathematician feels the sweep of it, and obeys, if he has talent, spark, genius, i.e., if he can communicate with this dialectic of ideas.

Now heuristic is concerned with the autonomous dialectic of mathematics and not with its history, though it can only study its subject through the study of history and through the rational reconstruction of history. (Lakatos 1961, 178)

A central theme in this passage is the claimed autonomous growth of mathematics in history, as it follows its own dialectic. This dialectic is seen as an internal logic, the skeleton structure that history fleshes out. Lakatos draws a line between the lives and social context of mathematicians, and the logical interplay of their disembodied abstract ideas. Hegel's ideas contribute an historicism to Lakatos's thought, but it is a limited use of history, subservient to an inner dialectic logic.

Lakatos's Hegelian synthesis. There is a striking similarity between Popper's logic of conjecture–refutation–new conjecture and Hegel's dialectic. Both begin with a proposition, move to a contradiction/refutation of it, followed by a new proposition. In some sense, both are internalist too, seeing their logic as transcending the brute reality of history. Popper is well aware of this analogy, but he dismisses it as a "superficial similarity" (Popper 1972, 126).[8]

What Hegel's triad supplies, which Popper's cycle does not, is the conceptual link between the new proposition (conjecture) and the original proposition, via its refutation, all embedded in history. Unlike Popper's Logic of Mathematical Discovery, Hegel's dialectic triad provides a model for conceptual continuity and change in the growth of knowledge, both logically and historically. My suggestion is that this aspect of Hegel's dialectic, deeply embedded in Lakatos's thought from his early days as a Marxist, provided the missing ingredient which allowed him to construct a synthesis which took him beyond Popper. Lakatos was able to develop a logic of mathematical discovery which applied to the methodological concerns of philosophy and which encompassed the history of mathematics as well. (Polya's role in opening up the processes of mathematical creation for Lakatos and enabling this synthesis to be applied to mathematics should not be underestimated).

By an irony that I am sure will not have escaped him, Lakatos's philosophy of mathematics is, in effect, the synthesis of Hegel's ideas (the thesis) with Popper's philosophy (the antithesis).[9]

Rejection of Hegel. In the transition from Lakatos's doctoral dissertation (1961) to "Proofs and Refutations" (1963–64), explicit references to Hegel are systematically purged. Thereafter, all of Lakatos's references to Hegel in his published work, barring those reprinted unrevised from his dissertation, are critical and disparaging. Lakatos was a reformed Hegelian-Marxist who strongly repudiated his past philosophy as youthful error. Indeed, his attitude to Hegel smacks of a loss of faith, almost the rejection of earlier uncritical allegiances by an ex-cult member.

Popper's ideas represent the most important development in the philosophy of the twentieth century; an achievement in the tradition—and on the level—of Hume, Kant or Whewell. Personally my debt to him is immeasurable: more than anyone else, he changed my life. His philosophy helped me to make a final break with the Hegelian outlook which I had held for nearly twenty years. [Continued in a footnote.] Since Hegel each generation has unfortunately needed—and has fortunately had—philosophers to break Hegel's spell on young thinkers who so frequently fall into the trap of "impressive and all-explanatory theories (like Hegel's or Freud's) which act upon weak minds like revelations." . . . Moore was the liberator in Cambridge before the first war, Popper in the London School of Economics after the second. (Lakatos 1978d, 139)

Why, given his evidently great intellectual debt to Hegel, should Lakatos turn so roundly on him? Lakatos suggests the basis of his change of mind in the above passage. The reaction of a lapsed (and persecuted) Marxist against the old ideology might be expected to be strong. But more importantly, there is the influence of his new milieu. From 1960, Lakatos worked closely with Popper and his followers in the philosophy department at LSE. The powerful influence of Popper and his school at LSE—and of Anglo-American philosophy in general, with its rejection of metaphysics—would predictably lead to a strong rejection of Hegelian ideas. Popper's demarcation of science from pseudoscience conceals a powerful rationalist, scientistic ideology which is sharply dismissive of metaphysics, idealism, and Hegelian ideas, perhaps even contemptuously so.[10] It would be hard for a newcomer who is a great admirer of Popper and seeking to become a professional philosopher and establish himself in a new country not to absorb such an outlook and its implicit values. I believe that exposure to the climate of ideas at LSE (and to professional Anglo-American philosophy in general) caused a radical shift in Lakatos's philosophical allegiances in the 1960s. Consequently, Lakatos rejected Hegelian and Marxist theory but appropriated its dialectics and historicism as part of his own philosophy of mathematics (and science).

Contradictions in Lakatos's thought. This admittedly speculative account suggests that the Hegelian historico-dialectic thesis and the Popperian logico-rationalist antithesis which underpinned the Lakatosian synthesis might suffer from some internal tensions. There might therefore be said to be a contradiction in Lakatos's thought, with both a critical, anti-formalist strand (evident in his philosophy of mathematics), and a rationalistic, demarcationist line (in his growing stature as a philosopher of science). This can be seen in his criticism of Toulmin and in his writings on science and education (Lakatos 1978c). Berkson characterizes these two strands in Lakatos as "progressive" and "reactionary."

> As his work was developed . . . one thing always puzzled me: his work seemed to contain such conflicting tendencies. He would continue developing his ideas along a progressive line, and suddenly insert an element which appeared to me to be quite reactionary . . . imbued with the spirit of Positivism . . . Both aspects concern the research program which has dominated both philosophy of science and philosophy of mathematics in the twentieth century. This research program is aimed at constructing a formal system in which all important disputes are rationally decidable. The progressive aspect of Lakatos's work was his critique of this program and his attempt to go beyond it. The reactionary aspect was his falling back into the program and attempting to produce decisive criteria for settling disputes. (Berkson 1981, 297)

Likewise, his brief writings on education also contain contradictions. On the one hand, his critique of the widespread deductivist approach to the teaching of mathematics as authoritarian is progressive and radical (Lakatos 1961, 1976). On the other hand, his later writings contain elements that are authoritarian and reactionary (Lakatos 1978c). The two strands which can be distinguished in Lakatos's thought largely feed into his philosophy of mathematics and his philosophy of science, which is his later and more "reactionary" strand (Berkson 1981).

An exploration of the development and contradictions in Lakatos's thought would not be complete without consideration of the claim made by the editors of Lakatos (1976) that in his later years Lakatos revised and ultimately rejected his fallibilist philosophy of mathematics. What J. Worrall and E. Zahar assert is twofold. First, the modern conception of valid inference as represented in formal deductive logic is "essentially infallible" (Lakatos 1976, 138) and, consequently, Lakatos was *mistaken* in denying this in his writings on the philosophy of mathematics. Second, Lakatos *changed his mind* in agreement with this claim (or could have been so persuaded) and would have revised his publications accordingly. These claims are made in footnotes to Lakatos 1976 and in a *new infallibilist ending to the Lakatosian dialogue* in chapter 2 (written by the editors), a revision that totally subverts Lakatos's text.[11]

What is the basis of the editors' claims? The totality of Lakatos's published writings, including the paper from 1973, provides no evidence that he changed his mind on the fallibilism of mathematics and logic. In contrast, his 1967 paper entitled "A Renaissance of Empiricism" (in Lakatos 1978c) reasserts and further elaborates his thoroughgoing fallibilism. However, even if Lakatos had changed his mind, as his editors claim, this would not affect the validity of his early philosophy of mathematics as published. For this must stand on its own merits. Any later change of heart by Lakatos would be biographically interesting, but it would not weaken his earlier philosophy of mathematics or detract from the arguments it is based on.

For whatever reasons, although they do not conceal their interventions, the editors of Lakatos 1976 illegitimately revise and misrepresent Lakatos. They seem intent on subverting the central thesis of Lakatos's philosophy of mathematics.[12]

In my view, the intrusion of the editors own opinions into Lakatos 1976 is astonishing and incorrect, irrespective of the merits of their opinions. Other commentators also feel strongly on this. Bloor (1978) carefully refutes the editors intervention, whilst Hersh (1978b, 133) calls it "gratuitous and embarrassing" and "jarring and inappropriate."[13]

Lakatos: Philosopher of Mathematics and Philosopher of Science

Both Toulmin (1976) and Berkson (1976) distinguish between Lakatos as a philosopher of mathematics and Lakatos as a philosopher of science. The parallel between the two sets of ideas is worth noting, and table 4.2 shows the strength of the analogy that exists between Lakatos's LMD and his methodology of scientific research programs (MSRP).

TABLE 4.2
A COMPARISON OF LAKATOS'S LMD WITH HIS MSRP
(BASED ON YUXIN 1990)

	LMD	MSRP
The Basic Structure		
Auxiliary vs. central	Lemmas	Protective Belt
assumptions	Main Conclusion	Hard Core
Heuristic Principles		
Loci of error vs.	The Principle of	Negative Heuristic
development	Retransmission of Falsity	
	The Basic Principle of	Positive Heuristic
	the Proof	
Alternative Methodologies		
Progressive vs.	The Method of Proof-	Progressive Problemshift
degenerative	Analysis	
methodologies	The Methods of Monster	Degenerating Problemshift
	and Exception-Barring	

Firstly, in LMD, a mathematical result is made up of a main conclusion, the theorem itself, and preliminary lemmas and conditions, which can be adjusted to preserve the conclusion. In MSRP, each scientific research program has "a characteristic hard core, stubbornly defended, with its more flexible protective belt" (Lakatos 1978d, 5). Each contains a core to be preserved, and a protective belt which bears the brunt of any criticism. Thus there is a strong structural analogy between the two positions.

Secondly, LMD is based on the retransmission of falsity as "a *regulative principle* for proof analysis" (Lakatos 1976, 48). According to this, "falsehood should be retransmitted from the naive conjecture to the lemmas, from the consequent of the theorem to its antecedent" (47), thus allowing the basic principle of the proof to be retained. Analogously in MSRP there is the negative heuristic specifying which paths researchers must avoid. It

> forbids us to direct the *modus tollens* at his "hard core." Instead we must use our ingenuity to articulate or even to invent "auxiliary hypotheses" which form a protective belt around this core, and we must redirect the modus tollens to these. (Lakatos 1978d, 48)

This builds on the Quine-Duhem thesis that falsification applies to a whole nexus of assumptions, and not just a central hypothesis (Losee 1980).

The positive heuristic of a program is a set of methodological rules or a metaphysical principle suggesting what research paths will preserve the hard core, thus paralleling the basic principle of the proof (in mathematics).

Thirdly, there is the analogy between progressive and degenerating methods in LMD and MSRP. The methods of monster-barring and exception-barring in LMD, like degenerating problemshifts in MSRP, represent a focus on ad hoc hypotheses fabricated to accommodate only known facts. In contrast, the method of proof analysis represents the heuristic means to develop the new, improved conjecture, advancing mathematical knowledge in LMD, just as the progressive problemshift should lead to the discovery of hitherto unknown facts in MSRP. Thus both positions allow the distinction between fruitful and sterile developments, indicating the analogy that exists between the criteria for evaluating developments.

Finally, although it is not surprising in view of the above analogy and the mechanisms underpinning it, Lakatos regards both MSRP and LMD as providing a basis for the autonomy of the development of their respective sciences. In each case, Lakatos proposes a logic of knowledge growth which not only concerns the justification of knowledge, but provides a rational mechanism embedded it in history describing the evolution of mathematical and scientific knowledge. In both spheres, this remains a very Hegelian notion.

This comparison shows the strong analogy that exists between Lakatos's philosophy of mathematics and his philosophy of science. It is clear that LMD with its associated historicism came first and was subsequently reapplied to the philosophy of science to develop MSRP. Consequently, another parallel is the use and importance ascribed to internalist accounts of history, central to Lakatos's philosophy of both mathematics and science. In each, a rationally reconstructed history is seen to reveal the underlying logical and conceptual development. So although it is important to distinguish the two philosophical positions, their mutual influence and interdependence should not be forgotten.

However, a disanalogy should also be noted. The spirit of Lakatos's philosophy of mathematics is antidemarcationist, concerned to break down the division between informal mathematics, which had hitherto been largely ignored in the philosophy of mathematics, and formal mathematical theories. Also to dissolve the impenetrable barrier that had been erected between the contexts of discovery and justification, and between the history and philosophy of mathematics (although only an internalist history is admitted). In each case this represents a broadening or liberalization of the scope of the philosophy of mathematics to be more descriptive of mathematical practice. This is a central feature of Lakatos's innovation.

In contrast, Lakatos's philosophy of science is demarcationist, prescriptive, and evaluative, being concerned to mark off "good" (progressive) scientific programs from those that are "bad" (degenerating). Thus, although there is an analogy between monster- and exception-barring and degenerating problemshifts, the former are temporary local moves, in defense of a conjecture, whereas the latter constitute a global shift of emphasis to protect a whole scientific research program. Ironically, in this respect, the MSRP comes closer to admitting external, contextual, even sociological factors from the practice of science, at least by analogy (e.g., with the self-protective interests of a group of researchers defending their program).

Overall, although there is a striking parallel between LMD and MSRP, there is a significant difference between the two philosophies. The recognition of contradictions in Lakatos's philosophical position is necessary, but there is also a unity to his thought that survives and integrates the shifts in emphasis.

LAKATOS'S LOGIC OF MATHEMATICAL DISCOVERY

Lakatos's most important contribution to the history and philosophy of mathematics is his detailed case-study based treatment of the LMD. This is intended as a contribution to the methodology of mathematics, a field of study which sits at the intersection of the history and philosophy of mathematics,

and at the intersection of the contexts of justification and discovery.[14]
LMD provides "the autonomous dialectic of mathematics" (Lakatos 1976, 146). In Lakatos's own words, the cycle is as follows:

> There is a simple pattern of mathematical discovery—or in the growth of mathematical theories. It consists (the historical pattern possibly slightly deviating from this heuristic pattern) of the following stages:
>
> 1. *Primitive conjecture*
> 2. *Proof (a rough thought-experiment or argument, decomposing the primitive conjecture into subconjectures or lemmas)*
> 3. *"Global" counterexamples (counterexamples to the primitive conjecture) emerge*
> 4. *Proof re-examined: the "guilty lemma" spotted, to which the global counterexample is a "local" counterexample. This guilty lemma may have previously remained "hidden" or may have been misidentified. Now it is made explicit, and built into the primitive conjecture as a condition. The theorem—the improved conjecture—supersedes the primitive conjecture with the new proof-generated concept as its paramount new feature.*
>
> (The fourth stage may precede the third: an ingenious proof-analysis may suggest the counterexample; and there may be a series of counterexamples forcing hidden lemmas into the open and a series of ever more careful proof-analyses suggesting a series of counterexamples.)
> These four stages constitute the essential kernel of the proof-procedure. But they may frequently be joined by some further standard stages:
>
> 5. *Hunt for the newly found lemma or new proof-generated concept in other proofs. This concept may be found lying on cross-roads of different proofs, and thus emerge as of basic importance.*
> 6. *Check the hitherto accepted consequences of the original and now refuted and improved conjecture.*
> 7. *Counterexamples are turned into new examples—new fields of inquiry open up.* (Lakatos 1961, 144–45, original emphasis)

This is an explicit statement of Lakatos's LMD. The most extended (although implicit) version of Lakatos's heuristic occurs in the celebrated Euler conjecture dialogue (Lakatos 1976, 6–125). This operates at a number of levels. First, the divisions of the dialogue and the subheadings (also given as the contents list) explicitly indicate the stages in Lakatos's heuristic. Second, within the dialogue there occur explicit statements of the heuristic. Third, the text comprises a classroom dialogue between a teacher and about a dozen pupils, as they (1) apply the heuristic to the Euler conjecture, in a sequence of conjectures, proofs, and refutations, representing a rational reconstruction of the history of the evolution of the conjecture and its proof, and (2) critically reflect upon their applications of the heuristic, making aspects of it explicit at times, as well as discussing philosophical issues raised by their application. Fourth, in the footnotes, Lakatos himself reflects on the dialogue and, most notably, relates the reconstructed history in the dialogue to the actual historical evolution of the problem and its solutions ("The real history . . . chime[s] in the footnotes," Lakatos 1976, 5).

Thus the dialogue serves a number of functions. First, it is an imaginative case study of the heuristics in action. In this way it illustrates the potential utility of the heuristics as a methodology of mathematical practice. Second, the methodology also constitutes the LMD, the pattern of knowledge growth and appraisal in mathematics. Third, it offers a rational reconstruction of a case study employing the LMD in the history of mathematics. This illustrates the logical development and conceptual change involved in the evolution of mathematical knowledge. Fourth, by offering in parallel an account of the actual historical development of the proof of the Euler conjecture it tests the historical reconstruction through LMD against the "facts" of history. Finally, it implicitly suggests that the heuristic serves a pedagogical end in arriving at mathematical knowledge developmentally, rather than following the traditional formal pattern of textbook presentations (definition, lemma, theorem, proof). This last reading of the dialogue is strengthened by Lakatos's own reference to the application of the "'fundamental biogenetic law' about ontogeny recapitulating phylogeny to . . . mathematical mental development" (Lakatos 1976, 4), as well as his explicit references to education.

Within the dialogue, there occurs a second explicit statement of Lakatos's heuristic,

> the *"method of proofs and refutations."* Let me state its main aspects in three heuristic rules:
>
> *Rule 1. If you have a conjecture, set out to prove it and to refute it. Inspect the proof carefully to prepare a list of non-trivial lemmas (proof-analysis); find counterexamples both to the conjecture (global counterexamples) and to the suspect lemmas (local counterexamples).*
>
> *Rule 2. If you have a global counterexample discard your conjecture, add to your proof analysis a suitable lemma that will be refuted by the counterexample and replace the discarded conjecture by an improved one that*

incorporates that lemma as a condition. Do not allow a refutation to be dismissed as a monster. Try to make all "hidden lemmas" explicit.

Rule 3. If you have a local counterexample, check to see whether it is not also a global counterexample. If it is, you can easily apply Rule 2. (Lakatos 1976, 50, original emphasis)

Rule 4. If you have a counterexample which is local but not global, try to improve your proof-analysis by replacing the refuted lemma by an unfalsified one. (58, original emphasis)

Rule 5. If you have counterexamples of any type, try to find, by deductive guessing, a deeper theorem to which they are counterexamples no longer. (76, original emphasis)

The language used here shows that this is a set of mathematical heuristics, prescriptive rules for the practicing mathematician constituting a proposed method of mathematics. My contention is that in LMD Lakatos's offers a unified theory of mathematical development, a methodology encompassing four functions, each pertaining to the genesis of mathematical knowledge. First, there is the descriptive philosophical function accounting for the genesis and justification of mathematical knowledge. This is the informal combined logic of mathematical discovery and justification, that is, the detailed epistemological pattern of mathematics. Second, there is the historical function in describing the actual development of mathematics, or at least its historical reconstruction. In this role it provides a simplified logical description of the pattern that such developments follow in reconstructed history, together with indications of the actual historical development plus a justification for some deviations by LMD. Third, there is the heuristic function, providing a method for practicing mathematicians, a set of guidelines for them to follow. Fourth, it also has a significant pedagogical function; it describes a method for teaching mathematics in a way that parallels history. These four functions are indissolubly fused in his unified theory (LMD), which he locates in the field of methodology of mathematics.

THEMES OF LAKATOS'S QUASI-EMPIRICISM

A number of central themes of Lakatos's quasi-empiricism, as he termed his philosophy of mathematics, can be identified although some occur more explicitly than others.

The Fallibilism of Mathematical Knowledge

Lakatos's major critical claim is that mathematical knowledge is fundamentally fallible and corrigible. This claim is based on two further subclaims.

First, any attempt to find a perfectly secure basis for mathematical knowledge leads to an infinite regress. Second, mathematical knowledge cannot be given a final, fully rigorous form.[15] His commitment to fallibilism in his early work is quite unequivocal, as a number of the quotations given above indicate.

The consequence for Lakatos's philosophy of mathematics is that the search for a basis for absolute certainty in mathematics is rejected, and mathematical knowledge is acknowledged to be fallible, corrigible, and without certain foundations. This makes it the latest expression of the skeptical tradition in epistemology, which claims that we cannot attain knowledge of the truth at all—and that even if we did attain it we would not know that we had.

> For more than two thousand years there has been an argument between *dogmatists* and *sceptics*. The dogmatists hold that—by the power of our human intellect and/or senses—we can attain truth and know that we have attained it . . . In this great debate, in which arguments are time and again brought up to date, mathematics has been the proud fortress of dogmatism. Whenever the mathematical dogmatism of the day got into a "crisis," a new version once again provided genuine rigour and ultimate foundations, thereby restoring the image of authoritative, infallible, irrefutable mathematics, "the only Science that it has pleased God hitherto to bestow on mankind" (Hobbes [1651] 1962, 15). Most sceptics resigned themselves to the impregnability of this stronghold of dogmatist epistemology. A challenge is now overdue. (Lakatos 1976, 4–5)

This locates Lakatos's philosophy of mathematics in the tradition of skeptical philosophy that goes back to classical Greece, and for which there has been no ready refutation. Furthermore, its significance extends more widely than does the philosophy of mathematics alone. Dogmatist epistemology rests much of its claim on the privileged position of mathematical knowledge. So the claims of quasi-empiricism, if established, represent a challenge not only to absolutism in the philosophy of mathematics, but also to dogmatist epistemology in general.

Koetsier (1991) distinguishes between two types of fallibilism and claims that Lakatos's work is more in keeping with weak than with strong fallibilism. He defines weak fallibility to be the view that mathematical theories are revisable but not refutable in their totality, and he claims this implies that the continuity of mathematics and the accumulation of "truths" are not accidental but due to the nature of mathematics. He defines strong fallibility to be the view that mathematical theories can be refuted as a whole (comparable to the refutation of scientific theories), and he implies that the continuity in the development of mathematics and the accumulation of "truths" could be accidental.

Koetsier tries to establish his claim by showing with historical cases that mathematics is weakly but not strongly fallible. A single counterexample is all that is needed to refute him, and Russell's refutation of Frege's *Grundgesetze der Arithmetik* (Russell 1902) can serve this purpose. However, Koetsier's line of reasoning is directed at establishing the validity of "weak fallibilism," and is not relevant in establishing the parameters of Lakatos's philosophy of mathematics. Another problem in these claims is that strong fallibility is not clearly enough defined. After all, even in empirical science, the refutation of a whole theory is problematic. According to the Quine-Duhem thesis, in refuting a theory empirically, the refutation can always be directed at ancillary hypotheses and not at the central theory itself. This analysis was adopted by Popper, and in particular by Lakatos, in distinguishing between the core and protective belt of a theory.

On the basis of Lakatos's writings, such as those quoted above, there is no reason to attribute a weak form of fallibilism to him. It is true that the central thrust of his work was to establish the rational but fallible nature of mathematical knowledge and progress. Thus he does not regard the development of mathematics as *arbitrary* (which rejection Koetsier calls his *rationality thesis* and links with the position of weak fallibilism). However Koetsier is mistaken in viewing this rejection as indicating Lakatos's acceptance of the *necessity* of mathematics. Instead, Lakatos showed how the development of mathematical concepts, proofs, and theories are *contingent* on a variety of circumstances, not least of which are the human powers of invention and criticism. *Contingency*, not arbitrariness, is the opposite of *necessity*, and contingency is the central notion which Rorty (1979) proposes as the basis of fallibilist epistemology.

The Primacy of Informal Mathematics

Lakatos rejects the traditional view that formal mathematical theories and proofs are philosophically primary. He asserts instead the primacy of informal over (relatively) formal mathematical theories. In fact, according to Lakatos, formal mathematical theories are rational reconstructions of informal mathematical theories (as given by mathematical practice and history), in which genetic structure is abandoned in favor of justificatory logic. Informal mathematical theories are the phenomena of mathematics that formal theories attempt to explain. Lakatos's aim is to provide a more accurately descriptive theory of mathematics that accounts for the genesis as well as the justification of mathematical knowledge, for its history as well as its logical proof structure. Lakatos's view is that in mathematical practice relatively formal and informal mathematical theories exist simultaneously and have important relationships. Informal mathematical theories are the source as well as the touchstone of all formal mathematics, and they have a primacy which must be accounted for in the philosophy of mathematics. Informal mathematics is the source of potential falsifiers of more formalized mathematics, and it provides individuals with the premises and conclusions of deductive mathematics (informal axioms, definitions, and conjectures) as well as the informal proofs through which the premises and conclusions are connected.

In addition, Lakatos is critical of the dichotomy between formal and informal theories in mathematics. His rejection of absolutism entails that there is no clear-cut distinction between formal and informal mathematical theories. Formal mathematical theories can never find an ultimate expression; and any formulation, no matter how rigorous, is permanently open to improvement, revision, and reformulation. Therefore the difference between formal and informal theories is thus always a matter of degree.

A Theory of Mathematical Knowledge Genesis

Lakatos (1976) proposes a theory of knowledge creation in mathematics, which may be represented as follows. Given a mathematical problem (P) and an informal mathematical theory (T) an initial step in the genesis of new knowledge is the proposal of a conjecture (C). The method of proofs and refutations is applied to this conjecture, and an informal proof of the conjecture is constructed and then subjected to criticism, leading to an informal refutation. In response to this refutation, the conjecture and possibly also the informal theory and the original problem are modified or changed (new problems may very well be raised), in a new synthesis, completing the cycle. This is illustrated schematically in table 4.3 as an induction step, the nth stage in the cycle.

Although Lakatos (1976) is explicit about the role of the conjectures, proofs, and refutations in this cycle, the part played by problems and informal theory are often implicit in his account. He does stress the role of problems in the development of mathematics in some places, such as at the end of his dia-

TABLE 4.3
CYCLIC FORM OF LAKATOS'S LOGIC OF MATHEMATICAL DISCOVERY

Stage	Context	Components of Cycle
Stage n:	Problem Set P_n	Conjecture C_n
	Informal Theory T_n	Informal proof I_n of C_n
		Informal refutation of C_n
Stage $n + 1$:	Problem Set P_{n+1}	Conjecture C_{n+1}
	Informal Theory T_{n+1}	

logue where the teacher states that "a scientific inquiry 'begins and ends with problems'" (Lakatos 1963–64, 336, quoting Popper).

LMD involves conceptual changes which may need to be reflected in changes in the underlying informal mathematical theory as well as in the conjecture itself. Meaning and definition changes may permeate a whole informal theory and cannot necessarily be confined to a conjecture. Lakatos regards the role of new lemmas in the overall process as highly significant, and the underlying informal mathematical theory also provides the lemmas with a context and positioning. So explicitly including the background factors of the underlying set of problems and the informal theory provides a more complete representation of the LMD cycle.

Lakatos provides further details of the logical process involved in LMD through the role of lemmas. In LMD, the production of an informal proof I_n of the conjecture C_n is followed by discovery of an informal refutation of the conjecture. Lakatos asserts that I_n can be analyzed and be shown to involve a number (k, say) of implicit lemmas $L_1, L_2, \ldots, L_k$. In this process, not only the proof but also the conjecture (and possibly the background informal theory and pool of problems) may be revised. So now a revised informal proof I_{n+1} purports to derive the conjecture C_{n+1} from the conjunction T_{n+1} & L_1 & $\ldots$ & L_k, consisting of the theory T_{n+1} and the k new lemmas.[16] This is stage $n + 1$ of LMD.

In more detail, the pattern of knowledge generation employs both analysis and synthesis. In the first part of stage n, the analysis of the conjecture C_n, the informal proof or thought experiment I_n (resulting from stage $n - 1$ of LMD, assuming there is one), and the assumptions it is based on leads to a sequence of increasingly fundamental lemmas, ending in a simple conjunction of assumptions (and definitions) A_n, say. In the second part, the process of synthesis reverses the direction (and results of this analysis), and starting with the statement of assumptions A_n, a deductive or informal proof of C_n is built up, resulting in an improved proof with the following skeleton structure: A_n, L_1, L_2, L_3, $\ldots$, L_k, C_n. All this takes place in the early parts of stage n of LMD. Typically, the next phase is the search for and discovery of a counterexample to C_n, or, more generally, a refutation.

Lakatos considers refutations of the conjecture C_n which are counterexamples, and distinguishes between a "global" counterexample, which directly refutes C_n, and "local" counterexample, which falsifies one of the proof-generated lemmas (L_i, say) and hence indirectly refutes C_n as well. The logical mechanism involved in this latter case is the retransmission of falsity back through the proof, to the "guilty" lemma L_i. Logically, the falsity of the conjunction of the premises is equivalent to the disjunction of their falsity, and this is localized in the identification of the falsified lemma L_i. All this occurs within stage n of LMD, and the scene is now set for the completion of this stage and progress to stage $n + 1$.

Overall, Lakatos's theory describes the logical mechanism involved in the genesis and testing of mathematical knowledge. In this process, a conjecture and a proof (including a sequence of lemmas and a number of definitions) are exposed to criticism; and, in an iterated cycle, they are reformulated in response to the criticism. One of the important features of this is that concepts, conjectures, and proofs may all be modified and changed in the process. The resulting proof may "not prove what it sets out to prove" and may "not explain what it sets out to explain" (Lakatos 1978c, 93, 97). The autonomous dialectic of LMD "improves" as it "proves," for each (successful) iteration overcomes the refutation of the old conjecture. Part of this process is the refinement and redefinition of the mathematical concepts involved, and hence also the conjecture as well as the proof.

Mathematics is Hypothetico-Deductive and Quasi-empirical

Lakatos, taking a perspective parallel to Popper's (1959, 1972) view of science, regards mathematics as hypothetico-deductive. Mathematics consists of hypothetical theories, and within each there are attempts to deduce the proofs of conjectures. Thus, for example, a conjecture C may be entertained within an informal theory T, and informal proofs constructed leading *to* C (represented by the inference $T \Rightarrow C$). In Popper's account, a scientific hypothesis H is entertained, and an empirical or observational consequence O is deduced *from* it (represented by the inference $H \Rightarrow O$). The directions of inference are opposite in Popperian and Lakatosian hypothetico-deductive systems. Deduction *from* the hypothesis in the former, versus deduction *of* the conjecture in the latter.[17]

Lakatos terms mathematics quasi-empirical because of the analogy between his Logic of Mathematical Discovery and Popper's (1959) Logic of Scientific Discovery for empirical science.[18] In traditional "Euclidean" mathematical theories the flow of truth in the logical structure is "downwards," from the axioms to their conclusions, the theorems. In empirical science there is an opposite flow of falsity from the refuted consequences of the theory (falsifying observations) "upwards" to the theory itself. Mathematics according to Lakatos is quasi-empirical because there is an "upward" flow of falsity, from a refuted conjecture to the premises or assumptions from which it is derived. The emphasis is thus not on the transmission of truth from premises to conclusions, but on the retransmission of falsity from falsified conclusions (contradicted by "falsifiers") to hypothetical premises.

Mathematics has no external source of observations to serve as potential falsifiers of theories or conjectures. Instead, according to Lakatos, the realm of informal mathematics serves this function. Informal mathematical theories supply both conjectures and potential "heuristic falsifiers." For example, in the case of the Euler conjecture, if the three-dimensional surface comprising two nested cubes is accepted as a polyhedron, then the informal theorem that this polyhedron is non-Eulerian constitutes a "heuristic falsifier." In the case of formal axiomatic theories, since they are the formalizations of already existing informal mathematical theories, their potential "falsifiers" are the informal theorems of the preexisting theory (the "heuristic falsifiers"), in addition to formal contradictions, which constitute the "logical falsifiers" of the theory. The existence of an informal theorem serving as an "heuristic falsifier" shows that the axiomatization has not validly expressed the informal theory, that is, its source (Lakatos 1978c). Indeed Womack (1995) argues that using "heuristic falsifiers" amounts to using a plausibility or relevance argument, not a logical, that is, "real" falsification as in empirical science.

Despite the differences noted above, the logic of the retransmission of falsity in Lakatos's LMD is similar to that in Popper's LSD. Thus if Y is deduced from X (i.e., $X \Rightarrow Y$), the falsification of Y is retransmitted back to X ($\neg Y \Rightarrow \neg X$), by *modus tollens*, refuting X. However, if it is not only X which entails Y, but a number of additional assumptions $A_1, A_2, \ldots, A_n$, then the original implication can be represented as $X \& A_1 \& A_2 \& \ldots \& A_n \Rightarrow Y$. Falsifying Y then refutes the whole antecedent conjunction ($\neg Y \Rightarrow \neg[X \& A_1 \& A_2 \& \ldots \& A_n]$), so the falsification refutes at least one of the original premises $X, A_1, A_2, \ldots$, or A_n.

This fits Popper's logic of scientific discovery with X representing the scientific hypothesis, Y the deduced observation, and $A_1, \ldots, A_n$ auxiliary hypotheses. In Lakatos's LMD, Y represents the conjecture, X the basic proof assumptions, and $A1, \ldots, A_n$ the hidden (enthymatic) lemmas uncovered in the proof analysis. This illustrates the strong parallel between the logical forms implicit in the retransmission of falsity in Lakatos's LMD and in Popper's empirical logic of scientific discovery.

Lakatos's quasi-empiricism reinforces his fallibilism, for it means that the validity of mathematical knowledge is at best tentative, is continually further tested by pragmatic means, and is not established once and for all by rigorous proof. In this process the consequences of mathematical assumptions are explored, just as the observational consequences of empirical theories are explored, with a view to fruitfulness as well as falsification. This is why mathematics is described by Lakatos (and others) as "quasi-empirical" or "quasi-experimental."

History is Central to the Philosophy of Mathematics

According to Lakatos the history of mathematics, being the history of the evolution of mathematical knowledge, plays a central and constitutive role in the philosophy of mathematics. Lakatos's LMD is offered both as the logic of the historical development of mathematical knowledge, revealed by the "rational reconstructions of history," as well as the epistemological mechanism of mathematical knowledge growth. A rational reconstruction of the development of the Euler conjecture and its proofs is the central theme and substance of his major work, *Proofs and Refutations*. This is characterized as a "distilled" history, which reconstructs the relationships of the concepts, methods, proofs, conjectures, and theories as they developed in history to demonstrate their logical development and ultimately to show the progress in knowledge that occurs, and how it is logically attained. Such a reconstruction aims to show the rational aspects of knowledge growth, those that can be modeled by means of logic, and in particular by LMD, and not "extraneous" external factors. Thus it is a depersonalized, decontextualized internalist history that he constructs. Lakatos (1976) indicates the discrepancies between rationally reconstructed history (in his text) and "factual" (i.e., empirical) history (in the footnotes), which he explicitly sets out *not* to write.

Although he first refers to the "rational reconstruction of history" in his 1961 thesis, based on Popper 1959, Lakatos articulates his views on the method most clearly in his philosophy of science, where he claims that philosophy "provides normative methodologies in terms of which the historian reconstructs 'internal history' and thereby provides a rational explanation of the growth of objective knowledge." He maintains the distinction between the internal history of a science (including mathematics) and its external history, which treats empirical factors concerning its social (and psychological) context: "any rational reconstruction of history needs to be supplemented by an empirical (socio-psychological) 'external history'" (Lakatos 1978d, 102). The "internal history" of the development of a mathematical conjecture or theorem is given by its rational reconstruction.

A rational reconstruction evidently imposes a theoretical framework on history, that is, it interprets history through a simplifying theoretical lens. Lakatos admits this: *"History without some theoretical 'bias' is impossible"* (Lakatos 1978d, 120, original emphasis). Thus Lakatos's position is that there is no "raw" or uninterpreted history—no set of basic, objective facts—as consistency with his fallibilist epistemology requires.

> Whether a proposition is a *"fact"* or a *"theory"* in the context of a test-situation depends on our methodological decision. "Empirical basis of a theory" is a monotheoretical notion, it is *relative* to some monotheoretical deductive structure. We may use it as a first approximation; but in case of appeal by the theoretician, we must use a *pluralistic model*. In the pluralistic model the clash is not "between theories and facts" but between two high-level theories: between an *interpretative theory* to provide the facts and an *explanatory theory* to explain them;

and the interpretative theory may be on quite as high a level as the explanatory theory. The clash is then not any more between a logically higher-level theory and a lower-level falsifying hypothesis. The problem should not be put in terms of whether a *refutation'* is real or not. The problem is how to repair an inconsistency between the "explanatory theory" under test and the—explicit or hidden—"interpretative" theories; or, if you wish, *the problem is which theory to consider as the interpretative one which provides the "hard" facts and which the explanatory one which "tentatively" explains them.* (Lakatos 1978d, 44, original emphasis)

This position can be immediately applied to the history of mathematics, since it offers a set of empirical theories, irrespective of the fact that they are located in a different disciplinary setting. Thus a rational reconstruction of the history of mathematics may impose a particular theoretical reading on history to reveal (or rather construct) a simplified logic of knowledge growth.

The quotation illuminates another important aspect of Lakatos's philosophy of mathematics discussed above. This is the relationship between informal mathematical theories (as given by mathematical practice and history) and formal mathematical theories. According to Lakatos's view, the latter are rational reconstructions of the former, in which genetic structure is abandoned in favor of justificatory logic. Informal mathematical theories are the phenomena of mathematics that formal theories attempt to explain. Consequently Lakatos locates the potential falsifiers of a formal theory among the informal theorems of the preexisting informal theory. Although falsifiers for mathematics and empirical science originate in different realms, they have much in common. Empirical observations are themselves theoretical hypotheses, originating from another "explanatory" theory. Likewise mathematical falsifiers are theorems of a background informal theory.

A CRITICAL APPRECIATION OF
LAKATOS'S PHILOSOPHY OF MATHEMATICS

Appraisals of Lakatos's Philosophy of Mathematics

Feferman (1981) challenges the accuracy of LMD as a theory of history and suggests that the method of proof analysis, central to the theory, first appears only at the mid-nineteenth century. If this is true, then the theory might fail to account for much of the history of mathematics. However Lakatos (1978c) does consider Pappus's method of analysis-synthesis, and Descartes's methods too, and shows at least a partial fit with his LMD, so it is not clear that the criticism can be sustained in full.

However the fact remains that Lakatos's theory of mathematical history has a narrow evidential base and has been poorly tested. It is largely based on a single case study from nineteenth-century mathematics, the Euler conjecture (plus a brief treatment of uniform continuity, in Lakatos 1976). In some domains, such as in number theory, conjectures concerning well-defined concepts (not needing redefinition, "monster barring," etc.) may be proposed in final form, simply needing proofs (for example, Ramanujan's conjectures proved by Hardy and Littlewood). In other domains, such as axiomatic set theory, it may not be possible to distinguish sharply between substance (concepts) and form (proofs), as Lakatos does in his case studies (Ernest 1977). In addition to work of the scholars cited, there is a growing literature critical of Lakatos's LMD for its historical inaccuracy or narrowness (e.g., Corfield 1995; Kvasz 1995).

For example, Feferman (1981) claims that internal foundational moves involving the reorganization of mathematical theories may not be the result of proof-analysis. Anapolitanos also argues that Lakatos's (1976) method of proof-analysis is not adequate to "play the role of the bare ultimate backbone for every plausible descriptional model of what we call mathematical discovery" (Anapolitanos 1989, 337). In his view, the method is inadequate for dealing with problems related to structural characteristics of crisis periods in the history of mathematics, such as sudden shifts of conceptual frameworks. The two crises in the history of mathematics cited are those besetting the Pythagoreans over incommensurability and the Cantorian set-theoretic foundational crisis. The claim is that in these cases the aim was to repair the fundamental conceptual framework, not merely to prove a conjecture, and that Lakatos's LMD cannot account for such situations or their historical outcomes, for example, the domination of set theory by the Zermelo-Fraenkel axioms. Anapolitanos acknowledges that the Lakatosian method of proofs and refutations can be abstracted from its concrete case study and extended, but he claims that this transforms it into an empty general schema that lacks both detailed descriptive content and explanatory force.

Thus Lakatos's LMD is criticized for applying only to a narrow range of historical developments. This criticism appears to be legitimate. Perhaps LMD applies best or only to those developments which offer the analogue in mathematics to periods of normal science in Kuhn's (1962) theory, as opposed to those paralleling scientific revolutions. Some limitation like this certainly seems to follow from the criticism of both Anapolitanos and Feferman. Both are critical of the ability of Lakatos's historical theory to account for foundational crises, which are not reducible to the search for improved proofs of a conjecture. Similarly, there is also the problem concerning the ability of LMD to accommodate the development of new theories, which may well not emerge from proof analysis. However the added specification of the background theory and problems, as in the above explication of LMD (table 4.3), provides the potential for generalization and extension—and hence possibly for circumventing the criticism. Anapolitanos's second criticism, that such a generalization results in an empty general scheme, is inadequately argued, in my view. Kvasz (1995), for example, offers a generalization of Lakatos's LMD which is rich in explanatory power.

An aspect of Lakatos's LMD that I wish to criticize is its exclusively internalist focus in history. Although a first accounting for history can legitimately focus on the internal logical development of mathematical knowledge, ultimately the dividing line between the knowledge produced and the social and material circumstances of its production cannot in my view be fixed and absolute, since the process is at base human and social. Lakatos regards his LMD as a contribution to a new field, the methodology of mathematics, which incorporates actual and possible theory growth and heuristics (and hence both the contexts of discovery and justification) but still remains separate from actual history. This is perhaps an instance of his demarcationist tendencies affecting the philosophy of mathematics (as in the philosophy of science). Lakatos believed that there is an objective and rational logic of mathematical discovery which can be treated entirely separately from the actual details of historical, individual, or social development of mathematical knowledge by means of "rational reconstruction."

My criticism is that although the methodology of mathematics is a legitimate and valuable subfield of interest, it should not be rigidly separated from the history of mathematics with its external, social factors. Lakatos himself has shown that logic (like mathematics) is fallible, changing, and context bound, not a priori and disconnected from empirical circumstances. To reinstate a methodological metalogic (LMD) at a higher level and claim that it can be considered apart from the external history of its deployment does not sit well with Lakatos's fallibilism. Lakatos has attacked the attempt to replace informal mathematical theories by formal theories. The latter may be useful, but they cannot supplant the former in all contexts, as Lakatos has shown. Likewise I wish to attack the replacement of the history of the development of mathematical knowledge by logical reconstructions of that history. The latter may be useful, but they cannot supplant the former in all contexts. Thus, contrary to Lakatos, I believe that the LMD cannot exclude a consideration of external historical factors, namely, the social context of mathematical knowledge creation.[19]

A second and related criticism concerns the logical basis of LMD. Lakatos takes the inspiration for this initially from Hegel and then justifies it in Popperian terms as applying, in effect, to an objectified realm of abstract ideas (Popper's World 3 or Hegel's realm of Absolute Spirit). Thus LMD represents the playing out of a pure logic in the realm of concepts and objective ideas, a realm in which the "logical essence" of historical development can be reconstructed abstractly. I wish to criticize this as a hidden form of idealism and Platonism.

The LMD in my view is the dialectical logic of human conversation and interaction, which is founded in Wittgensteinian language games and forms of life. It is not some abstract ideal logic but the alternating voices in dialogue, coupled with mathematical standards of criticism, which gives rise to LMD. Thus my criticism is that Lakatos mistakenly idealizes the LMD and neglects its origins in conversation. Acknowledging this, and ditching Lakatos's problematic idealism, removes the barriers that rigorously exclude external aspects of history from the realm of methodology, Lakatos's preferred seat for his LMD.

However, a caveat to this criticism should be stated. Lakatos writes of the autonomy of mathematics and how it alienates itself from the human activity which produces it. Whether or not he was still thinking of the Hegelian Absolute, there is no doubt that an important aspect of mathematics is at stake. As I shall argue, the objectivity of mathematics is realized in its strong autonomy and cultural momentum. Lakatos's idealism can be interpreted as a metaphor for this cultural autonomy, even though this is probably not what he intended. Nevertheless, he makes a space for this essential feature of mathematics, even if his terminology must be altered.

The Adequacy Criteria and Quasi-Empiricism

Quasi-empiricism offers a partial account of the nature of mathematical knowledge and its genesis, and in this Lakatos offers an account more extensive in scope than traditional philosophies of mathematics. He adds a new, lower stratum, namely, that of informal mathematical knowledge, to the traditional stratum of formalized mathematical knowledge. He also adds a dynamic to this extended system, one that shows not only how knowledge in the lower stratum develops, but also the relationship between the two strata. In particular, he shows how knowledge in the lower stratum is reflected upwards, by formalization, to form at the upper level idealized images, which are seen by absolutists as the indubitable truths of mathematics. Both the formalized and the informal levels of mathematics are organized into theories: a collection of well-defined axiomatic theories at the formal level and a collection of overlapping, more loosely defined theories at the informal level. This is a rich and more effectively descriptive account than hitherto found in the literature.

Lakatos accounts for the nature of mathematical knowledge as hypothetico-deductive and quasi-empirical. He accounts for errors in mathematical knowledge in such a way that there is a symmetry between "true" and "false" beliefs. The symmetry is that both types have been accepted as adequately justified by the mathematical community: the "truths" are not yet refuted, whereas the falsehoods have been refuted and are in the process of being revised.[20]

He provides an elaborate theory of the genesis of mathematical knowledge. This potentially accounts for much of mathematical practice and for its history, although his approach to the latter is internalist. Since Lakatos's theory of the genesis of mathematical knowledge puts it on a par in many respects with scientific knowledge, the success of the applications of mathematics are potentially explicable by analogy with science and technology. Regarding mathematics as quasi-empirical and rooted in informal theories allows for the impact of extradisciplinary problems and concepts on mathematics. Since LMD applies to conjectures stimulated by mathematical problems, which have either internal (mathematical) or external (scientific or social) origins, it is no longer any surprise that the resulting concepts, conjectures, proofs and theories have applications in realms beyond those of pure mathematics.

Lakatos's philosophy provides criteria for the evaluation, appraisal and choice of mathematical concepts, definitions, proofs, and theories, and in this he is almost alone. Hallett (1979), who had been his student, further develops the Lakatosian criteria for mathematical theory appraisal in terms of their fruitfulness in solving mathematical problems. In addition, a key strength of Lakatos's philosophy of mathematics is that it is not prescriptive but descriptive and that it attempts to describe mathematical practice and mathematics as it is historically, not as it ought to be practiced or reorganized in order to fulfill some foundationalist plan.

In terms of the adequacy criteria, quasi-empiricism therefore partly satisfies those concerning mathematical knowledge, applications, practice, and theories. What he offers are only sketches, as far as these issues are concerned, with the exception of the genesis of mathematical knowledge. Lakatos's treatment of the autonomy of mathematics offers the germ of an idea concerning the nature of mathematical objects, but he does not develop this enough to address the appropriate criterion. Lakatos gives no account of the nature of the objects of mathematics and devotes no discussion at all to ontological matters. This is a deficiency.

This review suggests that although Lakatos's quasi-empiricism is potentially very fruitful in terms of the adequacy criteria, it needs to be suitably elaborated and worked out to actually meet most of the criteria. Overall, in critical evaluation of Lakatos's philosophy of mathematics, I argue that the major weaknesses are (1) the overly internal focus of his LMD and (2) sins of omission concerning a lack of elaboration of his theory.

The Strengths of Lakatos's Philosophy of Mathematics

The rejection of absolutism in favor of fallibilism is a special feature and strength of Lakatos's philosophy of mathematics. Lakatos was the first philosopher of mathematics to do this clearly and unequivocally. He went beyond advocacy, for he also initiated a reconceptualization and implicit redefinition of the philosophy of mathematics. In doing this he further called into question the dominant orthodoxy in the philosophy of mathematics with regard to both its foundationalism and absolutism. Thus Lakatos might be considered to have potentially freed the philosophy of mathematics to reconsider its function, as well as to question the hitherto unchallenged status of mathematical truth. Although these are critical (i.e., essentially negative) achievements, their importance cannot be overestimated, in my view, in a field as conservative as the philosophy of mathematics.

A central and characteristic part of Lakatos's achievement is to reconsider the role of mathematical proof as an essential component of the context of discovery in mathematics. Traditionally proof has been seen as no more and no less than the method of warranting knowledge within formal mathematics, constituting the core of the context of justification. It took great vision on Lakatos's part to cast off this traditional perception and reconceptualize the role of proof in the growth of mathematical knowledge. This was the consequence of his desire to offer a philosophy of mathematics that treats its methodology descriptively, not prescriptively.

Lakatos made a particularly valuable contribution by offering a synthesis of epistemological, historical, and methodological aspects in his philosophy of mathematics. The result is a partially developed global theory of mathematics, offering insights for the history, philosophy, sociology, psychology, and practice of mathematics. What is offered may be hesitant and incomplete—due perhaps to the brevity of his career as a philosopher of mathematics and the paucity of his publications—but Lakatos has opened the door to a reconceptualized interdisciplinary account of mathematics that can take advantage of sympathetic development across the range of metatheories of mathematics. His adherence to a Popperian internalism limits his contribution in this dimension, although another commentator not committed to a social constructivist view of mathematics might see this as a strength. Nevertheless, the relationship between the history and philosophy of mathematics in Lakatos's theory emphasizes the novelty of his conception of the philosophy of mathematics. Lakatos rejects the traditional conception of the philosophy of mathematics that provides a remote logical rhetoric of mathematical practice but avoids engaging with its actual phenomena. Thus his historicist reading is a radical move which not only requires a reappraisal of the field but forces a new interdisciplinarity upon it. A consequence is the breakdown of the absolute distinction between the context of justification and the context of discovery. The admission of informal mathematics and history as central to the philosophy of mathematics means that their total separation can no longer be sustained without question.

Another significant strength of Lakatos's philosophy of mathematics is that it suggests a pattern for the development of mathematical concepts, conjectures, proofs, and theories as a collective enterprise and that it indicates the role and variety of interactions contributing to this development. It shows that, contrary to some of the traditional accounts that abound, creation in mathematics is not essentially an isolated individual activity. Mathematics is essentially a community activity (Marchi 1976). This position has recently become widespread among historians of mathematics (Schubring 1989). According to Lakatos, in addition to the work of individuals, a dialectical negotiation process plays an essential part. This fits well with accounts of the origin of mathematical reasoning and proof that locate it in interpersonal argument and dialectics (Szabo 1969).[21]

NOTES

1. My main sources of biographical detail are Worrall 1976; Hersh 1978a, 1978b; and Lakatos 1961, 1976, 1978d, 1978c.

2. Polya's heuristics have been widely adopted in mathematics education, following recommendations for including problem solving in school mathematics. See, for example, National Council of Teachers of Mathematics (1980, 1989); Cockcroft (1982); Her Majesty's Inspectorate (1985); Krulik and Reys (1980, inside cover).

3. Another exception is Paul Bernays's 1947 review of *How to Solve It.*

4. "I owe the suggestion that I should start with a careful and detailed case study in the history of the Euler-formula to Professor G. Polya. His encouragement and advice since 1957 has been invaluable" Lakatos (1961, 5).

5. The "picture frame" example; figure 9 in Lakatos 1976.

6. Lakatos (1961, 1963–64) parodies Galileo's dialogue, and knowing Renyi well he can be presumed to know his dialogues. Heyting's 1956 dialogue, his major contribution to the intuitionist philosophy of mathematics, is probably not an influence. It is cited in Lakatos 1963–64, but not in Lakatos 1961.

7. The references to Young 1802, 1817; Fresnel 1850; Lobatschewsky 1829; Bolyai 1850 in Lakatos's original have been deleted.

8. Popper (1962, 1957) is profoundly antithetical to Hegelian ideas. Williams (1983) even notes that Popper gave the word *historicism* a new pejorative meaning. Nevertheless, it would be interesting to explore the influence of Hegel and dialectics

on Popper's thought. After all, they share a fallibilism, a partly analogous "logic," and idealistic beliefs (Absolute Spirit versus World 3). Certainly the youthful Popper (1976) was a Marxist who read Marx and Engels, and he would have encountered dialectical materialism.

9. Lakatos once jokingly referred to the Zeitgeist as having descended on the LSE (London School of Economics), which again counterpoises Hegel and Popper in a characteristically witty way (Berkson 1976).

10. In 1945, Popper also directed a swingeing polemic at Hegel and Marx's political philosophy, treating the ideas of Hegel with contempt; to this he added an unrepentant twenty-eight-page addendum in 1961, the year Lakatos completed his thesis (Popper 1962).

11. Not only does this chapter close with the editors' own infallibilist dialogue, but a substantial chunk of dialogue concerned with the fallibility of proof is edited out of the beginning (Lakatos 1961, 98–108). Much of the previously unpublished material in Lakatos 1976 is substantially edited and rewritten by the editors; this is why I quote here only from passages written by Lakatos himself.

12. Probably because they were attached to the LSE philosophy department, with its Popperian orthodoxy.

13. I should add that the editors, both friends and colleagues of Lakatos, were probably sincerely acting as they thought he would have wanted them to do. However there is a chasm dividing the practice of an author revising his own work from that of his posthumous editors doing the same.

14. "But Popper who has laid down the basis of *this* logic of discovery was not interested in the meta-question of what was the nature of his inquiry and he did not realize that this is neither psychology nor logic, it is an independent discipline, the logic of discovery, heuristic" (Lakatos 1961, 174).

15. I have drawn on Lakatos's claims and arguments in chapter 1, and do not repeat them here.

16. In a formalized proof T_n would have to be represented in these premises as the conjunction of a finite set of axioms.

17. During the analysis phase of LMD, the heuristic process of proof genesis, the directions of working are opposite. However during the synthesis phase, in which the justificatory deduction of C is constructed, the directions of working coincide.

18. The term *quasi-empirical* is adapted from the description of mathematics as "quasi-experimental" in a 1756–57 editor's summary to Euler's work (Lakatos 1976, 9).

19. Lakatos (1978d, 1102) agrees that "any rational reconstruction of history needs to be supplemented by an empirical (sociopsychological) 'external history.'" But he contrasts the latter with "intellectual" history.

20. This is Bloor's (1976) symmetry criterion for an adequate sociology of mathematical knowledge.

21. Another of Lakatos's achievements, although implicit in his fallibilism and historicism, is the explicit identification and criticism of essentialism. For Lakatos (1961, 1976), concepts are always in the process of development in the dialectical relationship between formal and informal theories, and no formal (or other) definition can ever be said to capture the essence of a concept, i.e., there is no such "essence."

CHAPTER 5

THE SOCIAL CONSTRUCTION
OF OBJECTIVE KNOWLEDGE

THE NATURE OF SOCIAL CONSTRUCTIVISM

The Social in Philosophy

Over the course of the history of philosophy and epistemology there has been a tendency to neglect or repudiate the social dimension. Traditional epistemology objectifies discourse and knowledge and focuses either on the individual knower and cognizing subject or on objectivized knowledge. Knowledge is detached from the knower, and once warranted it remains knowledge irrespective of whether it is the property of one individual or is shared by many or all, including those of past and future generations. From this perspective, the social, representing a plurality of human beings, is irrelevant. Social acceptance is thus traditionally a contingent or empirical fact, rather than the province of epistemology.

There is an irony in this neglect, given the "linguistic turn" in the modern Anglo-American philosophical tradition. For language is both the quintessential social institution and the underpinning sine qua non of philosophy. Without language and its socially shared meanings, even if I could inscribe these words they would just be meaningless marks on a page. Any explicit human formulations of doubt, belief, or knowledge, encompassing all philosophy and other realms of scholarship, presuppose the social institution of language. This alone justifies and necessitates the admission of the social into philosophy at some point or other.

Of course the standard philosophical rejoinder to this is that it may be true that the social, including language, is essential to the genesis of individual knowledge, but this does not demonstrate its necessary contribution to the constitution or justification of knowledge. My argument is that meaning and the social institution of language are not just contingent aspects of knowledge and epistemology: they are presupposed by any discussion of the justification of propositional knowledge. Thus to explicitly dismiss issues of language and hence of the social in discussing propositional knowledge is incoherent.

Not all philosophers or philosophically minded theorists neglect the social dimension. Dewey (1950) stressed that social experiences play an essential role in the growth of knowledge. Mead (1934) elaborated pragmatism into a fully social philosophy. Wittgenstein's characteristic notions of "language game" and "form of life" introduce irreducibly social elements, not only into philosophy, but also into the philosophy of mathematics. Rorty (1979) uses the central social concept of conversation as a basis for his theory of knowledge, although he calls himself "post-epistemological." Searle (1995) has extended his linguistic "speech act" philosophy to include "the social construction of reality," which is close in spirit to the present enterprise, although he ends up on a different side of the relativism issue. As these exemplars illustrate, the concept of the social has a continued presence and growing currency in modern philosophy.

One area of philosophy in which the social dimension is not neglected is in the philosophy of the social sciences. There, a number of issues concerning the role of the social in philosophy are raised. Winch, who emerged from the post-Wittgensteinian tradition of ordinary language philosophy, goes so far as to say that "logical relations between propositions depend on social relations between men" (Brown 1979, 227). He argues that the social dimension must be included in discussions of epistemology: "the philosophical elucidation of human intelligence, and the notions associated with this, require that these notions be placed in the context of the relations between men in society" (Winch 1969, 40). He thereby claims that the cognizing subject of epistemology cannot be considered without bringing in the role of the social. This is a theme echoed by others.

> Thus the philosophically abstract conception of self-sufficiency of the individual mind, free and independent of others, serves to conceal its origins as a social product of rule-governed reflection. "I think therefore I am" totally obscures the social process whereby the use of the term "I" is acquired. (Doyal and Harris 1986, 86)

This is strongly reminiscent of Mead's ([1913] 1964) social view of the self, which will be drawn upon in chapter 7 below.

A central issue of concern in the philosophy of the social sciences is the relationship between, and the possibility of the reduction of, the social to the individual. The position of logical empiricists (e.g., Nagel [1961] and others such as Watkins [1968]) known as "methodological individualism" is that all social phenomena and laws can be reduced to those of individuals and their dispositions. Although there is some dispute over these claims in the philosophy of the social sciences, it does not bear directly on the issue of the legitimacy of the social for philosophy. As Lukes (1970) shows, the arguments in favor of methodological individualism do not rule out a consideration of "situations" or "interrelations between individuals" but, at best, lead to a rejection of some forms of "holism" and "historicism."

In contemporary philosophy the once incommensurable traditions of Anglo-American philosophy, philosophy of science, continental philosophy, and sociology of knowledge are now engaged in conversation. Hybrid positions straddling several of these traditions are emerging—such as social epistemology (Fuller 1988). Fuller argues not only that the neglect of the social in epistemology and philosophy of science is an omission but that it is commonly associated with fallacies concerning the character and justification of knowledge.

> As currently practiced, the branches of philosophy devoted to the nature of knowledge—epistemology and the philosophy of science—rest on a couple of elementary fallacies. On the one hand, philosophers treat the various knowledge states and processes as properties of individuals operating in a social vacuum. They often seem to think that any correct account of individual knowledge can be, ipso facto, generalized as the correct account of social knowledge . . . And insofar as this slide from the individual to the social has been implicit instead of argued, philosophers have committed *the fallacy of composition*.
>
> On the other hand, philosophical accounts of the individual knower are sometimes quite perspicuous, but not because they have isolated real features of individual cognition. Rather these accounts have identified inference schemas, so-called logics of justification, and scripts that have persuasive force in the public exchange of information . . . Consequently, philosophers can slip into committing *the fallacy of division* by assuming that a feature of the knowledge enterprise that appears primarily at the level of social interaction is, ipso facto, reproduced . . . as a feature of the minds of individuals engaged in the interaction. (Fuller 1988, xii–xiii)

Thus Fuller argues not only that the character of the social is necessary in discussions of knowledge but that the strategies employed to obviate the need for the social hinge on fallacious arguments.

There is a tradition in the philosophy of mathematics which tacitly admits the social dimension as central—namely, conventionalism (Priest

1973). Conventions, which lie at the heart of conventionalism, are essentially social agreements of one sort or another, and so this philosophical position implicates the social. Elements of a conventionalist philosophy of mathematics are to be found in Poincaré (1905), who asserts that certain geometrical hypotheses are freely but not arbitrarily adopted conventions. Similar elements are also to be found in Ajdukiewicz, who termed himself a radical conventionalist and argued that the linguistic basis of knowledge significantly determines its content (Giedymin 1982). Logical empiricists such as Carnap, Hempel, and Nagel; and philosophers such as Ayer and Quine; as well as others espouse versions of conventionalism. However, despite the widespread support for varieties of conventionalism earlier this century, it has rarely if ever been explicitly linked with the necessity for acknowledging the social dimension of mathematics.

Fuller (1988) distinguishes two senses of the term *convention* and argues that conventionalism is based on the first sense. This is a convention as an explicit agreement on a definition, assumption or a rule. However his second sense of convention is as "a practice that has emerged largely without design yet continues to be maintained" (56). This second sense resembles the rules and agreements of Wittgenstein's language games and forms of life (and Foucault's concept of discursive practice). This is more explicitly and constitutionally social, and recognizes the historical and institutional dimensions of the social.

In the philosophy of mathematics there has been a growth of social perspectives following from the admission of historical perspectives, evolutionary aspects of epistemology, and naturalistic approaches, concerned to *describe* the practices of mathematicians; this occurs in the work of Lakatos (1963–64, 1978c), Kitcher (1984), Rav (1989), Glas (1988), and a number of others including Davis and Hersh (1980, 1988), Tymoczko (1986b), Ernest (1991), Gillies (1992), and Tiles (1991). In addition, there is a growing number of researchers drawing on other disciplines to account for mathematics socially; these include Bloor (1976) and Restivo (1985, 1992) from sociology; Wilder (1981) and Livingston (1986) from cultural studies and ethnomethodology; Rotman (1987, 1988) from semiotics; and Asprey and Kitcher (1988), Joseph (1991), and Kline (1980) from the history of mathematics.

Thus although some of the main traditions in modern Anglo-American philosophy may reject or neglect the social dimension, there are a growing number of other strands of thought which do take it seriously in accounting for knowledge in general and mathematics in particular.

The Philosophical Roots of Social Constructivism

There are two main sources for the social constructivist philosophy of mathematics, Lakatos's and Wittgenstein's philosophies of mathematics.

First, there is the account of the genesis of mathematical knowledge and proofs in Lakatos's LMD. This describes the essentially social, dialectical process of mathematical knowledge creation and warranting. However, on the basis of the criticism that has been directed at it, this needs to be extended and generalized in the social constructivist account.

Lakatos's fallibilist critique of absolutist notions of formal proof in mathematics and the associated epistemological assumptions also necessitates a novel perspective on proof. I argue below that the philosophy of mathematics needs to recognize the rhetorical and socially persuasive role of proof in mathematics. This development would in all probability have been unacceptable to Lakatos, who rejected the concept of a social element in knowledge justification, and termed it "élitism" (Lakatos 1978c).

One of the fundamental problems that any philosophy of mathematics must face is the challenge of accounting for, or at least attempting to account for, the epistemological basis of mathematical knowledge. Whatever the orientation of an approach to philosophy of mathematics, the issue of the justification of mathematical knowledge is one that must be faced. This is especially pressing for a fallibilist philosophy of mathematics, as social constructivism is intended to be, since a well-articulated account of the foundations for mathematical knowledge is needed, an account that does not lapse into foundationalism.

It is on this epistemological issue that Wittgenstein's philosophy of mathematics plays a particular role in the formulation of the social constructivism. For Wittgenstein offers a unique account of the foundation of mathematical knowledge and its social basis. He locates the basis for logical necessity and mathematical knowledge in linguistic rules (be they tacit or explicitly articulated) and practices (which are embedded in socially enacted forms of life). Thus it is the social conventions, norms, and lived patterns of behavior, including above all socially accepted patterns of language use, that provide the basis for the notions of necessity and truth; these in turn provide the epistemological foundation for mathematics and logic.

Wittgenstein's profound contribution to the philosophy of mathematics, and to social constructivism, is thus to offer a far-reaching and thoroughgoing social theory of mathematical knowledge and logical necessity. However Wittgenstein's contribution is exclusively synchronic, and this needs to be developed to include a diachronic element. This has a dual impact. It both allows the history of mathematics to be accommodated and, by explicitly admitting historical tradition, adds weight to the forms of life on which the language games of mathematics rest.

The social constructivist philosophy of mathematics presented here accords an essential role to the social, on the grounds that there are epistemologically central social phenomena such as language, negotiation, conversation, and group acceptance that cannot be accounted for in purely individual or objectivist terms. Quite the reverse; social constructivism offers a theoretical social account of both "objective" and "subjective" knowledge in mathematics and describes the mechanisms underlying the genesis and warranting of these two types of knowledge socially. In each case, it claims that the mechanisms are analogous, being based on dialectical, socially situated interpersonal "conversations." Conversation can be seen as the shared underlying metaphor in the philosophies of Lakatos and Wittgenstein drawn upon here.

THE PROBLEM OF MATHEMATICAL KNOWLEDGE

Tacit and Explicitly Represented Knowledge

A traditional assumption of epistemology is that mathematical knowledge can be represented as a set of explicitly formulated sentences. This position contrasts with the view of knowledge in Wittgenstein's later work, in which to know the meaning of a word or text is to be able to engage in the appropriate language games and forms of life, that is, to use it appropriately. This suggests the distinction between being able to state knowledge in propositional form and being able to use it.[1]

There is a tradition going back to Aristotle which distinguishes between practical wisdom and theoretical knowledge. The dualism of Descartes makes a parallel, categorical distinction between mind and body and their associated forms of knowledge. Ryle (1949) rejects this as based on a categorical error, arguing that mind is embodied.[2] He distinguishes between the different types of knowledge that are possible for an individual knower. "Knowing that" refers to knowledge of propositions or statements. In contrast, "knowing how" refers to practical knowledge, skills, or dispositions, which are not immediately given in the form of propositions, even if they can (or cannot) ultimately be so represented.

The motivation for including "know how" as well as propositional knowledge as part of mathematical knowledge is that it takes human understanding, activity, and experience to make or justify mathematics—in short, mathematical know-how. Much that is accepted as mathematical knowledge consists in being able to carry out certain symbolic or conceptual procedures or operations. To know the addition algorithm, proof by induction, or definite integrals is to be able to carry out the operations involved, not merely to be able to state certain propositions. Thus what an individual knows in mathematics, in addition to publicly stateable propositional knowledge, includes her or his mathematical know-how, and this latter category needs to be accommodated in a naturistically adequate epistemology of mathematics.

A related conception, that of "tacit" or personal knowledge, is attributable to Polanyi (1964, 1966). Polanyi's epistemological thesis is that we know more than we can say explicitly. In particular, he emphasizes that all our propositional knowledge, that which is traditionally known as the sum of our knowledge, rests on tacit knowledge of language. He insists that the knower be acknowledged in a discussion of knowledge and argues that the explicit propositional knowledge could not be apprehended, and hence would not be known to the knower, without the tacit knowledge of language.

> While tacit knowledge may be possessed by itself, explicit knowledge must rely on being tacitly understood and applied. Hence all knowledge is *either tacit* or *rooted in tacit knowledge.* A *wholly* explicit knowledge is unthinkable. (Polanyi 1969, 144)

Although Polanyi intends tacit knowledge to extend beyond that of language, even when understood broadly, linguistic knowledge is clearly at the heart of his notion of tacit knowledge. I focus on tacit knowledge of language since this underpins propositional knowledge. What is clear is that for any propositional knowledge to be known by an individual or group of persons, the putative knowers must have knowledge of language. Part of this must be tacit, a precondition to understanding and assenting to the knowledge. Two immediate arguments in further support of this claim can be mounted on genetic and logical grounds.

The genetic argument is that knowledge of language is acquired experientially and that grammar and the laws of language thus learned are known to be tacit, inferred unconsciously by the learner from the pattern of her/his experiences (Miller 1964). In other words, much human knowledge of language evidently is tacit, certainly when it is acquired. There is no reason to suppose that all of this tacit knowledge ever becomes explicit—and, anyway, language acquisition can be a lifelong affair.

The logical argument is that the meaning of some concepts, terms, words, and phrases of natural language must be assumed, that is, must be known tacitly. For as is well known (see, e.g., Popper 1979) any attempt to define all of these parts of language explicitly must lead to an infinite regress. In other words, logically, some knowledge of language must remain tacit. Furthermore, although I have not treated them differentially, the argument holds for both the syntax and semantics of language. Knowledge of each must have a tacit component, since neither is reducible to the other.

The philosopher Marjorie Grene also argues for the indispensability of tacit knowledge. "There are constituents of knowledge which, though not only psychologically but epistemologically indispensable to it, are not stateable in the form of propositions or arguments" (Grene 1966, 204).

Finally, it should be noted that a notion of tacit knowledge or know-how is necessitated by Wittgenstein's philosophy of language (and mathematics), for a central part of knowing consists in being able to participate in language games embedded in shared forms of life. Sharing a form of life involves sharing norms, assumptions, and know-how which underpin the associated language games. Wittgenstein's philosophy of mathematics thus presupposes that all knowledge is irreducibly rooted in tacit knowledge.

Justification. An important issue is that knowledge *qua* knowledge must have a warrant or form of justification. Tacit knowledge can be legitimately so termed only if there are grounds for asserting it or if it is justified. Of course since the knowledge is tacit, then so too its justification must—at least in part—be tacit, on pain of contradiction. Thus the validity of some tacit knowledge will be demonstrated implicitly by the individual's successful participation in some social activity or "form of life." Not in all cases, however, need the justification be tacit. For example, an individual's tacit knowledge of the English language is likely to be justified and validated by conformity to the public norms of correct grammar, meaning, and language use. Thus a speaker's production of a sufficiently broad range of utterances appropriately in context can serve as a warrant for that speaker's knowledge of English. Practical know-how is also likely to be validated by public performance and demonstration. To know language is to be able to use it to communicate (Hamlyn 1978). As Ayer says "To have knowledge is to have the power to give a successful performance" (Ayer 1956, 9). Such a validation is to all intents and purposes equivalent to the testing of scientific theories in terms of their predictions. It is an empirical, predictive warrant. It is a weaker warrant than a mathematical proof, for no finite number of performances can exhaust all possible outcomes of tacit knowledge as a disposition (just as no finite number of observations can ever exhaust the observational content of a scientific law or theory). Thus I am claiming that tacit knowledge can be defended as warranted knowledge provided that it is supported by some form of justification or validation (possibly tacit) of which the knower or another judge of competence is, or can become, aware.

On the basis of these distinctions and arguments I shall therefore claim that, beyond traditional propositional knowledge, there is a category of tacit knowledge. The subjective knowledge of an individual includes both of these categories.

A Model of Mathematical Knowledge

One of the central notions introduced by Kuhn in his philosophy of science is the ambiguous notion of "paradigm" (Masterman 1970).

In the later development of his philosophy, Kuhn (1970) argues that scientists share, to a greater or lesser extent, a paradigm understood as a "disciplinary matrix": "disciplinary" because it refers to the common possession of the practitioners of a particular discipline; "matrix" because it is composed of ordered elements of various sorts, each requiring further specification. (Kuhn 1970, 182)

Kuhn describes a number of these elements: accepted statements comprising laws and so forth; metaphysical beliefs such as explanatory metaphors; scientific values concerning such things as preferred types of warrants and predictions; and exemplars, especially paradigmatic problem-solutions. Kuhn makes it clear that his list is exemplary rather than complete and that it includes "'tacit knowledge' which is learned by doing science rather than by acquiring rules for doing it" (Kuhn 1970, 191).

Thus Kuhn's conception of a disciplinary matrix is an elaborated complex of different forms of knowledge, values, and belief, a complex that extends far beyond the traditional conceptions of mathematical knowledge. This notion is developed and applied by Kitcher (1984), who as part of his quasi-empirical philosophy of mathematics proposes a systematic account of what he calls "mathematical practice." This serves as a model of mathematical knowledge which includes both explicit propositional and tacit knowledge components. Kitcher defines

a mathematical practice as consisting of five components: a language, a set of accepted statements, a set of accepted reasonings, a set of questions selected as important, and a set of meta-mathematical views (including standards for proof and definition and claims about the scope and structure of mathematics). As a convenient notation, I shall use the expression "<L,M,Q,R,S>" as a symbol for an arbitrary mathematical practice (where L is the language of the practice, M the a set of meta-mathematical views, Q the set of accepted questions, R the set of accepted reasonings, and S the set of accepted statements). (Kitcher 1984, 163–64)

Kitcher introduces this notion of a mathematical practice to account for the historical growth and development of mathematics; this parallels Kuhn's account of scientific change and incorporates the elements of a disciplinary matrix. However Kitcher extends this notion so that it accounts for mathematical knowledge in a more comprehensive way than is found elsewhere in the literature. Consequently, I shall adopt it as a tentative naturalistic model of mathematical knowledge. The five components of the model are as follows: the language L, accepted statements, accepted reasonings, mathematical questions, and metamathematical views.

The language L. The underlying language L of the mathematical practice is understood to be a mathematical sublanguage of English, or its equivalent in another language, supplemented with specialized mathematical symbolism and meanings. Because of this shared specialist symbolism, there is much in common between the mathematical sublanguages of different countries. Indeed, the more formal mathematical publications become, the more internationally accessible they become (to mathematicians). This may be interpreted as reflecting the cultural domination of professional mathematical work by its formalism world wide, as opposed to the absolutist interpretation that it stems from the essential universality of mathematics.

Understood broadly, the language of a mathematical practice is extensive, and it comes equipped with a large range of discursive objects, including mathematical symbols, notations, diagrams; terms, concepts, definitions, axioms, statements, analogies, problems, explanations, methods, proofs, theories, and texts. Mathematicians must *know* this mathematical sub-language, at least some central and substantial part of it, but much of this is know-how (Ryle 1949). Thus this knowledge is in large part *tacit,* but it is knowledge nonetheless.

Accepted statements. Second, there is the set of accepted statements. This is the body of mathematical knowledge in the traditional sense, the warranted propositions, theorems, or "truths" of mathematics. Its inclusion needs no new justification, as it is evidently an essential component of mathematical knowledge.

Accepted reasonings. Third, there is the set of accepted reasonings. This includes the justificatory warrants for the set of accepted statements and comprises the set of proofs accepted by the mathematical community as correct. It also includes informal and traditional proofs, which—although not accepted as adequate proofs—are regarded as having some valuable content. Finally, it includes accepted problem solutions, comprising analyses and computations other than just proofs.

Proofs are traditionally associated with mathematical knowledge, although they are often regarded as ancillary to the accepted statements. Technically, proofs can themselves be seen as a part of mathematical knowledge, since they are sequences of accepted statements.

However it is appropriate to accord proofs (and problem solutions) a knowledge category of their own, in view of the central role they play in mathematics. In mathematics proofs are understood to do more than merely serve as a warrant for the theorem they prove, as Kitcher claims. They can add to knowledge as well as reveal the connections of existing knowledge. They sometimes include the first applications of new mathematical methods and thus embody procedural knowledge. As Wittgenstein says, a proof reveals part of the meaning of a theorem not given in the statement alone. "A psychological disadvantage of proofs that construct *propositions* is that they easily make us forget that the *sense* of the result is not to be read off from this by itself, but from the *proof*" (Wittgenstein 1978, 162). Kitcher also regards accepted problem solutions, which may not be proofs or propositions, as a significant part of mathematical knowledge in this category.

Questions. Fourth, there is the set of mathematical questions and problems that the mathematical community regards as being of current importance; of future importance, such as the Hilbert Problems of 1900 (Kneebone 1963); or of past importance.

Many philosophers, such as Popper, Kuhn (1970), and Laudan (1977), attach great weight to problems in science and mathematics because of their role in stimulating the growth of knowledge. Indeed, Popper (1979) admits problems and questions as well as theorems and proofs into his realm of objective knowledge. In the philosophy of mathematics, Hallett (1979) proposes that problems play a key role in the evaluation of mathematical theories. Theories should be judged by the extent to which they aid the solution of outstanding problems. Thus Hallett identifies problems as central to the justification of mathematical theories, that is, to the "context of justification" in mathematics. Van Bendegem (1987) regards problems and methods to be the most important components of mathematical knowledge. He claims that these represent the central features of continuity in the evolution of mathematical knowledge. Lakatos also attaches great significance to problems in the genesis of mathematical knowledge and proofs. Thus there are good grounds for regarding problems as an important and legitimate part of mathematical knowledge.

Metamathematical views. Fifth, there is the set of meta-mathematical views; this includes "*at least* the following issues: (i) standards of proof [and definition]; (ii) the scope of mathematics; (iii) the order of mathematical disciplines; (iv) the relative value of particular types of inquiry" (Kitcher 1984, 189).

The first component is a set of standards for proof and definition in mathematics. This is the set of norms and criteria that the mathematical community expect proofs and definitions to satisfy if they are to be acceptable to that community. Kitcher claims that it is not possible for these standards to be made fully explicit. He argues that proof standards may be exemplified in texts taken as a paradigm for proof (e.g., Euclid's *Elements*), rather than in explicit statements. For the formal accounts and rules of proof and definition available in logic texts do not cover the forms actually employed in practice. A significant portion of these standards remains unarticulated and is a significant part of the tacit knowledge of mathematicians, that is, of mathematical knowledge. The same remarks hold for standards of definition, for in every era mathematicians create novel definition and proof forms while solving problems—and once their additions are accepted by the mathematical community, they thus add to the body of implicit and explicit knowledge of this type. This point is anticipated in Kuhn's philosophy of science, namely, that past exemplars serve as paradigms for the scientific community:

> the term "paradigm" is used in two different senses. On the one hand, it stands for the entire constellation of beliefs, values, techniques, and so on shared by the members of a given community. On the other, it denotes one sort of element in that constellation, the concrete puzzle solutions which, employed as models or examples, can replace explicit rules as a basis for the solution of the remaining puzzles of normal science (Kuhn 1970, 175)
>
> [For this second sense] I shall here substitute 'exemplars'. By it I mean, initially the concrete problem-solutions that students encounter from the start of their scientific education, whether in laboratories, on examinations, or at the ends of chapters in science texts. To these shared examples should, however, be added at least some of the technical problem-solutions found in the periodical literature that scientists encounter during their post-educational research careers and that also show them how their job is to be done. (Kuhn 1970, 187)

Likewise in mathematics, exemplary problems, solutions, definitions, and proofs serve as a central part of the accepted norms and criteria that definitions, proofs, and mathematical knowledge are expected to satisfy.

The remaining metamathematical views concern the values, scope, and structure of mathematics. They include organizing principles for the whole of mathematics: its set of subdisciplines or fields of study and their epistemological prioritization, as well as the modes of inquiry most valued. Thus these principles incorporate at least in part the shared beliefs (and values) of the mathematical community, at least insofar as they pertain to the field of study itself.

Each one of these views can be construed as concerning knowledge: knowledge of the scope of mathematics, of the order of mathematical disciplines, and of the relative value accorded to different types of inquiry. Like the accepted standards of proof, much of this knowledge is likely to be tacit and unarticulated. For example, knowledge of the relative value of particular types of inquiry is almost certain to be known similarly in terms of examples and paradigm cases. The warrant for such knowledge is its tacit acceptance as evidenced by its use by the mathematical community.

Reviewing the proposals. Understood as a naturalistic model of mathematical knowledge, Kitcher's theory is able to account for both tacit and explicit knowledge components. His last three components, questions, reasonings and statements, constitute explicit mathematical knowledge which is representable in sentential form. However, language and metamathematical views are largely made up of tacit knowledge elements. These represent, respectively, underpinning and overarching knowledge of the discipline of mathematics, rather than the knowledge claims of mathematics itself. Thus their tacit epistemological nature can be linked to the tacit, behind-the-scenes role they play in mathematics (Hersh 1988).

One of the strengths of a model of mathematical knowledge based on Kitcher's account is that it includes both the linguistic basis of mathematical knowledge, and the criteria for mathematical proof and for the acceptance of new mathematical propositions as knowledge. From the social constructivist perspective, these play a central role in the practice of mathematics. Each of these components is implicated in the "language games" of mathematics.

Like Kuhn's theory, which inspired it, Kitcher's model has the strength of being able to account for the historical development of mathematics. He demonstrates its applicability with reference to the shared views of contemporary pure mathematicians, as well as to those of the time of Newton, and he shows how his designated components have changed radically over time.

Kitcher's model of mathematical practice can be criticized on a number of fronts. First of all, it is not adequately representative of mathematical practice. A part, namely mathematicians' knowledge and beliefs, has been taken to replace a complex, socially situated whole, comprising a set of persons and a set of social relations and a discourse. While Kitcher's notion of a mathematical practice represents a significant naturalistic advance over the traditional conception of mathematical knowledge, it remains a simplified and depersonalized representation of a form of life. However, this criticism is irrelevant to the use made of the model here.

Second, there is the issue of omissions. There are a number of potentially significant components of mathematical knowledge or practice not properly accommodated. For example, the set of methods and procedures of mathematics is omitted. These are a central part of mathematicians' intellectual armory, which scholars such as Van Bendegem (1987) have argued are among the most important elements in the evolution of mathematics. Although Kitcher partly subsumes mathematical methods under accepted reasonings, the incorporation does not really reflect the significance of such methods as the "diagonal method" in recursion theory and logic.

Beyond methods, a case can be put for an element representing knowledge of the literature of mathematics: its texts, papers, journals, and so on. Consequently, although Kitcher's model may be taken as representing some central elements of mathematical knowledge, it should not be taken as final.

Finally, the question arises, How legitimate is it to take as Kitcher's model as explicating the notion of "mathematical knowledge" (or as forming the basis of such an explication)? Its legitimacy hinges on two assumptions, those of naturalism and tacit knowledge. The task I am attempting is to account for mathematics naturalistically, following the extended criteria for the philosophy of mathematics given in chapter 2. This involves accounting for the methodology of mathematicians as well as the finished products of their activity, that is, accepted mathematical knowledge. But mathematicians' practices, including the reconstructed logic of their methodologies in action, cannot be adequately accounted for without considering the language, reasonings and problems and their metamathematical views. Thus naturalism requires an extended domain of discourse. Because of the tacit nature of much of this "knowledge," this does not legitimate the extension epistemologically. But I have already argued that tacit knowledge is epistemologically legitimate, since it has a form of justification.

The Nature of Objectivity and Objective Knowledge

In a consideration of mathematical knowledge, an important issue is that of the nature of objectivity and objective knowledge in mathematics. In particular, a key distinction that I employ below is that between subjective or individual knowledge and publicly accepted or "objective" mathematical knowledge.[3] This is clarified by a consideration of Popper's (1979) definition of three distinct worlds and the associated types of knowledge: "We can call the physical world 'world 1', the world of our conscious experiences "world 2," and the world of the logical *contents* of books, libraries, computer memories, and suchlike 'world 3'" (Popper 1979, 74). Thus subjective knowledge belongs to World 2, and objective knowledge belongs to World 3. According to Popper, World 3 includes products of the human mind, such as published theories, discussions of such theories, related problems, and proofs; it is human-made and changing. In this sense it differs from Plato's World of Forms, which although equally objective is timeless, eternal, and unchanging. In contrast, World 3 knowledge can, potentially at least, be knowledge of entities or events of Worlds 1 or 2. It is the form and modality of World 3 knowledge which makes it objective—not solely its subject matter.

A problem for social constructivism and other fallibilist philosophies of mathematics is that of accounting for objective knowledge in mathematics by nonabsolutist means. To accomplish this, I shall use the term *objective knowledge* in a way that deviates radically from Popper's own usage. I shall instead use it to refer to knowledge that is intersubjective and shared (in the mathematical community). I wish to count all that Popper does as objective knowledge, including mathematical theories, axioms, problems, conjectures, and proofs (both formal and informal). However, I also want to include the shared (but possibly implicit) conventions and rules of language usage and the types of tacit understandings described above. These are shared and intersubjective in that they are deployed and used in public, for persons to witness. But they remain implicit in that only their instances and uses are made public, and the rules themselves may never be uttered. Thus I am referring to publicly shared, intersubjective knowledge as objective, even if it is implicit knowledge, which has not been fully articulated. This further extension is very likely unacceptable to Popper.

In fact what I am doing is to adopt, at least in part, the social theory of objectivity proposed by Bloor (1984), Harding (1986), Fuller (1988), and others.

> Here is the theory: it is that objectivity is social. What I mean by saying that objectivity is social is that the impersonal and stable character that attaches to some of our beliefs, and the sense of reality that attaches to their reference, derives from these beliefs being social institutions.
>
> I am taking it that a belief that is objective is one that does not belong to any individual. It does not fluctuate like a subjective state or a personal preference. It is not mine or yours, but can be shared. It has an external thing-like aspect to it. (Bloor 1984, 229).

Bloor argues that Popper's World 3 can defensibly and fruitfully be identified with the social world. He also argues that not only is the threefold structure of Popper's theory preserved under this transformation, but so are the connections among the three worlds. Naturally, the social interpretation does not preserve the *meaning* that Popper wishes to attach to objectivity, which transcends the social in that it appears to guarantee objectivity in an idealistic sense. Despite this, the social view is able to account for most, if not all, features of objectivity: the autonomy of objective knowledge, its external thing-like character (which is presumably the original meaning of *objectiv*ity), and its independence from any knowing subject's subjective knowledge. For the social view sees objective knowledge, like culture, developing autonomously in keeping with tacitly accepted rules and not subject to the arbitrary dictates of individuals. Since objective knowledge and rules exist outside individuals (in the community or, rather, in the realm of the social), they seem to have an object-like and independent existence.

Thus it can be seen that the social view accounts for many of the necessary characteristics of objectivity. Beyond this, it is worth remarking that Bloor's social view of objectivity explains and accounts for objectivity. In contrast traditional views (including Popper's) elaborate on—or at best *define*—objectivity (intensively or extensively), but they never account for or *explain* objectivity. For the autonomous, independent existence of objective knowledge is traditionally shown to be necessary, without any explanation of what of objectivity is or how objective knowledge can emerge from subjective human knowledge. In contrast, the social view of objectivity is able to offer an account of the basis and nature of objectivity and objective knowledge.

The social consists of human beings together with their patterns of interaction, the shared but always mid-renegotiated mutual use of signs, and the joint forms of life. At any one moment there seems to be no more than a vast collection of individuals, but their interrelationships, expectations, traditions, and histories of negotiations together make up the mortar that joins these individuals into a whole that is more than the sum of its human parts. The social is more than just the sum of individual humans, for they are engaging in an array of shared practices, learning and using tools and artifacts, and taking part in a conversation—sometimes intense, sometimes attenuated— that is as old as humankind.[4]

Thus my claim is that the social is constituted by individuals together with their shared forms of life. And because of this shared feature, with all of its complexity and human-constituting properties, it cannot be reduced to individuals alone. Thus the objective knowledge which rests in the social is based on shared language use, rules, and understandings, embedded in shared forms of life. It is essentially supported by the subjective knowledge of individuals, but because of their interrelations, it is correlated in a complex and ever changing way.

A problem that this social view must face is that of accounting for the necessity (or at least seeming necessity) of logical and mathematical truth. The answer given by Bloor (1983, 1984), and adopted here, is that this necessity (understood in a fallibilist sense) rests on linguistic conventions, rules, and accepted social practices, as Wittgenstein proposes.

In any language, whatever epistemology is assumed, there are elements of convention, since the relationship between signifiers and signified is established by convention. There is a sense in which such relationships are arbitrary, since no necessity attaches to the pairings. However once such conventions have been established, then it becomes contingently necessary to maintain the conventions as a foundation for linguistic communication and agreement. Maintaining conventions in any language game is definitionally necessary for participating in that game. Abnegating agreements terminates a game and withdraws the possibility of shared understanding of the rules employed, the roles adopted, and the moves made. Thus to participate in mathematical language games involves granting the necessity of some assumptions. Within that game, certain conclusions are therefore necessary.

Bloor's interpretation of Popper's World 3 as the realm of the social has been criticized by Fuller for being ahistorical: "According to my diagnosis,

Bloor's reliance on Wittgenstein causes him to neglect the historical dimension of knowledge transmission. Remedying this deficiency suggests a role for Foucault's 'archaeological' approach" (Fuller 1988, 51). Fuller (1988) himself promotes a view of "social epistemology" that not only meets Bloor's criteria but reinserts the social location and constitution of "objective knowledge" implicit in language games and forms of life back into the flux of history. This is a vital further dimension, as Lakatos's work shows. However, although it is apparently neglected by Bloor and Wittgenstein, it seems easy enough to include. These authors focus on a synchronous, structural account of epistemology. But such an approach is complementary to a diachronous genetic-historical account.[5]

Other scholars including "evolutionary epistemologists" have also criticized Popper's attempt to install an "epistemology without a knowing subject" in his treatment of World 3. Callebaut and Pinxten cite half a dozen researchers and conclude that "this programme is an utter failure . . . Once this is realised a thoroughly *social* epistemology becomes inescapable" (Callebaut and Pinxten 1987a, 34). Their position thus involves an unequivocal rejection of the concept of disembodied, superhuman "objective knowledge" in favor of a social conception.

Feminist philosophers have also wished to appropriate the concept of objectivity and understand it in terms of the social. Harding begins from the assumption that all knowledge is produced by socially situated persons and that there is no such thing as the "objective knower," whose knowing transcends all contingent aspects of her/his historicality and cultural location. She proposes a concept of "strong objectivity" based on the recognition that all knowledge is thus socially constituted and that knowledge increases in objectivity when its social roots and presuppositions are laid bare and acknowledged.

> Strong objectivity requires that we investigate the relation between subject and object rather than deny the existence of, or seek unilateral control over, this relation. (Harding 1991: 152)
>   In other words, we can think of strong objectivity as extending the notion of scientific research to include systematic examination of such powerful background beliefs. It must do so in order to be competent at maximizing objectivity. (149)

In the spirit of these proposals, the social constructivist philosophy of mathematics takes "objective knowledge" in mathematics to be that which is accepted as legitimately warranted by the mathematical community. Thus it is the mutually agreed upon, shared knowledge of that community, knowledge that satisfies its knowledge acceptance procedures and criteria, not something superhuman or absolute. Thus the next issue which needs to be addressed is how objective mathematical knowledge is warranted by the mathematical community.

OBJECTIVE KNOWLEDGE IN MATHEMATICS

The social constructivist account of objective mathematical knowledge simultaneously describes both the genesis and justification of mathematical knowledge, as in Lakatos (1976). Social constructivism begins with the assumption that mathematical practices and institutions are a given; they are historically constituted and have a life of their own. In other words, the starting point is the existence of mathematical "forms of life," with their own participants, representations of knowledge, and so forth (following Wittgenstein). Given this assumed background, a proposed new item of mathematical knowledge begins its candidacy upon publication, that is, when it is represented symbolically in the public domain.[6] Such knowledge claims are the immediate products of individuals or groups of individuals and are represented physically in some form. They are claims that may be regarded as utterances by one of the voices in a formally regulated conversation: a conversation that may be spoken face-to-face, but which is more likely to be carried out in written form between spatially and temporally distanced participants.

Social constructivism adopts the position that proofs are necessary to persuade the mathematical community to accept mathematical knowledge claims, so publication is necessary but not sufficient for such claims to become warranted. Formal dialectical conversational exchanges (based on Lakatos's logic of mathematical discovery) located in the social institutional centers of mathematics are the basis of the process whereby published knowledge claims become warranted knowledge of mathematics. In these exchanges, one of the "voices" utters the knowledge claim, that is, takes the role of proponent. That knowledge claim is part of a justificatory narrative which is couched in a way intended to persuade the other participants in the conversation. Other "voices" represent the role of opponent or critic. These depend on the criticism of mathematical claims and proofs, and the criticisms are at least partly rational based on shared criteria within a significant section of an academic mathematical community. These criteria are made up of both propositional and tacit knowledge (founded on knowledge of language, logic, and mathematics), including a case-history knowledge of what has been accepted in the current branch of mathematics and the currently accepted standards of mathematical rhetoric and proof.

Thus within the contexts of professional research mathematics, individuals use their subjective (personal) mathematical knowledge to (*a*) construct

mathematical knowledge claims (possibly jointly with others) and (*b*) participate in the social process of criticism and warranting of others' mathematical
knowledge claims. In each case, the individual mathematician's symbolic productions are (or are part of) one of the voices in the warranting conversation.
Maximal objectivity is attained, according to Faust (1984) and Fuller
(1993), by scientists and mathematicians alternating between these dual roles.
For they act as their own conjecturer, proposer, and advocate, in support of
their own immediate cognitive interests, and act as someone else's critic and
refuter, supporting the criteria and standards of their subspecialism, when
someone else's cognitive interests are at stake. They will also have internalized the roles of proponent and critic, both of which are usually deployed privately in the elaboration of mathematical claims before publication.

At the heart of production of mathematical knowledge is its approval by
representatives of the academic mathematical community. This consists of its
warranting in formal dialectical conversational exchanges. During these
processes the narrative knowledge claims are subjected to scrutiny and usually also transformed, to some degree or other. They are usually required to be
modified, following some process comparable to Lakatos's logic of mathematical discovery. They may of course be altogether rejected.

This, in schematic outline, is the social constructivist account of the
genesis and warranting of objective mathematical knowledge.

The Warranting of Objective Mathematical Knowledge

The claim of social constructivism is that all explicit objective mathematical knowledge, that which was traditionally termed mathematical *knowledge*, depends on linguistic utterance and symbolic representation, which
originates with and is rooted in human conversation. In particular, at the center of the social constructivist philosophy of mathematics is located a dialogical social process for warranting objective mathematical knowledge based on
Lakatos's logic of mathematical discovery (LMD). This utilizes a dialectical
form or logic, alternating between a thesis and its criticism—that is, between
contradictory voices—to arrive at a higher synthesis. However as the discussion in chapter 4 showed, Lakatos's LMD is insufficiently general to account
for the full range of knowledge developments in mathematics—such as revolutionary theory change—and so a generalized logic of mathematical discovery is proposed here.

The generalized logic of mathematical discovery. Some of the elements
of a more general LMD are clear. It needs to be cyclic, with each iteration producing what appears locally to be progress. It must be located in a scientific
or epistemological context, a pool of problems, concepts, methods, and informal theories, including all of the knowledge elements of Kitcher's model of

mathematical practice, within which the cycle acts. The production of mathematical knowledge requires a constructive act, the production of a text embodying the proposal of a conjecture, proof, problem-solution, or theory. They may be relatively novel, or they may be minor adaptations of existing intellectual objects. The submission of the would-be knowledge proposal into the social acceptance mechanism requires, and should elicit a formal conversational response from, the representatives of the mathematical community. This could be critical, made up of a criticism of the proposal such as a counterexample, a refutation, a counterargument. It could instead be a suggested extension of the proposal, or it could combine both response types. As a consequence of the response there is modification. Typically the proposer modifies the proposal in the light of the critique and resubmits it. Normally this would be a new proposal, such as a new or modified conjecture, proof, problem solution, theory, and so on. As such it would have a marginal effect on the scientific or epistemological context. However, the outcome might be more dramatic. It might involve a more far-reaching change to the scientific or epistemological context, with major changes to the pool of problems, the concepts, methods, informal theories, language, or metamathematical views of mathematics (analogous to a Kuhnian revolution). This modified or generalized logic of mathematical discovery (GLMD) is illustrated in table 5.1.

The GLMD in table 5.1 follows a cyclic pattern, as in Lakatos's LMD, and adopts the terms of the Hegelian dialectic that inspired Lakatos. The essential feature of GLMD, which it takes from LMD, is the pattern of dialectical interaction in the mathematical community; this enables the full range of discursive products of mathematics (including conjectures, proofs, problems, solutions, concepts, methods, and informal theories) to be developed. This development can include both the criticism and the elaboration of such products in the creation and warranting of objective mathematical knowledge. The GLMD is formulated in objectified and passive terms to highlight the locus of the evolving knowledge. Needless to say the human context provided by the mathematical community is essential and presupposed throughout. People make the proposals.

The whole process takes place within a background scientific and epistemological context, which includes problems, concepts, theorems, proofs, methods, informal theories, a mathematical sublanguage, proof criteria and paradigms, and metamathematical views. This is a cultural context, that of the group of mathematicians working in the appropriate mathematical specialism. In that context an individual or group proposes a conjecture, proof, problem-solution, or theory. Whether new or revised, it will most likely represent the outcome of a previous cycle of GLMD. This in turn generates a dialectical response to the proposal from a subsection of the mathematical community. On the one hand, this can be an acceptance response, in which case the pro-

TABLE 5.1
DIALECTICAL FORM OF THE GENERALIZED LOGIC OF MATHEMATICAL DISCOVERY

Scientific Context for Stage n
Background scientific and epistemological context, including problems, concepts, methods, informal theories, proof criteria and paradigms, language, and metamathematical views.

Thesis Stage n *(i)*
Proposal of new or revised conjecture, proof, problem-solution, or theory.

Antithesis Stage n *(ii) Dialectical and evaluative response to the proposal:*

Critical Response	*Acceptance Response*
Counterexample, counterargument, refutation, criticism of proposal	Acceptance of proposal. Suggested extension of proposal.

Synthesis Stage n *(iii) Reevaluation and modification of the proposal:*

Local Restructuring	*Global Restructuring*
Modified proposals: new conjecture, proof, problem-solution, problems or theory.	Restructured context: changed problem set, concepts, methods, informal theories proof paradigms and criteria, language or metamathematical views.

Outcome Stage n *+ 1*
Newly accepted or rejected proposal, or revised scientific and epistemological context.

posal is added to the body of accepted objective mathematical knowledge—although this response might also result in a suggested extension or elaboration of the proposal. On the other hand, the dialectical response to the proposal may be critical. It might result in members of the mathematical community offering counterexamples, counterarguments, a refutation, or other criticism of the proposal.

These two responses constitute contrasting evaluations of the proposal, and one outcome of a critical response is the rejection and abandonment of the proposal. This option is a perpetual possibility, and doubtless proposed contributions to mathematical knowledge are rejected frequently. Such proposals will sometimes be reformulated and submitted as new proposals, sometimes they will be resubmitted to other sets of representatives of the mathematical community, and sometimes the attempt to publish them will be abandoned altogether.[7]

If the proposal is retained for the sake of modification, then it will be reworked. The outcome will most likely be a modified proposal in the form of a new conjecture, proof, problem-solution, problem, or theory. This amounts to a local reformulation or restructuring of the original proposal.[8] Such an outcome may have a small effect on the background scientific and epistemological context by adding new terms or symbolic forms to the mathematical sublanguage. It may also help to clarify or add a little to the proof criteria and metamathematical views of the context.

However, a more radical outcome is also possible in the form of a global restructuring of the background context. This can involve a changed set of problems, concepts, methods, or informal theories, which are the explicit components of mathematical knowledge. It can also involve significant changes to the mathematical sublanguage, proof criteria and paradigms, and metamathematical views accepted by the mathematical community. These represent the tacit elements of accepted mathematical knowledge. Changes in them are very significant, for they can result in a shift in terms of what constitute acceptable linguistic formulations, proof paradigms and criteria for acceptable proofs, and the metamathematical views of the mathematical community. In particular, the outcome can include changes in (1) the accepted standards for proof and definition, (2) views of which types of inquiry are valuable, and (3) accepted views concerning the scope and structure of mathematics. Such changes can result in a profound reorientation of mathematics. The outcome of this radical restructuring is a new or revised scientific and epistemological context for mathematics.

This completes one cycle of GLMD. It may be expected that in any development there will be many iterations of the cycle, as proposals and counterproposals are suggested, tried out, and modified or rejected.

The generalized pattern allows it to describe not only the genesis of new definitions, theorems, and proofs, but also new theories. Analogous to Kuhn's theory of scientific revolutions, GLMD can account for "revolutionary" developments in mathematics, such as new theory developments and crises in the foundations. It can also account for routine developments (comparable to "normal science"), such as the creation and elaboration of conjectures, proofs, and refutations within an existing informal mathematical theory, as Lakatos's LMD does. In either case, there will be both continuities and discontinuities in the pool of problems, concepts, methods, or informal theories that are the explicit components of mathematical knowledge. It can also involve major changes to the mathematical sublanguage, proof criteria and paradigms, and metamathematical views accepted by the mathematical community

As with Kuhn's work, examples from history can be cited to illustrate such changes to the background scientific and epistemological context of mathematics. This has been done by a number of authors, including Lakatos (1976), Kitcher (1984), Gillies (1992), and Kvasz (1995). In terms of this structure, it is worth remarking that the claimed origin of such a change is the proposal of a conjecture, proof, problem-solution, or theory, that is, an item of explicit mathematical knowledge. The outcome may be a radical restructuring of a significant part of the background scientific and epistemological context, much of which constitutes tacit knowledge of the mathematical community. However, according to the theory, this is not the overt and initial proposal, which will concern explicit items of mathematical knowledge, especially proposed mathematical proofs.

Indeed, what GLMD does not show—because of its generalized form, which Lakatos's LMD does emphasize—is the central role of proof in mathematics. Proof serves as more than just a warrant for propositional knowledge in mathematics. It also provides such things as the central test of the fruitfulness of new concepts and definitions, the means to elicit the consequences of informal and axiomatic theories, the means to test proposed solutions to problems, and the way to establish the consequences of hypotheses and conjectures. Consequently, the public construction, scrutiny, and testing of proofs is undoubtedly the central activity around which GLMD revolves. Of course, epistemologically, providing the warrant for propositional knowledge is the most important function of proof. In this role, it can be seen that conversation and the dialectics of GLMD provide the platform for proof in its warranting role by means of social negotiation and acceptance. However, as is indicated above, a proposed proof can occasionally result in more far-reaching changes than just the local restructuring of knowledge.

In the activity initiated under GLMD by the proposal of a proof, shared standards and criteria are brought into play, both in the acceptance and in the criticism and rejection of proofs. The shared criteria and proof-standards are usually not fully and explicitly articulated, and they may involve the non-mechanical applications and extensions of accepted methods to the particular case under consideration. Such applications can result from the use of a particular proof or family of proofs as a paradigm, in which case the features and characteristics embodied in the model provide criteria and standards implicitly, by analogy. However the rejection of a proof for failing to meet the required criteria and standards will often be accompanied by an explicit indication of which steps or aspects of the proof are inadequate or insufficiently detailed, according to the prevailing standards (or those of the critic and judgement maker).

In addition to the deployment of the sometimes tacit standards of proof, the critical scrutiny of mathematical proposals also draws upon such meta-mathematical views of the mathematics community such as the value of particular types of inquiry. In particular, in such cases where GLMD results in a global restructuring of the context, other aspects of the metamathematical views of the mathematics community are very likely be called into play. These include the value attached to particular types of inquiry as well as more general views such as the scope of mathematics and the order of the mathematical disciplines. The role of the tacit knowledge of mathematics is explored in greater detail below.

In summary, the claim of social constructivism is that the warranting of fully explicit mathematical knowledge including propositions, sentences, and theorems as well as proofs themselves stems from the humanly situated GLMD. The outcome is objective mathematical knowledge in that it is publicly available for scrutiny and is socially accepted. Valid mathematical knowledge in the main is knowledge which is accepted on the basis of there being a public justification of the knowledge (a published proof) which has survived this dialectical process or been reformulated in the light of this public scrutiny and criticism. Indeed there is an analogy with the "replicability" criterion for experimental results and observations in physical science, which demands that results, for acceptance, should not be peculiar to a unique scientist but replicable. Likewise a mathematical proof has to be publicly surveyable by others, and this survey must result each time in acceptance, at least when scrutinized by a significant mathematician (one in a position as a mathematical knowledge gatekeeper). When it ceases to do so, which at some point might well happen, then it will no longer effortlessly pass muster when GLMD is applied to it. Instead it is rejected or revised. This is the essence of the process that underlies the fallibility of mathematical knowledge. As in empirical science, such knowledge never ceases to be open to scrutiny and revision (although it may fall into neglect without rejection).

In addition to propositions and proofs, mathematical questions, conjectures, concepts, definitions, methods, and theories can emerge from the social processes of GLMD with their importance and acceptance by the mathematical community warranted. Although there are significant issues of social valuation involved as well, the extended conception of mathematical knowledge developed includes these issues under the umbrella of the warranting of objective mathematical knowledge, and hence among the central concerns of epistemology in mathematics.

The varieties of mathematical creation. In the functioning of GLMD three modes of mathematical creation might be distinguished, although the distinctions are far from absolute or clear-cut. These modes consist of the local and global restructuring of mathematical knowledge and its reproduction.

Like science, mathematics is hypothetico-deductive, with mathematicians generally working and making their contributions within an established mathematical theory. Much of this work consists of the development of new consequences of existing aspects of the theory or the application of existing methods from within the theory to a range of problems. When fruitful, the results of such work might be termed "incremental additions" to the body of mathematical knowledge. Such contributions can be regarded as local restructurings of mathematical knowledge because, within a given context or theory, they result in new or modified proposals, such as new conjectures, proofs, problem-solutions, or theories. In such contributions, existing elements of mathematical knowledge are recombined in a novel way. These are likely to be the most common types of novel contribution to mathematics.

Mathematicians also utilize the concepts and methods from one mathematical theory in another, or establish links between two previously separate theories. Such work causes new structural links to be formed between separate parts of mathematics. This constitutes a larger-scale restructuring of mathematics, one that can be considerable if under the influence of the new links the two theories are reworked, reformulated, and drawn closer together (Corfield 1995). In addition, work in some theories, often directed at the solution of some particular mathematical problem, may generate a new mathematical theory. This may simply be an additional new theory, or it may subsume previous theories into a larger, more general theory. The move in mathematics toward increasing abstraction and generality (Wilder 1981), such as in this case, is a major factor in the restructuring of mathematical knowledge. For increasingly general theories are more widely applicable, and several more specialized, preexisting theories may fall within its more general structural patterns. An example is provided by Cantor's theory of sets, which initially seemed very specialized and recondite. Since its introduction, because of its wide generality and power, it has come to encompass many other mathematical theories and provide them with reformulated and unified foundations.

This second type of more widespread change to the body of mathematical knowledge is termed "global restructuring," since it involves more deeply seated changes (such as a restructured background scientific or epistemological context), including a changed pool of problems, concepts, methods, and informal theories (Dunmore 1992). Such changes can of course vary in their profundity and revolutionary nature. Thus, for example, rich new methods and theories emerge periodically in mathematics. Although they may result in a restructured background context, such innovations may not result in a radical restructuring of the epistemological background and context of mathematics. Such more radical changes will happen more rarely. When they do, they are likely to result in new theories emerging, and the epistemological shifts are often masked by the novelty of these new theories and thus seem to be the addition of new mathematical content, although deeper changes have taken place. Thus, global restructurings can vary in their scope and impact (Gillies 1992).

In addition to restructuring additions a third mode is the reproductive, as opposed to the productive, contribution to accepted mathematical knowledge. This is concerned with the representation and regeneration of existing mathematics, rather than the genesis of new mathematical knowledge in the form of new theorems or proofs. Such contributions are typically made in the form of textbooks or advanced expositions. Although they primarily serve an ancillary or supporting role, usually such new publications involve some novel notational or presentational devices. So they are not wholly reproductive. However the novelty in such productions is usually regarded by modern mathematicians as resulting from routine transformations of mathematical knowledge, not from creative problem solving or the derivation of significantly new items of mathematical knowledge.[9] Thus the classification of some mathematical productions as reproductive is far from absolute and depends largely on the metamathematical views of mathematicians.

Changes in the overall epistemological context. The deployment of GLMD takes place within an overall epistemological context, in which mathematicians' metamathematical views and values play an important part, especially in the acceptance of new knowledge. However, these areas of knowledge change over time, and thus what is acceptable to the mathematical community as a mathematical proof and as warranted mathematical knowledge vary with time. In particular, standards of rigor, expectation, and rhetorical expression change, as is amply illustrated by the history of mathematics (Wilder 1981; Dunmore 1992).

Thus, for example, infinitesimal-based proofs in analysis following the work of Newton and Leibniz were universally accepted, despite Berkeley's ([1734] 1901) strong criticism, until they were banished by new standards of mathematical rigor in analytic proofs introduced by Cauchy, Weierstrass, and Heine in the nineteenth century. This change reflects a shift in the nature and standards of proof, from those based on geometric intuition to those of arithmetical argument (Boyer 1968). Likewise, proof standards in geometry shifted from demonstrations relying on spatial intuition to a reliance on an axiomatic logical basis (Hilbert 1902; Richards 1989), followed by the move to an axiomatic basis in arithmetic proofs (Peano 1889), and the axiomatic rigorization of deductive logic itself (Frege [1879] 1967).

Another chapter in the history of analysis is the reintroduction of infinitesimal-based arguments in the proofs of nonstandard analysis (Robinson 1966). This reflects a further change in the nature and standards of proof accepted in analysis, from those based on arithmetic to those of axiomatic first-order logic and the theory of nonstandard models (Lakatos 1978a; Robinson 1967).

Many other such examples can be cited. These include the shift of standards of proof in algebra in the nineteenth century from intuitive generalizations of arithmetic to a deductive axiomatic basis (Richards 1987). The conceptual difficulties in making this transition should not be underestimated. The rigid attachment to the field-structure of number, crystallized in such laws as Peacock's "principle of the permanence of equivalent forms" constituted what Bachelard terms an "epistemological obstacle" to reconceptualizing the nature and epistemological basis of algebra. It took the great mathematician Hamilton ten years to overcome this obstacle in inventing his noncommutative ring of Quaternions. In doing so, he enabled a reconceptualization which heralded a revolution in the nature of algebra and the basis of proof in the subject.

These examples illustrate changes that took place in the background epistemological context during global restructurings of mathematical knowledge. The changes especially include the criteria and standards of rigor and proof upon which the mathematical community bases its judgement. The objectivity of these standards, which are employed publicly across the appropriate mathematical subcommunity, are by no means compromised by the acknowledgment that they change over the course of history or vary when applied by different individuals or in different contexts.[10]

What is compromised by such changes is the absolutist notion that absolute and unvarying criteria and standards underpin mathematical rigor. It is clear that standards of rigor and mathematical knowledge acceptance vary over history. Even today different standards of proof differ in different mathematical subcommunities. Constructivists claim epistemological priority for their standards, but their constructive proofs are often disregarded by the classical mathematics establishment (Rosenblatt 1984). Classical mathematicians themselves disagree on whether their standards of rigor extend so far as to include unsurveyable computer assisted proofs (Tymoczko 1986b). In addition, nonstandard logics proliferate endlessly (Routley *et al.* 1982; Haack 1974; Hughes and Cresswell 1968). Thus many competing sets of standards coexist in different mathematical subspecialisms.

The overall epistemological context of mathematics is at least partly implicit, and it changes and grows alongside the rest of mathematical practice. When changes have taken place new justifications for them may be offered. However, often it is mathematical practice itself, including the acceptance of exciting new bits of mathematical knowledge, that is responsible for current acceptability criteria for mathematical proof. One need only think of the proofs of the four-color theorem, the classification of simple groups, and the proof of the nonexistence of the projective plane of order 10, to find modern examples of theorems that have forced a revaluation of the rules of acceptability of proofs. Each of these proofs is unsurveyable by a single human; either because it is, at least in part, computer generated, or because it results from a gargantuan collaborative effort. Such proofs would have been unacceptable, perhaps inconceivable, only fifty or one hundred years ago.

Conceptual continuity in mathematics. Mathematical knowledge is made up of a variety of meaningful components, including mathematical symbols, notations, and diagrams; terms, concepts, definitions, axioms, statements, analogies, problems, explanations, applications of mathematical methods, and proofs; and references beyond the given text to named theorems, to theories, and to other texts. These components vary in scope, from the small scale (e.g., a symbol or term) to the large scale (a major proof or method application). Knowledge in each mathematical subspecialism is based on a literature combining selections of all of these elements. A new item of mathematical knowledge will combine a selection of such components from this literature in a novel way. Novelty is almost certain to occur at the large-scale level, in that a new text has been constructed, but it will usually occur at other levels too. However the overwhelming bulk of the material in any new piece of mathematics is not new, and it represents the reutilization of existing mathematical knowledge components. Thus many of the parts of a mathematical text are identical with (in the case of small-scale components) or closely resemble (on the medium- and large-scale level), preexisting components. Thus there is a high degree of conceptual continuity in mathematics.

A number of authors have stressed different elements in this continuity. Lakatos (1976) stresses continuity and change in concepts, definitions, theorem statements, and proofs. Van Bendegem (1987) explicitly stresses the continuity of problems and methods, and the complexes of their interrelationships, and he offers a theory of conceptual continuity in mathematics. Hallett (1979) and Koetsier (1991) emphasize the continuity of problems, as does Wilder (1974, 1981), who also emphasizes concepts. In a case study Fisher (1966) emphasizes the development, continuity, and ultimately the temporary extinction of a mathematical theory. This is a larger unit of continuity, and its progress is probably almost coextensive with the mathematical subcommunity involved in the study of the particular theoretical subspecialism.

It is fair to claim that conceptual continuity in mathematics is often localized within theories. These represent not only a selection of mathematical knowledge around a particular subject matter, but also a social grouping of mathematicians working on a theory. In addition to Fisher, several of those mentioned above stress conceptual continuity within theories.

Overall, considerations of conceptual continuity indicate another vital issue concerning the social acceptance of mathematical knowledge, one which has been neglected until now. New knowledge which emerges from the social mechanism of GLMD as warranted is not all on a par. A crucial issue concerns the extent to which the knowledge is disseminated and, above all, used. The extent to which an item of mathematical knowledge is used depends on the extent to which its components are used in subsequent texts or to which it is cited in texts. There are substantial qualitative differences in the extent to which different items of accepted mathematical knowledge are used in mathematics, differences that indicate the extent of the influence and impact on the development of mathematical knowledge overall. Acceptance is thus only a necessary or threshold condition for a new item to contribute to the discipline. Accepted items of mathematical knowledge which suffer neglect by the mathematical community represent inactive contributions, whereas central contributions which are used in many mathematical knowledge subspecialisms are significant as the core of active and hence potentially of future mathematical knowledge developments.

This issue of mathematical knowledge use adds a new dynamic which potentially weakens the import of GLMD, for what is accepted as new mathematical knowledge does not of itself necessarily have a privileged existence: it is merely a resource that mathematicians (and appliers, recontextualizers, and teachers of mathematics) can draw upon.

Perhaps the most thoroughgoing theory of mathematical knowledge use (and continuity) is that of Van Bendegem (1987). He suggests that sets of problems and their variations remain at the center of active mathematical work if they are associated with sets of mathematical methods which are successfully applied to the problems. Continuity is also possible if the methods are transferred to variant sets of problems. He argues that a set of problems or methods is determined by its "makeup"—the constituent mathematical "things" (objects), operations, and properties—and that changes in such sets are fundamentally due to shufflings or redistribution of this makeup.

The certainty of mathematical knowledge. Having described the social constructivist theory of the genesis and warranting of mathematical knowledge by means of the GLMD, it is possible to give a partial account of the certainty of mathematical knowledge. *Certainty* is a term sometimes used to describe the highest degree of belief—absolute conviction[11] rather than absolute, unshakable knowledge—so it is apposite for a fallibilist account. In brief, the certainty of mathematical knowledge to a large extent results from the warranting process of the GLMD. For knowledge claims, based on the traditions of mathematics, are offered to the warranting mathematical community and are scrutinized, rejected if regarded as inadequate or criticized and made stronger if any weaknesses are noted, or accepted. The process is one of deliberate selection, whereby only the "fit" (according to the judgement of representatives of the mathematical community) are permitted to survive and to enter into the realm of accepted mathematical knowledge. Since mathematical knowledge claims are usually texts comprising propositions and proofs, only those proofs which convince their judges that they establish their conclusions impeccably, that is, that establish their mathematical knowledge claims with certainty, are accepted. Since mathematical propositions and proofs and their components, in various forms, have often been worked on by mathematicians in many stages over a prolonged period of time, and improved in the process, it is not surprising that in their latest form they are very strong. All of the objections and criticisms of the knowledge scrutineers have been met, and the outcome is mathematical knowledge that is accepted with certainty.

This is only part of the account, because there is the issue of the content of mathematical knowledge and what the nature of its claims consist of. This is treated in the next chapter.

The Nature of Mathematical Knowledge: Conclusion

This chapter has offered two important perspectives on mathematical knowledge. It has offered the GLMD as a social mechanism by means of which mathematical knowledge is generated and justified. This generalization of Lakatos represents the kernel of the social constructivist philosophy of mathematics proposed here.

The second perspective is one which perhaps opens the proposals up to criticism. It concerns the nature of knowledge. Throughout the chapter I have proposed ways of broadening the underpinning conception of the nature of mathematical knowledge. I have included know-how as well as propositional knowledge, tacit as well as explicit knowledge; the five components of Kitcher's theory of mathematical practice as a model of mathematical knowledge (plus some additional elements), and finally, in the last section, all of the elements and meaningful combinations of mathematical knowledge as parts of it themselves.

On the one hand, these enlargements of the domain are justified because a practicing mathematician knows and needs to know items of all of the categories mentioned. On the other hand, these items can be justified as being mathematical *knowledge*, since any of them is either explicitly warranted, or is warranted by its use in practice. To *know* one of these items is to be able to offer a valid justification for it, if it is explicit, or is to be able to demonstrate that knowledge through appropriate behaviors.

Nevertheless, it must be acknowledged that my account of mathematical knowledge goes beyond the norms of epistemology. However, accounting for mathematics naturalistically, in a satisfactory way, has required this conceptual extension. The traditional conception of mathematical knowledge is too narrow to achieve this, and hence to satisfy the criteria proposed in chapter 2.

NOTES

1. Austin's (1962) "performative" theory of language suggests that sentences or propositions do not have a fixed meaning outside of their context of utterance anyway

and that the intention of their utterance or use, and other contextual factors, constitute an essential component of their meaning. Initially he tried to distinguish "constative" utterances of statements or facts (which might be taken to include mathematical propositions) from "illocutionary" utterances, but he came to doubt his distinction (Horn 1995, 159).

2. There is a tradition in modern thought that argues that mind and the knower are embodied and that knowledge is actively derived. Marx is at root a materialist and argues that material conditions are the final causes of the intellectual. The pragmatists Peirce, James, and Dewey saw knowing as irrevocably related to lived experience. Husserl, and later Heidegger and Merleau-Ponty, saw "being in the world" as an essential prerequisite of knowing. It is reported that both Wittgenstein (Kenny 1973) and Ryle (Urmson and Rée 1989) studied Husserl's work before developing their mature philosophies. Finally it is worth mentioning that there is a tradition in philosophical psychology that knowing is embodied, a position articulated by, for example, Piaget; Johnson; and Varela, Thompson, and Rosch (1991).

3. Here and elsewhere I use the term *objectivity* without subscribing to, or committing myself to, absolutism in the epistemological realm or idealism in ontology.

4. A factor I downplay here is that persons have rule-like roles and expectations in the context of social institutions: semi-permanent forms of life usually associated with certain determinate places, material resources, and human relations.

5. Furthermore, Wittgenstein's notion of a form of life carries within it an implicit recognition of history, for it is an organized pattern of social living laid down and established over time.

6. By "publication" I mean here the material representation of the knowledge claim prior to the processes of refereeing, warranting, etc. that precede "official publication" in a journal.

7. Sometimes the submitter will attempt to evade the outcomes of the GLMD by publishing the claim privately. For example, recently *The Mathematical Intelligencer* carried a paid announcement of a purported proof of the inconsistency of ZF set theory, including a rejecting reviewer's remarks (Knowles 1995).

8. See below for a discussion of the importance of the transformation of mathematical texts.

9. Below I highlight the import of transformations of mathematical texts and their under-recognized role in defining identity and difference in mathematics.

10. Even the styles of mathematical thought and writing vary significantly from one mathematical subspecialism from another, as Knuth's (1985) comparison of texts in nine mathematical subspecialisms illustrates.

11. See, e.g., the *Concise Oxford Dictionary*, 7th ed., s.v. "certainty."

CHAPTER 6

CONVERSATION AND RHETORIC

CONVERSATION AND RHETORIC IN MATHEMATICS

The Nature of Conversation

Currently, an increasing number of fields of thought, especially in the social sciences, are adopting conversation as a basic metaphor. Thus, for example, Young (1987) proposes a phenomenological theory which, following Goffman, Berger, Luckmann, and others, takes the realm of conversation to be basic. Another example is that of social constructionism:

> Central to the social constructionist ontology . . . is the view (shared with Gergen and Harré) that the primary human reality is conversation. (Shotter 1991a, 13)

Conversation is taken as central to philosophy by modern authors in diverse traditions including Mead, Oakshott, Peters, Rorty, and Gadamer. Conversation presupposes a group of persons talking together in a common language.

> The original form of conversation can also be seen in derivative forms in which the correspondence between question and answer is obscured. Letters, for example, are an interesting transitional phenomenon: a kind of written conversation, that, as it were, stretches out the movement of talking at cross purposes before seeing each other's point. (Gadamer 1979, 332)

Thus "immediate" conversations in which the conversants are face-to-face, communicating by direct means such as speaking or signing, evidently engaged in a language game and a shared form of life, can be distinguished from nonimmediate conversations in which the conversants communicate out of "real time" by some intermediary symbolic technology or medium such as written texts.

There is an important difference between speech and writing and the role of conversation in each. Writing is much more than symbolized speech and has a life and history of its own (Harris 1986; Rotman 1994). Although "live" conversation might be identified as speech, the exchange of written texts and other representations constitutes a vital extension of conversation beyond this original form. This important difference notwithstanding, technological advances which allow the exchange of digitized conversations by telephone over long distances and written texts in "real time" by e-mail—not to mention the editing and manipulation of all forms of representation including audio and video speech—mean that the distinction between speech and writing is blurring.

What is intended by the concept of a conversation is as follows. A conversation is a sequence of linguistic utterances or texts in a common language (or languages) made by a number of speakers or authors, who take it in turn to "speak" (contribute) and who respond with further relevant contributions to the conversation (Grice 1975; Sperber and Wilson 1986).[1]

The Epistemological Role of Conversation

Conversation in the form of written dialogue has been used in philosophy and epistemology since the time of the ancient Greeks. One of Socrates's distinctive contributions is "the use of dialogue as a means to uncover truth" (Ferguson 1970, 15). Dialogue is used by many other important philosophers and scientists, including Plato, Boethius, Alcuin, Bruno, Galileo, Fontenelle, Berkeley, Leibniz, Hume, Nietzsche, Renyi, Heyting, and Lakatos.[2] Their purpose is to show and contrast multiple perspectives on the problems under discussion; to counter proposals with criticism; and to lead, via disputation, to clear and persuasive conceptions, if not consensus.[3] Of course conversation is a more obvious metaphor for philosophy than for mathematics or science, for in philosophy old positions (such as skepticism, dogmatism, realism, and idealism) and the disputes between them never die, whereas in mathematics or science a single paradigm is perceived to prevail.

Conversation is taken as a basis for epistemology by a number of philosophers.[4] Collingwood, for example, proposes the epistemological project of substituting a conversational or dialectical "logic of question and answer" for a logic of propositions. He argues that what is of epistemological significance is not the individual proposition, but a complex consisting of questions and answers.

The structure of this complex had, of course, never been studied by propositional logic; but with help from Bacon, Descartes and others I could hazard a few statements about it. Each question and each answer in a given complex had to be relevant or appropriate, had to "belong" to the whole and to the place it occupied in the whole. Each question had to "arise"; there must be that about it whose absence we condemn when we refuse to answer a question on the ground that it "doesn't arise." Each answer must be "the right" answer to the question it professes to answer.

By "right" I do not mean "true." The "right" answer to a question is the answer which enables us to get ahead with the process of questioning and answering. Cases are quite common in which the "right" answer to a question is "false." (Collingwood 1944, 29–30)

Collingwood argues that knowledge growth requires participation in the dialogical process of question and answer, whether the question is posed by oneself or by another. He also evidently distinguishes knowledge growth from the search for absolute truth.

There are other philosophers who adopt a similar view. For example Gadamer (1979, 333) argues that the hermeneutic quest for knowledge "contains within itself the original meaning of conversation and the structure of question and answer." Again, Bakhtin (1986, 110) argues that "Truth is not to be found inside the head of an individual person, it is born *between people* collectively searching for truth, in the process of their dialogic interaction."

Rorty adopts conversation explicitly as the cornerstone of epistemology: it is the human reality underpinning and supporting knowing, including mathematical knowledge. He states that conversation is "the ultimate context in which knowledge is to be understood" (1979, 389). He proposes that we should "see knowledge as a matter of conversation and of social practice, rather than as an attempt to mirror nature" (171). "Conversational justification, so to speak, is naturally holistic, whereas the notion of justification embedded in the epistemological tradition is reductive and atomistic" (170). "The point of edifying philosophy [as opposed to systematic foundationalist philosophy] is to keep the conversation going, rather than to find objective truth" (377).

Habermas (1987, 316) also gives a central role to conversation: "In the theory of communicative action, [conversation is] the feedback process by which the lifeworld and everyday communicative practice are intertwined."

Gergen surveys several fields of thought and remarks on

the emergence of a thoroughgoing social epistemology, or an epistemological standpoint from which knowledge claims are viewed as quintessential constituents of social interchange . . . *Knowledge* claims may properly viewed as forms of discourse . . . The latter claims may be viewed as moves in the process of discourse. (Gergen 1988, 36–37, original emphasis).

On the most abstract level, we might say that what we count as knowledge are temporary locations in dialogic space—samples of discourse that are accorded status as "tellings" on given occasions. More concretely, this is to say that knowledge is in continuous production as dialogue ensues. (Gergen 1993, 13–14)

The key role attributed to conversation by these thinkers raises the issue of its epistemological status.

The Epistemological Role of Conversation

In traditional epistemology and logic, it is conventional to treat the sentence as the fundamental unit of knowledge. There are a number of different forms that have been used, including the judgement, assertion, thought, belief, and proposition as well as the sentence. However each of these alternate forms corresponds in one way or another to the sentence.

Deductive proof is another privileged form in epistemology because of role of proofs as the main providers of justificatory warrants for mathematical and other forms of *a priori* knowledge. A proof is a string of sentences with a structure, the relation of inference or transformation, relating previously established or assumed sentences to new ones within the sequence. Mathematical and logical proofs, together with linguistic sentences, are epistemologically privileged units. The subdivision of either involves some loss of this unitary character.[5]

Not all philosophers accept the sentence or proposition as the basic epistemological unit, as the following quotation shows:

Logicians have almost always tried to conceive the "unit of thought," or that which is either true or false, as a kind of logical "soul" whose linguistic body is the indicative sentence . . . There have always been people who saw that the true "unit of thought" was not the proposition but something more complex in which the proposition served as an answer to a question. Not only Bacon and Descartes, but Plato and Kant come to mind as examples. When Plato described thinking as a "dialogue of the soul with itself," he meant (as we know from his own dialogues) that it was a process of question and answer, and of these two elements the primacy belongs to the questioning activity, the Socrates within us. When Kant said it takes a wise man to know what questions he can reasonably ask, he was in effect repudiating a merely propositional logic and demanding a logic of question and answer. (Collingwood 1944, 28)

Thus Collingwood regards the proposition or indicative sentence as too small a unit to represent knowing adequately. To stand alone a sentence must be abstracted from the human context where it serves a purpose, namely, participating in a dialogical process by answering a question, whether posed by oneself or by another; that is, in a conversation.

Building on this, I wish to consider—in addition to sentences and proofs—conversation (including dialogue and dialectical reasoning) as a special and privileged epistemological form. Thus my claim is that conversation constitutes an epistemological unit for mathematics and the philosophy of mathematics. A case can also be made for its broader significance, as the parallels in other disciplines suggest.

The claim that conversation is needed as a privileged epistemological unit requires that I show that it has a character that is essential for mathematical knowledge and that cannot be subdivided or eliminated in favor of some other less complex form of expression. Traditionally, sentences and proofs play the role of epistemological units in the philosophy of mathematics. They both serve an indispensable function in mathematics, and indeed in knowledge in general. But a deficiency they share as epistemological units is that they are abstracted from any context, human or otherwise, and do not seem to depend on human knowers.

The argument for accepting that conversation has a special role to play in epistemology is that language and discourse play an essential role in the genesis, acquisition, communication, formulation, and justification of mathematical knowledge. Conversation is the dialogical deployment of language, and its social exchange dimension—in the form of acceptance, elaboration, reaction, criticism, and correction—is essential for feedback. This dimension underpins the justification of objective mathematical knowledge and the ratification of personal knowledge. Without conversation and its feedback mechanisms, the individual appropriation of collective knowledge cannot be conducted or validated. Likewise, the social construction and acceptance of objective mathematical knowledge cannot take place. This depends, following Lakatos, on the mechanism of the GLMD. The underlying dialectical form of these processes needs to be accommodated in my account of the epistemological foundations of social constructivism. This can be done only by conversation or another variant of dialogue which embodies dialectics in its deep structure.

Two immediate objections to adopting conversation as a privileged epistemological form can be anticipated. First of all, it might be argued that conversation and dialogue, including dialectical reasoning, are concerned with the genesis of mathematical knowledge, not with its justification. Therefore, to accord conversation or dialogue some special epistemological role is to confuse the context of discovery with the context of justification. However, if it is accepted, as I argue, that the warranting of mathematical knowledge is a social act, then this criticism breaks down, for the complete separation of these two contexts cannot be sustained.

The second immediate objection concerns the adoption of a larger complex entity, conversation or dialogue, as a privileged epistemological form in place of a smaller and simpler vehicle of knowledge, namely, the sentence. Surely, the objection might run, the sentence is an atom of knowledge, whereas what I suggest is a complex molecule or aggregate of knowledge. Therefore, should not primacy be claimed for the sentence as an element of knowledge, into which the larger unit can be analyzed?

My response is that to reduce conversation to a string of sentences is to sacrifice the structure within speech, essential for proofs, as well as its intrinsically social and interactive aspect. Hence sentences cannot be substituted for conversation as an epistemological form unless it is conceded that the social, contextual element of mathematical knowledge is inessential and an add-on extra. This would contradict the assumption of the essentially social nature of knowledge and knowing, an assumption that forms the basis of social constructivism, including both the genesis and justification of knowledge.

THE DIALECTICAL RHETORICAL NATURE OF MATHEMATICS

The Dialectical Nature of Mathematics

The social constructivist view of mathematics, following Wittgenstein, is as a collection of language games sited in various forms of life. From this perspective mathematical knowledge is at base conversational, and mathematical proof is a special kind of narrative. Indeed, proof may be regarded as having evolved from, and still having the functions of, a particular type of segment of dialogue. It is a text designed to persuade members of the mathematical community to accept a proposition or certain propositions as mathematical knowledge.

Contributions to mathematical knowledge are textual utterances which are largely made up of written mathematical proofs, so the utterances are a level removed from spoken dialogue. Even if spoken, such as at a mathematical conference, the forms of acceptable proof reflect the standard written models and paradigms in the literature. Furthermore, lecture presentations are generally supported textually, by writing on the chalkboard, slide displays, or printed notes, since diagrams and complex symbols cannot easily be presented orally.

Although mathematics is primarily textual knowledge, social constructivism takes it to be conversational and to have an underlying dialectical form. This is not a strict Hegelian dialectics, which would impose an absolute, metaphysical order on the world and thought which is inconsistent with fallibilism. Mathematics is dialectical because of the dialogical form of human conversation, with its ebb and flow, its assertion and counterassertion, reflecting the basis of the social: language games in process, embedded in human forms of life.

Thus mathematics is claimed to be conversational and based on "dialogic" (dialectical logic). However, this "logic" is not intended to challenge or supplant the vital role of deductive logic in mathematics and in warranting mathematical proof. As Rosen argues:

> logic and dialectic are joined together in the texture of everyday modes of reasoning. There is no natural competition between logic and dialectic, and my task is never to reduce one to the other. However . . . dialectic is the broader of the two functions of thought. It is surely uncontroversial to observe that there cannot be a logical justification of logic [on pain of contradiction]. Even such defenses as by Aristotle of the principle of noncontradiction are dialectical. (Rosen 1989, 118)

However, utilizing two strategies, traditional absolutist accounts deny and conceal the dialogical nature of mathematics. The first strategy is to accept at face value the ideologically motivated historical assimilation, absorption, suppression, and final denial of the dialogical components within mathematics itself. Since the time of the ancient Greeks, mathematics has been associated with a desire for certainty and has been presented so as to persuade others that it achieves this state. Thus indications of dialogue and criticism and traces of the authorial subject are eliminated from presentations of mathematical knowledge. The second strategy is to locate the remaining irrepressibly dialogical aspects of mathematics in its pragmatic, human, and social penumbra, which are then labeled as immaterial to the nature of mathematical knowledge and its justification. The denial and suppression of its dialogical aspect is perhaps an inevitable part of the ascendancy of the formal and deductive dimension of mathematics and its largely successful quest for objectivity. This development represents a great cultural achievement: the articulation of mathematics as a collection of formal, abstract, and largely structural systems. However a reevaluation of the dialogical aspects of mathematics is not a challenge to this achievement.

Although it is claimed that the dialogical nature of mathematics has been hidden, it is still evidenced in a number of ways (Ernest 1994a). These include the role of language and symbolism in mathematics, the constitution of some mathematical concepts, the origins and basis of proof, and the epistemological basis of mathematics.

Mathematical language. Mathematics is primarily a symbolic textual activity that uses written inscription and language to create, record, and justify its knowledge (Rotman 1993). However, despite the traditional view of mathematical discourse as isolated and abstracted from human realities and concerns *"The sign may not be divorced from the concrete forms of social intercourse"* (Volosinov 1973, 21). All texts are regarded by theorists such as Bakhtin, Gergen, Halliday, Lotman, and Volosinov as dialogical.

> Utterance, as we know, is constructed between two socially organized persons, and in the absence of a real addressee, an addressee is presupposed in the person . . . The *word is* [always] *orientated towards an addressee . . .*
>
> In point of fact, *word is a two-sided act.* It is determined equally by whose word it is and for whom it is meant. As word, it is precisely *the product of the reciprocal relationship between speaker and listener, addresser and addressee.* (Volosinov 1973, 85–86, original emphasis)

Viewed semiotically as comprising texts, mathematics is inescapably conversational and dialogical in an immediate way, for by its very nature text addresses and thus presupposes a reader.

Mathematical proof is a special form of text, which since the time of the ancient Greeks, has been presented in monological form (Skovsmose 1994). This reflects the absolutist ideal that total precision, rigor, and perfection are attainable in mathematics through objectivizing and abstracting its form from the context of utterance. But as a proof is an argument intended to convince, a listener/reader is presupposed. The monologicality of proof tries to forestall the listener and render her response obsolete by anticipating all of her possible objections.[6] So the dialectical response is condensed and subsumed into the ideal perfection of a monological argument, one in which no sign of speaker or listener remain except for the idealized and perfected utterance, the proof itself. This style is an essential part of the rhetorical form of mathematics, as discussed below.

More evidence of the dialogical nature of mathematics arises from an examination of mathematical language. A detailed analysis of mathematical texts, proofs, and algorithms reveals that the verb forms employed are in both indicative and imperative moods. The declarative case of the indicative mood is used by the writer to make statements, claims, and assertions. According to Rotman (1988, 1993), drawing on the work of C. S. Peirce, these are claims about relations between mathematical objects and the outcomes of mathematical processes, claims that describe the future outcomes of thought experiments which the reader can perform, or can simply decide to accept. "By such a process . . . like mathematical reasoning, we can reach conclusions as to what would be true of signs in all cases" (Peirce, cited in Rotman 1993, 76). (This is consistent with Lakatos's [1976] view of informal proofs as thought experiments.)

The imperative mood is used for both inclusive and direct imperatives, which are shared injunctions, or orders and instructions issued by the writer to the reader.

> The speaker of a clause which has selected the imperative has selected for himself the role of controller and for his hearer the role of controlled. The speaker expects more than a purely verbal response. He expects some form of action. (Berry 1975, 166)

Thus mathematical texts comprise specific assertions and imperatives directed by the writer to the reader. The reader or addressee of mathematical text is therefore either the agent of the mathematician-author's will—an agent whose response is an imagined or actual action—or a critic seeking to make a dialectical response. In both cases mathematical knowledge and text can be claimed to be dialectical or dialogical. A full explication of the semiotics of mathematics requires more space than is appropriate here (see Rotman 1988, 1993; Ernest 1993b, 1995).[7]

Mathematical concepts. Dialogic and dialectical processes underpin a substantial class of modern mathematical concepts and content. Some examples include aspects of analysis (ε-δ definitions of the limit, well known to have a dialogical interpretation), statistics (hypothesis testing involving H_0 versus H_A), probability (the analysis of multiplayer wagers, betting games), game theory (the alternation of moves by opponents), constructivist logic (interpretation of quantifiers: $\forall x \exists \, y P(x, y)$ means "You choose x, and I show how to construct y *such that* . . ."), number theory (Conway's 1976 game theoretic foundations of number), set theory (the game-theoretic version of the axiom of choice and the diagonal argument in which for any enumeration of a set you provide, I construct an omitted element), recursion theory (the arithmetical hierarchy with its alternation of quantifiers, e.g., $\forall \exists \forall \exists \forall \exists$, with meanings like those in constructivist logic). In each of a wide selection of examples the dialogical alternation of voices can be located in (or read into) the structure of the mathematical concept involved.

Thus dialectical interpretations can be given to significant concepts from some of the main branches of mathematics (number theory, analysis, foundations, deductive logic) and form an essential underpinning of others (game theory, stochastics). Since mathematics arises through conversation and is the science of abstract form, some of the structural features of conversation are abstracted and are found embedded in the conceptual basis of the discipline.

Origins and basis of proof. Mathematical proof, certainly in its axiomatic form, appears to have developed in classical Greece. Cornford, Kolmogorov, Restivo, Struik, and others have argued that the emergence of proof in ancient Greek mathematics reflected the social, political, and cultural circumstances of the time. These included, most notably, the democratic forms of life in which dialectical argument and disputation were valued and widely practiced, skepticism and speculation about hypotheses and ideas, and an idealistic outlook associated with an aristocratic slave society. It seems very probable that the emergence of proof in ancient Greece, in the fields of mathematics, philosophy, and logic, was in large part due to the widespread and central cultural practices of disputation and dialectical reasoning, which were intrinsic to the democratic public institutions of the society.

The word *dialectic* already had a number of shades of meaning in the time of the ancient Greeks. In its earliest sense dialectic is the name for the method of argument which is characteristic of metaphysics and is derived from the verb meaning "to discuss."

> dialectic means a co-operative inquiry carried out in conversation between two or more minds that are equally bent, not on getting the better of the argument, but on arriving at the truth. A tentative suggestion (*'hypothesis'*) put forward by one speaker is corrected and improved until the full meaning is clearly stated. The criticism that follows may end in complete rejection or lead on to another suggestion which (if the examination has been skillfully conducted) ought to approach nearer to the truth. (Cornford [1935] 1960, 30)

Szabo (1967, 1969) claims dialectics in this sense as the source of the axiomatic method, following the use of indirect reasoning by the Eleatics, such as Zeno of Elea. He argues that a key development concerns the rejection of empirical evidence as a source for mathematics and the acceptance of abstract logical reasoning instead. He suggests that axioms were originally a common, basic starting point for two disputants in a dialectical argument.

Fritz (1955) also locates the source of deductive mathematics and logic in dialectical argument and disputation. This fits well with the more general view that the dialogical nature of Greek public life is a crucial source of proof in both philosophy and mathematics. Which actually came first is perhaps immaterial, according to Lloyd (1990). Indeed Knorr (1975) disputes Szabo's account and argues that philosophy and mathematics developed in parallel.

What does seem to be above dispute, though, is the conversational, dialectical origin of proof in mathematics. Although some of the detailed published proposals are conjectural, and there is controversy over the source of the axiomatic method, there is unanimity that disputation and dialectical reasoning play an essential part in the historical origins and the development of logic and mathematics in classical Greece (Boyer 1968). Thus it may be concluded that the origins of mathematical proof are dialectical and dialogical.

In modern proof theory, some of the main developments treat mathematical proofs as if they are offered in a dialogue. In them a proponent attempts to convince an opponent of her claims, while the opponent challenges what is asserted but accepts a number of agreed basic rules of reasoning and facts. Thus these developments have been dialogical, if not always explicitly dialectical.

Heyting ([1931] 1964) describes how every proposition asserted in intuitionistic mathematics signifies a promise offered to an opponent, namely, that of providing an intuitionistic proof of it. Thus such propositions are claims that are valid only if the opponent can be convinced.

Natural deduction techniques likewise allow a mathematician to build up a proof of a theorem by means of inferential schemes. Once sufficient assumptions or hypotheses have been agreed by the proposer and opposer, then a chain of deductive inferences is built up using the schemes until the theorem is established. (This strikingly resembles Szabo's and Cornford's accounts of ancient dialectical proof.)

The method of semantic tableaux is even closer to a dialectical logic of conversation, since it represents an explicit attempt to refute the claim (or story) as put forward by another in dialogue (Bell and Machover 1977). One of its originators, Hintikka, also proposes a system of game theoretic semantics for tableaux that emphasizes the strategic, dialogical aspect of the choice of terms in instantiating quantifiers.

The most fully developed dialogical interpretation of proof is that of Lorenzen, for constructive logic. Lorenzen's (1970) method is based on the interaction between two disputants where one tries to maintain a thesis over the other's objections. He suggests a dialogical interpretation of the logical constants incorporating both the proponent's claims and conclusions, and the opponents queries and claims. Lorenzen's proposals represent an explicitly conversational, dialectical basis for logical reasoning and mathematical proof; this basis, he claims, is not another arbitrary formal system but reflects mathematical practice (Roberts 1992).

What can be concluded overall is that both the beginnings of logic and mathematical proof and their modern developments confirm that mathematical proof is at root dialectical, based in human dialogue and conversational exchange.

Epistemology and methodology. Lastly, conversation plays a key role in the epistemology and methodology of mathematics. Conversation and dialectical processes are immediately present in the warranting dialogue of Lakatos's LMD and the GLMD presented in chapter 5. There it was shown that the underlying logic of the GLMD is dialectical and that this underpins the genesis and warranting of mathematical knowledge. In that mechanism, mathematical proofs and other proposals are offered to the appropriate mathematical community as part of a continuing dialogue. They are addressed to an audience and are tendered in the expectation of reply, be it acceptance or critique. Thus not only has mathematical proof evolved from dialogical form, but its very function in the mathematical community as an epistemological warrant for items of mathematical knowledge requires the deployment of that form.

Finally, a word of caution is needed. Although mathematics is claimed to be at root conversational, it is also the discipline par excellence that hides its dialogical nature under its monological appearance and that has expunged the traces of multiple voices and of human authorship behind a rhetoric of objectivity and impersonality. This is why the claimed conversational nature of mathematics might seem surprising: it is the exact opposite of the traditional absolutist view of mathematics as disembodied and superhuman, a view critiqued above. To explore this more fully, it is necessary to consider the rhetoric of mathematics.

The Rhetorical Nature of Mathematical Knowledge Claims

According to the social constructivist account, new mathematical knowledge claims are constructed by individual persons, or groups of individuals working jointly, within the context of a mathematical practice or tradition. They are formulated linguistically (understood broadly to include diagrams, mathematical symbols, and other forms of representation) with reference to traditions of their form and content (composing part of the tacit knowledge of mathematics).

What needs to be stressed beyond the account given in chapter 5 is that there are powerful rhetorical constraints on form which play a crucial role in the acceptance of new mathematical knowledge claims. The primary function of new knowledge claims in mathematics is to persuade other members of the mathematical community, notably critics, referees, and other "gatekeepers" of the domain of accepted knowledge, to accept them. Thus from an outsider's perspective, both the form and content of new knowledge texts are designed to accomplish this persuasion and the gaining of legitimacy. From an insider's (i.e., mathematician's) perspective, new knowledge claims are put in the "correct form" required by the discipline of mathematics. My claim is that these two perspectives are accounts of the same thing and that rhetorical form plays an essential part in the expression and acceptance of all mathematical knowledge (of course such perspectives may differ in terms of the underlying epistemology). At base, "rhetoric is about persuasion" (Simons 1989, 2), and logic and proof provide the strongest rational means of persuasion available to humankind.[8]

A critic might reasonably raise the issue of the importance of the contents of which persons are persuaded and argue that the content of mathematics precedes its persuasive form. In rebuttal I shall argue that form and content are not wholly separable, particularly in mathematics, where the content is primarily defined by a set of textual relationships.

The rhetoric of mathematics and the sciences. In rhetoric there is a tradition, dating back to Aristotle and the Sophists, concerning the modes and styles of linguistic expression. However, in an opposing tradition dating back at least to the time of Plato, rhetoric has been dualistically opposed to content. For example, in modern times Frege's 1892 seminal analysis of linguistic meaning views rhetoric as "the coloring and shading which poetic eloquence seeks to give to the sense. Such coloring and shading are not objective, and must be evoked by each hearer or reader according to the hints of the poet or the speaker" (Frege [1892] 1966, 60–61).

However Frege's view that rhetoric is mere ornament in style or subjective "coloring and shading" is based on what are now questionable philosophical assumptions. Frege assumes or posits that each sentence has a unique and fixed meaning or sense that is its objective content. He also assumes that sentences designate propositions with determinate truth values. Rhetoric, for Frege, is just the "dressing" overlying the signification of these objects. In Frege's case, these problematic views are bound up with a Platonistic conception, for he asserts that senses of sentences (propositions) and their references (truth values) are superhuman abstract objects. Such Platonistic notions receive double support, first, from the tacit Cartesianism which infused scientific thought in the last century and much of modernism in general. This assumes that thus just as each material human body has a mind, existing in some other realm of existence, so too each sentence corresponds to a sense or meaning, in some Platonic realm of meanings. As Collingwood (1944, 28) says, the truth value serves "as a kind of logical 'soul' whose linguistic body is the indicative sentence." Second, the forms of language encourage reification of meanings. If a sentence has a meaning, then it follows that there is a meaning expressed by it. Ergo, meanings exist somewhere. Nominalization is a well known phenomenon in natural language which approaches reification (Chomsky 1965). Elsewhere I argue for the importance and prevalence of the reification of abstract objects in mathematics, originating in linguistic and psychological factors (Ernest 1991).

The Fregean model of meaning and assumptions about language are inconsistent with the view that objectivity is social (Bloor 1984) and with the related Wittgensteinian notion that meaning is bound up with language games. According to this conception, meaning is something far less tangible. It includes a set of linguistic rules which are part of a complex evolving human practice, not all aspects of which can be made explicit. Thus from this perspective it is fallacious to impute or attribute a unique, fixed, and determinate sense to a text. Given that it is to be understood socially, the meaning attributed must vary according to the social group making the interpretation, as their language games and group understandings vary. Certainly the sense attributed to mathematical texts has varied in history as the epistemological outlook of mathematical communities has changed.

This assumption lies at the heart of certain modern philosophical movements, such as the holistic view of meaning of Quine (1960) and others as well as natural language ("speech act") philosophy from Wittgenstein, Austin, and Grice to Searle (1995). Outside of the Anglo-American analytic tradition more support can be found, including that of hermeneutics (Anderson *et al.* 1986; Gadamer 1979), poststructuralism (Anderson *et al.* 1986; Dreyfus and Rabinow 1982) and deconstruction in philosophy (Derrida 1989; Norris 1983). Each of these traditions rejects the notion that a text embodies a unique or determinate meaning. This view is shared by semiotic theory ("Texts generate or are capable of generating multiple [and ultimately infinite] readings and interpretations" [Eco 1984, 24]), and also by scholars concerned with the rhetoric of the sciences ("The underlying reality of a representation is never fixed and always able to change with occasion of use. This means that it is not in principle possible to establish an invariant meaning for any given representation" [Woolgar 1988, 32]). Thus the notion that a text expresses a fixed meaning is under serious and widespread challenge.

The complexity of "objective meaning" which does not allow it to be made explicit or claimed to be fixed, prevents the separation of rhetoric and content. For if the meaning of a sentence or text cannot in principle be uniquely specified or individuated, there is no way either in principle or in practice of wholly separating rhetoric and content in any text. Meaning cannot any more than style (including rhetoric) be abstracted from its textual expression. A text may be modified to change its meaning with little rhetorical effect, or to change style and not meaning. But given the conceptual validity of the distinction all this shows is that there are transformations of rhetoric and meaning which are socially accepted as leaving one of them unchanged.

Overall, the claim is that no hard-and-fast distinction can be drawn between rhetoric or form, on the one hand, and logic, sense or content, on the other, especially in natural language. This does not make them indistinguishable, but it does make rhetoric, or the *form* of discourse, inseparable from its *content*.

Scholarship uses argument, and argument uses rhetoric. The "rhetoric" is not mere ornament or manipulation or trickery. It is rhetoric in the ancient sense of persuasive discourse. In matters from mathematical proof to literary criticism, scholars write rhetorically. Only occasionally do they reflect on that fact . . . even writers attacking an earlier rhetoric pay no attention to their own. Modern scholars usually deny their rhetoric. (Nelson, Megill, and McCloskey, 3–4)

To elaborate this point, the rhetorical styles adopted within disciplines, or within research communities, play a deep but often unrecognized epistemological role. For in every such context, rhetoric needs to conform to disciplinary conventions and expectations to have any hope of being persuasive. The validated rhetoric of a discipline is but one of many ways of communicating knowledge in it, but it embodies the one mode of expression or "voice" that speaks with authority and is listened to.

In recognition of these issues, a number of scholars are analyzing the rhetoric of the social sciences (Billig 1991; Firestone 1987; McCloskey 1985), the physical sciences (Markus 1987; Woolgar 1988), and even mathematics (Kitcher 1991; Rotman 1988). A shared theme in such analyses is the identification of the speakers and the voices underlying the discourse and texts; the tropes, metaphors, metonymies, and other discursive devices, and the role they are intended to fulfill in their respective disciplines. A widespread conclusion shared by these scholars is that depersonalized, objective rhetorical style serves to support an implicit absolutist epistemology in many disciplines.

Thus, for example, McCloskey (1985) claims that the arguments of economics are couched in the language of mathematics to give them more authority and persuasive power. Woolgar argues that the impersonal style of scientific writing is designed to communicate objectivity and that underpinning this rhetoric are covert metaphysical assumptions of a realist ontology and an absolutist epistemology. These assumptions imply the ultimately knowable nature of the known but leave the knower out of the picture. "The scientist needs to be the trusted teller of the tale but at the same time, should not be seen as intruding upon the object" (Woolgar 1988, 18). Starting instead from the assumption of the fallible nature of human knowledge, Woolgar argues that a shift to a more open rhetorical style is necessary if the absolutist epistemology of science is to be abandoned.

Poststructuralists, like Foucault, argue that discourse, encompassing both rhetoric and meaning, serves to create and establish "truth," rather than merely describe it. This, it is argued, is because it is a human construction which arises from people's projects, purposes, and perspectives and, consequently, is also irreducibly tied up with power.

Each society has its regime of truth, its "general politics" of truth: that is, the types of discourse which it accepts and makes function as true; the mechanisms and instances which enable one to distinguish true and false statements, the means by which each is sanctioned; the techniques and procedures accorded value in the acquisition of truth; the status of those who are charged with saying what counts as truth. (Foucault 1980, 131)

Central to this view is the claim that rhetoric as much as logic contributes to the construction of this truth. Foucault bases his position on a series of historical studies tracing several bodies of professional knowledge and practice ("discursive practices") and noting how the discourses and the "reality" they describe are interdependent. Brown likewise traces the different forms that rationality has taken in different cultures over the course of history and concludes that reason itself has a varying, rhetorical, and socially constructed character.

Absolute judgements of truth claims are dubious even within a given canon of validity, since the interpretation and application of such canons are inevitably symbolic acts intended to persuade an audience according to some interest. In addition, such canons themselves exist in social and historical contexts. Canons of validity, and epistemologies generally, are legitimations of belief. As such, they are rhetorical in character. (Brown 1987, 188)

The claim is twofold. First, that rhetoric plays an essential methodological role in the textual communication of knowledge, one in which the form and style of a text are inseparable from its content. Second, that the rhetoric of discourse is a function of the underlying epistemology assumed by the speaker or text and serves to validate its content. The different disciplines and research communities associated with different epistemological paradigms have different circumlocutions or *façons de parler* and characteristic means of expression necessitated by their different attitudes to meaning, truth, and knowledge. In mathematics, this is illustrated by the difference between the texts of constructivists and classical mathematicians. Their different rhetorical styles, including what is acceptable as a definition or proof, are based on their different theories of truth.

Rotman (1988) has pointed out that the rhetoric of mathematics plays an essential role in maintaining its epistemological claims. As in science, a depersonalized style eschewing all deixis (with other features considered below) is adopted to establish the impersonal and objective nature of mathematical truth. Thus, the rhetoric of mathematics plays a key role in the acceptability of new mathematical knowledge. This is echoed by Kitcher (1991, 3) *even in the most austere case, namely mathematics*, a rhetorical function is served by the presentation of the proof. Given two presentations of the same proof, one may be effective in prompting members of a particular audience to undergo the intended/reliable process of belief formation, while the other may not. Relativization to audiences is crucial here.

In pointing out the rhetorical aspects of mathematics my goal is not necessarily to critique or reject them. There are good reasons for eschewing deixis and for adopting an objectivist style in mathematics. It can be argued that such a style has served historically as a safeguard against lapses into unintended errors of subjectivism and psychologism in mathematical proofs. However a critical analysis of the rhetoric of mathematics and the social conventions on which it depends is a necessary part of a social constructivist enquiry into the nature of mathematics. Furthermore, since rhetoric can serve epistemological and sometimes even ideological functions, its consideration and critical scrutiny is necessary.

Acceptance Criteria for New Mathematical Knowledge

I argued in chapter 1 that the proofs accepted as warrants for mathematical knowledge do not follow the explicit canons of formal logic and proof, as expressed in texts of mathematical logic, for example. Instead, proofs and other mathematical texts have a powerful rhetorical function, namely, to persuade mathematical critics and referees. To persuade mathematical critics is not to fool them into accepting unworthy mathematical knowledge; it is to convince them that the actual proofs tendered in mathematical practice are worthy. But persuasion is necessary since fully rigorous formal proofs are rarely, if ever, tendered in mathematics. This phenomenon has important implications for the acceptance criteria for new mathematical knowledge. It also ties in with the fact that mathematical knowledge has a tacit dimension in addition to the explicit forms of knowledge as propositions and proofs, for what it indicates is that the acceptance of new items of mathematical knowledge depends to a large extent on the tacit knowledge and professional expertise of suitably situated mathematicians. Two major new issues are raised by this claim. First of all, there is the issue of the persons involved and their positioning with regard to the social institution of mathematics. This must take account of the crucial issues of power and legitimacy in their positioning with regard to the institution of mathematics; it is treated in the next section.

Second, there is the issue of the content and rhetorical style of texts constituting new items of mathematical knowledge or, at least, putative ones. Needless to say, this too depends on the persons involved and their social roles. The claim is that both the content and style of texts play a key role in the warranting of mathematical knowledge, and both are judged with reference to a mathematical tradition, rather than with reference to any specific explicit criteria. Thus judges of mathematical knowledge-candidates use their mathematical expertise based on tacit knowledge to evaluate submissions in terms of their content and rhetorical style. Although ultimately the rhetoric and content of any mathematical text are inseparable, it is convenient to distinguish criteria for them. Thus, in particular, a central claim of the social constructivist account is that there is an accepted rhetorical style of mathematics, or rather a set of styles, for different mathematical communities and subspecialisms and that conformity with these styles is a very significant factor in the warranting and acceptance of new mathematical knowledge.

Detailed empirical studies will enable the provisional sets of criteria below to be augmented and validated. The following are offered as an initial theoretical analysis.

Criteria for the rhetoric of mathematical texts. With regard to rhetorical style, some of the key criteria for acceptance are that the mathematical text should:

1. Use a restricted technical language in conformity with accepted usage for the mathematical subspecialism
2. Use the standard accepted mathematical notation of the mathematical subspecialism
3 Avoid deixis, that is, eschew pronouns or any other terms referring to the spatiotemporal location or identity of the writer[9]
4. Use a very spare, clipped form of expression with minimal grammatical conventions observed, no superfluous linking or explanatory prose used, and formal symbols predominating
5. Be succinct and preferably brief (the longer the text, the less the likelihood of journal acceptance, other things being equal)
6. Use expressions conforming with the various accepted models of style for introductory ("motivating") prose, linking prose, definition, exposition, proof, and so on, at appropriate points in the texts
7. Represent standard mathematical methods of computation, transformation, or proof in the accepted and recognized ways
8. Justify proof steps in accordance with accepted rhetorical practice, often with minimal justification if the steps are judged small
9. Make recognizable reference to central mathematical theorems, results, definitions, methods, problems, texts, or mathematicians and either use the standard names for these items or refer to standard or canonical texts and references in the literature

10. Relate any new problems, methods, or results to extant ones in a current or recognized mathematical theory
11. Except in rare and exceptional circumstances produce a text that is expressed so as to minimize its novelty, and be largely familiar, and as far as is possible represent a slightly novel rearrangement of known elements
12. Provide a persuasive logical narrative establishing any claims made to the satisfaction of the audience

These are general criteria or categories; they would not enable a mathematician to make judgements of acceptability as they stand, because the key additional source employed is tacit knowledge of previous cases from which judgements are inferred informally. Thus this list and those that follow confirm that any attempt to make the acceptance criteria fully explicit fail. In fact such criteria vary according to time, context, purpose and mathematical specialism.

One issue of importance is that the rhetoric of mathematics described here as involving, for example, the "slightly novel rearrangement of known elements," belies the difficulty and effort involved in the intellectual labor of mathematics. Creating mathematical texts and manipulating mathematical symbols meaningfully is very difficult intellectual labor involving great knowledge, flair, and insight, in view of the complexity of the conceptual and linguistic systems involved and the extensive range of constraints and criteria that must be respected and satisfied. The "slightly novel rearrangement of known elements" is a crucial aspect of virtually all areas of creative endeavor, including scientific inquiry and report writing, novel writing, ballet, music composition, jazz performance, and so on. However I use this phrase to emphasize the continuity of tradition, instead of the often emphasized novelty of individual contributions.[10]

Criteria for the content of mathematical texts. With regard to content, some of the key criteria for acceptance are that the mathematical text should:

1. Address accepted or recognizable mathematical problems, especially problems of current community interest, within a "live" mathematical theory
2. Utilize accepted or recognizable mathematical methods of computation, transformation of mathematical objects or notations, and proof
3. Employ accepted or recognizable mathematical objects, concepts, or definitions, especially those of current community interest
4. Provide a new result in the context of comprehensible and recognizable mathematical content; thus it should usually involve the statement of a new relation between existing mathematical objects, or the creation of a new mathematical object by the application of an existing mathematical method to known objects

5. Offer a novel conceptual resource in terms of power: the generality and abstraction of the result and its potentially broad domain of application
6. Be "elegant," that is, conform to the aesthetic ideals of mathematicians in terms of succinctness, ingenuity, surprise, power (i.e., breadth of applicability), and generality
7. Address an issue of importance or significance for mathematics: in particular, some of the novel features of the content treated should be judged powerful as generators of new knowledge, including the linking of existing mathematical knowledge

As the above lists show, it is not possible to entirely distinguish criteria for rhetoric and content in mathematics, just as it is not possible to separate form and content in texts. Nonetheless it remains illuminating to try to distinguish their different emphases. Neither of the two lists given above is complete. Furthermore, the criteria in use, which are in the main tacit, are likely to vary in different subcommunities of mathematicians pursuing different specialisms. The different employment of such criteria in different contexts is a matter that needs to be investigated empirically. Knuth (1985) compared page 100 in nine mathematical texts from different subspecialisms in mathematics and found very significant differences in style and content.

A third and as yet unexplored criterion also related to the previous two lists concerns the identity and pedigree or provenance of the submitting author. Although this is a relatively minor criterion compared to the two above, it constitutes a plausibility threshold that predisposes critical readers to look more seriously at would-be mathematical knowledge. Failure to cross the threshold may easily result in rejection if a submission fails some of the above criteria or concerns an area of mathematics that receives a great deal of "amateur" interest (e.g., the Delian angle trisection or circle squaring problems, the four-color theorem, Fermat's last theorem, etc.).

Criteria for judging the status of mathematicians. According to this criterion the author—to have submission taken more seriously—should be in at least one of the following categories:

1. A known or recognized mathematician who has published in accepted journals or given papers at the appropriate mathematical specialism conferences
2. A student or protégé of a known and respected mathematician
3. A student or academic faculty member of a known mathematical institution
4. A distinguished mathematician from another branch of mathematics and known for contributions to that field who is now contributing to another specialism

Failure to meet one or more of these criteria means that a submission may not receive a great deal of professional attention and scrutiny and is at risk of summary rejection.[11]

Overall, my claim is that both the content and rhetorical style of texts play a key role and that both are judged with reference to a living historical mathematical tradition, within which the critic is immersed and has completed an apprenticeship, rather than with reference to any specific explicit criteria. What this means is that the judges or critics of submitted mathematical knowledge claims are within a mathematical tradition, masters, who have successfully served out an apprenticeship, during which time they have absorbed the tacit knowledge of their mathematical specialism. This includes knowledge of the questions, language, proof criteria, and other metamathematical views, knowledge, and values, distinguished above, which play a central role in the acceptance of new mathematical knowledge.

What this account omits is reference to the subjectivity of the mathematician. Subjectivity is strenuously excluded from mathematical texts, but the process of creating and judging texts has an overwhelming subjective dimension.[12] What I mean by this is that mathematicians when reading mathematical texts have a strong belief that (1) that they are reading about existent objects and their relations in some mathematical realm and (2) that the proofs in texts offer ironclad warrants for theorems, by describing logically necessary conclusions and the inevitable results of constructions. Thus to describe a major component of mathematical texts as persuasive rhetoric seems to falsely describe the mathematicians' lived experience of irrefutable existence and certainty. It seems to devalue the strengths of the discipline as well as to misdescribe the experiences of mathematicians. My response is that both the existence of the objects of mathematics and the certainty proofs of mathematics have an objectivity that allows them to be subjectively experienced in strong and shared ways by mathematicians, but that these features of objectivity (and of subjective experience) rest to a large degree on mathematicians' overall knowledge of mathematics, especially its tacit dimension, which is acquired over a lifetime's enculturation. It can be anticipated that mathematicians will remark on the mismatch between the account of the significance of the rhetoric of mathematics given here, their own experiences of the subject, and their beliefs about the nature and significance of mathematics (which often include ideological elements of Platonism and absolutism).

The Role of Mathematical Proof

A mathematical proof is a special text with both a structure and a social function. The social function is to persuade the mathematical community to accept the theorem proved as mathematical knowledge. The structure or form, often identified with the proof-text itself, plays an essential role in fulfilling this social function. The textual form of a mathematical proof makes a unique and essential contribution to its persuasive role, as the above account of the rhetoric of mathematics indicates. However, my claim is that without fulfilling its social role a proof-text does not constitute a mathematical proof.

The main epistemological role and function of mathematical proof is evidently to provide a warrant for the assertion of mathematical knowledge. Mathematically proofs can serve other roles too, such as showing explicitly which assumptions a theorem rests upon, demonstrating how a mathematical entity can be constructed, and showing that an assumption leads to untoward or inconsistent consequences. However my interest here is restricted to the main epistemological function of mathematical proof. I have argued that the role of mathematical texts, especially proofs, is rhetorical, designed to persuade mathematicians to accept their conclusions. In extreme cases it might even persuade them to extend their criteria for judgement, so that the theorem satisfies the newly extended set. This social view of proof is shared by a growing number of mathematicians and philosophers such as Manin, Evert Beth, Piaget, Wilder, and Rorty:

> A proof becomes a proof after the social act of "accepting it as a proof." This is as true of mathematics as it is of physics, linguistics and biology. (Manin 1977, 48)

Rorty not only presses the case for the social, persuasive nature of proof, but explicitly bases it on the underlying notion of conversation.

> If, however, we think of "rational certainty" as a matter of victory in argument rather than of relation to an object known, we shall look toward our interlocutors rather than to our faculties for the explanation of the phenomenon. If we think of our certainty about the Pythagorean Theorem as our confidence, based on experience with arguments on such matters, that nobody will find an objection to the premises from which we infer it, then we shall not seek to explain it by the relation of reason to triangularity. Our certainty will be a matter of conversation between persons, rather than an interaction with nonhuman reality. (Rorty 1979, 156–57)

Thus the structure of a mathematical proof is a means to its epistemological end of providing a persuasive justification, a warrant for a mathematical proposition. To fulfill this function, a mathematical proof must satisfy the appropriate community, namely, that of mathematicians, that it follows the currently accepted criteria for a mathematical proof.

Criteria for the Acceptability of Mathematical Proof

I have claimed that the criteria for the acceptability of proofs and hence of mathematical knowledge are deployed in the decision-making activity of the current mathematical community (rather: multiple communities). Their source is the tradition of the community that preceded and created them, a tradition moderated by current practice; and they are not based on any fixed, absolute, or explicitly formulated basis. However, the members of any particular mathematical community do not vary the criteria they inherit from tradition on an arbitrary or whimsical basis. Any changes to tradition are hard fought and won. Nevertheless, the criteria for what constitutes an acceptable mathematical proof are not permanent or unchanging. Furthermore any changes to these criteria need not be restricted to minor ones reflecting only improvements in past procedures. It is been argued that revolutions in mathematics come about when there are major shifts in the underlying epistemological paradigm of mathematics, including these rules and criteria (Ernest 1992, Dunmore 1992). "**Revolutions may occur in the metaphysics, symbolism and methodology of mathematics** . . . Also subject to revolution are standards of rigor in mathematical proof" (Wilder 1981, 142–43, original bold face).

A crucial determinant of the acceptability of an item of would-be mathematical knowledge is the structure and properties of its proof. A central question therefore concerns how the nature and structure of proof contribute to its role as a warrant for propositional mathematical knowledge. Although I stress above the social and rhetorical aspects of persuasive demonstration in mathematics, the centerpiece of justification in mathematics is an argument usually consisting of a deductive proof. Thus the social and rhetorical aspects supplement but cannot replace the logical dimension of proof. However, as the analysis in chapter 1 shows, mathematical proofs are almost never rigorous formal proofs. This is because of the assumptions and inferences which are accepted as legitimate. These include the following elements of proof accepted in mathematical practice.

1. Previously accepted results. Proofs assume previously accepted mathematical knowledge, typically previously established theorems. Thus proofs are seldom if ever self-sufficient, for they refer to and presuppose the correctness of other proofs and items of mathematical knowledge. This is a legitimate position, for all knowledge assumes and builds on past knowledge. However the argument for this practice is that such assumed results are reducible to primitive assumptions (via proofs) in principle. This is a questionable justification for their inclusion, as was shown in chapter 1, for it is not possible for practical or theoretical reasons to make most or all proofs fully rigorous.

2. Definitions. A second source of assumptions introduced into proofs consists of definitions, such as Peano's inductive definition of '+'. They are conventions by *fiat*, are simply laid down as such and accepted without formal justification. Such assumptions are far from arbitrary and must conform to accepted criteria and standards of mathematical definition that are based on both tacit and overt mathematical knowledge (analogous to proof standards). Definitions either will explicate an informal notion belonging to an informal mathematical theory or may define novel formal concepts in the context of a mathematical theory. In this latter case, they will be admitted into proofs as hypothetical, as an auxiliary conceptual construction within the proof. Their acceptance by the mathematical community in broader contexts than a single proof will depend on pragmatic factors, typically, their facilitating role in developing a mathematical theory. An example of a novel concept or construction accepted in axiomatic set theory on such grounds is that of 'forcing' of Cohen (1966). Similar novel concepts abound in most if not all branches of mathematics.

3. Mathematical rules. The steps in a proof may include compound rules or principles, such as the "pigeon hole principle," and the standard account of their justification or warrant is that they are reducible to simpler assumptions, namely, basic mathematical and logical rules. This parallels case one, discussed above. As in that case it needs to be acknowledged that such assumptions depend on the knowledge and assent of the appropriate mathematics community. Different mathematical specialisms and the associated communities of mathematicians have different compound rules and principles. Knowledge of these, and the contexts and warrants of their application, will be part of the mathematical knowledge of the appropriate community and may be, in part, tacit. Thus although derived rules or principles of mathematics and logic are logically reducible to simpler assumptions, so that no stronger assumptions are introduced into proofs by their use, they nevertheless add to the assumed and accepted body of mathematical knowledge which needs to be known in order to warrant proofs and allow the telescoping of proof steps in abbreviating proofs.

4. Large proof steps and proof by analogy. Inferential steps in a proof may be justified by the claim that the step is justified by a combination of elementary inference steps, or by analogy with a proof given elsewhere. Such claims are to the effect that certain token replacements for missing proofs or proof-segments are sound. They are in effect promissory notes, promising validity; and they are often accepted at face value by the mathematical community on the grounds that they are believed or conform to tacit knowledge of accepted proof models and paradigms. The claim that a proof step is justified by an elementary combination of the previous types of steps is rarely verified and often not feasibly verifiable.[13] What is accepted as convincing by the mathematical community therefore is determined by tacit rules and conventions of acceptability that are defined and realized by the pattern of acts of acceptance, challenge, and rejection. Once accepted, such a proof-step is claimed to be verified, or verifiable in principle. This is equivalent to the claim of a function being "computable in principle" (Bell and Machover 1977) and does not entail that any mathematician intends to actually try to verify it.

The warranting of a proof or proof-segment by analogy with a similar proof depends on a judgement as to how convincing the analogy seems to be. Thus it depends on the knowledge of proof paradigms, that is, of the range of proofs or proof types accepted as models in the specific branch of mathematics concerned. Given an existing proof model, it also depends particularly on the relationship (the analogy and parallels) between the characteristics of that which is proved (or to be proven) and those of the proof itself. Thus, a wide ranging tacit knowledge of cases, proofs, and their properties and relationships is required, as is a metamathematical knowledge about values and preferred areas of inquiry or methods in mathematics.

5. *Informal assumptions.* A further source of assumptions consists of the informal "truths" or rules of accepted informal mathematical knowledge; they are embedded in informal mathematical language and may also have independent formalizations (e.g., arithmetic, set theory). They represent elementary truths that are accepted as part of the body of mathematical knowledge (or at least of some subdomain of it) including logic. They are imported into a proof, and used without explicit statement or justification. (Once stated they can be justified as in case one above.)

Altogether, the passing of judgements as to the correctness or acceptability of proofs in mathematics involves the deployment of considerable professional skill, judgement, and knowledge, in view of the range of acceptable or possibly acceptable strategies that can be employed and which must be evaluated. It has been shown that in addition to the explicit knowledge of formal mathematical and logical proof, and the criteria for their correctness and validity, a wide range of tacit knowledge is also brought to bear. Since proofs in practice are virtually never fully formalized, judging their correctness entails far more than the mechanical application of rules. Instead, such decisions are far less clear-cut and depend on the exercise of judgement by well-informed mathematicians deploying explicit, tacit, and metamathematical knowledge of mathematics.

The requirement for extensive tacit knowledge is further exacerbated since, in practice, all the different proof-step justifications are likely to be compounded, admixed, and abbreviated, according to what is acceptable to the particular mathematics community involved. In addition, there are a variety of different formulations of the mathematical logic that may be assumed to be the bedrock or foundation on which the proofs rest. Thus the mathematical knowledge involved in judging the acceptability of mathematical proofs goes well beyond a simple knowledge of the laws of mathematical logic.

THE SOCIAL POSITIONING OF MATHEMATICIANS

I do not wish to give the impression that there is unanimity among mathematicians in their decisions concerning the acceptance of mathematical knowledge. There is disagreement and conflict, and the dimension of power plays a central role in the acceptance of new mathematical knowledge as warranted. Indeed, any such act of acceptance represents power at work. Nevertheless, decisions as to the acceptance or rejection of new mathematical knowledge may normally be regarded as rational, for they constitute the application of norms and criteria in the making of professional judgements of acceptance (or otherwise). However, fully explicit justifications are not and cannot be given for all decisions made, for expert judgement, values, and tacit knowledge are involved in an essential way.[14] Thus rationality depends to a large extent on the norms and knowledge of the mathematical subspecialisms, tacit or otherwise, deployed in acceptability decisions. In particular, the acceptance of new mathematical knowledge will depend on the criteria described above, including the rhetorical style and content of mathematical texts.

Rationality is one of the central concepts of the philosophy of science, and there are different interpretations of its meaning. Fuller (1993, 144) distinguishes "the difference in the conception of *rationality* presupposed by the social epistemologist (i.e., one of systemic efficiency) and the more classical philosopher of science (i.e., one of methodical self-consistency)." The notion I use is the broader and more traditional one: A rational choice is one that is or can be justified by a plausible argument, based on recognized principles. Rationality is thus based on reasoning or reason. Arguments in law, scientific explanations, philosophical arguments, administrative decisions, and mathematical proofs and the decision to accept them, are all potentially rational.

However, decision-making processes concerning mathematical knowledge may also depend on nonrational factors (with respect to the mathematical community and its norms and criteria). Such decisions can be influenced by the positioning and relationships of mathematicians within the social institution of mathematics. They can also depend on the personal interests of the decision makers, or on pressure or power exerted upon them, such as by explicit or implied promises of sanctions or rewards. In such cases the resulting decision making could no longer be said to be rational with respect to the criteria and norms of the mathematical community involved (although it could be seen as rational from the perspective of the involved person's own interests).

Finally, it should be said explicitly that rational decision making by mathematicians concerning the acceptance of new mathematical knowledge by no means needs to involve unanimity or shared reasons. Two mathematicians could well have different reasons for accepting an item of mathematical knowledge. Equally, two mathematicians might easily disagree on the acceptability of a proposed item of mathematical knowledge and give plausible, if different, reasons for their judgements. However within a mathematical subspecialism there tends to be a move towards shared norms and judgements, and this may very well be facilitated by a shared absolutist epistemology which admits no ambiguity with regard to mathematical correctness and truth.

Mathematical Communities

At the heart of the social institution of mathematics is the group of persons called "mathematicians." However, mathematicians do not constitute a single homogenous group. Thus a subject such as mathematics is not monolithic, that is, it should be seen not as a group

> of individuals sharing a consensus both on cognitive norms and on perceived interests, but rather as constantly shifting coalitions of individuals and variously sized groups whose members may have, at any specific moment, different and possibly conflicting missions and interests. These groups may, nevertheless, in some arenas, all successfully claim allegiance to a common name, such as "mathematics." (Cooper 1985, 10)

In practice the set of mathematicians is made up of many partly overlapping subsets pursuing research in subfields, each subfield with a similar substructure, but loosely interconnected through various social institutions (journals, conferences, universities, funding agencies).

As Crane noted in her analysis of science, "Science as a whole appears to consist of hundreds of research areas that are constantly being formed and progressing . . . through stages of growth before tapering off" (Crane 1972, 29). Thus mathematicians are organized in multiple and complex ways. First of all, the set is structured into overlapping subsets constituting different subspecialisms and interests. Some mathematicians will belong to many of these subsets (including some outside of what is termed by its practitioners "proper mathematics," such as mathematics education, philosophy, computer science, cognitive science, mathematical physics, statistics, mathematical economics, and so on). Within each subset there are relationships based on shared interests, cooperative work, and so on. Another organization of the set of mathematicians is based on geography: shared institutional affiliation, collegiality, contiguity, and so on. An additional structure on the set of mathematicians is based on power (and status). Although power is exercised within localized institutions (e.g., mathematics departments at a university), from the point of mathematical knowledge acceptance the major dimensions of power concern the critical scrutiny and possible acceptance of mathematical texts embodying potentially new mathematical knowledge.

Some members are institutionally more powerful than others in the roles they play in warranting mathematical knowledge. Thus journal editors and referees, conference organizers and paper referees, and book and monograph series editors and referees all exercise power in making their professional judgements about which knowledge claims to accept, require to be revised, or reject. These are the persons involved in the dialectic of the GLMD. The power exercised by these persons plays an essential role in quality control in mathematics. The warranting of mathematical knowledge essentially involves a process of discrimination.

Discrimination also plays a further role after acceptance, namely, the use and citation of certain texts by mathematicians in their own texts. Within each mathematical specialism this is to some extent regulated by the norms of rhetoric, as was indicated above (i.e., which are the acceptable and most appropriate authorities or texts to cite within a given mathematical specialism). But it also depends on content: which mathematical concepts, results, methods, proofs, and texts are currently central to the practices and specialism of a particular mathematical subcommunity.

Less directly concerned with knowledge, but more concerned with the material conditions which support the construction of new mathematical knowledge, are those persons concerned with disbursing grants and contracts and with hiring and firing personnel. Their activities also constitute an important dimension of the exercise of power within the social institution of mathematics, although much of this power is exercised from outside, too.

This account is primarily *synchronic*, concerning the existing structure of the institution of mathematics. However, the set of mathematicians and the relations on it are continually changing, and thus mathematics is continuously evolving. As new members join, existing members shift in their interests, relationships, and exercise of power; and old members reduce their involvement or leave. From this *diachronic* perspective, the changing institution of mathematics and the changing temporal positions and relations between mathematicians become foregrounded. Collins (1993) explores the relations among mathematicians, scientists, and philosophers in the fifteenth and early sixteenth centuries and indicates the centrality of interpersonal networks and relations. He singles out three types of relationships: master-pupil ties, acquaintance or correspondence, and conflict. He suggests that although conflicts occur within all of the fields (and between all types of scholars), they remain unresolved in philosophy but are resolved, with consensus achieved, in science and mathematics.

In discussing the range of career positions of mathematicians and master-pupil ties it is useful to adopt Lave and Wenger's (1991) definition of situated learning or apprenticeship as legitimate peripheral participation. Lave and Wenger describe participation in social practices as having three stages: first, apprenticeship; second, master status; third, "grand" master status (attained when one has held apprentices who have themselves achieved master status). Thus novice mathematicians can be seen as apprentices who are peripheral participants in the social institution of mathematics. Their primary function is to engage in knowledge production work, often under the guidance of current masters. Such novices could be research students, research assistants, or junior college faculty at the start of their academic career. Mathematical masters, of both levels, not only engage in knowledge production work, but also participate centrally in the knowledge warranting process. The grand masters are likely to have more power in warranting knowledge and in the control of material resources. As Collins's analysis indicates, a significant dimension of power or influence is exercised through master-pupil ties. As a mathematical grand master, a mathematician exercises a strong, if indirect, influence through master-pupil ties, for the grand master's contributions to mathematical knowledge can include the laying down of new paradigms of proof, new mathematical methods, or new problems or theories which will potentially form or modify the core of a research program or subspecialism. This will often be the central focus of the grand master's influence through master-pupil ties. A number of studies, such as Fisher 1966 and Anellis 1989, have illustrated such impacts in the development of mathematical subspecialisms via the influence of master-pupil ties.

Becoming a mathematician thus requires an apprenticeship stage involving participation and enculturation in the institutions of mathematics and, presumably, the adoption of some of the values and culture of the mathematics subcommunity (Davis and Hersh 1980; Tymoczko 1986a). The apprenticeship stage might be roughly equated with the period of doctoral studentship and the first years as a contributing creative mathematician. For it is during this period that the apprentice mathematician first undertakes major self-directed research under guidance, and if successful the products of this will be offered to the mathematical community for warranting.

The apprentice stage follows and depends upon an extended period of schooling in mathematics, beforehand (discussed more extensively in chapter

7). During this phase the novice mathematical apprentice will have been enculturated into the social and cultural contexts of school mathematics and subsequently university mathematics. This process of enculturation results in personal knowledge of mathematics, the norms of mathematical content and rhetoric, and the social institution of mathematics. Those that complete the process have successfully learned (appropriated) part of the official body of mathematical knowledge (tacit and explicit) and have been "socialized" into mathematics. This is a necessary, but not sufficient condition for entry into the set of mathematicians, for next comes the stage of apprenticeship described above. This requires a more personal interaction with other mathematicians, and in particular, with one or more "masters" (e.g., doctoral supervisor or supervisors).

The Social Basis of Mathematicians' Truth

One of the outcomes of viewing the social institution of mathematics from a *diachronic* perspective is to stress the importance of socialization in the development and careers of mathematicians; that is, individual mathematicians' personal "historical" development. As they pass through the stages of studenthood, apprenticeship, master status, and then grand master status, mathematicians at first increasingly absorb the concepts, norms, rhetorical style, and other aspects of mathematical knowledge and culture, both tacit and explicit. During this period, their immersion in the culture, knowledge, and truths of mathematics leads to the personal appropriation of the cultural world of mathematics (or at least a corner of it) and, consequently, to an increasing commitment to and belief in its conceptual world and truths. Later, as they progress to master and grandmaster status, mathematicians' ontological and epistemological beliefs about mathematics become reinforced and buttressed by their "living in" the social institution of mathematics and "working in" the world of the cultural objects of mathematics (White 1947).

Foucault's (1980, 1984) concept of a "regime of truth" provides a useful tool in accounting for this process. This concerns the historical truth-status of a socially accepted model, perspective, or worldview. When for historical reasons important sectors of a community or society have come to accept such a perspective and act as if it is true, then a regime of truth prevails. A regime of truth concerns not individually warranted propositions but an overall metaphysical worldview. Such a perspective may seem as well grounded as a foundationalist account of knowledge, but the basis of such truths is the social acceptance and lived nature of the underlying presuppositions. A regime of truth is hegemonic, and it is held in place by a discursive practice, a set of language games embedded in a form of life, parallel to Wittgenstein's notions.

A possible criticism of this account is that it sounds as if persons have been fooled or coerced into accepting error. In mathematics this sounds ridiculous, little different from Orwell's (1949) hero Winston in the chilling novel *1984*, who finally concedes under torture that 2 + 2 = 5. This criticism is based on a misconception. A regime of truth enables people to see what *is* as what *has to be*; to identify historically grounded but contingent truths—not errors—as necessary truths. Mathematics is the subject par excellence, in which necessity abounds. Once certain assumptions, definitions, and rules are accepted the greater part of mathematics *does* follow by logical inference, that is, by necessity. But that necessity rests on a set of assumptions that are not themselves necessary. Therefore the fallibilist claim of social constructivism is that some crucial elements of mathematical knowledge are contingent truths and that consequently the body of mathematical knowledge as a whole is contingent truth.

Foucault's theory of regimes of truth provides an historical explanation of the strength of the widespread belief in the certainty of logical and mathematical knowledge. Because the historically received metatheoretical views of knowledge include its status as absolute and incorrigible, based on the Euclidean and Cartesian paradigms, that status is confirmed. Since mathematical knowledge and the objects of mathematics have considerable degrees of autonomy and permanence, these views are confirmed and entrenched.

In terms of traditional philosophy of mathematics, the account I am urging comes closest to that of conventionalism. However there are different forms of conventionalism, and they hinge on different interpretations of the concept of 'convention'. As described in chapter 5, Fuller (1988) distinguishes two senses of the term. First, there is the more artificial sense of convention as an explicit agreement on a definition, assumption, or a rule. This might be termed a "rational convention." The standard versions of conventionalism in the philosophy of mathematics adopt this sense and propose in one way or another that the conventions on which mathematics rests (i.e., the foundations of mathematics) are chosen for pragmatic reasons. According to such views the rest of mathematical knowledge, the superstructure, follows by logical means from the conventional basis. In the extreme form which Dummett termed "full-blooded" conventionalism and attributes to Wittgenstein, there is no base-superstructure division and all mathematical knowledge is directly adopted by convention. This position is untenable, given the universally acknowledged role of inference in mathematics, and no philosophers subscribe to it.

Fuller's (1988, 56) second sense of convention is "a practice that has emerged largely without design yet continues to be maintained." Convention in this sense is close to what is implied by participation in what Wittgenstein terms language games and forms of life, and in Foucault's "discursive practices." For to participate in a form of life and its language games is to follow the roles and norms and engage in the expected practices, that is, to observe the conventions of the form of life. This sense of convention is at least partly implicit, since usually no explicit statement of the conventions will be made; rather, participants must infer the conventions from observed behaviors and from others' corrections of their own infractions. This might be termed "historical convention," since it is based on preexisting practices. Fuller (1988, 56) argues that a convention in this second sense is "maintained in virtue of the beneficial consequences accrued to the individuals who adhere to it." Whilst this may often be the case, the beneficial consequences may be the indirect gains from participation in language games and forms of life, and it could be envisaged that an individual might adhere to a personally disadvantageous convention because of commitment to the form of life.

TEXTS AND THE OBJECTS OF MATHEMATICS

One "mystery" or central problem that any philosophy of mathematics must account for is that of the existence and nature of the objects of mathematics—and indeed their objectivity itself. This might be rephrased as the question, How can one obtain the benefits of Platonism without adopting its questionable ontology?

The social constructivist approach to this problem is that the objects of mathematics are among the social constructs of mathematical discourse. As Rotman (1993, 140) puts it, "one can say that mathematical objects are not so much 'discovered out there' as 'created in here,' where 'here' means the cultural circulation, exchange, and interpretation of signs within an historically created and socially constrained discourse."

According to the social constructivist view the discourse of mathematics creates a cultural domain within which the objects of mathematics are constituted by mathematical signs in use. Mathematical signifiers and signifieds are mutually interacting and constituting, so the discourse of mathematics which seems to name objects outside of itself is in fact the agent of their creation, maintenance, and elaboration, through its use.[15] Furthermore, because of the historically constituted nature of the objects of mathematics and the discourses in which they subsist, mathematicians join and learn to participate in a preexisting and already populated realms of discourse. By doing this they are appropriating and recreating their own corner of this world as well as ultimately contributing to its maintenance. Elsewhere I describe some of the ways that language and linguistic practices contribute to this phenomenon psychologically (Ernest 1991). Here I discuss the relationship between the objects of mathematics and texts.

In chapter 2 I recounted Rotman's (1988) semiotic account of the success of Platonism as philosophy for the working mathematician. He argues that it views mathematics as a full sign system, comprising both signifiers and signifieds, and thus accommodates human signifying activity concerning shared, objective meanings—something essential for mathematical practice. In this respect Platonism was judged superior to formalism and logicism (which prioritize mathematical signifiers) or intuitionism (which prioritizes the signified). Thus Platonism, according to Rotman, treats mathematical knowledge as inseparably tied up with mathematical texts (and their objective meanings).

Popper (1979) links objectivity and abstract objects with texts in one of his defenses of World 3. He argues that even if all machines and tools disappeared from the world (World 1) and all knowledge of science and abstract concepts from individuals' minds (World 2), then persons (or even intelligent creatures from space) would be able to reconstruct our scientific knowledge from texts. Thus the contents of texts is objective knowledge; and according to Popper, there is a unique objective meaning that is associated with scientific texts and is independent of the physical world or subjective knowledge. Popper makes it clear that he thinks discussions of meaning are futile—preferring to discuss truth instead—but he does describe World 3 as including the contents of journals, books, and libraries. For him such texts have unique contents and it is these that populate World 3.

There is one particular strength of Popper's account (and Plato's) which needs to be acknowledged: its recognition of the strong autonomy of the objects of mathematics and of the population of World 3 in general. The social constructivist account has to explain how something so apparently flimsy as a shared fiction created by texts (in context) can become so solid, robust, and autonomous as World 3 objects. There are also number of powerful objections to Popper's view to be put, but before embarking on a further critique I wish to elaborate the consequences of his view further.

Texts and Their Meanings

The traditional Platonistic or Popperian view is that objective knowledge, information, propositions, meanings, and the objects of mathematics are independent entities existing in a some superhuman realm (World 3 or the realm of Plato's Forms). Furthermore these abstract objects may be referred to or signified in multiple ways. For example, 2, 1 + 1, 99–97, 4/2, 200 percent, and 1.999 . . . all signify the number two. Similarly, the different sentences "Two is the only even prime number," and "The unique even prime number is two," are normally understood to express the same proposition, that is, to have identical senses and references. These are almost trivial illustrations of a virtually ubiquitous phenomenon of ambiguity. The way that such ambiguities are accommodated is to distinguish signifier from signified, and then to attribute a many-one relation between the signifying expressions (terms or sentences) and the signified "entity," which is mathematical object or proposition, respectively.

Another traditional problem lies in distinguishing between 2, 2, 2 and 2, for example. Each of these is a numeral for two, but drawn differently, or as here, presented in a different typeface.[16] This problem is dealt with by distinguishing signifier tokens—the physical inscription or utterance—and signifier types—the intended symbol (or the class of tokens standing for it). As before we have a many-one relation: many actual and possible inscribed tokens standing for or instantiating the intended signifier.

In the two cases described, each signifier and signified is regarded as an object. Furthermore, each one is an abstract object, except in the case where the signifying relation is one of direct reference and the signified referred to is a physical object, action, or event. In Popperian terms, although signifier tokens are part of World 1 (the physical world), signifier types are in World 3 (the domain of objective knowledge). Likewise, except when signifieds are physical objects, actions, and events (World 1) or mental states (World 2), they are abstract objects (World 3). Thus, since in all but trivial mathematics signifier types and signifieds are abstractions, they are both inhabitants of World 3 and part of objective knowledge.[17] An outcome of this view is that World 3 objects are prioritized—certainly in mathematics—and that Platonism or mathematical realism is virtually inescapable.

Discussing mathematical signifiers or texts, on the one hand, and the mathematical objects, contents or knowledge signified by them, on the other hand, raises the issue of the synonymy (and nonsynonymy) of texts or signifiers, and the identity and diversity of the abstractions signified, respectively. A Platonistic account of such relations prioritizes the realm of the abstract. Consequently, mathematical signifiers are synonymous if they refer to the same mathematical object, that is, have the same signifieds. Mathematical inscriptions can be regarded as identical if they represent the same signifier type. There is nothing wrong with these definitions except that the establishment of identity, synonymy, or equivalence is based on recourse to abstract and intangible World 3 objects. A problem for metaphysics that is unsolved (and is insoluble in my view) is how the identity and diversity of abstract objects might be ascertained without recourse to signifiers or discourse. For those, such as myself, Bloor (1984), Rotman (1993), and the many others wishing to question or unwilling to accept the ontological assumptions of Platonism, and the epistemological problems it brings, this is deeply problematic.

Platonism and Popper's World 3 are perspectives that arise out of ontological considerations, but they have profound consequences for epistemology.

Following Frege's introduction of predicate logic and its semantics, the reference of a mathematical term is its value, which for a numerical term is its numerical value, and the reference of a sentence is its truth value.[18] But to know the truth value of a sentence is to have information about its epistemological status. For example, to know that the sentence $x^3 - 3x^2 + 3x - 1 = 0 \rightarrow x = 1$ is true, is to know that 1 is the solution to the cubic equation. Likewise, to know the numerical value of a complicated term or functional expression is to know the outcome of a calculation. Thus knowing what some mathematical expressions signify is to have substantial mathematical knowledge. Furthermore the implicit realism in prioritizing the abstract signifieds of mathematics suggests that answers and truth-states preexist their human discovery. According to this perspective, the values exist, and it is only human wit that lags behind in discerning what these values of terms and sentences are. Thus in this account the identity of terms arises from their sharing the same value, and the equivalence of sentences arises from their sharing the same truth values.[19]

Social Constructivism, Texts, Meanings and Objectivity

Social constructivism rejects the priority and prior existence of abstractions and thus overturns these notions of identity and equivalence. If embodied physical existence is taken as the bedrock of ontology, it is tokens which are the empirically real signifiers. Signifier types are cultural artifacts—the sign intended and, to a greater or lesser extent, understood—when signifier tokens are perceived. But this notion of the intended signifier or sign underlying each inscription or utterance is something that arises from human agreement in language games and forms of life. That is, from a social constructivist perspective, it is a secondary and derived (albeit more important) phenomenon. Likewise, signifiers have ontological priority over the signified—especially in mathematics, for the signifiers can be inscribed and produced, or at least instantiated, whereas the signified can be indicated only indirectly, always mediated through signifiers. The questions, When do two signifier tokens represent the same signifier type? and, When do two signifiers indicate the same signified? must be answered differently from this perspective. The social constructivist answer is that the accepted practices of mathematical language games are what determine the answers. The identity and equivalence of linguistic forms and expressions that are admitted vary according to time, community, and context; and they are not given once for all. Indeed the history of mathematics can be seen partly in terms of the growth and elaboration of relations of equivalence of linguistic expressions, as a brief excursion into this history illustrates.

In five thousand years of written mathematics, a number of areas of mathematics have grown immensely. There has been, first of all, the great profusion of domains of mathematical knowledge, which can be described as mathematical theories, language games, and contexts. According to Høyrup (1994), mathematics first emerged as a discipline through the unification of the three protomathematical practices of primitive accounting, practical geometry, and measurement. This took place late in the fourth millennium B.C.E. in Mesopotamia through the common application of numeration and arithmetic to these applications in scribal training. By the late twentieth century the number of distinct modern mathematical subspecialisms was estimated at thirty-four hundred (Davis and Hersh 1980), indicating the explosive growth of the discipline.

Second, within each of these specialisms, and shared across many of them, is the large and still-growing range of mathematical symbols, diagrams, inscriptions, and notations. Beginning with simple symbols serving as numerals, mathematical notation has grown over history into a very elaborate set of special and dedicated symbols, icons, and figures. Indeed, so important is this development in supporting mathematical calculation, reasoning, and conceptualization that the history of mathematics might be viewed as the history of the development of mathematical symbolism.

Third, an intrinsic part of each mathematical language game is a set of rule-based symbolic transformations, which are regarded as preserving some features of mathematical expressions or texts as invariant. These include identity transformations of terms and equivalence transformations of sentences and formulas. Many of these transformations are built into the uses of symbols, irrespective of context, and are thus shared across many mathematical language games. Thus identity (used in expressing the identical transformations of terms) is an equivalence relation with the properties of reflexivity, symmetry, transitivity, and substitutivity, and this relation is probably used in all mathematical language games.[20]

Platonism and mathematical realism suggest a reading of the history of mathematics in which increasingly refined sets of mathematical signifiers have evolved to describe the universe of mathematics. The social constructivist account reverses this prioritization and argues that the development of the increasingly elaborate systems of mathematical symbolism have helped bring into being and scaffold the imaginary universes of mathematical ideas.

Invariance and Equivalence in Mathematics

Structural invariance is widely established as a central feature in both the content and the development of modern mathematics (Weyl 1947). Thus continuous functions, homeomorphisms, homomorphisms, isomorphisms, isotopies, and other structure preserving maps, functions, and functors; their properties; and the relations between their domains and codomains are pivotal in the mathematics of the past two hundred years. Likewise, in the elaboration, extension, or abstraction of theories in the historical development of mathematics, certain designated central relations and structures are preserved faithfully, and the extent of this preservation is often the deciding factor in community acceptance (Corfield 1995).[21]

Above I discussed the following problems of identity (and the traditional solutions). On what basis are different signifiers of mathematics regarded as identical? Under what conditions are distinct signifiers regarded as having the same signified? The social constructivist answer is that the conditions for identity depend on traditions and rules for the identification of signifiers located in language games and situated in mathematical forms of life. In particular, in mathematics there are usually explicitly permitted sequential transformations of symbols which convert a signifier into an equivalent one. Thus terms are converted into equal terms, equations are converted into equivalent equations, and, more generally, sentences and formulas are transformed into equivalent sentences and formulas. This raises the question, What is the basis for the permitted transformations? The answer is normally that they are transformations that preserve the signifieds, or at least some central feature or property of signifieds such as truth value. Thus permitted transformations of numerical expressions and terms are those that keep the numerical values of expressions and terms invariant. Permitted transformations of sentences and formulas are those which preserve truth values.[22] Typically, such transformations are introduced and defined constructively, with a certain number of basic transformations admitted (as demonstrable preservers of value signified), and compound transformations are defined inductively as finite combinations of the basic ones. However, in the limit, classical mathematics is not inhibited from introducing infinite sequences of operations provided there is a guarantee that some underlying invariant is preserved. Thus equivalence transformations of mathematical expressions are admitted stepwise because it can be shown that they preserve a central feature of the fictional objects which are accepted as the underlying signifieds.

One area of especial importance for mathematics which exploits these issues is that of (explicit) definition. This is a stipulation of identity (of terms) or of equivalence (of sentences and formulas) in which the definiendum is substitutable for the definiens *salve veritate* (i.e., truth value preserving).[23] In fact, because a definition is a stipulated synonymy, meaning as well as truth is preserved in such substitutions.

Texts and Objects

There is a series of developments in modern philosophy of direct bearing on the issues of mathematical texts and the objects they signify. The position of Quine (1970) on the meanings of texts is well known. He argues, first of all, against the idea that the meaning or sense of a sentence is a proposition. His argument is that propositions cannot be individuated satisfactorily and that therefore it makes no sense to claim they exist. His second and earlier claim is the more general argument that synonymy is indefinable (Quine 1953b). In justifying this he first shows that the boundaries of the concept (relation) are ill defined and cannot be rendered precise. He also shows that substituting synonyms for each other need not in all cases preserve truth values, which is a sine qua non of synonymity. Third, he argues for meaning-holism, that is, the view that the meaning of a linguistic expression cannot be divorced from its linguistic context or the background theory.

Although Quine's position is quite distinct from that of Wittgenstein, his holism supports the latter's view that the meanings of textual objects cannot in general be individuated, as Platonism seems to require. Wittgenstein's holist conception of meaning as use in specific contexts is a central underpinning conception of social constructivism.

It is worth mentioning that there is a whole modern tradition stemming from modern continental philosophy including postmodernism (Derrida, Lyotard, Norris), poststructuralism (Foucault, Lacan, Dreyfus) and Hermeneutics (Gadamer, Ricoeur, Palmer) which tradition has deeply influenced modern literary criticism (Eagleton, Fish) concerning the thesis that texts do not have unique signifieds. However much the meaning of an expression appears transparent, literal, or unique, in adopting a favored or apparently correct interpretation "a thousand possibilities will always remain open" (Derrida 1977, 201).

> In writing, the text is set free from the writer. It is released to the public who find meaning in it as they read it. These readings are the product of circumstance. The same holds true even for philosophy. There can be no way of fixing readings . . . (Derrida in Anderson *et al.* 1986, 124)

Derrida of course takes up an extreme position on the indeterminacy of textual meaning, namely, that meaning is infinitely open. However such a broad consensus exists within this tradition and beyond, including the rhetoric of the sciences and the social studies of science movements, that it is a mistake to assume the existence of a unique meaning or "correct" interpretation of a text.

Support for this thesis can also be found within mathematics from the generalized Lowenheim-Skolem theorem (Bell and Machover 1977), for this theorem states that any set of sentences expressed in a first-order language which has an infinite model also has models of every infinite cardinality.[24] This means that first-order axiomatizations of Peano arithmetic admit uncountable models of the natural numbers, for *every* infinite cardinality. Another consequence is that first-order axiomatizations of the field of real numbers and of set theory admit denumerable models (although they would appear uncountable from within the theory itself, Schoenfeld 1967). These are well known and explicable but nevertheless counterintuitive results indicating that even the most precise theories of mathematics cannot uniquely determine their meanings or domains of interpretation (Tiles 1991).

The conclusion to be drawn is that the signifiers of mathematics do not correspond to unique signifieds. The relation is one-many, not a mapping, let alone a one-to-one correspondence. Mathematical language is not therefore a map, model or, "mirror" of a Platonic or World 3 reality (Rorty 1979). The case I want to argue is that signifieds are individuated instead by the admission of a class of textual transformations accepted as preserving the signified. The signifieds themselves of mathematics are unreachable, except through other signifiers. Ultimately, the accepted notion that there is something autonomous and real behind the signifiers is the result of the reification of abstract objects that are part of mathematical culture.

In Ernest 1991, I argued that the objects of mathematics are reifications in three senses: philosophical, sociological, and psychological. I shall discuss the thesis that the objects of mathematics are psychological reifications in the next chapter, when I treat subjective knowledge in mathematics.

Sociologically, there is a tradition epitomized by Marx in which concepts are understood as reifications which become cultural objects and things in themselves. "The productions of the human brain appear as independent beings endowed with life, and entering into a relation both with one another and with the human race" (Marx [1867] 1967, 72). He argues that the form of products becomes reified and fetishized into an abstract thing: money, value, or commodity (Lefebvre 1972). This argument has been extended to show how mathematical objects and knowledge are abstract reifications of more concrete conceptions and operations, and the transitions to the more abstract and autonomous objects of mathematics can be identified historically (Hadden 1994; Restivo 1985, 1992).

In philosophy there are a number of traditions that are relevant. First of all, there is a tradition going back to ancient philosophy concerning problem of universals. Aristotle's view is that the objects of mathematics do not exist apart from their instances. Similarly, the nominalism of the Schoolmen, especially William of Ockham, suggests that concrete individuals are what is first known, and the abstract concept corresponding to a class of individuals is a name whose meaning is identical with its extension, that is, the individuals it represents. Universals or abstract concepts are derived from the individuals they represent and may thus be seen as reifications. It is impossible to do justice to the problem of universals in the history of philosophy in a paragraph.

However, these indications suffice to show that there is a long tradition that rejects realism in mathematics and, instead, views abstract concepts as based on the particulars to which they apply.

Another tradition is that of intuitionism, which regards the objects and sentences of mathematics as representing constructions, that is, the construction of an individual or the claim that a proof of a sentence can be constructed, coupled with guidance on how they should be implemented (Troelstra and van Dalen 1988). An alternative reading is that objects and sentences represent promises by the utterer that such constructions have been or will be made (Heyting 1956). Thus according to this perspective, mathematical objects are constructions. Going beyond this position Machover (1983) and Davis (1974) argue that the objects of mathematics are reifications—reified constructions, as the former puts it. This explanation is intended not only to account for the genesis of mathematical concepts, but also to account for the nature of mathematical objects and the truth conditions associated with their properties, that is, to function as an ontological and epistemological account.

Rotman's (1993) semiotic theory of mathematics also interprets mathematical inscriptions as recipes, instructions, or claims about the outcomes of procedures. This is based on Peirce's ideas and those of modern semiotics, and also arises from a linguistic analysis of mathematical texts.

The Autonomy of the Objects of Mathematics

Moving from a realist to a social constructivist account of the objects of mathematics brings with it certain problems. For all their weaknesses, Platonism and realism in mathematics offer an account of an autonomous realm of mathematical objects. Objects found there (projected there by the imagination, according to social constructivism) have apparent—but nonetheless convincing—stability, "solidity," autonomy.

The claim that I am making in this section is that the objects of mathematics, as well as the theorems and other expressions of mathematical knowledge, are cultural constructions. In terms of their genesis these represent the reification of more primitive operations, but they are no less convincing for that. Like many other cultural artifacts such as moral rules and taboos, money and the value attached to objects and work, Shakespeare's plays, Beethoven's symphonies, the gods and saints of organized religions, and Bugatti cars, they appear to have an essential "inner nature" which is inevitable and necessary and transcends the contingent. Furthermore, each in this more-or-less arbitrary list of cultural objects is woven into multiple layers of networks of social usage, expectation, and necessity which provides stability and "solidity" buttressing their autonomy. Such ramifications and bonds, being those of logical necessity, are even stronger in the case of the objects of mathematics, where, in addition, shifts in the material basis of the objects can be perceived as irrelevant.

Overall, the claim is that the ontology of mathematics is given by the discursive realm of mathematics, which is populated by cultural objects, which have real existence in that domain, just as money does in the domain of human economic affairs. In a remark judged influential by others in the field (Wright 1980; Shanker 1987), Kreisel (1965) has claimed that the key issue is not so much the existence of mathematical objects so much as the objectivity of mathematical knowledge that is at stake. This objectivity is clear (under the reinterpretation of objectivity as cultural and social *à la* Bloor 1983 and Harding 1986). My claim is that mathematical discourse as a living, cultural entity creates the ontology of mathematics.

Within the philosophy of mathematics and philosophical logic there is also a widespread if technically formulated view that discourses entail, and perhaps even create, the universes of objects they refer to. In particular, a mathematical theory or discourse brings with it a commitment to the objective existence of a set of entities. Quine (1953c) identifies bound individual variables within an informal or formal mathematical theory as giving the clearest indications of its ontological commitments.

Model theory is the branch of mathematics (or mathematical logic) concerning the interpretation of formal mathematical theories within the domain of mathematics itself. It is glossed in terms of mathematical realism and the correspondence theory of truth by Tarski (1936) and others. However, from a social constructivist perspective, the provision of formal interpretations of mathematics within itself serves to illustrate the mutual constitution of signifier and signified in mathematics, and how mathematical discourse, if not actually self-referential, constitutes a closed system. This account finds support from some technical developments within mathematics itself. For example, Henkin ([1949] 1969a, [1950] 1969b) derived completeness proofs for the first-order predicate calculus and the theory of types in which he constructs models of the language in terms of *the objects of the language themselves*. Thus he makes the objects of the language serve a dual role, as both linguistic entities (signifiers) and as the objects (self-)signified. In this case, the signifiers not only create the signified but are one and the same—but viewed from different perspectives.[25]

NOTES

1. This definition foregrounds the pattern of communicative interactions, and rests on a number of background assumptions, including the following. Conversations take place between human beings who share:

1. a common language;
2. some forms of life, which give lived meaning to shared language and language games;
3. a view of each other as cognising moral beings, at least some mutual respect and concern, and a mutual acknowledgment of each other in at least partially equal roles in the conversation;
4. an ability to attend to others and a willingness to subserve strictly personal interests in the interest of the conversation.

Thus, according to this account, there are irreducible moral aspects to conversation. This is also recognised by Habermas, in his "discourse ethics." It is also present in the work of Gergen, Harré, and Shotter.

2. In recent times Bateson, Hofstadter, and others have also used dialogues philosophically.

3. There are also different styles of philosophical conversation, and Moulton (1983) contrasts the aggressive adversary method, designed to defeat opponents in the eyes of others, and the Socratic *elenchus*, intended to persuade an opponent of the weakness of their own position. This is discussed further in chapter 8.

4. The "speech act" theory of sentence meaning of Austin, Grice, Searle, and others according to which the meaning of a sentence depends on the intention and context of utterance also presupposes conversation as the underlying frame. This is unsurprising since it developed from Wittgenstein's later philosophy.

5. A compound sentence or proof can of course contain a subordinate sentence or proof, respectively, as a proper part, although an atomic sentence and a primitive proof may contain no such parts. Subordinate sentences and proofs do not, however, have the same content (i.e., sentential meaning or deductive warrant, respectively) as their superordinate sentence or proof.

6. If the "proof" is uttered by one voice, the antiphonal "refutation" is uttered by another. Traditionally, this back-and-forth dialogical flow is broken, and the "proof" draws nourishment from the "refutation" until the former grows stronger and the latter can be discarded as an empty shell. This leaves one voice, one pronouncement. This metaphor is implicit in the quotation from Lakatos (1961, 25) given in chapter 4, which also indicates that the resultant monological proof represents only one complete cycle of the dialectic, and in all liklihood the dialectic continues.

7. The elaboration of this perspective constitutes the author's next project and will be treated in a future book tentatively entitled *The Semiotics of Mathematics*.

8. Writing of Socrates as an orator and Sophist who used logic as one of his most powerful rhetorical devices, Ferguson (1970, 13) quotes the witticism of the columnist pen-named Beachcomber: "Logic is an unfair means sometimes used to win an argument."

9. Some proofs might use the pronoun *we* in phrases such as "we see that . . ." to indicate that the arbitrary reader is assumed to agree with the author. Such usage does not essentially involve the identity of the reader or writer.

10. The emphasis on the latter is a characteristic of the individualistic ideology of scientific invention that prevails (see, e.g., McBride 1994).

11. The impact of this dimension is sometimes minimized by the practice of "blind refereeing."

12. The terms *subjective* and *subjectivity* are used here to foreground the texture of a person's lived experience, not to background objectivity or to suggest whimsicality.

13. Also relevant here is a technical result in proof theory, the Craig interpolation lemma (Craig 1957; Smullyan 1968). According to this result, for each step in a proof of the form A implies B, say, there is always an interpolation formula X, which includes the mathematical concepts occurring in both A and B, such that A implies X and X implies B. In other words, no step from A to B in a proof is above further analysis, and there are no ultimate basic proof steps into which a published mathematical theorem can be analyzed.

14. Just as the justifications for mathematical claims are not usually fully explicit mathematical proofs.

15. Not all signifieds of mathematics are claimed to be textual, as Piaget (1972) shows. At the basic level, some mathematical terms denote or are abstracted from actions and operations.

16. Actually, what matters here is not that the twos are drawn differently, but that they are different and hence nonidentical instances of the numeral. By using different styles (or typefaces, as here) I am inserting an additional many-one relation; namely, that there are different types for the same signifier.

17. Signifiers as often treated as part of World 1 through the elision of signifier tokens and types. For most purposes, this causes no problems, although it is of course strictly inaccurate.

18. More generally, the reference of a mathematical formula is the truth valued function which maps the domain of interpretation of the variable letters into the set of truth values.

19. The synonymy of sentences (and predicates and formulas) arises from their sharing the same meanings and ultimately the same truth values (or truth valued functions, respectively).

20. By 'substitutivity' I mean the property of preserving identity of terms and equivalence of formulas when one term is substituted for an identical one. (If $s = t$, then $f(s) = f(t)$ and $P(s) \equiv P(t)$, where s and t are terms, f is a function with argument x and $f(s)$ represents f with s substituted for x throughout, P is a formula with free variable x, and $P(s)$ represents P with s substituted for x throughout).

21. Corfield (1995) describes the rival theories of Kronecker and Dedekind in attempting to extend the property of unique factorization to general number fields. Dedekind's ideal-theoretic approach with its field-relative prime ideals initially appeared superior. But Kronecker's divisor-theoretic approach, in which the divisors are not so relative, in the end proved more fruitful and contributed centrally to Grothendieck's program in category theory. The faithful preservation of invariant factorization properties by Kronecker seems to have been a decisive factor.

22. What I have described are equivalence transformations which would satisfy reflexivity, symmetry, and transitivity. Such operations have a group structure because the operations are reversible (and there is closure, associativity, and the identity transformation). Of course in mathematics some transformations are permitted which are not equivalence but linearly ordered transformations. Thus numerical terms can be transformed by inequality transformations, which decrease ($\geq$) or increase ($\leq$) the value of the value signified. Sentences are transformed by implication transformations, which preserve undiminished ($\leq$) the truth value signified. In each case the transformation has the structure of a weak linear ordering, namely, satisfying reflexivity, asymmetry, and transitivity. (Strict orderings are also possible for terms, in which case irreflexivity holds).

23. This can be illustrated with the elementary number-theoretic notions of divisor and prime. n is a divisor of m if, and only if, there is a number which multiplied by n gives m: $ndivm =_{def} \exists x \in N(x \times n = m)$. p is a prime number if, and only if, its only divisors are 1 and p itself: $Primep =_{def} \forall n \in N(ndivp \rightarrow n = p \vee n = 1)$.

24. Strictly speaking, if the set of sentences has infinite cardinality c, then it has models of every cardinality $\geq c$.

25. Technically, the interpretation of an individual term t is the equivalence class made up of terms provably equal to t, i.e., the set of terms s in the given language such that the formula $s = t$ is derivable from the axioms of the system. This device is the formal means of dealing with the informal problems of many-one mappings in signifier-signified relations discussed above.

CHAPTER 7

THE SOCIAL CONSTRUCTION
OF SUBJECTIVE KNOWLEDGE

CONVERSATION AND LANGUAGE IN LEARNING MATHEMATICS

In chapter 6 it was claimed that conversation underpins mathematical knowledge in its public objective forms. In this chapter the argument is extended to individual thought and subjective knowledge of mathematics.

Conversation in the Formation of Mind

The idea that thought is a form of internalized speech goes back at least to Plato, as the following extract from the *Theatatus* shows:

SOCRATES: I wonder if your description of the thought process agrees with mine?
THEATATUS: How do you describe it?
SOCRATES: As a discourse that the mind carries on with itself about any subject it has under consideration . . . I have an idea that when the mind is thinking, it is simply conversing with itself, asking and answering questions, and affirming or denying. When it arrives at a decision (whether slowly, or by a sudden leap) when doubt is resolved and agreement reached, we call that its "judgement." I therefore describe thinking as discourse, and judgement as a statement expressed, not aloud to someone else, but in silence to oneself. (Plato 1961, 127)

Through the mouth of Socrates Plato claims that thought is a discourse—a mental dialogue—and that the judgement of an individual may be arrived at by an inner dialectical process of opposition and resolution. Of course, given Plato's theories of forms and of learning, it cannot be said that he claims that thought is *internalized* dialogue, for he might argue that the private precedes the public use.

Hobbes, however, in Leviathan suggests that thinking and understanding result from speech: *"understanding* [is] nothing else than conception caused by speech" (Hobbes [1651] 1962, 80). More recently Peirce wrote ([1868] 1931–58, 265), "We have no power of thinking without signs."

In modern times, one of the first to develop a social linguistic theory of thought and mind is Mead ([1913] 1964, 146), who says, "The mechanism of thought . . . is but an inner conversation." Mead argues that "We import the conversation of the group into our inner sessions, and debate with ourselves" (Mead 1964b, 358). Thus "Thinking is the process of conversation with one's self when the individual takes the attitude of the whole group" (Mead 1964a, 34). Mead terms the imagined self with which one converses the "generalized other." "The generalized other is the internalized audience with which the thinker converses" (Mills 1963, 60) Mead's theory of mind is thus complex and multiple. He distinguishes the agentic, present 'I' from the 'me', which includes the past of the 'I', its social context, and thus the generalized other.

A little later, independently, Vygotsky developed a parallel view of thought as internalized speech.

> Language arises initially as a means of communication between the child and the people in his environment. Only subsequently, upon conversion to internal speech, does it become an internal mental function . . . reasoning occurs in a children's group as an argument intended to prove one's own point of view before it occurs as an internal activity. (Vygotsky 1978, 89–90)

Vygotsky offers a theory of the primary mediating factor shared by both thought and language. "The conception of word meaning as a unit of both generalizing thought and social interchange is of incalculable value for the study of thought and language" (Vygotsky 1978, 9). Based on this essentially semiotic position, he makes "the claim that human action, on both the social and individual planes, is mediated by tools and signs" (Wertsch 1991, 19).

Vygotsky also offers a theory of the genesis of higher level thought from language use. He distinguishes between spontaneous, intuitive concepts that the child first develops and the subsequent higher level or scientific concepts acquired through language. The acquisition of the latter through participation in speech brings together and radically transforms these two tributaries of the child's functioning, leading to thinking which is qualitatively different from earlier mentation.

> The history of the process of the *internalization of social speech* is also the history of the socialization of children's practical intellect. (Vygotsky 1978, 27)

Every function in the child's cultural development appears twice, on two levels. First, on the social and later on the psychological level; first between people as an interpsychological category, and then inside the child as an intrapsychological category. This applies equally to voluntary attention, to logical memory and to the formation of concepts. The actual relations between human individuals underlie all the higher functions. (Vygotsky 1978, 128)

Overall, Vygotsky offers a

schema of development—first social, then egocentric, then inner speech . . . Egocentric speech emerges when the child transfers social, collaborative forms of behaviour to the sphere of inner-personal psychic functions . . . something happens, we believe, when the child starts conversing with himself as he has been doing with others. When the circumstances force him to stop and think, he is likely to think aloud. Egocentric speech, splintered off from general social speech, in time leads to inner speech, which serves both autistic and logical thinking. (Vygotsky 1986, 35)

Many scholars have and continue to elucidate and elaborate the rich and suggestive theory bequeathed to us by Vygotsky's premature death in 1934. One of the more important of these is Rom Harré, whose grand project in social philosophy is to theorize "ways of being," including social being (1979), personal being (1983), and physical being (1987). Harré explicitly asserts that "The primary human reality is persons in conversation" (Harré 1983, 58).

I take the array of persons as the primary human reality. I take the conversations in which those persons are engaged as completing the primary structure, bringing into being social and psychological reality. Conversation is to be thought of as creating a social world just as causality generates a physical one . . . By 'conversation' I mean not only speech exchanges of all kinds, but any flow of interactions brought about through the use of a public semiotic system . . . I am not suggesting that persons and their talk exist prior to social reality and engender it as an effect. People and their modes of talk are made by and for social orders, and social orders are people in conversation. I shall be arguing for a thoroughgoing reciprocity between the social and the personal . . . not only human individuals, but collectives too can have "psychological" attributes and be the locations of psychological processes. (Harré 1983, 64–65).

Harré has developed a theory of "Vygotskian space," based on two polarities of thinking or speech, as part of his theory. These two polarities consist of manifestation or display (this can be public or private) and social location (this can be collective or individual). He combines these in a Cartesian product to make four quadrants (table 7.1). The four quadrants have a cyclic relationship in the development (and location) of mind, following the order of their labels, which also defines the cycle of the "appropriation and testing of knowledge" (Harré 1983, 46). He uses the terms *Appropriation, Transformation, Publication,* and *Conventionalisation* to describe the successive passage of thought and knowledge (and even the construction of personal identity) from one quadrant to the next, beginning with Q_1.

The person (presumably a child) first meets language in Quadrant 1, in the form of a public manifestation which is located in the collective, not in any individual. Thus the child participates in a shared, collective linguistic activity. In appropriating collective language, the child uses speech in an egocentric way (speaking to herself as if she were an "other" in a conversation) in Quadrant 2. This is a private manifestation, but it still employs a collectively located form of language.[1] The person "internalizes" (and personalizes and individualizes) the speech in the form of thought in Quadrant 3, and this is a private manifestation, located in the individual. It involves the transformation of the collective speech or thought into something individual and personal. Next the person may make a personal public statement in Quadrant 4 (publication). This is a public manifestation located individually, for the linguistic form used is the personalized construction of the individual. The acceptance of this statement or personal innovation as part of a shared conversation or collective performance which belongs to the group of speakers returns the utterance to Quadrant 1, as a public manifestation located (and owned) collectively. Harré terms this "Conventionalisation." The cycle has thus completed one full revolution.

To quote Harré:

according to the constructionist viewpoint, "development" must occur through the transfer of rules and conventions that govern public conversation and other social practices from Quadrant 1, via Quadrant 2, to

TABLE 7.1
HARRÉ'S MODEL OF 'VYGOTSKIAN SPACE'

	Social Location	
Manifestation	Individual	Collective
Public	Public & Individual Q_4	Public & Collective Q_1
Private	Private & Individual Q_3	Private & Collective Q_2

Quadrant 3 . . . The first step is the privatization of language of the local social group. But in fact, "the Vygotskian space" allows us to think of the mind of another person as spread out over all four quadrants. (Harré, quoted in Shotter 1991b, 211)

The successive passage of thought and knowledge from one quadrant to the next, beginning with Q_1, describes the development of speech and thinking, the project of developing a personal identity as well as the cycle of knowledge creation. I draw the parallel with this last aspect in elaborating the social constructivist account of mathematical knowledge below. Overall, Harré offers a well-developed social theory of mind, building on the seminal insights of Vygotsky (and Mead) and drawing upon the central metaphor of "persons in conversation."

Key elements and concepts in this account are employed by other theorists working in parallel but distinct traditions. Thus Ricoeur also uses the notion of "appropriation" to denote a relationship with text which results in an enhanced and enlarged self.

The theory of appropriation . . . follows from the displacement undergone by the whole problematic of interpretation . . . To understand is not to project oneself into the text; it is to receive an enlarged self from the apprehension of proposed worlds. (Ricoeur 1981, 182)

For Ricoeur and Hermeneutics it is clear that this appropriation results from the conversational "dialectic of question and answer in the hermeneutical experience" (Palmer 1969, 233).

Berger and Luckmann, in describing the "social construction of reality" offer a model almost identical to that of Harré and Vygotsky, but based on the sociological tradition.

. . . society is understood in terms of an ongoing dialectical process composed of the three moments of externalization, objectivation and internalization. As far as the societal phenomenon is concerned, these moments are *not* to be thought of as occurring in a temporal sequence . . . In the life of every individual, therefore, there *is* a temporal sequence, in the course of which he is inducted into the societal dialectic. The beginning point of this process is internalization . . . (Berger and Luckmann 1967, 149)

Again, the dialectical process described here is fundamentally dialogical or conversational.

To put these developments in perspective, it can be said that the adoption of a social view of mind is a widespread phenomenon, although it goes against the grain of the dualist Cartesian view of mind in traditional Anglo-American philosophy and psychology. Thus a number of authors in different disciplines propose more or less well developed social theories of mind, including Soviet activity theorists (Davydov, Gal'perin, Leont'ev, Luria, Vygotsky), symbolic interactionists and ethnomethodologists (Blumer, Garfinkel, Goffman, Mead), social constructionists in social psychology (Coulter, Gergen, Harré, Secord, Shotter), sociologists (Collins, Goffman, Mills, Restivo, Schütz), sociolinguistic theorists (Bakhtin, Halliday, Sapir, Volosinov, Whorf), situated cognitionists (Cole, Lave, Rogoff, Wenger), post-structuralists (Foucault, Henriques et al., Lacan, Walkerdine), postmodernists (Culler, Derrida, Lyotard, Rorty), and last but not least late-Wittgensteinian philosophers, preeminently Wittgenstein himself.

What these and other thinkers agree upon is that persons and their minds are uniquely shaped, right from the moment of birth, by their conversations and social interactions with other persons. In the years that follow, children participate in social interactions with their caregivers and others and consequently learn to participate in a growing range of different social contexts or forms of life. As a central part of this they learn to use language and to understand and use other forms of communication, such as gestures, facial expressions, body movements, diagrams, etc. In short, they participate in a growing range of language games. Most importantly, they develop a sense of self, and moral and caring relations with others, as they develop into young human beings. These early preschool experiences, certainly in industrialized countries and probably everywhere, involve some learning of early mathematical language and modes of thinking as they relate to and occur in some of the language games and forms of life in which children participate and through which they are formed.

The position I am adopting here is that socially situated conversation between persons plays a crucial role in the formation of mind. Consequently it is also a central underlying feature of the use of mind. Even the private and individual functions of mind are socially formed, although once formed they can take on a life of their own and operate a long way removed from any collective or public conversation. In this context it is worth repeating a quotation used previously:

> Thus the philosophically abstract conception of self-sufficiency of the individual mind, free and independent of others, serves to conceal its origins as a social product of rule-governed reflection. "I think therefore I am" totally obscures the social process whereby the use of the term "I" is acquired. (Doyal and Harris 1986: 86)

This directly challenges the Cartesian dualist conception of mind which it might be said ushered in the modern conception of philosophy. Instead, I have argued for a view of mind which is social because (1) individual thinking of any complexity originates with and is formed by internalized conversation, (2) all subsequent individual thinking is structured and constitutively shaped by this origin, and (3) some mental functioning is collective (e.g., group problem solving). In addition, This social view of mind rejects Cartesian dualism because mental functioning is both individual and collective, it is both private and public, and, above all, it is always materially embodied. Thus, for example, the use of manipulatives or public forms of representation which can be transformed or manipulated in public, constitutes public, embodied thought. Human thinking and doing are all of a piece, according to the social view of mind (Wertsch 1991; Restivo and Collins 1991).

Brain studies also confirm that the constitution and powers of the human cognizing subject depend heavily on the experiences and interpersonal relationships of the person during the course of development (Trevarthen 1987). Thus the human being with its time-dependent powers and constitution cannot be subsumed under an abstracted and timeless concept of Cartesian cognizing subject. A central characteristic of the social constructivist view of the person as a cognizing subject is that she has cognitive capacities and powers that change qualitatively over her course of development. With this development, the identity of the individual, Mead's "I" and "me," also change.[2]

One criticism can be immediately anticipated, namely, that the newborn baby develops an awareness of its environment through its senses prior to acquiring speech. Therefore the origins of mind are not conversational or social. In fact babies engage in preverbal dialogical interaction with persons around them and are genetically adapted to attend to humans, especially the human face, long before they acquire speech. The social knowledge acquired in this way becomes interwoven with babies' models of the world based on sensory perception. Nevertheless, babies undoubtedly do develop a sensory based awareness before acquiring speech and developing a social mind.[3] This is a necessary prerequisite for awareness of other persons (as well as the environment). However once they acquire language and speech their thought is transformed and restructured. Thus a new type of thinking—and even a new type of mind—is formed through conversation. So it is correct to say that consciousness precedes verbal conversation. But once they become users of language the thoughts and minds of children are shaped in an irrevocably transformed and different way and become socialized minds (Sapir 1949; Whorf 1956).

Of course the position I have adopted here is controversial, and "there is currently a dispute over both whether mind is located in the head or in the individual-in-social-action, and whether mathematical learning is primarily a process of active cognitive reorganization or a process of enculturation into a community of practice" (Cobb 1994, 13). Clearly I am emphasizing the second of each of these two alternatives here.

The Basis of Language in Mathematics

The acquisition of language involves participation in conversation, that is, the exchange of utterances with other individuals in shared activities with common purposes located in a social and physical context. Such interaction provides encounters with and immersion in rule governed and purposive linguistic behavior. It represents the confrontation with, and accommodation to, collective features of language, in the context of shared activities. The acquisition of linguistic competence results from a prolonged period of social interaction and conversation, situated in such shared forms of life. During this period of acquisition, which of course never ends, individuals learn to use language in accordance with the rules and conventions of collective language use, in the communities and forms of life in which they participate. Quine refers to the 'objective pull', which brings about adequate levels of agreement between individuals' utterances and behavior: "Society, acting solely on overt manifestations, has been able to train the individual to say the socially proper thing in response even to socially undetectable stimulations" (1960, 5–6).

Halliday (1978) describes linguistic competency in terms of the mastery of three interlocking systems, namely, the forms, meanings, and (social) functions of language. Language forms, functions, and meanings-in-use are publicly manifested systems and thus lend themselves to correction and agreement. Individuals develop their social and linguistic functioning in all the contexts in which they operate and live (including schooling and mathematics) through their experience of, and interaction with, the physical and social worlds, in both the physical-action and speech modes. The shaping effect of experience, to use Quine's metaphor, must not be underestimated: this is where the full impact of human culture occurs and where the rules and conventions of language use are internalized and reconstructed by individuals, with the extensive functional outcomes manifested around us in human society.

The preexisting norms, rules, and conventions of linguistic behavior that every speaker meets, in some form, when entering into a linguistic community are part of a preexisting form of life, the enacted rules of linguistic behavior shared by speakers with shared tasks and purposes. Indeed, these regularities and constancies exist only through their repeated concrete manifestations in conversation. It is the existence of such regularities which permits the possibility of a mesh between speakers and listeners. Such a mesh depends on the extent to which the actors are drawn from communities which share the same collective speech forms, patterns, and norms arising from conversation woven around shared activities and purposes.

A consequence of this view that symbolic and linguistic meanings reside in the social contexts of use is the denial that there are meanings inherent in books or written mathematical proofs. Such meanings are attributed by communities, by cultures; they are social constructions. In other words, there is no meaning that can be located exclusively in books and proofs. Such meanings are a function of the social contexts in which texts are used and purposes for which they are used. Thus, although the meaning of a text remains, in the sense of Derrida, "infinitely open," certain specific attributions of meaning are presupposed and privileged by particular cultural groups, such as mathematicians. What this underlying "infinite openness" does do however, even when concealed by a conventional reading, is to perpetually maintain the possibility of change in the interpretation of texts, as the community's language games and forms of life change.

Consider the elementary example of mathematical text $2 + 2 = 4$. In elementary school contexts, this signifies an achievement, the endpoint of a procedure "when 2 is added to 2 the answer is 4." Research shows that for many young learners "=" has the asymmetric meaning of "becomes" (Kieren 1992). In many other contexts, $2 + 2 = 4$ signifies an axiomatic truth, one that is so basic that it stands for the unchallengeable certainty of mathematics (Restivo 1984). In this book and Ernest 1991,[4] as well as in Nagel 1956, an equivalent fact $(1 + 1 = 2)$ stands for a theorem, a derived piece of knowledge whose underpinning assumptions and chains of derivation are exhibited. Restivo 1984, 1993; Davis 1972; and Davis and Hersh 1980 show many more contexts and meanings for these facts, both in and out of mathematics, thus illustrating how the meaning is a function of social context and use. Needless to say, many individuals participate in several of these contexts and elicit the appropriate meaning(s) according to the context in which they are operating.

In this account, I have looked ahead of the development of the acquisition of linguistic and mathematical competencies, including written text-related competencies, to consider the range of contexts in which such competencies are acquired and deployed (often simultaneously). Vygotsky offers a theoretical account of how such competencies develop in the child's interactions with others, beginning with socially situated conversation.

Vygotsky's theory of the development of semiotic functioning in the child starts with spoken language. This is followed by the gesture. "The gesture is the initial visual sign that contains the child's future writing as an acorn contains the future oak. Gestures . . . are writing in air, and written signs frequently are simply gestures that have been fixed" Vygotsky (1978: 107). "The second realm that links gestures and written language is children's games. For children some objects can readily denote others, replacing them and becoming signs for them, and the degree of similarity between the plaything and the object it denotes is unimportant" Vygotsky (1978, 108). This is a very important dimension that I return to below. The third contribution is from the realm

of children's drawing: "make-believe play, drawing, and writing can be
viewed as different moments in an essentially unified process of development
of written language" (116).

> written language . . . is a particular system of symbols and signs that
> whose mastery heralds a critical turning point in the entire cultural
> development of the child. A feature of this system is that it is second-
> order symbolism, which gradually becomes direct symbolism. This
> means that written language consists of a system of signs that designate
> the sounds and words of spoken language, which, in turn, are signs for
> real entities and relations. Gradually this intermediate link, spoken lan-
> guage, disappears and written language is converted into a system of
> signs that directly symbolize the entities and relations between them . . .
> The developmental history of written language, however, . . . does not
> follow a single direct line in which something like a clear continuity of
> forms is maintained. Instead it offers the most unexpected metamor-
> phoses, that is, transformations of particular forms of written language
> into others . . . it is as much involution as evolution. This means that
> together with processes of development, forward motion, and appear-
> ance of new forms, we can discern processes of curtailment, disappear-
> ance and reverse development of old forms at each step. (Vygotsky
> 1978, 106)

There is one vital aspect of Vygotsky's theory that, although mentioned above,
needs to be considered at greater length. This is his of theory of play and its
importance in the social and individual construction of multiple realities or
meanings, and in the development of semiotic functioning.

First of all, he argues "that in play a child creates an imaginary situation . . . [But] play involving an imaginary situation is, in fact, rule-based play.
One could go even further and propose that there is no such thing as play
without rules. The imaginary situation of any form of play already contains
rules of behaviour, although it may not be a formulated game with rules laid
down in advance" Vygotsky (1978, 93–94). It is clear that Vygotsky is
describing the development of something like language games in certain early
shared forms of life. Certainly the features of rules and play are central to
Wittgenstein's notion, and both are socially situated. Vygotsky goes on to
describe the change in the nature of children's games over their course of
development: "The development from games with an overt imaginary situation and covert rules to games with overt rules and a covert imaginary situation outlines the evolution of children's play" (96).

In describing this development Vygotsky encompasses both the ontoge-
netic development of games in individuals and the phylogenetic development

for humanity as a whole. Before continuing, it is worth remarking that the same pattern holds true for the development of mathematics. This begins, both ontogenetically and phylogenetically, as ways of operating in an overt concretely given situation (e.g., counting pebbles or sheep) constrained by contextually determined but implicit rules (e.g., each concrete pebble or sheep constitutes an instance of the counting act or unit). Later mathematics such as algebra has overt rules of symbolic manipulation but, because it is abstracted, refers only to a covert imaginary situation.

However, Vygotsky has much more to say about the role and importance of play in the development of thought.

> The influence of play on a child's development is enormous. Play in an imaginary situation . . . is a novel form of behaviour liberating the child from constraints . . . Since a situation is communicated psychologically through perception, and since perception is not separated from motivational and motor activity, it is understandable that with her consciousness so structured, the child is constrained by the situation in which she finds herself. But in play, things lose their determining force. *The child sees the thing but acts differently in relation to what he sees. Thus a condition is reached in which the child begins to act independently of what he sees* . . . Action in an imaginary situation teaches the child to guide her behaviour not only by perception of objects or by the situation immediately affecting her, but also by the meaning of the situation . . . A divergence between the fields of meaning and vision first occurs at preschool age. In play thought is separated from objects and action arises from ideas rather than from things: a piece of wood begins to be a doll and a stick becomes a horse . . . [T]his is such a reversal of the child's relation to the real, immediate, concrete situation that it hard to underestimate its full significance . . . [T]he structure of human perception could be figuratively expressed as a ratio in which the object is the numerator and the meaning is the denominator (object/meaning) . . . For the child the object dominates in the object/meaning ratio and meaning is subordinated to it. At the crucial moment when the stick becomes the pivot for detaching the meaning of the horse from a real horse, this ratio is inverted and meaning predominates, giving meaning/object . . . The child at play operates with meanings detached from their usual objects and actions . . . The creation of an imaginary situation is not a fortuitous fact in a child's life, but is rather the first manifestation of the child's emancipation from situational constraints . . . Play continually creates demands on the child to act against immediate impulse . . . Thus the essential attribute of play is a rule that has become a desire . . . In short *play gives a child a new form of desires*. It teaches her to desire by relat-

ing her desires to a fictitious "I," to her role in the game and its rules. In this way a child's greatest achievements are possible in play, achievements that tomorrow will become her basic level of real action and morality . . . Now we can say the same about the child's activity that we said about objects . . . Whereas action dominates early in development [action/meaning], this structure is inverted; meaning becomes the numerator while action takes the place of the denominator . . . While action begins as the numerator of the action/meaning structure, now the structure is inverted and meaning becomes the numerator . . . The separation of meaning from objects and actions has different consequences, however. Just as operation with the meaning of *things* leads to abstract thought, we find that the development of will, the ability to make conscious choices, occurs when the child operates with the meaning of *actions*. (Vygotsky 1978, 96–101)

In this excerpt, Vygotsky introduces and develops a number of important ideas. It is through play that children learn to be able to construct multiple interpretations of social situations beyond what is presented by perception. In other words, perceptions of social situations are mediated by a greatly enhanced power of interpretation that can call up different "realities." It is only when this level of operating is achieved that the rich cultural overlay and meaning of social situations can be brought into play by participants in language games and forms of life. Play occupies a special place in which meanings are imposed on objects and actions, rather than vice versa, in the development of semiotic functioning. Through play the basic semiotic fraction of signifier/signified begins to become a powerful factor in the social (and hence personal) construction of meaning. Symbols (e.g., the stick that stands for a horse) become a semiotic means for creating and then calling up alternative "play realities" (i.e., the meanings and overall imaginary situation of games), thus providing the mediating factor for accessing (as well as constructing) multiple individual and social realities. Rules also occupy a special place in the interpretation of construction of "realities" and enable a rich overlay of meanings to be associated with social contexts. Play, through roles, also provides the platform for the development of multiple, context-related, personal identities (paralleling Mead and anticipating modern social constructionists and poststructuralists such as Foucault). The construction of the interpretation of social contexts is driven by motives and goals, and desires are displaced onto signs and rules (paralleling Freud and Lacan) through play. The processes described in the separation of meaning from objects and actions leads to abstract symbolic thought and to the ability to make conscious choices and plans for action. Bearing all these areas of significance in mind, as Vygotsky indicates, it would be hard to overestimate the full significance of play in the development of human thought, semiotic functioning, and the construction and interpretation of multiple realities.

It is worth anticipating and noting in this account two aspects of the child's thought beginning to develop, aspects that are central to later mathematical knowledge and functioning. The first is participation in and voluntary submission to rule-governed symbolic contexts. The second is the ability to form and enter into imaginary realms of meaning. These are two interrelated underlying and necessary modes of knowing in mathematics.

The theme of play and the construction of alternative realities is further developed by Winnicott (1971, 47), who describes play as occurring in the space between "external or shared reality and the true dream." Winnicott thus echoes and extends Vygotsky's insight that play together with signification allows the creation of multiple individual and social realities, beyond those given immediately by perception. Winnicott argues that the "transitional" zone of play is or "becomes the source of all experienceable novelty and cultural creativity" (Rotman 1993, 145). Rotman goes on to argue that this is the source of the mathematical imagination, the individual realm of mathematical thought and intuition constituted by and underpinning signifying practices. In the next section I shall link such facilities with the "mathematical reality" that mathematicians inhabit and experience.

The Role of Intuition and Subjectivity in Mathematics

One important feature that an adequate philosophical account of mathematics should offer is describing mathematics in such a way that it accounts for the subjectivity of mathematicians. In other words, the account should be able to accommodate what it feels like to be a mathematician, working in a world of mathematical objects and constructing new mathematical knowledge and proofs. Therefore, given the above account of mathematical objects as cultural fictions, how can they feel or be experienced as so real?

As described above, the psychologists Vygotsky and Winnicott look to children's play as a key factor in the construction of alternative realities and in social and cultural realities. Winnicott (1971, 47) describes play as occurring in the potential space between persons, the arena of cultural reality.

(a) To get the idea of playing it is helpful to think of the *preoccupation* that characterizes the playing of a young child. The content does not matter. What matters is the near withdrawal state, akin to the *concentration* of older children or adults. The playing child inhabits an area that cannot be easily left, nor can it easily admit intrusions.
(b) This area of playing is not inner psychic reality. It is outside the individual, but it is not the external world.

(c) Into this play area the child gathers objects or phenomena from external reality and uses these in the service of some sample derived from inner or personal reality. Without hallucinating, the child puts out a sample of dream potential and lives with this sample in a chosen setting of fragments from external reality.

(d) In playing, the child manipulates external phenomena in the service of the dream and invests chosen external phenomena with dream meaning and feeling.

(e) There is a direct development from transitional phenomena to playing, and from playing to shared playing, and from this to cultural experiences . . .

(i) Playing is essentially satisfying. This is true even when it leads to a high degree of anxiety. (Winnicott 1971, 60–61)

Winnicott thus stresses the need for signification in play and argues that this is a means not only of constructing highly motivated personal realities, but also of entering cultural traditions.

> I have used the term cultural experience as an extension of the idea of transitional phenomena and of play . . . In using the word culture I am thinking of the inherited tradition. I am thinking of something that is in the common pool of humanity, into which individuals and groups of people may contribute, and from which we may all draw *if we have somewhere to put what we find.* There is a dependence here on some kind of recording method . . . in any cultural field *it is not possible to be original except on a basis of tradition* . . . The interplay between originality and the acceptance of tradition [is] the basis for inventiveness. (Winnicott 1971, 116–17, original emphasis)

Thus playing, according to both Winnicott and Vygotsky, is originally something that children do, but that forms the basis of adult cultural life and the creation of cultural realities. These experienced realities, I want to claim, include the discursive cultural worlds of mathematics inhabited by mathematical objects. Schooled by immersion in a tradition, mathematicians find themselves inhabiting or at least accessing these worlds. A number of theorists including Rotman (1993) and Maher (1994) have argued that the potential or cultural space is not only the source of the mathematical imagination constituted by and underpinning signifying practices, but also the source of mathematical reality (and creativity).[5]

The social constructivist account of the objects of mathematics is thus a combination of the above accounts of (1) mathematical imagination and intuition which emerges from the human capability to construct (in stages) and hence to recall or retrieve imagined worlds (i.e., mathematics-worlds of the imagination) and (2) human cultural, discursive signifying practices, which, having been individually appropriated, provide the resources for (1).

The individual mathematician's experience of doing mathematics is not just that of being immersed in such a mathematics-world of the imagination. It is of doing, that is, of carrying out imagined or notated transformations of imagined objects or signs. Many such transformations (of images, concepts or text) are tentative, tried out in the pursuit of some goal (proving a conjecture, carrying out a calculation, finding a particular function, etc.). These are self-initiated transformations. In addition, there are transformations of imagery brought about by reading a text or a proof, following a presentation, and so forth. In each case, transformations of signs and images are involved.

The case I wish to make is that mathematicians are inducted into a discourse and practice in which a number of elements converge. First of all, they have devoted many years to completing mathematical exercises and problems by carrying out textual and conceptual transformations. Many of these involve equivalence relations, and the outcome is a sense of the solidity of the underlying (mathematical) objects. Second, but related to this, is the tendency in language and culture to reify constructions into self-subsistent entities. Mathematical knowledge constructions thus become the objects of mathematics. Third, the language games of mathematics are particularly rich with rules and constraints, and indeed mathematics can be regarded as the study of abstract rules. These rules and constraints become reified into logical necessity and the fixed constraints of mathematical reasoning. Fourth, the discourse of research mathematics is one which presupposes the rich and multifarious ontology of mathematics. These factors combine with the psychological mechanisms described above so that mathematicians progressively appropriate and develop their own world of mathematical objects, which they experience as tangible and rule governed, until they are full participants in the cultural realm of mathematical objects. The paradoxical outcome is that the realm of mathematical objects and the rules that constrain them are appropriated and personally reconstructed by the individual mathematician gradually until they seem real, ever-present, and eternal.

Conversation in the Learning of Mathematics

Mathematics, like any other area of knowledge, is learned through individuals (learners) participating in language games embedded in forms of life. Personal knowledge of language, mathematics, and logic are all "acquired" through prolonged participation in many socially situated conversations in different contexts with different persons. Initially, as I have suggested, the forms of life will be domestic and out of school. These provide a central set of resources which young persons draw upon when they enter into the novel and formalized settings for learning in schools and other educational institutions. Schools, of course, represent only one cluster of contexts and social practices into which young learners enter and participate, and they continue to learn over their whole life spans from all of the forms of life in which they participate. Nevertheless, within this motley of contexts and situations, some are planned learning situations in which the teaching of mathematics is deliberate. In the context of such intentional forms of mathematics education (in or out of formal institutional settings) individuals (paradigmatically teachers) structure mathematical conversations on the basis of their own knowledge and institutionally sanctioned texts, in order to offer mathematical experiences to learners. Their aim is to teach, to develop learners' mathematical competencies, i.e., to communicate mathematical knowledge to them.

However, the public representation of collective, socially accepted mathematical knowledge within a teaching-learning conversation (including its textual variants) is necessary but not sufficient for such knowledge to become the personally appropriated mathematical knowledge of an individual learner. Sustained two-way participation in such conversations is also necessary to generate, test, correct, and validate mathematical performances, with the aim of ensuring that the learner has appropriated the collective mathematical knowledge and competencies, and not some partial or distorted version. Appropriated mathematical knowledge is potentially unique and idiosyncratic, because of human creativity in sense making (one of the deep insights of constructivist learning theory).[6] This possibility also arises because school mathematical knowledge is not something that emerges out of the shared meaning and purpose of a pregiven form of life. Instead it is a set of artificially contrived symbolic practices, a significant part of the meaning of which is not already given but deferred until the future.

The mesh of a learner's knowledge of mathematics with that of others is brought about by prolonged personal interaction and shared participation in deliberately structured forms of life. Of course the acquisition of mathematical competence by individuals and its use in socially situated performances are irrevocably interwoven. For only through utterance and performance are the individual construals or their consequences made public and confronted with alternatives, extensions, corrections, or corroboration. Continual participation in dialogue, including the various stylized and institutionalized forms employed in education, is necessary for the personal appropriation and internalization of mathematical knowledge, if it is to mesh with the utterances of others and, hence, with their knowledge. Ultimately, such interactions are what allows an individual's personal knowledge of mathematics to be regarded as an interiorization of collective knowledge.

Within educational contexts individuals with the specific social role of teacher use their personal knowledge of mathematics and mathematics education to direct and control mathematics learning conversations both (*a*) to present mathematical knowledge to learners directly or indirectly (i.e., teach) and (*b*) to participate in the dialectical process of criticism and warranting of others' mathematical knowledge claims (i.e., engage in assessment). These two functions normally overlap, although in their extreme forms, such as in expository lecturing and the marking of externally set assessments, they can be temporarily and conventionally separated. Typically, it is the latter form of interaction that serves as the basis for the warranting and certifying the mathematical knowledge of a learner, up to a specified level.[7]

The Role of Semiotic Tools and Rhetoric in Learning Mathematics

One of Vygotsky's important contributions is his insight that, in order to facilitate and further their purposes, human beings have created psychological tools analogous to the use of physical tools in the world of work.

> Psychological tools are artificial formations. By their nature, they are social, not organic or individual. They are directed towards the mastery or control of behavioral processes—someone else's or one's own—just as technical means are directed toward the control of processes of nature. The following can serve as examples of psychological tools and their complex systems: language; various systems for counting; mnemonic techniques; algebraic symbol systems; works of art; writing; schemes, diagrams, maps, and mechanical drawings; all sorts of conventional signs; etc. (Vygotsky 1979, 137)

Vygotsky's insights have been extended by a number of Soviet and other theorists (in some cases independently) including Luria, Leont'ev, Bakhtin, Volosinov, Lotman, and others.

> Texts have functional dualism, being either univocal or dialogical. The first "requires maximal semiotic ordering and structural uniformity of the media used in the process of reception and transmission." (Lotman 1988, 35)

> The second function of the text is to generate new meanings . . . the very essence of a text's function is to serve as a "thinking device." (Lotman 1988, 36–37)

Thus Lotman stresses the role of language and text both as the means of passing on orders and information and as psychological tools which serve as a thinking devices.

Vygotsky, alongside other semioticians and sociolinguists, explicitly recognizes the function of mathematical symbol systems as semiotic tools which must be socially acquired and mastered (changing the learner in the process) in any acquisition of mathematical competence and knowledge. Thus a key stage in the learning of mathematics is the acquisition of competence in its written (and figural) linguistic forms and symbolism. For collective mathematical knowledge not only is recorded and transmitted largely by means of written text, but it also uses its own specialized and abstracted codes and symbolism. The gradual appropriation and mastery of this symbolism is an activity that takes the young learner of mathematics many years.

A semiotic analysis of mathematical texts, proofs, and algorithms reveals many important rhetorical features, such as the mood or verb forms employed (indicative and imperative), the presupposed "natures" of the "speaker" (writer) and the "listener" (reader), and the genre and rhetorical style (Kitcher 1991; Rotman 1988, 1993). This has important implications not only for the nature of mathematics, but also for research on the learning of mathematics.

An analysis of the linguistic forms used and the types of mathematical activity most common in school mathematics suggest the overwhelming presence of imposed tasks in which the learner is required to carry out symbolic transformations (Ernest 1993b). During most of their mathematics learning career in school, from five to sixteen years and beyond, learners work on textual or symbolically presented teacher-set tasks. They carry these out, in the main, by writing a sequence of texts (including figures, literal and symbolic inscriptions, etc.), ultimately arriving, if successful, at a terminal text—"the answer." Sometimes this sequence consists of the elaboration of a *single* piece of text (e.g., the carrying out of three-digit column addition). Sometimes it involves a *sequence of distinct* inscriptions (e.g., the addition of two fraction names with distinct denominators, such as $1/3 + 2/7 = 1 \times 7 / 3 \times 7 + 2 \times 3 / 7 \times 3 = 7/21 + 6/21 = 13/21$); or it may combine both activities. The magnitude of such activity may be underappreciated. A reasonable supposition is that the typical British school student attempts a mean of between five and a hundred mathematical tasks per day over the course of their compulsory schooling, from five to sixteen years. This is a plausible estimate, as research on children's classroom mathematics (e.g., Bennett *et al.* 1984; Ernest 1993b) and on mathematics texts (e.g., Christiansen *et al.* 1986) show. Such a typical student will consequently attempt between ten thousand and two hundred thousand individual mathematical tasks in their statutory school career. Many of these exercises will be shown to the teacher. Naturally the student's teacher cannot respond to every item or mark each item that is attempted individually. Nevertheless, the student will doubtless experience hundreds or thousands of teacher responses in mathematics classes over the whole period. Evidently the learning conversation is very elaborate and protracted.[8] The sheer repetitive nature of this activity is underaccommodated in many current accounts of mathematics learning, where the emphasis is more often on the construction of meaning than on the acquisition and deployment of semiotic tools and, given that texts are being produced and marked, the rhetorical style of school mathematics. (Notable exceptions include Christiansen, Howson, and Otte 1986; Pimm 1987; Mellin-Olsen 1987; Morgan 1995.)

From the above discussion and evidence it is clear that tasks concerning the transformation of mathematical signs are central to school mathematics. Typically a task is a text presented by someone in authority (the teacher); it specifies a starting point, intends to elicit and utilize a set of textual transformation skills (and possibly a set of sign meanings), and indicates a goal state: where the transformation of signs is meant to lead. The types of transformations to be deployed may be determinate algorithms in the application of routine mathematical skills, or strategically and creatively combined elements of mathematical knowledge in problem solving or investigative work. In either case, from a semiotic perspective, a completed mathematical task is a sequential transformation of, say, n signs (S_k) inscribed by the learner, implicitly or explicitly derived by $n - 1$ transformations $(\Rightarrow)$.[9] This can be shown as the sequence: $S_1 \Rightarrow S_2 \Rightarrow S_3 \Rightarrow \ldots \Rightarrow S_n$. S_1 is a representation of the task as initially construed (the text as originally given, curtailed, or some other mode of representation employed by the student, such as a figure). S_n is representation of the final symbolic state, intended to satisfy the goal requirements of the task as interpreted by the learner. Viewed narrowly, without attention to the social context, such an account of school mathematics tasks fits with cognitive science approaches in mathematics education (Davis 1984; Skemp 1982; Ernest 1985, 1987a, 1987b).

Beyond an information processing view, the rhetorical requirements of the social (i.e., classroom) context determine which sign representations (S_k) and which transformational steps $(S_k \Rightarrow S_{k+1}$, for $k < n)$ are acceptable. Indeed, the rhetorical mode of representation of these transformations, together with the final goal representation, S_n, is the major focus for negotiation between learner and teacher, both during production and after the completion of the transformational sequence. In response to a learner's working of a school mathematics task, the focus of the teacher's attention (and correction) usually includes both the "answer" and the method and working exhibited as well as the mode of representing it as a text, for the object is commonly to produce a text in the appropriate form, which deploys certain textual transformations in achieving the answer. In extended, sequentially represented tasks, the learner is often expected to explicitly write out a sequence of steps and then to label the final answer as such (Ernest 1993b). Another feature noted in this reference is the disparity between the learner's carrying out of a mathematical task and representing it as a text. One of the lessons of the rhetoric of school math-ematics is that the text produced as answer to a mathematics task does not exactly match the learner's process of deriving the answer, or even the scrib-blings the learner made on paper in deriving the answer. The written text is in fact a "rational reconstruction" (Lakatos 1978d) of the derivation of the answer, and the disparity between the genetic process and the public record is usually determined by the rhetorical demands of the context. The rhetorical style demands are not arbitrary, they represent an elementary justification of the answers derived in tasks. They provide evidence for the teacher that the intended processes and concepts are being applied.

Teacher-pupil dialogue (typically asymmetric in classroom forms) usu-ally takes place at two levels: spoken and written. Spoken dialogue may be one-to-one or one-many, and it can take a number of forms, including social and task instructions, direct exposition of content, question-and-answer ses-sions, and so on. In written "dialogue" pupils submit texts (written work on set tasks) to the teacher, who responds in a stylized way to its content and form (ticks and crosses, marks awarded represented as fractions, crossings out, brief written comments, etc.). However, there are significant variations in the rhetorical demands of teachers in different contexts, indicating that they are to a large extent conventional. For example, the introduction of problem solving or investigational work in school mathematics usually involves a major shift in rhetorical style. Instead of representing only formal mathemat-ical algorithms and procedures, with no trace of the authorial subject, the text produced by the student may also describe the judgements, conjectures, and thought processes of a mathematical subject. This represents a major shift, and there are often difficulties associated with it, both from the perspective of the learner and from the perspective of the teacher (Ernest 1993a; Lerman 1989; Morgan 1995).

Drawing on a semiotic analysis of mathematics (e.g., Rotman 1988, 1993), a more detailed analysis of the textual nature of mathematics and school mathematics tasks is possible. According to the seminal analysis of Saussure, Peirce, and others, signs or sign representations can be regarded as a pair made up of signifier and signified. Each step $S_k \Rightarrow S_{k+1}$ in a school math-ematics task is a transformation of signs which can thus be understood on two levels, those of signifier and signified. So the performance of the task can be analyzed as a dual-level transformation, acting on the level of signifier or sig-nified, or on both levels. The completed task must be represented as a text, i.e., a sequence of signifiers. However the implicit justification (intended by the learner, or read by the teacher) for each step in this sequence may be at the level of signifier (explicit external use of a symbolic rule or tool of sign trans-formation) or signified (use of the properties of the signified or meaning of the sign to justify the transformation). Elsewhere more elaborated accounts of such analyses have been made (e.g., in Skemp 1982 and Ernest 1985, 1987a, 1987b, 1993b).

Of course this is a very general and simplified account and a few caveats are needed. First of all, signifieds cannot be exhibited publicly (except through other means of signification) while signifiers can be, so it must be stressed that significations overall, and signifieds in particular, vary with interpreter and context and are far from unique. An intended outcome of the educational process is to teach learners to use symbols in collectively accepted ways. Although a second intended outcome is to facilitate the appropriation of mathematical concepts and meaning-structures by learners, this can be inferred only from the former outcome.

Second, I have discussed only the structure of a successfully completed task, represented linearly as a text. This does not show the complex process of its genesis, which if represented would almost certainly be non-linear.[10] In engaging with and performing mathematical tasks (especially nonroutine tasks) the learner may pursue a number of different lines of enquiry, may be making effort and success-likelihood estimations, and might even disengage from the goals and give up the task or seek assistance from others. The learner may lack confidence and need reassurance or may not be able to make the transformations unaided (i.e., lack a tool, or not know which to apply), in order to achieve the goal. If assistance enables the learner to make the symbolic transformations, then the task lies within what Vygotsky termed the learner's zone of proximal development. Guidance helps her to extend her domain of competence so that ultimately she can undertake this challenging type of task unaided, in the given context, and complete the transformational sequence alone. None of these overlays of subtlety and complexity is indicated in the simple linear scheme.

Third, the account does not indicate that the text is a contingent product and far from unique, that different texts could be produced, and that reference is made only to the one which happens to have been constructed. Last, the levels of signifier and signified are relative; they are all the time in mutual interaction, shifting, sliding, reconstructing themselves, with signifiers changing and reemerging as signifieds or parts thereof. The instability of signs, signifiers, and signifieds is one of the insights of the poststructuralism of Foucault, Derrida, Lacan, and so on; and what constitutes a sign itself varies. For example, any teacher-set task is itself a sign, with the text as signifier and possibly its goal as signified.

This account of the role of semiotic tools and rhetoric in learning mathematics stresses the transformations of signs. Typically these are identity- and equivalence-preserving transformations that are applied to written terms and expressions. As recounted in chapter 6, the years of cumulative experience in carrying out such transformations play a major role in constructing the mathematician's mathematical ontology, for carrying out such transformations helps to develop and reinforce the idea that the mathematical objects underlying the signifier chains are invariant. Thus the seeds of the research mathematicians' Platonism are sown in the mathematics classroom.

Social Context in the Learning of Mathematics

I have recounted a tradition in the modern philosophy of science and mathematics which views knowledge as having a significant tacit and embodied element (Kuhn, Kitcher, Polanyi, Toulmin, Feyerabend). Some but not all of these philosophers also view knowledge as social, shared among members of a culture or community, as do many others[11] including Wittgenstein (1953), who argues that knowledge and meaning reside in various language games embedded in organized social forms of life. This view suggests that mathematical knowledge items (utterances or texts) differ in significance and meaning according to the context, that is, according to the language games and forms of life of which they are a part.

From the perspective of the mathematics classroom, it can be said that there are already extensive developments in the psychology of mathematics education which recognize this, including various forms of situated cognition of Lave and Wenger (1991), Saxe (1991), Solomon (1989), Walkerdine (1988), and others. Typical of these views is the notion that some parts of learners' mathematical knowledge relate to shared social activities, namely, the contexts of acquisition and use, and are not easily detached from them or transferred. In particular, such aspects of mathematical knowledge are often elicited in their contexts of origination as part of an automatic component of recognition and engagement with the specific social situations to which they relate. Research on the transfer of learning suggests that particular and tacit knowledge do not transfer well from the context of acquisition, whereas general and explicit knowledge are more susceptible to transfer (Kilpatrick 1992). Needless to say, fully social knowledge cannot be transferred to another context, unless the group moves context (if such a thing is possible) or unless the knowledge is transformed into something personal which is later recontextualized (Bernstein 1975).

The semiotic and rhetorical features of school mathematics are one aspect of its overall social constitution and context, and some more inclusive theorization of this context is necessary for any acceptable account of the learning of mathematics. There are a number of sources on which such a theorization of the social context in general, and of the mathematics classroom, in particular, can be based.

Wittgenstein's key contribution is to recognize that mathematical knowledge is based not on absolute logical compulsion, but on the acceptance of a language game's rules, which are grounded in preexisting social forms of life shared by a community. Wittgenstein thus acknowledges not only the primacy of social context, but also its multifaceted nature. He anticipates the notion that human activities fall into a set of different practices with different purposes, associated language games, resources, and participants. However Wittgenstein's approach is synchronic rather than diachronic, thus he emphasizes existing social structures and linguistic use-patterns, at the interpersonal level, but not their historical development and change (although the contingency of the rules is explicitly stressed). This missing feature is one of Foucault's great contributions, through his "archaeology of knowledge" project (Fuller 1988). He introduces the dimensions of personal positioning and power, as well as the notion that knowledge consists of vast discursive formations that are inseparable from the institutions that formed them and are always changing together. His central concept is that of a 'discursive practice', which is a social practice with an associated discursive formation or body of knowledge.

> Whenever one can describe between a number of statements, such a system of dispersion, whenever, between objects, types of statement, concepts, or thematic choices, one can define a regularity (an order, correlations, positions and functionings, transformations), we will say, for the sake of convenience, that we are dealing with a *discursive formation*—thus avoiding words that are already overladen with conditions and consequences, and in any case inadequate to the task of designating such a dispersion, such as "science," "ideology," "theory," or "domain of objectivity." The conditions to which the elements of this division (objects, mode of statement, concepts, thematic choices) are subjected we shall call the *rules of formation*. The rules of formation are conditions of existence (but also of coexistence, maintenance, modification, and disappearance) in a given discursive division. (Foucault 1972, 38)

Some of the other features of this conceptualization are the positions and functionings of persons (i.e., roles and power relations); the social circumstances and environments in which they find themselves (including material resources); the social purposes and objects; and the language, discourse, and knowledge structures involved (the objects, statement types, concepts, themes); their interrelations; and their overall conditions of formation, existence, transformation, and disappearance.

Foucault's concept of a discursive practice or discursive formation has as much to do with objective knowledge as it does with subjective knowledge, because of his view of their mutual interdependence and constitution (as is argued here for social constructivism). It is therefore of interest to examine his treatment of discursive formations and, in particular, of mathematics as a scientific discipline.

It is possible to describe several distinct emergences of a discursive formation. The moment at which a discursive practice achieves individuality and autonomy, the moment therefore at which a single system for the formation of statements is put into operation, or the moment at which the system is transformed, might be called the threshold of positivity. When in the operation of a discursive formation, a group of statements is articulated, claims to validate (even unsuccessfully) norms of verification and coherence, and when it exercises a dominant function (as a model, a critique, or a verification) over knowledge, we will say that the discursive formation crosses a threshold of epistemologization. When the epistemological figure thus outlined obeys a number of formal criteria, when its statements comply not only with archeological rules of formation, but also with certain laws for the construction of propositions, we will say that it has crossed a threshold of scientificity. And when this scientific discourse is able, in turn, to define the axioms necessary to it, the elements that it uses, the propositional structures that are legitimate to it, and the transformations that it accepts, when it is thus able, taking itself as a starting-point, to deploy the formal edifice that it constitutes, we will say that it has crossed threshold of formalization. (Foucault 1972, 186–87)

There is perhaps only one science for which one can neither distinguish these different thresholds, nor describe a similar set of shifts: mathematics, the only discursive practice to have crossed at one and the same time the thresholds of positivity, epistemologization, scientificity and formalization. The very possibility of its existence implied that which, in all other sciences, remains dispersed throughout history, should be given at the outset: its original positivity was to constitute an already formalized discursive practice (even if other formalizations were to be used later). Hence the fact that their establishment is both so enigmatic (so little accessible to analysis, so confined within the form of absolute beginning) and so valid (since it is both valid as an origin and a foundation); hence the fact that in the first gesture of the first mathematician one saw the constitution of an ideality that had been deployed throughout history, and has been questioned only to be repeated and purified; hence the fact that the beginning of mathematics is questioned not so much as a historical event as for its validity as a principal of history: and hence the fact that, for all other sciences the description of its historical genesis, its gropings and failures, its late emergence is related to the meta-historical model of a geometry emerging suddenly, once and for all, from the trivial practices of land measuring. (Foucault 1972, 188–89)

Fascinating and powerful as Foucault's overall theory is, there is no doubt that he is mistaken about mathematics. He has fallen victim to the popular myth about the origins of mathematics in Greece; according to this, it sprang fully developed, like Athene, from the head of Zeus. In fact, mathematics as a discipline or discursive formation crossed the thresholds of positivity and epistemologization in Mesopotamia, long before the ancient Greek culture came into being. Mathematics emerged as a scribal art and discursive practice, and exercised a dominant role over both knowledge and the professionalism of the scribes, over the course of the third and second millennia B.C.E. (Høyrup 1994). Something of the order of two thousand years were to pass before it crossed the threshold of formalization in the hands of Euclid. These origins, according to Høyrup, bring us back to the social context of schooling, because "the creation of mathematics in Sumer was specifically a product of that school institution which was able to create knowledge, to create the tools whereby to formulate and transmit knowledge, and to systematize knowledge" (Høyrup 1987, 45). This illustrates once again the inseparability of personal and public knowledge, of subjective and objective knowledge, and of the institutions that generate and reproduce them. Although the ideology of professional research mathematics stresses the discovery of new knowledge, that is, the production of objective knowledge as its goal, the institution of mathematics has always had a second goal, namely, teaching or the inculcation of personal knowledge. This second goal is not a mere incidental activity but, from the outset, has been the primary and originary activity of the institution of mathematics.

Having critically examined Foucault's conceptualization of the social context, it is appropriate to consider some alternatives for conceptualizing the learning of mathematics. Halliday (1978) offers a somewhat parallel semiotic analysis of the social context or situation into the mode (the symbolic organization), the field (social meaning of the situation), and the tenor (the role relationships). Where it falls short of Foucault's conceptualization is in understressing the underlying knowledge formation and the potential for historical change. However, Foucault's focus is on entire social institutions and cultural formations, rather than the concern with local (interpersonal) social contexts as in Halliday and Wittgenstein.

Another conceptualization of social practice is that of Lave and Wenger.

Briefly, a theory of social practice emphasizes the relational interdependency of agent and world, activity, meaning, cognition, learning, and knowing. It emphasizes the inherently socially negotiated character of meaning and the interested, concerned character of the thought and action of persons-in-activity. This view also claims that learning, thinking and knowing are relations among people in activity in, with, and arising from the socially and culturally structured world. This world is socially constituted; objective forms and systems of activity, on the one hand, and agents' subjective and intersubjective understandings of them, on the other, mutually constitute both the world and its experienced forms. Knowledge of the socially constituted world is socially mediated and open ended. Its meaning to given actors, its furnishings, and the relations of humans with/in it, are produced, reproduced, and changed in the course of activity (which includes speech and thought, but cannot be reduced to one or the other). In a theory of practice, cognition and communication in, and with the social world are situated in the historical development of ongoing activity. (1991, 50–51)

This account emphasizes well the mutual creation/recreation of persons and social practices, the goal-oriented nature of practices as "activities," and their historical growth and development. What it underplays is the role of discourse and knowledge, although elsewhere the authors stress the importance of semiotic tools and mediation.

Drawing on these theorists, I suggest that a theorization of social contexts needs to consider the purposes, social relations, material resources, and discourse involved, and to acknowledge its temporal shifts and reformations (i.e., the historical dimension). Consequently, the social context of the school mathematics classroom can be described as a complex, organized, and evolving social form of life (or set of forms of life) which is constituted by the following components (although they are not necessarily disjoint or exhaustive):

1. The aims and purposes of the activity or activities which take place in the social context of the classroom and for which the context is created and through which the context is given shape and direction.
2. The persons involved and their interpersonal relationships, patterns of authority, pupil-teacher roles, modes of interaction, and so forth.
3. The discourse of school mathematics and its social regulation, including:
   a. The content of school mathematics; the symbols, concepts, conventions, definitions, symbolic procedures, and linguistic presentations of mathematical knowledge
   b. Modes of communication: written, iconic and oral modes, modes of representation and rhetorical forms, including rhetorical styles for written and spoken mathematics (i.e., the rhetoric of school mathematics)

    c. The language and discourse of the social regulation of the classroom as it relates to, embodies, and communicates the underlying ideology of pupil-teacher relationships, patterns of authority, modes of interaction as in (1) above

4. The material resources of the classroom, including writing media, texts, electronic calculators, microcomputers, software, displays, learning equipment, teaching resources, furniture, an institutionalized location, space, and routinized times.[12]

First, there are the aims and purposes of classroom activities and organization, for schooling is an intentional and purposive activity. The various actors involved may have different views of these purposes, may have quite distinct purposes from each other, and indeed may not know what their aims are. Nevertheless, it is only through these purposes that the social context of the classroom is animated. The purpose of the context is the social analogue of desire in the individual mind or organism. It is what drives its activity and gives it shape and direction.[13]

The second of these components is crucial. In schooling, teachers establish a set of procedures and norms as well as their role, relationships, and interaction expectations with a class of pupils. The teachers have the power to impose much of this, and they are supported by the regulatory structures of schooling (including such procedures as school sanctions, exclusion, referral to educational psychologists, and so on). However the details of the interpersonal aspects of the social context are determined through the patterns of interactions with the pupils, as teacher expectations have their impact via actions of day-to-day life in the classroom. (As Foucault 1981 says, power is always manifested through concrete individual instances of personal interaction.)[14] The discourse of the social regulation of the classroom both provides the means by which teacher power is exercised, and carries the ideology and preconceptions on which its based.

Third, there is the discourse of school mathematics. This is manifested in the living conversations and personal interactions in the mathematics classroom, in the ritualized written interactions largely concerned with pupil work and its assessment, and in semiotic artefacts upon which schooling depends so much. As indicated above, it is possible to distinguish conceptually the content of school mathematics and the modes of communication, including the rhetoric of the school mathematics classroom. In reality, content and form are always inseparably fused. The discourse of school mathematics is the central component of the culture of school mathematics. Mastery of this discourse (or rather of a specially delimited part) is the main intended learning outcome of school mathematics. This third component also includes the discourse of the social regulation of the classroom, which again cannot ultimately be separated from the regulation of the learner within the discourse of school mathematics itself. For, typically, mathematical tasks are presented as instructions or commands.

The fourth set of components compose the material resources and conditions of schooling. These have much to do in establishing the specific features of the social context of schooling. In particular, this component contributes some of the vital semiotic artefacts that to a large extent constitute the nature of schooling. As was discussed above, collective semiotic tools must first be represented publicly before learners can appropriate and interiorize them. Some of the tools, including calculators, microcomputers, texts, manipulatives, and structured learning aids, remain collective and public throughout learners' use of them.

Many of the features I have indicated as contributing to and constituting the social context of the mathematics classroom are indications of the continuity—the regular and more or less constant features—of that context. There are relatively constant relationships between the pupils and teachers in terms of power and their respective roles. (Consequently, participating in the social practices of mathematics learning results in the construction of the mathematics learner in certain particular and contingent ways, and hence contributes to the identity of the developing person.) Likewise, the material resources, texts, furniture, institutional location, and routinized times are enduring and relatively constant. There are regular and enduring, if emerging, features of the discourse of school mathematics, including both the content of school mathematics and its rhetorical forms, as described above. Similarly, the purposes and aims of school mathematics as enacted in the classroom have or achieve a measure of stability. Already this account indicates that there is slow but steady change taking place in the social context of the mathematics classroom. Roles and power relations have to be negotiated or imposed through the discourse of the social regulation of the classroom—as do the aims and purposes of classroom activity—and thus they vary over time. The material resources change over time as artifacts become used and worn or are withdrawn, replaced or added to, and as spaces become appropriated and laden with conventions and material representations. The discourse of school mathematics deployed in day-to-day interactions is intended to develop progressively, as learners apply their growing skills and knowledge in systematically more complex and demanding tasks. Thus the social context of the classroom and its microculture evolve, develop, and gradually change, and many of its features emerge over the course of time, as detailed studies have shown (Bauersfeld 1980; Cobb 1987; Yackel 1987; Yackel, Cobb, and Wood 1991).

However, it must also be recognized that there are significant discontinuities as well as constancies in the fabric of the culture and social context of the classroom. Every pupil during the course of her schooling will experience several such ruptures. Three main types of discontinuity are worth singling out. First, the change from school to school. At the very least, in Britain and, indeed, in most of the world pupils will attend a primary or elementary school in their preteenage years and a secondary or high school afterwards. As is well known, the culture and most aspects of the social organization and relationships in these types of school are very different, in each of the dimensions discussed above. Likewise, the transition from secondary to tertiary education in mathematics involves a major discontinuity in culture (Bibby 1985).

Second, as pupils progress from year to year they frequently change teacher and classroom. Consequently major components of the social context of the classroom are modified in these transitions. Each new set of conditions, such as a new teacher and classroom, will construct a different culture and social context in the classroom. Over the course of her learning career a typical pupil in a developed country can expect to have many different teachers, dozens, in fact, including perhaps ten different mathematics teachers.

Third, as pupils progress through schooling another break will occur. There is commonly a shift from one-class teacher teaching all school subjects, including mathematics, to ten or more specialist teachers teaching different subjects, including specialist mathematics teaching. Thus there is a more pronounced division between school subjects, in which not only the discourse of the subject alters, but also the teacher (and usually the location too) changes in the shift from subject to subject. Later on, in the middle to late teenage years, in further education or preparation for higher education, this specialization often goes further. At this point, the different branches of mathematics, such as pure and applied mathematics and statistics, are commonly taught by different teachers.

Thus throughout their schooling, learners are not only making sense of, accommodating, and recreating through their participation the social and cultural contexts of school mathematics. They are also having to adjust to quite different cultures and social contexts under the same label of "mathematics." To these multiple social contexts and cultures of school mathematics must also be added the preschool, out-of-school, and postschool contexts in which persons encounter and use mathematics (i.e., mathematical discourse and semiotic tools, both material and intellectual). Thus *ab initio*, mathematics is not a unity as is traditionally presupposed, and as the use of a single name, *mathematics* suggests. Instead it is manifested in a multiplicity of different and distinct although sometimes overlapping social contexts in and out of school, and in and out of the institutions of professional (research) mathematics. Furthermore, such individual mathematical contexts, despite some invariants and enduring features, are themselves all the while evolving and changing and, sometimes, coming into being or ceasing to be. Learners trace a trajectory through a sequence of such contexts, bearing in mind that they are multiply positioned (e.g., both in and out of school), that they are in part constructed as persons through their participation in these contexts, and that, reciprocally, they are also constructors or reconstructors of the contexts too, which only exist through the participation (and conversation) of the persons involved.

Dowling (1991a, 1993) offers a rich model of mathematical practices, based on the work of Foucault and Bernstein, which accommodates some of this multiplicity. He distinguishes four fields of socially based mathematical activity in terms of the modes of engagement with knowledge. These are the fields of *production* (the context in which mathematical knowledge is created), *recontextualization* (the context in which mathematical knowledge is selected and transformed for educational purposes, such as the writing of pedagogical texts), *reproduction* (the context in which mathematical knowledge is relayed to learners), and *operationalization* (the context in which mathematical knowledge is utilized or applied practically). He also distinguishes a second orthogonal dimension of the social space within which mathematical practices are elaborated, that of different occupational practice-sites. There are four sites in the model, namely the academic site (of higher education), the school site (of primary, secondary, and further education), the work site (of economic activities), and the popular site (of consumer and domestic activities). Dowling suggests that it is logically possible to combine these two dimensions to give sixteen potential types of social context for mathematics, each with its own distinct social space, practice, and discourse (see table 7.2). However, Dowling makes it clear that the possibilities (the cells labeled A to P in the figure) may not all be actually realized in practice, with some likely remaining void, and that overly simple accounts of their adjacency or mutual influence should be avoided. It is important to realize that Dowling uses the term 'text' in a broad and inclusive way to include context.

> The boundaries between the fields of reproduction and those of operationalization correspond to those between transmission and acquisition. The field of reproduction produces transmission texts—teaching practices; the field of operationalization produces acquired texts—student practices. Transmission texts are pedagogic texts embedded within specific forms of social organisation of the classroom, and which are under the control of the teacher. (Dowling 1988: 114)

One of Dowling's central purposes in producing this model is to describe subjects' multiple positioning in these practices, both synchronically and diachronically. He suggests that in the popular site, all subjects are positioned in field of operationalization P (i.e., as shoppers and persons with

TABLE 7.2
DOWLING'S MODEL OF CONTEXTS FOR MATHEMATICAL PRACTICES

Fields of Mathematical Activity	Academic	School	Work	Popular
Production	Creation of mathematical knowledge in university (A)	Creation of mathematical knowledge in school (B)	Production of work situated mathematical knowledge (C)	Production of popular mathematical knowledge (D)
Recontextualization	Production of university teaching texts by producers (mathematicians) (E)	Production of school teaching texts and resources (F)	Production of work training texts and resources (G)	Production of recreational and popular mathematical texts (H)
Reproduction	Teaching of mathematics by producers (mathematicians) (I)	School teaching of mathematics by teachers (J)	Training in applied mathematical techniques for work (K)	Demonstration of applied popular mathematical techniques (L)
Operationalization	Learner produced texts in university (M)	School learner produced texts (N)	Use of contextual mathematical knowledge in labor (O)	Use of contextual mathematics in consumer or domestic activity (P)

domestic lives). Not only do they develop this subjectivity through a form of apprenticeship (immersion in the practice), but they are also prepared to become reproducers in the popular site as parents, guiding their children as consumers (L). Likewise, in the work site, subjects are positioned in field of operationalization O (i.e., as workers) and through an apprenticeship progress vertically through K, G, and C (if C is nonvoid). In the academic site, subjects are first positioned in field of operationalization M (i.e., as university mathematics students) and subsequently as producers A (creative mathematicians) often before becoming reproducers E (university mathematics lecturers). However, many graduate students of mathematics also teach, and so are (at least) doubly positioned.

In the school site, on the other hand, transmission texts within the field of reproduction (which are, themselves, recontextualizations of pedagogic texts produced within the field of recontextualization) construct a

very small number of pedagogic subjects (students) as having a potential academic career. Pedagogic subjects are thus differentiated according to their academic or work destinations, and united in their popular
destination. What is of particular significance is that transmission texts
cannot construct a destination within the school career since i) an academic career must precede such as destination and ii) pedagogic and
transmission texts seek to transmit that which is produced in other
careers rather than that which is produced within their own: mathematics teaching is about mathematics, not teaching. Thus the pedagogic
subject within popular and work careers is an apprentice, the career
structure being vertical, whilst the school pedagogic subject is a proto-
apprentice prior to distribution, there being no career structure within
schooling. The academic career structure is part vertical and part dis-
tributive, with pedagogic subjects being differentiated as having academic, school or work destinations; higher education students being at
least partially autonomous in terms of domestic, consumptive and political practices, their popular destinations may already have been
reached. (Dowling 1991a, 115–16)

Dowling makes a number of key points about the site of schooling.
First, it recontextualizes and reproduces not its own discourses, but those from
other sites. It has no field of production of its own (B is void). Second, the
texts to be recontextualized that relate to academic mathematics are collected
from the field of production of mathematical knowledge A (and possibly M).
Texts are also collected from work and popular sites in "vocational" and
"mundane" forms, which are to be recontextualized in the school site. Much
of Dowling's (1991b, 1991c, 1993) subsequent work has been devoted to analyzing school mathematics texts from the point of view of their coding, the
source of their textual and mathematical knowledge content, and the implied
outcomes for the pedagogic subject in terms of sites (academic, work, or popular).

In the present context, the value of the model is that it explicitly distinguishes between the social contexts and mathematical practices of schooling
and academia; and it indicates the key social spaces in the career trajectories of
mathematics students, and the range of differentiated outcomes. It thus offers a
theoretical structure within which the social construction of the mathematician
takes place. Of course there are many things that it does not show, such as the
fact that the (mathematical) social practice indicated by each cell is not a unity,
but a shifting diversity of different practices. What might appear to be a shared
unity is brought about by an overarching discourse, creating unity as a regime
of truth. Thus productive academic research mathematics, as was discussed
above, is a multiplicity of social practices, with no more than "family resem-

blances." Actually, they do have something more, as Dowling's model suggests: a shared overarching discourse. This is permeated with the ideology of mathematical uniqueness and, hence, of unity. This is one of the consequences of the widespread belief in mathematical absolutism (and of essentialism, in general).

Another problem of the Dowling model is the lack of articulation of the contexts of reproduction and operationalization. Even though these might be different conceptually, in the school site, for example, these contexts permeate and interpenetrate each other. The discourse and texts of teaching mathematics and of the learning of mathematics are part of a whole, the social context of the mathematics classroom as theorized above. Also, in the light of classroom power relations and positionings, the discourse of teaching mathematics dominates and controls that of learning mathematics. I am not sure to what extent a separate discourse of learning mathematics exists. Pupil production of texts in the classroom, in the home (homework), or in the examination hall are all part of, and controlled by, the discourse of mathematics teaching. Even when students carry out open-ended problem solving, project, or investigational work, this is usually regulated by the discourse of school mathematics. Nevertheless, a distinct theoretical site for the location of students (operationalization) can certainly be envisaged, even if its discourse is dominated by that of recontextualization.

Finally, the model does not indicate the way in which neighboring practices and discourses not shown on the map also impact. For example, the other, unseen discourse(s) of schooling are powerful and go far beyond mathematics-specific ones, and impact significantly upon it. So mathematics teaching *may be* about mathematics, but it is surely *also* about teaching, education and the overall institutions of schooling. In fact, in the academic site, there is also the production of texts concerning education (and mathematics education), psychology, sociology, and so on; this has an impact on both the contexts of recontextualization and reproduction in schooling (a point partly conceded by Dowling). There is also the production of educational knowledge by teachers in the schooling site ("action research") that is validated in the academic field of production. Dowling locates himself in cell F (the field of recontextualization in the school site), but in fact he is also to be located in the field of production in the academic site, not as a mathematician, but as an educator or educational theorist.

In summary, the significance of the theorizations offered in this section is that mathematics is part of and implicated in a number of quite distinct social contexts; that there are major discontinuities between the discourses, knowledge formations, and even the assumed (or created) mathematical subjects operating in these contexts. Any consideration of the trajectory of mathematical knowledge, or of the career paths of would-be or actual mathematicians must accommodate these contexts and the transitions between them.

THE INDIVIDUAL MATHEMATICIAN

The Social Construction of the Mathematician

Becoming a mathematician involves an extended period of study in school mathematics to acquire the necessary knowledge, modes of thought, skills, and discourse of school mathematics. The intended outcome of school mathematics is the development of an individual's mathematical powers and dispositions. It requires the would-be mathematician to be enculturated into the various contexts of school mathematics (the field of operationalization in the school mathematics site). This is followed by further study in the field of operationalization of the academic mathematics site. For those destined to become mathematicians, this is usually succeeded by an apprenticeship as a research student in mathematics followed by a first appointment as a university mathematician. Both these latter stages take place in the field of production, in the academic mathematics site. This apprenticeship entails participation in the public and collective institutions of mathematics.

The learning of mathematics thus requires prolonged participation in the social contexts of school and university mathematics. These in turn require interaction with other mathematicians and teachers, use of material resources and information-technology artefacts (books, papers, software, etc.), and immersion in and partial mastery of the discourse of mathematics. Over an extended period this results in personal knowledge of mathematics and of the norms of mathematical content and rhetoric and, to some extent, of the social institution of mathematics.

Enculturation into mathematics is to a large extent achieved through the use of key texts, as Kuhn (1970) points out for scientists, which for mathematicians have in the past included Euclid's or Bourbaki's *Elements*, Van der Waerden's or Birkhoff and MacLane's *Algebra*, and Rudin's *Principles of Mathematical Analysis*. It should not be forgotten that many, probably most students, fall away during this process (see, e.g., Cockcroft 1982; Howson and Kahane 1990). Those that remain have successfully appropriated part of the body of collective mathematical knowledge and have been "socialized" into the social institution of mathematics. These are necessary, but not sufficient, conditions for becoming an accepted professional mathematician. It should also be noted that would-be mathematicians may have internalized and appropriated a widely shared basis to their mathematical knowledge, but there will also be large variations according to which subfields or mathematical specialisms the mathematician contributes to (Davis and Hersh 1980).

Thus over a period of time, as a consequence of participation in social practices, individuals develop and enlarge personal knowledge of and competence in mathematics. This knowledge is manifested in linguistic behaviors and symbolic productions in "conversations" situated in a variety of different social contexts. Some of the would-be knowledge components distinguished by Kitcher (1984), including the largely tacit components such as the mathematical sublanguage, proof and definition criteria, metamathematical principles, and views of mathematics, are part of the background scientific and epistemological context of mathematics and make up the discourse and culture of mathematics. This plays an central role in the generalized logic of mathematical discovery. As part of this background context, these components tend to be taken for granted, since, apart from the mathematical sublanguage, they remain largely constant while new problems, concepts, theorems, proofs, methods, and informal theories become part of the body of accepted mathematical knowledge. Thus the background components, although part of the accepted tacit knowledge of mathematics, are accepted as the enduring backdrop of mathematics, part of the definition and very nature of the discipline. An exception is the mathematical sublanguage, which will be seen to change by the accretion of new terms, concepts, definitions, symbols, conventions, and so on. Although knowledge of the sublanguage of mathematics remains tacit in the main, changes in its usage are public and visible.

Participation in Mathematical Conversation

Mathematical knowledge is manifested in linguistic behaviors and symbolic productions in conversations situated in a variety of different social contexts. The full range of contexts includes those of (*a*) professional academic or research mathematics; (*b*) mathematics education, both within formal institutional settings and outside them; and (*c*) a whole variety of other contexts, such as those of work, everyday, recreational, technical or academic applications, and uses of mathematics. Each of these classes represents a wide range of contexts, as was indicted in the discussion above

Within the contexts of professional research mathematics (i.e., the field of production in the academic mathematics site), individuals use their personal knowledge of mathematics and mathematical discourse in two ways. These are to: (*a*) construct mathematical knowledge claims (possibly jointly with others) and (*b*) participate in the dialectical process of criticism and warranting of others' mathematical knowledge claims. In each case, the individual mathematician's symbolic productions are one of the voices (or part of it) in the warranting conversation. In case (*a*), the textual products that are constructed, whether individually or jointly, are always nascent, forming, in process. Many revisions take place, often many in case (*a*), and some in case (*b*) where as a result of the dialectical processes of criticism and warranting, the textual products are further revised.

Within the contexts of mathematics education (i.e., the fields of reproduction in the school and university mathematics sites), individuals use their
personal knowledge of mathematics and mathematics education to direct and
control mathematics learning conversations (*a*) to present (recontextualized)
mathematical knowledge to learners directly or indirectly (i.e., by teaching)
and (*b*) to participate in the dialectical process of criticism and warranting of
others' mathematical knowledge claims (i.e., by assessment of learning).

In all of these contexts the actors are embedded in and at least partly
constituted by (i.e., developed through) their location within the social contexts and discourses of mathematics and schooling. Thus in each case the
actor's individual actions and knowledge must be seen as inescapably part of
the social contexts; something evinced by the actor in those contexts, and not
necessarily something brought to or transferable out of context. As discussed
in chapter 6, individuals' subjective knowledge can be assessed both as
explicit knowledge (demonstrated by their stating the items of knowledge and
the associated justifications explicitly) and as tacit knowledge (demonstrated
by its successful application). Strictly regulated and institutionalized forms of
testing individuals' abilities to apply their mathematical knowledge up to a
certain level of competency results in the officially (i.e., institutionalized) certified mathematical knowledge. This process indicates the parallel between
the justification of "objective" mathematical knowledge as described by
GLMD and the assessment of its learning by individuals (as subjective knowledge).

Summary: The Social Construction of Subjective
and Objective Knowledge of Mathematics

At the center of social constructivism lies an elaborated theory of both
individual or subjective knowledge and social or objective knowledge of
mathematics—equally weighted (although in traditional epistemology the latter is prioritized)—and the dialectical relation between them. There is, first of
all, a powerful structural analogy between subjective and objective knowledge of mathematics through the role of conversation. For the two types of
voice in conversation are those of the knowledge constructor (proponent) and
critic, types that figure in the construction and warranting of both personal
and public knowledge of mathematics. Second, these types of knowledge are
dialectically interrelated and implicated in each other's creation and warranting. However this mutual recreation does not follow some abstract Hegelian
scheme, but is constituted by concrete conversations using materially embodied texts in social contexts.

A schematic overview of the interrelated social construction of subjective and objective knowledge of mathematics in a creative and reproductive

cycle is illustrated in figure 7.1. Because this figure illustrates a cycle, it is possible to begin to describe at any point. I shall begin at the point where there are persons with individual knowledge of mathematics. Such persons may be active in a number of mathematical and other contexts, of which the illustrated research (academic) context and the educational (school) context are the most important, because they are the sites of the creation and warranting of objective and subjective mathematical knowledge, respectively.

The creative mathematician is an active participant in the academic context of research mathematics. Such individuals have an extensive personal knowledge of mathematics, knowledge they draw upon when entering into the conversation of research mathematics. First they must put forward in public some new mathematical proposal, claim, or text. It must be physically represented (in print, electronically, in writing, or as the spoken word). Publication is necessary (but not sufficient) for an individual's personal mathematical knowledge production to become objective mathematical knowledge, for it must participate in the generalized logic of mathematical discovery. This plays the central role in the social construction of mathematical knowledge in the academic context, because it constitutes the dialectical (conversational) mechanism whereby newly proposed knowledge claims are the object of public scrutiny and approval in the academic warranting context. The outcome for successful claims, possibly after reformulation, is the admission of newly warranted knowledge texts to the pool of currently accepted "objective" mathematical knowledge.

All this takes place in the academic domain of mathematics. In that domain there is an archive of texts, including books in libraries and on mathematicians' shelves, similarly papers in journals, reprints and preprints, proceedings and presented but unpublished conference papers, and the various other optical and electronic representations of mathematical texts. This physically embodied but distributed archive is the cultural pool of mathematical knowledge—the source which mathematicians constantly refer (and add) to; which can be searched and used as a resource for research and teaching; and elements of which can be ignored, resurrected, or critiqued. This is the body of publicly shared and accepted (i.e., objective) mathematical knowledge, and it is made up of physical objects. However there is a perpetual vagueness about the boundary of this domain, and different subcommunities of mathematicians will disagree about the membership of some more peripheral texts, particularly during or following a mathematical revolution (i.e., they will question the legitimacy of some texts).

The figure shows how the academic domain of research mathematics and that of schooling are interrelated and interdependent. Texts produced and warranted in the former domain are selected for and recontextualized in the latter.

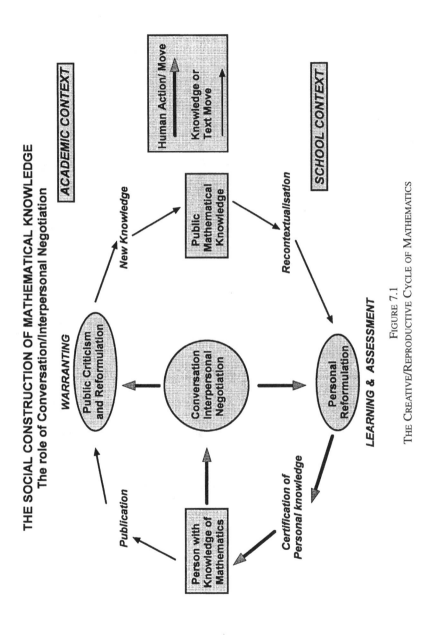

THE SOCIAL CONSTRUCTION OF MATHEMATICAL KNOWLEDGE
The role of Conversation/Interpersonal Negotiation

ACADEMIC CONTEXT

SCHOOL CONTEXT

Human Action/ Move

Knowledge or Text Move

New Knowledge

Public Mathematical Knowledge

Recontextualisation

WARRANTING

Public Criticism and Reformulation

Conversation Interpersonal Negotiation

Personal Reformulation

LEARNING & ASSESSMENT

Publication

Person with Knowledge of Mathematics

Certification of Personal knowledge

FIGURE 7.1

THE CREATIVE/REPRODUCTIVE CYCLE OF MATHEMATICS

Subjective knowledge of mathematics is acquired in the school context as internalized, reconstructed versions of the objective knowledge represented in texts. This knowledge is potentially idiosyncratic, but it is made to fit with social expectations by means of conversation and personal interaction with others (most notably teachers). Personal knowledge fostered, developed, and certified in the domain of schooling travels with individuals, who then utilize it in different ways in either domain (and elsewhere too, not discussed here). In the academic context they may produce new knowledge or act as critics of would-be additions to knowledge. In the school context they interact with learners in teaching or assessment conversations.

The cycle is evidently analogous to Harré's model of Vygotskian space. "Appropriation" corresponds to the individual internalization of collective mathematical forms. "Transformation" corresponds to the individual reconstruction and personalization of that knowledge. "Publication" explicitly occurs as the offering of new mathematical knowledge to the community. "Conventionalisation" corresponds to the process whereby that knowledge having been judged and accepted is added to the pool of objective mathematical knowledge.[15]

Overall, figure 7.1 summarizes how collective objective mathematical knowledge and personal knowledge of mathematics recreate each other in a cyclic process that alternates between the academic and the school contexts. This is both a creative and reproductive cycle, in which existing mathematical knowledge is reproduced and new knowledge is added to the stock of accepted representations.

One important feature of this overall model from an epistemological perspective is the parallel between the justification of both subjective and objective knowledge. In each case the warranting is by means of a social and hence public procedure. The difference, however, is that in one case (subjective knowledge) it is the individual person who is certified as being in possession of mathematical knowledge, to a given level. In the second case, it is the individual text item that is warranted as objective knowledge. All mathematical knowledge it is claimed is embodied in texts and personal knowledge, and objective mathematical knowledge is to be found socially in the interrelations and interactions of these texts and persons within the culture and institution of mathematics.

NOTES

1. Young (1995) conducted a detailed longitudinal case study of two young children talking which suggests a more refined conversational sequence in the acquisition of speech/thought, including the following stages: (1) answering or imitating adult other, (2) initiated speech to present other, (3) initiated speech to passive or imagined other (not self), and (4) speaking to self.

2. This is not the place to offer a full account of mind, and it will doubtless be the case that aspects of the account that have been offered will need revision. An account which offers a clear and detailed account of the formation of the individual as multiply positioned in social contexts, and which stresses the role of language as much as the Vygotskian account offered, can be found in Henriques *et al.* (1984). Although I hope the account offered here is consistent with this poststructuralist approach, it may be the latter that best supports the discussion of social context below. However, the primary philosophical aim of this in accounting for mathematical knowledge in its various aspects means that it is not possible to delve too deeply into psychological theory.

3. It could be argued that the preverbal exchanges that a baby enters into with its primary caregiver is proto-conversation and the resulting development and formation of mind and self is therefore social from the outset.

4. It is also made clear that the status of this fact depends on the mathematical context assumed, i.e., whether it is considered in Peano or standard arithmetic, Boolean algebra, or base 2 modular arithmetic, in which cases $1 + 1 = 2$, $1 + 1 = 1$, and $1 + 1 = 0$, respectively.

5. By immersing themselves in the "potential space" of mathematics with its cultural artifacts, by "playing" with the signs and objects of mathematics, as Winnicott suggests, mathematicians are able to be creative through transforming, reconfiguring, and reassembling these cultural objects in novel and meaningful but rule-governed and tradition-respecting ways.

6. This insight is also shared by many other perspectives including the personal construct theory of Kelly; hermeneutics; phenomenology; the sociology of knowledge of Schütz, Berger, and Luckmann; poststructuralism; etc. Unlike constructivism, many such perspectives talk about the *social* construction of reality.

7. The certification (assessment) of personal knowledge of mathematics in the educational domain is analogous to the justification of objective mathematical knowledge in the domain of research mathematics.

8. The learning conversation extends beyond the teacher-pupil interaction. In school contexts there are attenuated conversations including learner interactions with textually presented and computer presented answers, and learner-peer interactions. In out-of-school contexts there are also learner-parent and learner-significant other interactions.

9. Note that these transformations can vary from strict deduction, at one extreme, to sequentially adjacent steps in an informal chronological representation of the working of the task, at the other extreme.

10. Samuels (1993) provides one of the few published examples of a record of an unsuccessful attempt to solve a mathematical problem, warts and all, with an unquestionably nonlinear structure.

11. Fully social views of knowledge are found, for example, among sociologists (Berger and Luckmann, Schütz), sociologists of knowledge (Barnes, Bloor), social

epistemologists (Fuller), social constructivists (Restivo, Collins), poststructuralists (Foucault), and social constructionist psychologists (Gergen, Shotter, Harré).

12. In this account four components (aims and purposes, persons and relationships, discourse and knowledge, material resources) have been chosen as central and constitutive of a social or discursive practice. However, although none of the elements mentioned can afford to be overlooked in such a theorization, the components could be constituted differently, and perhaps unremarked elements could be brought forward. Thus what is offered is a tentative working model, and no finality or definitiveness is claimed.

13. Of course there may be different goals and purposes simultaneously coexisting—antagonistic goals even—held by the participants or even by a single participant. These might be viewed as a set of vectors in "goal space" with some overall resultant.

14. "Power is not something that is acquired, seized or shared, something that one holds on to or allows to slip away, power is exercised from innumerable points, in the interplay of non-egalitarian and mobile relations . . . Power comes from below" Foucault (1981, 94).

15. The cycle can also occur in miniature, with "publication" corresponding to uttering or doing mathematics, such as in class or in an examination, and "conventionalisation" corresponding to the public acceptance and ownership of the mathematics produced.

CHAPTER 8

SOCIAL CONSTRUCTIVISM:
EVALUATION AND VALUES

This chapter rounds out the presentation of social constructivism as a philosophy of mathematics. It does not further elaborate the theory, but addresses issues of justifying and evaluating the proposals and discussing some possible criticisms. It concludes by considering the values of mathematics and suggesting that an outcome of a social constructivist philosophy of mathematics is the need to recognize the social responsibility of mathematics.

RELATIVISM AND SOCIAL CONSTRUCTIVISM

One of the features shared by many social approaches to philosophy and knowledge including social constructivism is their relativism. But there is a long-standing controversy between relativism and absolutism, and the proponents of these two positions are still engaged in hot debate. Thus in evaluating social constructivism it is necessary to anticipate and reply to the criticism that since it is a relativistic account in epistemic terms it is therefore unable to account adequately for mathematics.

In reply, my claim is that the epistemology offered by social constructivism is indeed relativistic, but that it is a defensible form of relativism. One of the problems that a relativist epistemology such as social constructivism must face is that it seems to give up the attributes of necessity, stability, and autonomy for mathematical knowledge. These are features which, according to fallibilism, have been overemphasized in absolutist philosophies of mathematics to the extent of distorting the accounts of knowledge given, by claiming permanency and objectivity beyond all bounds. But in relinquishing absolutism, it appears that these properties of knowledge are sacrificed completely.

This is not the case, although in the account given the necessity, stability, and autonomy of social constructivist mathematics are relativized to the community of knowers.

The social constructivist position is that there is a great deal of stability in a discipline like mathematics while at the same time there are virtually no essential or necessary features handed on down through the millennia. Thus part of an answer to the charge of relativism concerns the momentum of historical tradition, as stressed by Foucault (1972). Mathematicians often contrast necessity with arbitrariness and implicitly argue that if relativist mathematics has no absolute necessity and essential characteristics to it, then it must be arbitrary, and consequently anarchy prevails and anything goes. However as Rorty (1991) has made clear in philosophy, contingency, not arbitrariness, is the opposite of necessity. Since to be arbitrary is to be determined by or arising from whim or caprice rather than judgement or reason, the opposite of this notion is that of being selected or chosen. I wish to argue that mathematical knowledge is based on both contingency, due to sociohistorical accident, and deliberate choice by mathematicians, which is elaborated through extensive reasoning. Both contingency and selection are active throughout the long history of mathematics. I also wish to argue that the adoption of certain rules of reasoning and consistency in mathematics mean that much of mathematics follows, without further choice or accident, by logical necessity.[1]

The discussion of epistemological relativism is clarified through a consideration of the Perry (1970) theory of the stages of intellectual and ethical development, as Gowri (1994) suggests. Perry distinguishes a number of positions including multiplicity and contextual relativism, in his theory of the intellectual and ethical development of persons. Although his theory is psychological, it offers a useful analogy for classifying different forms of relativism.

He summarizes multiplicity as follows.

> Multiplicity. A plurality of "answers," points of view or evaluations, with reference to similar topics or problems. This plurality is perceived as an aggregate of discretes without internal structure or external relation, in the sense "Anyone has a right to his own opinion," with the implication that no judgements among opinions can be made. (Perry 1970, end-chart)

Thus multiplistic views acknowledge a plurality of "answers," approaches, or perspectives in epistemology, but they lack a basis for rational choice between alternatives. Any selection of axioms, knowledge, framework, and so on that is made is therefore arbitrary, or at least whimsical. This position therefore has much in common with the crude form of relativism mentioned above in which the opposite of necessity is taken as arbitrariness. This position sometimes figures in "knockdown" critiques of relativism. It is a weak and possibly insupportable "straw person" of a position and certainly does not represent the epistemological relativism adopted by social constructivism.

Perry summarizes contextual relativism as follows:

> Relativism. A plurality of points of view, interpretations, frames of reference, value systems and contingencies in which the structural properties of contexts and forms allow of various sorts of analysis, comparison and evaluation in Multiplicity. (Perry 1970, end-chart)

Epistemologically, contextual relativism acknowledges multiplicity but requires that knowledge, justifications, and conclusions be seen as dependent upon features of the context and be evaluated or justified within principled or rule-governed systems. There is an underlying basis for knowledge and rational choice, but that basis is context-relative and not absolute.

Although crude, the distinction between multiplistic relativism and contextual relativism in Perry's work is useful in marking off the insupportable former position, often the target of antirelativist attacks by absolutists, and the latter position, which approximately describes the stance of social constructivism.

A more refined analysis is given by Harré and Krausz (1996) who distinguish "varieties of relativism." They define absolutism (or rather absolutisms) as being based on principles of universalism, objectivism, and foundationalism. The following three theses are based on those of Harré and Krausz, but instead of referring to meaningfulness, as they do, I refer to meaning and truth. (They also include ethical and aesthetic elements, which I omit here). The main difference between their theses and my version therefore lies in claims about assessments of meaning and truth instead of meaningfulness. However to be able to judge truth presupposes being able to assess meaning, and this in turn presupposes being able to judge meaningfulness. But one can judge that some act or speech is meaningful without being able to understand its meaning, and to understand the meaning of a claim does not entail believing in it, let alone knowing it as a truth. Thus the following theses are stronger than those of Harré and Krausz, who define relativism (or rather relativisms) as arising from the denial of one or more of the three principles which may apply in the epistemological domain (which they term discursive) or ontological domain.

1. *The Thesis of Universalism:* All people at all times in all cultures could be brought to agree on the assessment of meaning, truth, and existence.

2. *The Thesis of Objectivism:* The assessment of meaning, truth, and existence and their foundations can be presented so that they are independent of the point of view of persons, cultures, and humankind.
3. *The Thesis of Foundationalism:* There is a unique and permanent foundation for all assessments of meaning, truth, and existence.

Social constructivism denies all three theses with respect to both mathematical knowledge and the ontology of mathematics, but this denial is because the claims are too strong, not because "anything goes." There is, it concedes, something close to universalism and objectivism with regard to meaning, truth, and existence in mathematics. Many people at many times in many cultures have been or could be brought to agree on the assessment of meaning, truth, and existence in mathematics. But since, according to social constructivism, mathematics is a discipline developed in specific cultures over specific periods in the history of humanity there is no reason to assume that universal understanding and assent is guaranteed to be attainable, a priori, among all people past and future. Even less so, a fortiori, is universal understanding and assent guaranteed among other intelligent creatures that might exist in the universe.

Implicit in thesis 1 is the assumption of a fixed or largely constant universal rational epistemic subject. This subject has cognitive powers so that it understands and is rationally compelled to assent to the logical warrants, theorems, and established truth claims of mathematical discourse. Social constructivism rejects the assumption of a universal rational subject of this type, and it regards the human subject as as much a sociocultural and time-dependent product as mathematical knowledge is. Thus for persons or other creatures to understand and assent to modern mathematical knowledge and existence claims requires them to be educated over many years in school, and possibly university mathematics, and to learn to successfully participate in mathematical language games and forms of life. These persons will no longer be personally or culturally the same subject at the end of this process. Furthermore there is no reason to believe that they will all conform to the requirements of thesis 1. Currently it is not the case that even a majority in developed countries are successfully brought to the agreement required.

This counterargument depends in part on the claim in earlier chapters that knowledge in general, and knowledge of mathematics in particular, can be divided into tacit and explicit knowledge and that the former is necessary for individuals if they are to develop, assert, or justify the latter. Much of this tacit knowledge can be acquired only through participation in appropriate language games and forms of life. Thus it not enough to be a rational being; an extensive shared history in certain forms of life is also necessary. Furthermore, it is not clear that this can be successfully achieved for all.[2]

Harré and Krausz (1996) suggest that many forms of relativism reject universalism on the grounds of incommensurability or untranslatability of languages, conceptual frameworks, paradigms, or bodies of knowledge. However, incommensurability and untranslatability are notoriously difficult positions to maintain, as the large literature concerning the Kuhn/Popper debate (e.g., Lakatos and Musgrave 1970) and Quine's (1960) and others' views demonstrate. Strong claims about the incommensurability of theories or traditions and the untranslatability of languages have mostly been refuted. The social constructivist position is that the explicit knowledge of different cultures might well be intertranslatable, in principle at least, but that by definition, tacit knowledge cannot be completely translated. It would first have to be made explicit; and while this can be partially done, there must always be a residue of knowledge that remains tacit and remains bound to the forms of life that give it meaning. This residual knowledge is untranslatable, even when its boundary shifts. To understand it, a person must participate in the relevant form of life. Thus social constructivism is based on the assumption that the social is irreducible and cannot be reduced to discourse or knowledge.

On these same grounds, social constructivism also rejects the thesis of objectivism, that the assessment of meaning, truth, and existence and their foundations can be presented so that they are independent of the point of view persons, cultures, and humankind. For knowing, it is argued, has an irreducible social element situated in historical participation in forms of life. The assessment of meaning, truth, and existence is always, to some extent, circumscribed by the forms of life of the persons or groups involved, and there is no transcendent rational epistemic agent which can detach itself from these human contexts completely. Social constructivism accepts a weakened objectivism to the extent that there is such a thing as objective knowledge which transcends every individual knower in a form of life, and which can often be recontextualized in other forms of life. But such knowledge is not independent of the point of view all cultures or of all of humankind. Likewise, our knowledge of the objects of mathematics depends on the cultural viewpoint of mathematics too.

Another aspect of objectivism is our knowledge of the material world. The social constructivist view of empirical truth is pragmatic. We have working theories of the world, both explicit and implicit. However, as modern philosophers of science assert, our theories are logically underdetermined by our observations. Furthermore, our observations are not beyond the reach of possible revisions either, and they are best regarded as low-level hypotheses rather than facts. As participants in multiple forms of life, we have expectations about ourselves and other persons and about the material world and the impact of tools and technology on it. However, no matter how well entrenched these expectations may be, we cannot rule out the possibility that we may have to modify them.

The strongest criticism from the social constructivist perspective is directed at the thesis of foundationalism. As argued in chapters 1 and 2, there is neither a unique nor a permanent foundation for all assessments of meaning, truth, and existence in mathematics. This is partly demonstrated by the motley and variety of mathematics and epistemologies in history, which evidently do not rest on a unique foundation. Of course it can be rejoined that the failure to achieve this foundation in history does not mean that it will not be discovered. However social constructivism locates the roots of mathematical knowledge in the material—whether it be social or textual—which means that there can be no transcendent foundation waiting to be discovered. If one should emerge out of human agreement, it will never be able to arrogate to itself the right to claim eternal life and unrevisability, for human agreement would be its foundation, and the erosion of that agreement can never be ruled out *a priori*.

Thus social constructivism rejects all three of the theses of absolutism put forward by Harré and Krausz or, rather, the stronger versions of these theses listed above. In fact, by abandoning a central role for truth, validity, and correctness and the associated claims for its universality in their version of absolutism Harré and Krausz are already moving to what many absolutists would view as a weak form of relativism.

One of their major concerns is to deny a number of strong relativist claims, including:

1. Knowledge must be relativized to each individual knower
2. We know nothing about the world or its existence
3. We must take an arbitrary decision whether to accept or reject every putative item of knowledge

But each of these three claims is also rejected by social constructivism:

1. Public knowledge is independent of individual knowers and subject to strong test and agreement by communities of knowers which have traditions of knowledge assessment and partly rational means of making such judgements.[3]
2. Informally, we know a great deal about the world and its human and material inhabitants, and this knowledge presupposes the existence of the world and much of its contents. The precondition of our knowing anything, let alone participating in philosophical debate, is to be experienced conversationalists with extensive knowledge of language games in several human forms of life. This also presupposes extensive agreement in practical judgements concerning both bodily and discursive experiences in forms of life. However, our knowledge is always provisional, in that it is ever open to confirmation, elaboration, revision or change.

3. We do not make arbitrary decisions whether to accept or reject every putative item of knowledge. In particular, in mathematics knowledge forms systematic language games and having explicitly agreed to or tacitly accepted
the presuppositions and conventions upon which these language games rest,
the acceptance of subsequent knowledge items follows from the rules.

As Vico said, we can prove geometrical theorems because we invented
the system and its rules. "The rule and criterion of truth is to have made it . . .
We can know nothing that we have not made" (Vico [1710] 1858, 131).

As was made clear in chapters 1 and 2, this claim must be circumscribed
by the knowledge that mathematical proofs are rarely wholly rigorous or per-
spicuous, unless trivial, and that there is always an element of tacit knowledge
in applying mathematical knowledge and rules or in judging mathematical
knowledge claims. Nevertheless we come as close to certainty as is currently
humanly possible in mathematics, because it consists of self-contained language games which we humans have constructed purely by ourselves.

Critics of the possibility of relativism in mathematics claim that alternative
mathematics or logic is inconceivable; this confirms the necessity and unique status of mathematics and logic. This raises the question, What would an alternative
mathematics or logic look like? Bloor (1976) asks this question and illustrates his
answer with alternative notions of number, calculus, and so on, from the history
of mathematics. A critic's reply to this might be that although our conceptions
have evolved and changed throughout history, they were just steps on the path to
the necessary modern notions. If the questionable teleological aspect of this
claim is ignored, then it is necessary to exhibit simultaneous competing alternatives for mathematics to answer the criticism. However, a preliminary question
needs to be asked, How different does an alternative mathematics need to be to
count as alternative (and hence to refute the uniqueness claim)?

The answer I propose is that an alternative mathematics or logic should
be based on concepts defined differently, with different means of establishing
truths, and it should result in a significantly different body of truths. Furthermore, if the alternative is to be taken seriously, there should be a respectable
body of mathematicians who adhere to the alternative and who reject standard
mathematics. This, in my view, is an adequately strong characterization of an
alternative form of academic (as opposed to culturally embedded) mathematics. Strong as it is, it is not difficult to satisfy this requirement. Intuitionist
mathematics fits the requirement perfectly. Intuitionist concepts—from the
logical connectives *not* and *there exists* to the concepts of 'set', 'spread', and
the 'continuum'—differ in meaning and in logical and mathematical outcomes from the corresponding classical concepts, where such exist. Intuitionist axioms and principles of proof are also different, with the rejection of the
classical law of the excluded middle, $\neg\neg P \leftrightarrow P$ and $\neg\forall x\neg P(x) \leftrightarrow \exists x P(x)$. Intu-

itionist mathematics has its own body of truths (including the countability of the continuum, the Fan theorem, and the Bar theorem) which do not appear in classical mathematics, and it also rejects the bulk of classical mathematics. Finally, since the time of Brouwer, intuitionism has always had a cadre of respected adherent mathematicians who are committed to intuitionism (or constructivism) and reject classical mathematics (e.g., A. Heyting, H. Weyl, E. Bishop, A. Troelstra). Thus there is an alternative mathematics, which includes an alternative logic.

During this century there has also been an explosion other alternative or "deviant" logics, including many-valued logics, Boolean-valued logic, modal logic, deontic logic, relevant logics, paraconsistent logics, and quantum logic. These show that further alternatives to logic not only are possible but exist. However these deviant logics may not satisfy the last criterion given above, that is, the adherence of a group of mathematicians who reject classical logic.

The example of intuitionism shows that classical mathematics is not necessary, unique, or universal, for an alternative is not only possible but exists. It also shows that there are alternatives to classical logic. The example also demonstrates the relativism of mathematics, subject to the constraints discussed above, since there are two mathematical communities (classical and intuitionist) with their own opposing notions and standards of mathematical truth and proof. In previous chapters the absolutist view of mathematics as a body of immutable and necessary truth was refuted and a fallibilist view argued in its place. This weakened the claim of necessity for mathematics. This has now been supplemented with an example of a genuine alternative, dispelling any possible claims of uniqueness, necessity, or universality for mathematics.

There are, of course, absolutist rejoinders to this example. It is a fact that that the concepts and connectives of intuitionist mathematics can be translated into classical terms and that in suitably translated form the axioms and rules of deduction of intuitionist logic can be derived from those of classical logic, and vice versa. Consequently it might be asserted that classical and intuitionist mathematics are not essentially different since they are intertranslatable. However this argument first of all ignores the different meanings, traditions, and discursive practices associated with these two versions of mathematics, and it identifies them solely with the formal representations of their knowledge. Second, it adopts "formal intertranslatability in principle" as an equivalence relation between such knowledge domains. This approach is so powerful that if transposed to the domain of natural languages it would assert that all languages are essentially the same. The only possible alternative mathematics that could be excluded by such a criterion is one that is wholly incommensurable with any existing tradition. Social constructivism rejects the idea that there are absolutely incommensurable bodies of knowledge, yet it argues that there are significantly different knowledge traditions.

Just as social constructivism is relativist on epistemological issues, so too it is relativist in the sense indicated above on ontological issues in mathematics. The objects of mathematics are taken to exist only within systems of thought and culture. They are semiotic objects brought into being by conversation rooted in forms of life, and it is as meaningless, according to social constructivism, to speak about the absolute reality of their existence as it is for that of unicorns, Anna Karenina, the maximum number of angels on the head of a pin, or the Retail Price Index. They are discursive objects whose existence has no meaning outside of the human conversations in which they figure.

Criticism. Social acceptance is not the same as objectivity.

Reply. An account has been given of objective mathematical knowledge, but objectivity has been reinterpreted to mean socially accepted (Bloor 1984, 1991; Harding 1986, 1991). Thus it is true to say that objectivity (understood socially) is used to mean something different. In defense of the social interpretation the following has been argued. First, the important properties of objectivity, such as impersonality and verifiability, are preserved. Second, objective existence in mathematics means consistently postulable. The immense ontological consequences of this definition for mathematics distort the meaning of "objectivity" far beyond the sense of "existing like an object." Third, the social interpretation provides an explanation of the nature of objectivity in mathematics, which other accounts of objectivity, such as those of Frege ([1884] 1968) and Popper (1979), fail to do (Bloor 1991).

In conclusion, social constructivism adopts a relativist position on meaning, knowledge, and existence in mathematics because it roots these in language games and forms of life. These bases are historically formed and have an ineliminably contingent factor; that is, aspects of mathematical language games are shaped by events of history and not solely by their inner logic and rules, which are themselves the partly contingent products of history. Because human beings form a single biological family, speak languages descended from a single ur-language, and live together in overlapping and interacting forms of life in the same world, there is much agreement between them. Where agreement is lacking, cultural diffusion is closing the gaps. Nevertheless, this agreement where it exists, should not be mistaken for evidence of the absoluteness of our knowledge.

EVALUATING THE PROPOSALS IN TERMS OF THE CRITERIA

In chapter 2 I argued that the philosophy of mathematics should be reconceptualized and indicated what was needed through a set of six adequacy criteria. It is therefore appropriate to evaluate the social constructivist proposals against these criteria.

1. Mathematical Knowledge

According to this criterion the philosophy of mathematics should account for mathematical knowledge and its character, genesis, and justification, with special attention to the role of proof. Criterion 1 includes the traditional epistemological focus of the philosophy of mathematics, but adds a concern with the genesis of mathematical knowledge.

It is clear that social constructivism is primarily concerned with the character of mathematical knowledge and its justification at both the subjective and objective levels. One of the novelties and strengths of the account is that it interrelates knowledge at these two levels and offers a theoretical social mechanism whereby they create and recreate each other. In offering this account, social constructivism presents itself as a interdisciplinary theory, drawing on sociology, psychology, semiotics, and the history of mathematics as well as on epistemology, philosophy, and the traditional philosophy of mathematics.

In offering a naturalistic account of mathematical knowledge it is found necessary to include the dimension of tacit as well as explicit knowledge in order to accommodate the full theoretical "knowledge economy" of mathematics. Despite the growth of knowledge-related factors beyond those more commonly treated by philosophy, the primary aim of social constructivism is to accommodate a full account of mathematical knowledge genesis and justification, including all the secondary factors involved.

In the account of objective mathematical knowledge, social constructivism joins the emerging "maverick" tradition in the philosophy of mathematics in rejecting the widespread absolutist conception of mathematical knowledge. Instead it offers a social account of mathematical knowledge based on a new element of epistemological analysis, conversation. It also argues for the necessity of extending current thought about the import of rhetoric in the empirical sciences to mathematics. This is a central aspect in the social constructivist account of the role of proof in mathematics, and a necessary concept to interpose between conversation, on which the account is based, and a social epistemology.

Some specific criticisms concerning the treatment of knowledge in social constructivism can be anticipated.

Criticism 1. A number of inconsistent theories concerning knowledge (particularly those of Wittgenstein and Lakatos) have simply been glued together.

Reply. It is true that there are inconsistent elements concerning knowledge in the work of Wittgenstein and Lakatos. However, the ideas of these two philosophers have not simply been glued together. Selected elements of their philosophies have been combined in social constructivism, based on conversation as the shared basis. Wittgenstein's language games and forms of life provide a socially situated conceptual foundation for human conversation. This in turn provides an epistemological basis for knowledge generation and justification. Lakatos offers a dialectical logic of mathematical discovery as a sociohistorical mechanism for generating and warranting mathematical knowledge. This likewise can be understood to depend on a conversational basis for knowledge generation and justification. These elements of the philosophers' work treat complementary aspects of conversation as a foundation for mathematics, offering both the synchronic (Wittgenstein) and diachronic (Lakatos) dimensions which neither provides on its own.

Another shared feature is their fallibilist epistemology of mathematics. Both reject the absolutist foundations of mathematical knowledge and offer complementary grounds for its contingent character. Wittgenstein stresses that mathematical knowledge rests on agreements and decisions located in language games based in forms of life. Lakatos stresses the historically contingent nature of mathematical knowledge.

Where there is apparent inconsistency (and I ignore Lakatos's later antipathy toward Wittgenstein[4]) is in Lakatos's belief in the underlying autonomous rationality of mathematical knowledge growth and logic. This coexists with his early strong fallibilism in the form of a Hegelian dialectic, later becoming transmuted into a belief in a Popperian World 3. My interpretation is that early Lakatos, whose ideas I elaborate on here, was a full-blooded fallibilist who believed that everything including all of mathematics and logic are mutable, fallible, and nonabsolute, while simultaneously hankering for some immutable absolute lurking behind the phenomenal world. Ignoring this latter, metaphysical aspect of Lakatos's thought, which after all remains speculation, his overt early fallibilism is consistent with the late Wittgenstein's views of mathematics and logic as based on habitual practices rather than epistemological or metaphysical necessity.

A difference may, however, be inferred in the two thinker's views of the autonomy of mathematics. Lakatos is quite firm on this, throughout his career.[5] Wittgenstein sees the "motley of mathematics" as having a momentum through being already constituted as an existing set of discursive practices (language games embedded in forms of life). But this conception does nothing to prevent ruptures, discontinuities, or novelties from emerging, although Wittgenstein does not treat any such historical issues. Lakatos's LMD offers more stability and continuity in the history of mathematics perhaps. But Lakatos has been criticized for the lack of a mechanism to accommodate major changes in mathematical practice, and the GLMD has been proposed to overcome this limitation. It is not clear, however, that Lakatos's philosophy of mathematics provides for the *absolute* autonomy of mathematics (which I would wish to reject) any more than it provides for absolutism in epistemology.

Criticism 2. The discussion of mathematical knowledge fails to accommodate its stable, necessary character.

Reply. One of the problems that a relativist epistemology such as social constructivism must face is that it seems to give up any necessity, stability, or autonomy for knowledge. Admittedly, according to fallibilism, these are attributes which have been overemphasized by absolutists to the extent of distorting the account of knowledge. But in rejecting absolutism, it appears that these properties of knowledge must be relinquished and sacrificed.

The social constructivist position is that there is a great deal of stability in a discipline like mathematics while at the same time there are virtually no essential features necessarily handed on through the millennia. The main source of stability in mathematics is its long, robust, and semiautonomous history. Mathematics is semiautonomous because of its powerful inner conservative forces and intellectual constraints and continuities. The bulk of mathematical knowledge, understood broadly, is passed on from one generation to the next. Furthermore, neglected past academic mathematical knowledge still exists in textual form and can always be brought back into circulation.

Part of the seemingly stable and necessary character of mathematics arises from the fact that the methods and concepts of mathematics are all the while being reapplied to restructure existing mathematical knowledge and theories. Typically, structures are defined or extended to preserve certain invariances, and so the repeated emergence of "nice" properties in mathematics suggests autonomy and inevitability. But the seemingly "natural" occurrence of these features is the outcome of extensive directed intellectual labor—that is, it is constructed, rather than inevitable.

However mathematics is not fully stable, because there are both internal and external forces resulting in change. The internal forces may not challenge its autonomy; but external circumstances including the funding of mathematical research, the applied problems mathematics is required to address, developments in adjacent fields such as theoretical physics, and technological developments such as those in numeration and digital computing have an impact on the problems, solutions, language, concepts, proof standards, and overall shape of mathematics as a discipline and social practice. Even the logic of justification is not immune to these forces and shifts, perhaps imperceptibly for long periods, but also more dramatically at other times. Typically this would be in response to inner developments and changes. Adjacency with applied fields provides not only external impetus for change, but also external constraints on inner change. For mathematics is a language, a *calculus ratiocinator*, and much of its rationale derives from its continued use in other academic areas of study.

Fuller (1988) stresses the import of unanticipated consequences within mathematics as a indicator of the autonomy and objectivity of mathematics.

Since mathematical concepts, methods, and proof-procedures are highly explicit and rule governed, many of the consequences of mathematical theories follow inevitably from them, just as checkmate for white may follow inevitably in three moves from a certain chess configuration. Thus in mathematics, so long as a set of assumptions is agreed, as are the rules to be applied to them, the consequences are inevitable, and different persons will come to the same conclusions independently.[6] As reported above, almost three hundred years ago Vico (1710) had the insight to realize we can know the truths of mathematics with certainty, not because they describe an absolute Platonic realm, but because we have invented the game of mathematics.

Since, according to the social constructivist position, mathematical knowledge rests on conversation rather than some absolute foundation, the inevitable and necessary consequences of a mathematical system still rely on agreement. Mostly, because of the precision and explicitness of mathematics and the shared perspectives of its practitioners, there is little dispute over what follows from given rules and systems in mathematics. However agreement is achieved through consensus or victory in language games and forms of life rather than by reference to extramathematical absolutes, even if the rhetoric of such agreement uses the language of extramathematical absolutes.

The novelty of social constructivism (and some other fallibilist philosophies of mathematics) is to realize both that mathematical knowledge is necessary, stable, and autonomous but that this coexists with its contingent, fallibilist, and historically shifting character.

Criticism 3. The treatment of mathematical knowledge makes little explicit reference to the content of mathematics per se and could be described as a social constructivist account of anything.

Reply. The social constructivist account can be generalized to include a number of other areas of knowledge, as the parallels in psychology and sociology show. However the account given relies on specific aspects of mathematics as a discipline and set of discursive practices in a number of ways. The following are each discipline specific:

1. Discussion of the justification of mathematical knowledge and the role of proof in it
2. Analysis of the different practices involved in mathematics and its applications
3. Analysis of the discourse of mathematics
4. Discussion of the objects of mathematics
5. Recognition of the unique and characteristically mathematical features of the knowledge, theories, methods, and values of mathematics and mathematicians.

Thus although the schema underlying social constructivism is generalizable, there are a number of mathematics-specific features to the account. One aspect which is only sketched here is the semiotics of mathematics. Based on the work of Rotman (1988, 1993), it treats the particular symbols and meanings of mathematics. When further elaborated and fully integrated into social constructivism, this has the potential to provide further mathematics-specific aspects of the concepts and texts of mathematics.

2. Mathematical Theories

According to criterion 2 the philosophy of mathematics should account for mathematical theories, both constructive and structural; account for their character and development, and discuss their appraisal and evaluation. This criterion adds a concern with the form that mathematical knowledge usually takes: that is in mathematical theories. It allows as admissible the notion that theories evolve over time and can be appraised. This criterion requires that the philosophy of mathematics should provide a framework for discussing the appraisal and evaluation of mathematical theories, as appropriate. It also recognizes the dual nature of mathematical theories and concepts, which can be either constructive or structural, and it recognizes that both types play central roles in mathematics (Kreisel and Krivine 1967).

In general, the treatment of mathematical theories in the philosophy of mathematics is too often cursory and neglectful, given the importance of the place of theories as units of organization (epistemological role) and contexts of mathematical research (methodological role). The proposals incorporated here begin to rectify this.

There are two main ways in which mathematical theories are accommodated by social constructivism. The generalized logic of mathematical discovery is specifically concerned with theories, either as part of the backdrop against which changes in a theorem or proof need to be considered, or as primary objects of mathematical development themselves. Theory change is one of the novel features treated by GLMD, and this broadening over Lakatos's scheme was incorporated to overcome criticism about the narrowness of scope of his logic of mathematical discovery, thus offering a mathematical parallel to Kuhn's (1962) "structure of scientific revolutions." This represents a novel and substantial way of accommodating mathematical theories, which have tended to be largely overshadowed by the significance of theorems, in the philosophy of mathematics.

Overall, the account given begins to treat mathematical theories as significant entities in mathematics and philosophy of mathematics. More detailed work is need on the philosophy of particular theories and philosophical issues concerning constructive versus structural theories. More work is also needed on theory appraisal and evaluation, analogous to that in the philosophy of science. There are obvious differences, however, as mathematical theories can coexist rather than necessarily compete for acceptance, as they do in physics. Nevertheless, evaluation criteria are deployed both within and without mathematical theories, and the philosophy of mathematics needs to discuss the rational aspects of their constitution and deployment. However it is not yet clear how many of the issues raised can be treated in general. Many require detailed analyses of mathematical theories and of their history and reception, analyses that would go beyond the scope of accounts like the present one.

3. Mathematical Objects

According to criterion 3 the philosophy of mathematics should account for the objects of mathematics and their character, origins, and relationship with the language of mathematics. This criterion incorporates the traditional ontological focus of the philosophy of mathematics but adds a concern with the genesis of the objects of mathematics, as well as with the language in which mathematical knowledge is expressed and mathematical objects named.

Social constructivism adopts an approach to mathematical objects perhaps best described as nominalist, regarding them as linguistic/conceptual objects. It finds, like Carnap 1956, the traditional realist discussion about the ultimate ontological nature and status of mathematical objects meaningless, since it locates them in the language games and cultural space of mathematics, rather than in the abstract and intangible world of Forms (Plato) or World 3 (Popper). This shift avoids what can be regarded as an error (Harré and Krausz 1996; Rorty 1979; Wittgenstein 1953): the assumption of a correspondence theory of truth and a representational theory of meaning, in which signs denote signifieds in some abstract and immaterial realm. Instead, the Wittgensteinian notion adopted by social constructivism takes the meanings of signs as given by their uses in discursive practices. However the objects of mathematics are not "washed away" by this. Psychological and sociological, as well as semiotic and cultural, accounts of mathematical objects have been given to account for their subjective and objective presence, potency, and force.

One of the central concepts in this account is that of genealogy or historical development. It is claimed that only by understanding the growing individual's developing involvement in the language games and discursive practices of school and university mathematics can the subjective reality of the objects of mathematics be understood. For the meaning of these objects for individuals is something that must be constructed over a period of many years. Likewise, only through tracing the developing complexity of mathematics and mathematical language over the course of history can the evolution and hardening objectivity of mathematics and the objects of mathematics be understood. Our modern conceptions of numbers, shapes, and functions is qualitatively different from that of our mathematical predecessors (Wilder 1974; Spengler [1927] 1956), and the cultural space inhabited by mathematical objects is more thickly and differently populated than it used to be. Social constructivism suggests a similar mechanism (namely, reification) in both the subjective and objective domains through which these objects are constructed. Lastly, social constructivism interrelates the two levels of subjective and objective knowledge of mathematics; they recreate each other and the objects of mathematics in the knowledge creation cycle described above.

Criticism 1. The objects of mathematics are claimed to have a genetic relationship with the language of mathematics, but this is never adequately treated.

Reply. Some indications of the rudiments of a semiotics of mathematics are provided, but a full treatment cannot be included alongside social constructivism as a philosophy of mathematics. The semiotics of mathematics will be further developed in a subsequent book, which is intended to develop the seminal ideas in this direction in Rotman's *Ad Infinitum—The Ghost in Turing's Machine.* However the discussion of the personal and social reification of processes and concepts here and in Ernest 1991 provides a general, if partial, indication of how the objects of mathematics are generated through the language of mathematics.

Criticism 2. Regarding the objects of mathematics as cultural objects does not suggest the solidity and autonomy that mathematicians and persons in general feel them to have.

Reply. I have emphasized an important factor that contributes to the perception of the objectivity of the objects of mathematics. This is the acceptance by mathematicians and others of an extensive and broadening facility (over the course of their development as mathematicians) to identify and mutually inter-transform signifiers that are regarded as equivalent into each other. The creation of equivalence classes in this way is an important mechanism for developing the objective properties of mathematical objects. I do not expect this to persuade a committed mathematical realist, nor anyone entrenched in a similar philosophical or ideological position. It does however provide an account of the central features that characterize objectivity—the multisidedness and apparent permanence of the objects of mathematics—since it describes how they can be approached from many "directions" (i.e., signifiers).

4. Applications of Mathematics

According to criterion 4 the philosophy of mathematics should account for the applications of mathematics; its effectiveness in science, technology, and other realms; and, more generally, the relationship of mathematics with other areas of knowledge and values. This criterion goes beyond the traditional boundaries of the philosophy of mathematics by admitting the application of mathematics and its relations with other areas of human knowledge as legitimate philosophical concerns.

Social constructivism describes mathematics as a set of socially situated discursive practices. Persons always learn or use mathematics within a range of such contexts and are multiply positioned in them. Mathematical knowledge itself is recontextualized, reproduced, and operationalized within multiple contexts. That is, it is transferred from academic to more mundane contexts (Dowling 1991a). However historically, the transfer has gone both ways. Quantitative practices in various mundane contexts have been codified and appropriated by educational and academic contexts (Høyrup 1994).

Similarly, there is mutual recontextualization of knowledge between neighboring academic contexts. Thus aspects of theoretical physics and mathematics have mutually developed and inter-transferred. Mathematics and other areas of knowledge are thus richly and organically interconnected, with both persons and knowledge contextualizations having multiple presences throughout a wide range of discursive practices from the mundane to the academic. The outcome is an interconnected web, using Quine's (1960) metaphor, albeit one that changes its character within distinct discursive practices. This web reflects the origin of mathematics as a language to describe, predict, and regulate quantitative and spatial phenomena. Thus the web is linked both historically and psychologically with worldly contexts, and these links are repeatedly strengthened and validated by the multiple positioning of persons and texts. Through these links concepts, tools, and frameworks are imported and exported—appropriated from or recontextualized into other contexts—and thus further reinforced.

In terms of justification, mathematical language helps to provide a viable description of aspects of empirical and social realities. It is anchored to multiple external practices via these applications and is highly constrained by the need to describe, quantify, and predict events in the physical and human worlds effectively. Mathematics is also, in part, a set of independent language games which have developed their own inward-looking forms and practices. In this aspect it is constrained by the widespread demand for consistency in and between language games, applied in its inner logic of conjectures, proofs, and refutations. Thus not only does mathematics have its feet rooted in the reality of external discursive practices, but its "upper" (pure and theoretical) parts have to survive the rigorous public procedures of justification and criticism, based on the thoroughgoing application of a small number of rational principles.

Thus mathematical knowledge is mediately linked with other discursive practices, both academic and personal, which are dependent on or provide models of the world. These requirements of viability and pragmatic success mean that the effectiveness of mathematics in the physical sciences and beyond not only is reasonable (*contra* Wigner 1969) but is an inevitable consequence of its modes of genesis and justification.

5. Mathematical Practice and History

According to criterion 5 the philosophy of mathematics should account for the character of mathematical practice and the activities of mathematicians, present and past. This demand goes beyond the traditional boundaries of the philosophy of mathematics by admitting human mathematical practice and its history as legitimate philosophical concerns. This also admits the social aspects of mathematics as proper areas of philosophical enquiry.

It is clear that social constructivism not only opens up the possibility of satisfying this criterion, but is also at least partially able to satisfy it. The generalized logic of mathematical discovery offers a model of current and historical mathematical practice, and this, drawing on and extending the work of Lakatos, is one of its central contributions.

Criticism 1. Instead of improving upon Lakatos's methodology of mathematical practice, social constructivism provides even less methodological guidance.

Reply. One of the disadvantages of extending and generalizing Lakatos's logic of mathematical discovery is that attention is not paid to specific episodes in the history of mathematics or to specific methodological guidelines for mathematicians. This is simply unavoidable, and it must be compensated for by other, more empirically orientated research. Such a focus does not fall within the aims of the present project.

Criticism 2. The account is primarily sociological as opposed to philosophical, particularly since it relies on a number of empirical social assumptions and theories.

Reply. Part of the novelty of social constructivism is that it is offered as a philosophy of mathematics which adopts both a social approach to epistemology and an interdisciplinary approach to knowledge. Although traditional epistemology has neglected the social dimension, it is to be found in many modern currents of thought, as is discussed above. Thus shifting to a social account of knowledge is not the same as becoming a part of sociology. One significant difference is that social constructivism is concerned with the justification of mathematical knowledge, which is a philosophical rather than sociological concern. Indeed, the central theme running through social constructivism is the task of accounting for mathematical knowledge naturalistically, which is primarily a philosophical rather than sociological concern.

In addition, social constructivism incorporates a quasi-empiricist approach to epistemology, which denies the existence of an absolute boundary between the a priori and empirical knowledge, and this erases, or at least smudges, the traditional boundaries between philosophy and other disciplines, such as sociology. Thus matters that might be traditionally the exclusive business of sociology are partly treated by social constructivism. Although a small number of empirical theories and assumptions may be included in the account, these elements are marginal and are largely replaceable, should they be falsified. Most of social constructivism concerns general theories justified by analytic argument and reasoning.

Finally, it should be noted that the interdisciplinary approach to the philosophy of mathematics adopted here is necessitated by the desire to offer an adequate, fully descriptive account of mathematics. This is expressed in the proposed adequacy criteria for the reconceptualized philosophy of mathematics.

6. The Learning of Mathematics

According to criterion 6 the philosophy of mathematics should account for the learning of mathematics, notably its character and role in the onward transmission of mathematical knowledge, and in the creativity of individual mathematicians. This criterion concerns the problem of how mathematics is transmitted onwards from one generation to the next and, in particular, how it is learnt by individuals and the dialectical relation between individuals and existing knowledge in creativity.

A unique aspect of social constructivism is that it regards the learning of mathematics as a central and unavoidable matter for the philosophy of mathematics. The account given is inevitably only an outline, but it incorporates the genesis and warranting of subjective knowledge of mathematics in the educational context as a central part of the social institution of mathematics.

The account of learning in social constructivism supplies the historical dimension of personal knowledge growth, paralleling the historical growth of the discipline, as well as tracing the genealogy of the knowing subject. The mathematician does not suddenly spring into being, equipped with all her powers. Throughout her school education she is developing the mathematical tools within her reach, extending her stock of relevant experience and understanding, and developing herself as a knowing subject. Two aspects of this have been stressed above. The first is the ability to bring into being and sustain an appropriated personal world of mathematical objects and relations, a corner of the cultural domain of mathematics. The second is the ability to transform mathematical signifiers and texts in the performance of symbolic mathematical tasks. These two facilities are interrelated, since the signifiers and their equivalences help define and create the objects of mathematics for the individual, and the realm of mathematical objects and operations gives meaning to its texts. The road to the full development of these two aspects of the mathematician as a knowing subject is long and arduous, and it involves extensive and sustained involvement in mathematical exercises over many years.

The social constructivist account of the learning of mathematics makes a central contribution to its treatment of epistemological and ontological issues, for mathematical knowledge and existence are rooted in the culture of mathematics, which depends on persons participating both publicly and privately to create and sustain it. Likewise, mathematical knowledge in appropriately contextualized forms makes a central contribution to the creation of the mathematical identity of persons as mathematicians (or as users of mathematics) via the teaching and learning of mathematics.

Criticism 1. The account is primarily psychological and is thus open to empirical falsification. In addition, it is not primarily philosophical.

Reply. The grounds for adopting conversation as the central underpinning concept and metaphor for social constructivism are philosophical rather than psychological. Subsequently psychological theories which draw on this central concept have been utilized to account of the subjective knowledge elements of social constructivism. Since these are at least partly empirical they are open to falsification, and could be rejected. However, the elements of the psychology of Vygotsky and Winnicott adopted are philosophical and general in tone and unlikely to be falsified. If this were to occur, the social constructivist account would need to be modified.

The second criticism that the account is primarily psychological and not philosophical is answered analogously to the charge (criticism 2 in the discussion of criterion 5) that it is primarily sociological. In particular, the central aim of social constructivism is to account for mathematical knowledge naturalistically, which is primarily a philosophical rather than psychological concern.

Criticism 2. The account does not account for the creativity of individual mathematicians as specified by criterion 6.

Reply. The social constructivist account of the emergence of the individual mathematician includes the appropriation and elaboration of two facilities, which are those of mathematical intuition concerning the ability to access imagined mathematics-worlds and the signifying practices involving the symbolism of mathematics and its transformations. Thus mathematicians appropriate the imaginary and linguistic resources of mathematics as well as their underlying rule-governed bases. They learn to carry out imagined or notated transformations of signs and images; and they are able to develop and recombine the objects, elements, methods, expressions, and structures of mathematics in novel ways. Out of these disciplined combinations emerge new mathematical knowledge creations.

Overall Evaluation

In order to make an overall assessment as to whether the account of social constructivism is adequate, two approaches can be adopted. First, the question can be posed as to whether any social epistemology is acceptable. I have argued this point previously and indicated a number of parallel developments in modern thought which support a socially orientated approach. However, a number of stringent criticisms can be anticipated springing from a rejection of the underlying assumptions of the whole enterprise. One which has been anticipated is that the account is deeply and pervasively relativistic and hence fails to give an adequate account of knowledge *qua* knowledge. Although I have addressed the problems and weaknesses of an absolutist account of mathematical knowledge and the issue of relativism above, it is clear I cannot claim to have settled the absolutism/relativism issue, which goes back to the skepticism/dogmatism controversy of antiquity. I have offered one possible way of accounting for the necessity, objectivity, and autonomy of mathematical knowledge and mathematical objects within what I consider to be a moderately relativistic framework.

The second way of judging if the account is adequate concerns the persuasiveness of the particular social account given. In making a judgement on this issue, social constructivism must be evaluated relative to two bases: the underlying concepts and the overall theoretical scheme which links them. The philosophy will stand or fall on this conceptual foundation. Beyond these central pillars there a number of details which can be improved or changed without threat to the entire philosophy. These include such things as the details of the GLMD, the criteria for the acceptance of proof, specifics of the semiotic interpretation of mathematical language and proof, the details of the growth of mind, and the context of learning mathematics. Each of these, as well as other features, is open to improvement and "fine tuning."

One of the features that emerges in the evaluation in the previous section is that social constructivism satisfies or offers partial satisfaction of each of the six adequacy criteria. Where what it offers is sketchy, it at least opens the possibility of a more fully developed version of the position satisfying the criteria. As it stands, social constructivism is thus a potentially unique multidisciplinary descriptive philosophy of mathematics that links into consonant historical, sociological, psychological, educational, and semiotic social constructivist theories of mathematics.

One of the problems social constructivism faces is the consistency of its different aspects and components as they draw upon different disciplinary traditions and utilize different conceptual bases, explanatory metaphors, and rhetorical styles. If a multidisciplinary account as is proposed is legitimate then there is the possibility that any such dissonance can ultimately be smoothed out. Thus social constructivism is offered both as a philosophical position, largely worked out, and as a research program needing further elaboration.

VALUES AND SOCIAL RESPONSIBILITY

This final section extends the account of social constructivism by briefly addressing the issues of the values, ethics, and social responsibility of mathematics. Treating these issues exceeds the primary objective of social constructivism in accounting for mathematics and mathematical knowledge naturalistically. However one of the novelties of social constructivism is that it does have implications for this highly significant area concerning the relationship between mathematics and society. A full account of the values, ethics, and social responsibility of mathematics would itself require a book-length treatment, and what follows is therefore just a brief and selective sketch of some of the issues raised.

Mathematics and Values

Mathematicians have a strong set of values that are constitutively central to mathematics. For example, Hardy (1941) argues that the most important mathematical theorems have both beauty and seriousness, which means they have generality and depth and contain significant ideas. Within mathematics, problems, concepts, methods, results, and theories are routinely claimed to be deep, significant, powerful, elegant, and beautiful. These attributions cannot be simply dismissed as subjective, because mathematicians and absolutists claim that at least some of these properties reflect objective features of the discipline.

Human interests and values play a significant part in the choices of mathematical problems, methods of solution, concepts and notations constructed in the process, and criteria for evaluating and judging the resulting mathematical creations and knowledge. Mathematicians choose which of infinitely many possible definitions and theorems are worth pursuing, and any act of choice is an act of valuation. The current upsurge of computer-related mathematics represents a large scale shift of interests and values linked with social, material, and technological developments; and it is ultimately manifested in the production of certain types of knowledge (Steen 1988). The values and interests involved also essentially form, shape, and validate that knowledge too; and they are not merely an accidental feature of its production. Even what counts as an acceptable proof has been permanently changed by contingent technological developments (De Millo, Lipton, and Perlis 1986; Tymoczko 1979).

Overt or covert values can thus be identified in mathematics underlying the choice of problems posed and pursued, the features of proofs, and the concepts and theories that are valorized. Deeper still, values underpin the conventions, methodologies, and constraints that limit the nature of mathematical activity and bound what is acceptable in mathematics (Kitcher 1984). These values are perhaps most evident in the norms that regulate mathematical activity and the acceptance of mathematical knowledge. At times of innovation or revolution in mathematics, the values and norms of mathematics become most evident when there are explicit conflicts and disagreements in the underlying values. Consider the historical resistance to innovations such as negative numbers, complex numbers, abstract algebra, non-Euclidean geometries, and Cantor's set theory. At root the conflicts were over what was to be admitted and valued as legitimate, and what was to be rejected as spurious. The standards of theory evaluation involved were based on metalevel criteria, norms, and values (Dunmore 1992). Since these criteria and norms change over the course of the history of ideas, they show that the values of mathematics are human in origin, not imposed or acquired from some timeless source.

The values of absolutist mathematics. A further broad selection of values can be identified in mathematics—including the valuing of the abstract over the concrete, formal over informal, objective over subjective, justification over discovery, rationality over intuition, reason over emotion, generality over particularity, and theory over practice. These may constitute many of the overt values of mathematicians, but they are introduced through the traditional definition of the field. Only that mathematics which satisfies these values is admitted as bona fide, and anything that does not is rejected as inadmissible.[7] Thus warranted mathematical propositions and their proofs are legitimate mathematics, but the criteria and processes used in warranting them are not. The rules demarcating the boundary of the discipline are positioned outside it, so that no discussion of these values is possible within mathematics. Once metarules are established in this way, mathematics can be regarded as value free. In fact, the values lie behind the choice of the norms and rules. By concealing the underpinning values, absolutism makes them virtually unchallengeable. It legitimates only the formal level of discourse as mathematics (i.e., axiomatic theories, not metamathematical discussion), and hence it relegates the issue of values to a realm which is definitionally outside of the discipline.

An absolutist can reply that the list in the preceding paragraph is a matter not of preferred values, but rather of the essential defining characteristics of mathematics and science, which may subsequently become the values of mathematicians. Thus, the content and methods of mathematics, by their very nature, make it abstract, general, formal, objective, rational, theoretical, and concerned with justification. There is nothing wrong with the concrete, the informal, the subjective, or the particular or the context of discovery—they are just not part of the character of justified mathematical or scientific knowledge (Popper 1972).

Absolutist philosophies of mathematics thus have internalist concerns and regard mathematics as objective and free of ethical, human, and other values. Mathematics is viewed as value neutral, concerned only with structures, processes, and the relationships of ideal objects, which can be described in purely logical language. Any intrusion of values, tastes, "flavors," or "coloring" is either an inessential flourish or misrepresentation of mathematics due to human fallibility.

Similar ideas dominated the thought of the British Empiricists, who sharply distinguished primary and secondary qualities (Morris 1963). Primary qualities were the quantifiable properties describable in the mathematics of the day, that is, the properties attributed to things-in-themselves. These include mass, shape, and size; the mathematical attributes of a mechanistic worldview. Secondary qualities include color, smell, feel, taste, and sound; they are understood to be the human subject's responses to things, not the inherent properties of objects or the external world. By analogy, human values, tastes, and interests can be factored out from "objective" knowledge as human distortions and impositions. This resembles Frege's ([1892] 1966) view, as I showed in chapter 6. Thus there is a long intellectual tradition which distinguishes values and interests from knowledge, and which dismisses the former as subjective or human responses to the latter.

The claim that mathematicians and their practices display implicit or explicit values is not denied by absolutist philosophies of mathematics. It is acknowledged that mathematicians have preferences, values, and interests and that these are reflected in their activities and choices and even in the genesis of mathematics. But mathematical knowledge once validated is objective and neutral, based solely on logic and reasoning. Logic, reason, and proof discriminate between truth and falsehood, correct and incorrect proofs, valid and invalid arguments. Neither fear nor favor nor values affects the court of objective reason. Hence, the absolutist argument goes, mathematical knowledge is value neutral.

However, the fallibilist view is that the cultural values, preferences, and interests of the social groups involved in the formation, elaboration, and validation of mathematical knowledge cannot be so easily factored out and discounted. The values that shape mathematics are neither subjective nor necessary consequences of the subject. Thus at the heart of the absolutist neutral view of mathematics, fallibilism claims to locate a set of values and a cultural perspective, as well as a set of rules which renders them invisible and undiscussable.

The values of social constructivist mathematics. One of the central thrusts of social constructivism as a philosophy of mathematics is to challenge a number of traditional dichotomies as they pertain to mathematics. Thus it has been argued that it is not possible to keep disjoint a number of domains, including the philosophy of mathematics and the history of mathematics, the context of justification and the context of discovery, mathematical content and rhetoric, epistemology and objective knowledge as opposed to the social domain. An outcome of the breakdown of these traditional dichotomies is that mathematics ceases to be independent of values and interests and therefore cannot escape having a social responsibility.

Although the traditional absolutist stance is that values are excluded in principle from matters logical and epistemological, and hence can have no relevance to mathematics or the philosophy of mathematics, social constructivism argues that this claim is based on assumptions that can be critiqued and rejected. Mathematics may strive for objectivity, and consequently the visibility of values and interests within it is minimized. However, if the pairs of categories in the above oppositions cannot be regarded as entirely disjoint, it follows that mathematics and mathematical knowledge reflect the interests and values of the persons and social groups involved, to some degree. Once conceded, this means mathematics cannot be coherently viewed as independent of social concerns, and the consequences of its social location and social embedding must be faced.

In particular, a strong case has been made for the ineliminably contingent character of mathematical knowledge. If the direction of mathematical research is a function of historical interests and values as much as inner forces and logical drives, mathematicians cannot claim that the outcomes are inevitable, and hence free from human interests and values. Mathematical development is a function of intellectual labor, and its creators and appliers are moral beings engaged in voluntary actions. Mathematicians may fail to anticipate the consequences of the mathematical developments in which they participate, but this does not absolve them of responsibility. Mathematics needs to be recognized as a socially responsible discipline, just as much as science and technology.

This does not merely apply to the genesis of mathematics and the context of discovery or the applications of mathematics. As has been argued, it applies equally to logic and the context of justification, for logic, reason, and proof have also been shown to be contingent. They include historically accidental features, reflecting the preferences or inclinations of their makers and their source cultures. Thus even the most objective and dispassionate applications of logic and reasoning incorporate a tacit set of values and preferences.

The Social Responsibility of Mathematics

Social constructivism regards mathematics as value laden and sees mathematics as embedded in society with social responsibilities, just as every other social institution, human activity, or discursive practice is. Precisely what this responsibility is depends on the underlying system of values which is adopted, and social constructivism as a philosophy of mathematics does not come with a particular set of values attached.[8] However, viewed from this perspective mathematicians and others professionally involved with the discipline are not entitled to deny on principle social responsibility for mathematical developments or applications.

The same problem of denial of responsibility does not arise in the contexts of schooling. It has always acknowledged that education is a thoroughly value laden and moral activity, since it concerns the welfare and treatment of young persons. If, as in many education contexts, social justice values are adopted, then additional responsibility accrues to mathematics and its related social institutions to ensure that its role in educating the young is a responsible and socially just one. In particular, mathematics must not be allowed to be distorted or partial to the values or interests of particular social groups, even if they have had a dominant role in controlling the discipline historically. An extensive literature concerning gender and race in mathematics education treats criticisms of this sort. It has been argued that white males of European origin have dominated mathematics and science in modern times and that the androcentric values of this group have been attributed to knowledge itself (Ernest 1991; Walkerdine 1988; Walkerdine and the Girls and Mathematics Unit 1989; Bailey and Shan 1991). To the extent that this complaint can be substantiated, and there is significant confirmatory evidence, there is a value imbalance in mathematics and science which needs to be rectified. Such distorted values may permeate not only teaching but also the constitution of the subjects themselves in their modern formulations. I will not pursue this further here except to remark that social constructivism, by admitting the value-laden nature of mathematics and its social responsibility, necessitates the facing and addressing of these issues.

Social constructivism links together the contexts of schooling and research mathematics in a tight knowledge reproduction cycle. This cycle is concerned with the formation and reproduction of mathematicians and mathematical knowledge and thus is deliberately mathematics centered. But if the reproduction of the social institution of mathematics were to be adopted as the leading aim for schooling in the area of mathematics, the outcome could be an educational disaster. For although in most developed and developing countries virtually the whole population studies mathematics in school, fewer than one in one thousand go on to mathematics research. Letting the needs of this tiny minority dominate the mathematical education of everyone would lead to an ethical problem, not to mention a utilitarian one. This problem is further exacerbated by the fact that the needs of these two groups are inconsistent. I will not go into the educational details here except to say that what is needed is differentiated school mathematics curricula to accommodate different aptitudes, attainments, interests, and ambitions. Such differentiation must depend on balanced educational and social judgements rather than exclusively on mathematicians' views of what mathematics should be included in the school curriculum. Mathematicians are often concerned only with improving the supply of future mathematicians, and many of their interventions in the mathematics curriculum have been to increase its content coverage, conceptual abstraction, difficulty, and rigor. While this may be good for the few, the outcomes are often less beneficial for the many (Ernest 1991).

A further issue is that of the social import of differing perceptions of mathematics. There is an interesting division between the mathematicians' and the public's understanding and perceptions of mathematics. Mathematicians typically regard mathematics as a rational discipline which is highly democratic, on the grounds that knowledge is accepted or rejected on the basis of logic, not authority, and potentially anyone can propose or criticize mathematical knowledge using reason alone. Social standing, wealth, and reputation are immaterial to the acceptability of mathematical proposals, so the argument goes. This claim is an idealization, and I indicated in chapter 6 that social standing does matter to some extent with regard to the acceptance of new knowledge. Furthermore it is not pure, context-free reason but the context-embedded reason and rhetoric of the mathematics community that serves as the basis for proposing or criticizing mathematical knowledge. This caution must be borne in mind in evaluating the mathematicians' claims. However, given this caveat, the claim of the mathematicians' is largely correct. The mathematical community greatly values reason and attempts to minimize the role of authority in mathematics.

In contrast, a widespread public perception of mathematics is that it is a difficult but completely exact science in which an elite cadre of mathematicians determines the unique and indubitably correct answers to mathematical problems and questions using arcane technical methods known only to them. This perception puts mathematics and mathematicians out of reach of common sense and reason, and into a domain of experts, to whose authority they are subject. Thus mathematics becomes an elitist subject of asserted authority, beyond the challenge of the common citizen. Such absolutist views attribute a spurious certainty to the mathematizations employed, for example, in advertising, commerce, economics, and politics and in policy statements. The use of carefully selected statistical data and analysis is part of the rhetoric of modern political life, used by political parties of all persuasions to further their sectional interests and agendas. An absolutist perception of mathematics helps to prevent the critical questioning and scrutiny of such uses of mathematics in the public domain, and is thus open to antidemocratic exploitation. If democratic values are preferred over authoritarian ones, as presumably they are in most countries of the world, then part of the social responsibility of mathematics is to support a climate of critical questioning and scrutiny of mathematical arguments by the public. Although superficially this is consonant with mathematicians' views of the rationality of mathematical knowledge, it does not always fit with the public image of mathematics they communicate. Being aware of this, I wish to claim, is part of the social responsibility of mathematics. There are also important implications for schooling (Ernest 1991; Frankenstein 1983; Skovsmose 1994).

Social constructivism has adopted conversation as an underlying metaphor for epistemological reasons, to enable the social aspects of mathematical knowledge to be adequately treated within the philosophy of mathematics. But ethical consequences also follow, and it is worth dwelling a moment on the ethics of conversation. Part of the difference between monological and dialogical argument in conversation is the space and respect given to voices other than the proponent's. I have shown how modern proof theory in trying to remain close to mathematical practice—not for ethical reasons— has admitted the legitimacy of the multiple voices of both proponent and opponent. Habermas (1989–91) draws upon the dialogical logic of Lorenzen and his Erlangen school in order to ground the philosophical theory of communicative action in human actions and conversation. Much of his motive is ethical in that he posits an ideal speech community in which the alternating voices of persons are listened to with respect. Habermas's arguments for the ethical import of conversation offer support to the position defended here. The analogy with democracy is also clear—namely, the legitimacy of multiple voices seeking to persuade, as opposed to the imposed monologue of the dictator.[9]

A feminist critique of logic and the Western philosophical tradition claims that, first of all, the traditional monologic has been the male voice of authority and power, a voice that denies the legitimacy of challenge except from others speaking with the same voice (Nye 1989). This may seem to be an extreme reading, but it shares a number of points in common with the argument presented above. The social constructivist position is to acknowledge that, to be heard, a voice must be from someone who is already a participant within a shared language game. But discursive practices grow and change, and one generation's peripheral or excluded voice can become central in the next.[10] The very "natures" of rationality and logic are shifting. There is a reflexive point to be made here too, in that social epistemologies like social constructivism have traditionally been excluded from philosophy and the philosophy of mathematics. However their voices are now being listened to and the traditional boundaries of the philosophy of mathematics are being widened to admit the "maverick" tradition.

A second feminist criticism is that, even where contestation is admitted, the adversary method of traditional philosophy seeks not to employ the dialectics that counterpoises the voices of proponent and critic in the quest for a shared higher synthesis. Instead, the adversary method is a

> model of philosophic methodology which accepts a positive view of aggressive behaviour and then uses it as the paradigm of philosophic reasoning . . . The adversary method requires that all beliefs and claims be evaluated only by subjecting them to the strongest, most extreme opposition. (Harding and Hintikka 1983, xv)

These authors, with Moulton (1983), offer in contrast to the adversary method, the *elenchus*, the method of refutation employed in the Socratic dialogues of Plato, to lead people to see their views are perceived as wrong by others. Thus the ethics of conversation requires turn-taking in respectful listening as well as in talking.

Social constructivism takes the primary reality to be persons in conversation, persons engaged in language games embedded in forms of life. These basic social situations have a history, a tradition, which must precede any mathematizing or philosophizing. We are not free-floating, ideal cognizing subjects but fleshy persons whose minds and knowing have developed through our bodily and social experiences. Only through our antecedent social gifts can we converse and philosophize. I have argued for epistemological fallibilism and relativism, but instead of rendering social constructivism groundless and rootless, I have found its grounds and roots in the practices and traditions of persons in conversation. In addition to providing a reply to the criticism that social constructivism is relativistic, this conversational basis is also one that is irrevocably moral, for ethics arises from the ways in which persons live together and treat each other. Thus an outcome of social constructivism as a philosophy of mathematics is that questions of interhuman relations and ethics cannot be avoided and must be addressed. What is now needed, I wish to claim, is an ethics of mathematics, one that acknowledges the social responsibility of mathematics and how it is implicated in the great issues of freedom, justice, trust, and fellowship. It is not that this need follows *logically* from social constructivism: It follows *morally*.

In his *Ethics of Geometry*, Lachterman (1989, back cover), quotes Salomon Maimon's emblematic dictum: "In mathematical construction we are, as it were, gods." I have argued that in the social construction of mathematics we act as gods in bringing the world of mathematics into existence. Thus mathematics can be understood to be about power, compulsion, and regulation. The mathematician is omnipotent in the virtual reality of mathematics, although subject to the laws of the discipline; and mathematics regulates the social world we live in, too. This perspective perhaps resolves the enigma, mystery, and paradox of mathematics that I wrote of in the introduction. But in accepting this awesome power it also behooves us to strive for wisdom and to accept the responsibility that accompanies it.

NOTES

1. Much of mathematics follows by logical necessity from its assumptions and adopted rules of reasoning. However this does not contradict the fallibilism of social constructivism, for I deny that the rules, reasoning, and logical necessity in mathematics are absolute or context-independent. Mathematics consists of language games with very entrenched rules and patterns that are very stable and enduring but always remain open to the possibility of change and, in the long term, do change.

2. This caution is not meant to be elitist. There are persons or groups of persons who might not willingly participate in the enculturation process to become mathematical subjects.

3. Knowledge assessment cannot be fully explicit and rational because it rests in part on tacit knowledge of language games and forms of life.

4. This would be somewhat undermined were it possible to verify Hacking's (1979) claim that Lakatos wrote *Proofs and Refutations* with Wittgenstein's *Remarks on the Foundations of Mathematics* open on his desk beside him. A partial verification is provided by Gillies (1996), who recalls that in the 1960s Lakatos showed him a copy of *Remarks* annotated in Hungarian in his own hand. Lakatos stated that some of the annotations were positive, so he must have looked sympathetically at Wittgenstein's philosophy of mathematics in the 1950s. According to Gillies, Lakatos's tone was one of surprise at rediscovering that he had once thought well of Wittgenstein.

5. Yet, ironically, Lakatos's later methodology of scientific research programs suggests that social shifts in interests, resources, and other contingent or pragmatic factors might influence or determine the course of the sciences, including mathematics. For a progressive research program might die for lack of funding, while a degenerating one might survive due to generous funding.

6. Similarly, mathematicians make simultaneous discoveries because they address the same knowledge configurations and currents in the culture of mathematics (Wilder 1981).

7. These values and the associated powers of exclusion figure in a number of powerful feminist critiques of mathematics and science; see, for example, Ernest 1991, Harding 1991, Walkerdine 1988.

8. Elsewhere in the context of education I explored the consequences of a set of values largely consonant with social constructivism (Ernest 1991). Nevertheless, any such set of values is strictly independent of the philosophical position.

9. I argued in chapter 6 that the emergence of proof in ancient Greek mathematics, at least in part, reflected the prevailing democratic forms of social organization of the time.

10. Sometimes an excluded voice becomes strong in a second language game and then is listened to in the first on the basis of that strength.

BIBLIOGRAPHY

Aiken, H. D., ed. 1956. *The Age of Ideology*. New York: Mentor Books.

Alston, W. P. 1992. Foundationalism. In *A Companion to Epistemology*, edited by J. Dancy and E. Sosa. Oxford: Blackwell.

Anapolitanos, D. A. 1989. Proofs and Refutations: A Reassessment. In Gavroglu et al. 1989.

Anderson, A. R. 1964. Mathematics and the Language Game. In Benacerraf and Putnam 1964. Originally published in *The Review of Metaphysics* 11: 446–58.

Anderson, G. 1978. The Problem of Verisimilitude. In *Progress and Rationality in Science*, edited by G. Radnitzky and G. Anderson, Dordrecht: Reidel.

Anderson, R. J., J. A. Hughes, and W. W. Sharrock. 1986. *Philosophy and the Human Sciences*. Beckenham: Croom Helm.

Anellis, I. H. 1989. Distortions and Discontinuities of Mathematical Progress: A Matter of Style, A Matter of Luck, A Matter of Time, . . . A Matter of Fact. *Philosophica* 43, no. 1: 163–96.

Ascher, M. 1991. *Ethnomathematics*. Pacific Grove, Calif.: Brooks/Cole.

Aspray, W., and P. Kitcher, eds. 1988. *History and Philosophy of Modern Mathematics*. Minnesota Studies in the Philosophy of Science, vol. 11. Minneapolis: University of Minnesota Press.

Austin, J. L. 1962. *How to Do Things with Words*. Edited by J. O. Urmson. Oxford: Oxford University Press.

Ayer, A. J. 1946. *Language, Truth, and Logic*. London: Gollancz.

———. 1956. *The Problem of Knowledge*. London: Penguin Books.

Azzouni, J. 1994. *Metaphysical Myths, Mathematical Practice.* Cambridge: Cambridge University Press.

Bailey, P., and S. J. Shan. 1991. *Multiple Factors: Classroom Mathematics for Equality and Justice.* Stoke-on-Trent: Trentham Books.

Bakhtin, M. M. 1986. *Speech Genres and Other Late Essays.* Austin: University of Texas Press.

Barcan Marcus, R. 1967. Modalities and Intensional Languages. *Synthese* 27: 303–22. Reprinted in *Contemporary Readings in Logical Theory*, edited by I. M. Copi and J. A. Gould. New York: Macmillan, 1967.

Barwise, J., ed. 1977. *Handbook of Mathematical Logic.* Amsterdam: North-Holland.

Bauersfeld, H. 1980. Hidden Dimensions in the So-Called Reality of a Mathematics Classroom. *Educational Studies in Mathematics* 11: 23–41.

Bell, E. T. 1952. *Mathematics Queen and Servant of Science.* London: G. Bell and Sons.

Bell, J. L., and M. Machover. 1977. *A Course in Mathematical Logic.* Amsterdam: North-Holland.

Bell, J. L., J. Cole, G. Priest, and A. Slomson, eds. 1973. *Proceedings of the Bertrand Russell Memorial Logic Conference* [Denmark 1971]. Leeds: Bertrand Russell Memorial Logic Conference, Mathematics Department, The University.

Benacerraf, P., and H. Putnam, eds. 1964. *Philosophy of Mathematics: Selected Readings.* Englewood Cliffs, N.J.: Prentice-Hall.

———. 1983. *Philosophy of Mathematics: Selected Readings.* 2nd rev. ed. Cambridge: Cambridge University Press.

Bennett, S. N., C. W. Desforges, S. Cockburn, and B. Wilkinson. 1984. *The Quality of Pupil Learning Experiences.* London: Erlbaum.

Berger, P., and T. Luckmann. 1967. *The Social Construction of Reality.* 1966. New York: Doubleday. reprint, London: Penguin Books.

Bergeron, J. C., N. Herscovics, and C. Kieran, eds. 1987. *Proceedings of PME 11 Conference.* 3 vols. Montreal: University of Montreal.

Berkeley, G. [1710] 1962. *The Principles of Human Knowledge.* Fontana Library. Glasgow: William Collins.

———. [1734] 1901. *The Analyst; or, A Discourse Addressed to an Infidel Mathematician.* In G. Berkeley, *Works*, edited by A. C. Fraser. 4 vols. Oxford: Clarendon Press.

Berkson, W. 1976. Lakatos One and Lakatos Two: An Appreciation. In Cohen *et al.* 1976.

———. 1981. The formal and the Informal. In *Proceedings of the Philosophy of Science Association Annual Conference 1978*. vol. 2. LaSalle, Illinois: Philosophy of Science Association.

Bernays, P. 1934. On Platonism in Mathematics. In Benacerraf and Putnam 1964.

———. 1947. Review of *Polya* [1945]. *Dialectica* 1: 178–88.

———. 1964. Comments on Wittgenstein's Remarks on the Foundations of Mathematics. In Benacerraf and Putnam 1964. Originally published in *Ratio* 2: 1–22.

Bernstein, B. 1975. *Class, Codes and Control*. Vol. 3, *Towards a Theory of Educational Transmissions*. London: Routledge and Kegan Paul.

Bernstein, R. 1983. *Beyond Objectivism and Relativism*. Philadelphia: University of Philadelphia Press.

Berry, J. 1975. *Introduction to Systemic Linguistics I*. London: Batsford Books.

Bhaskar, R., ed. 1991. *Harré and His Critics*. Oxford: Blackwell.

Bibby, N. 1985. *Curricular Discontinuity: A Study of the Transition in Mathematics from Sixth Form to University*. Education Area Occasional Paper 12. Falmer: University of Sussex.

Billig, M. 1991. *Ideology, Rhetoric, and Opinions*. London: Sage.

Bishop, A. J. 1988. *Mathematical Enculturation*. Dordrecht, North Holland: Kluwer.

Bishop, E. 1967. *Foundations of Constructive Analysis*. New York: McGraw-Hill.

Blanché, R. 1966. *Axiomatics*. London: Routledge and Kegan Paul.

Bloor, D. 1976. *Knowledge and Social Imagery*. London: Routledge and Kegan Paul.

———. 1978. Polyhedra and the Abominations of Leviticus. *Studies in the History and Philosophy of Science* 29, no. 4: 245–72.

———. 1983. *Wittgenstein: A Social Theory of Knowledge*. London: Macmillan.

———. 1984. A Sociological Theory of Objectivity. In *Objectivity and Cultural Divergence*, edited by S. C. Brown. Royal Institute of Philosophy Lecture Series, 17. Cambridge: Cambridge University Press.

———. 1991. *Knowledge and Social Imagery*. 2nd rev. ed. Chicago: University of Chicago Press.

Boyer, C. B. 1968. *A History of Mathematics*. New York: Wiley.

Brouwer, L. E. J. [1913] 1964. Intuitionism and Formalism. In Benacerraf and Putnam. Originally published in *Bulletin of the American Mathematical Society* 20: 81–96.

————. [1927] 1967. Intuitionistic Reflections on Formalism. In Heijenoort 1967.

Brown, R. 1987. Reason as Rhetorical. In Nelson et al. 1987a.

Brown, S. C., ed. 1979. *Philosophical Disputes in the Social Sciences*. Brighton: Harvester Press.

Brown, S., J. Fauvel, and R. Finnegan. 1981. *Conceptions of Inquiry*. London: Methuen, in association with the Open University Press.

Callebaut, W., and R. Pinxten. 1987a. Evolutionary Epistemology Today: Converging Views from Philosophy. In Callebaut and Pinxten 1987b.

————, eds. 1987b. *Evolutionary Epistemology*. Synthese Library, vol. 190. Dordrecht: Reidel.

Carnap, R. [1931] 1964. The Logicist Foundations of Mathematics. In Benacerraf and Putnam 1964. Originally published in *Erkenntnis* 1931.

————. 1956. *Meaning and Necessity*. Enlarged ed. Chicago: University of Chicago Press.

Chihara, C. S. 1990. *Constructibility and Mathematical Existence*. Oxford: Clarendon.

Chisholm, R. 1966. *Theory of Knowledge*. Englewood Cliffs: Prentice-Hall.

Chomsky, N. 1965. *Aspects of the Theory of Syntax*. Cambridge, Mass.: MIT Press.

Christiansen, B., A. G. Howson, and M. Otte, eds. 1986. *Perspectives on Mathematics Education*. Dordrecht: Reidel.

Church, A. 1962. Mathematics and Logic. *Logic, Methodology and Philosophy of Science* (edited by E. Nagel, P. Suppes, and A. Tarski). Stanford: Stanford University Press.

Cobb, P. 1987. A Year in the Life of a Second Grade Class: Cognitive Perspective. In Bergeron et al. 1987, vol. 3.

————. 1994. Where is the Mind? Constructivist and Sociocultural Perspectives on Mathematical Development. *Educational Researcher* 23; 7: 13–20.

Cockcroft, W. H., chair. 1982. *Mathematics Counts*. London: Her Majesty's Stationery Office.

Cohen, M. R., and E. Nagel. 1963. *An Introduction to Logic*. London: Routledge and Kegan Paul.

Cohen, P. J. 1966. *Set Theory and the Continuum Hypothesis*. New York: Benjamin.

Cohen, R. S., P. K. Feyerabend, and M. W. Wartofsky, eds. 1976. *Essays in Memory of Imre Lakatos*. Boston Studies in the Philosophy of Science, vol. 39. Dordrecht: Reidel.

Collingwood, R. G. 1944. *An Autobiography*. 1939. Reprint, London: Penguin Books.

Collins, R. 1993. *The Causes of Philosophies*. Unpublished paper.

Confrey, J. 1981. Conceptual Change Analysis: Implications for Mathematics and Curriculum. *Curriculum Inquiry* 11, no. 5: 243–57.

Conway, J. H. 1976. *On Numbers and Games*. London: Academic Press.

Cooper, B. 1985. *Renegotiating Secondary School Mathematics*. Lewes: Falmer Press.

Corfield, D. 1995. Research Programmes, Analogy and Logic: Three Aspects of Mathematics and its Development. Ph.D. diss. King's College, London.

Cornford, F. M. [1935] 1960. *Plato's Theory of Knowledge*. London: Routledge and Kegan Paul.

Craig, W. 1957. Linear Reasoning: A New Form of the Herbrand-Gentzen Theorem. *Journal of Symbolic Logic* 22: 250–68.

Crane, D. 1972. *Invisible Colleges: Diffusion of Knowledge in Scientific Communities*. Chicago: University of Chicago Press.

Crowley, A. [1929] 1991. *Magick in Theory and Practice*. Reprint, Secaucus, N.J.: Castle Books.

Currie, G. 1979. Lakatos's Philosophy of Mathematics. *Synthese* 42: 335–51.

Curry, H. B. 1951. *Outlines of a Formalist Philosophy of Mathematics*. Amsterdam: North-Holland.

D'Ambrosio, U. 1985. *Socio-cultural bases for Mathematics Education*. Campinas, Brazil: UNICAMP.

Dancy, J., and E. Sosa, eds. 1992. *A Companion to Epistemology*. Oxford: Blackwell.

Davis, C. 1974. Materialist Philosophy of Mathematics. In *For Dirk Struik*, edited by R. S. Cohen, J. Stachel, and M. W. Wartofsky. Boston Studies in the Philosophy of Science, 15. Dordrecht: Reidel.

Davis, P. J. 1972. Fidelity in Mathematical Discourse: Is One and One Really Two? *American Mathematical Monthly* 79, no. 3: 252–63.

Davis, P. J., and R. Hersh. 1980. *The Mathematical Experience*. Boston: Birkhauser.

———. 1988. *Descartes' Dream*. London: Penguin Books.

Davis, R. B. 1984. *Learning Mathematics: The Cognitive Science Approach to Mathematics Education*. Beckenham, Kent: Croom Helm.

De Morgan, A. 1835. Review of *A Treatise on Algebra*, by George Peacock. *Quarterly Journal of Education* 9: 91–110, 293–311.

Dedekind, R. [1888] 1901. *Was sind und was sollen die Zahlen?* Translated by W. W. Beman. In *Essays on the Theory of Numbers*, edited by R. Dedekind. Chicago: Chicago University Press.

De Millo, A., R. J. Lipton, and A. J. Perlis. 1986. Social Processes and Proofs of Theorems and Programs. In Tymoczko 1986a. Originally published in *Communications of the ACM* 22, no. 5: 271–80.

Dennett, D. 1992. *Consciousness Explained.* New York: Viking.

Derrida, J. 1977. *Limited Inc.* Supplement to *Glyph* 2: 162–254. Baltimore: Johns Hopkins University Press.

———. 1989. *Edmund Husserl's Origin of Geometry: An Introduction.* Translated by J. P. Leavey, Jr. Lincoln: University of Nebraska Press, Bison Books.

Descartes, R. [1637] 1955. *A Discourse on Method.* Translated by E. S. Haldane and G. R. T. Ross. In R. Descartes, *Philosophical Works*, vol. 1. New York: Dover Press.

Dewey, J. 1938. *Logic: The Theory of Inquiry.* New York: Holt, Rinehart and Winston.

———. 1950. *Reconstruction in Philosophy.* Rev. ed. New York: Mentor Books.

Dowling, P. 1991a. The Contextualising of Mathematics: Towards a Theoretical Map. In *Schools, Mathematics and Work*, edited by M. Harris. London: Falmer Press.

———. 1991b. Gender, Class and Subjectivity in Mathematics: A Critique of Humpty Dumpty. *For the Learning of Mathematics* 11, no. 1: 2–8.

———. 1991c. A Touch of Class: Ability, Social Class and Intertext in SMP 11–16. In Pimm and Love 1991, 137–52.

———. 1993. Mathematics, Discourse and Totemism: A Language for Practice. In NECC Mathematics Commission, *Proceedings of Second International Conference on Political Dimensions of Mathematics Education.* Johannesburg: National Executive Curriculum Commission.

Doyal, L., and R. Harris. 1986. *Empiricism, Explanation and Rationality.* London: Routledge and Kegan Paul.

Dreyfus, H. L., and P. Rabinow. 1982. *Michel Foucault: Beyond Structuralism and Hermeneutics.* Brighton: Harvester Press.

Dummett, M. 1964. Wittgenstein's Philosophy of Mathematics. In Benacerraf and Putnam 1964. Originally published in *Philosophical Review* 68 (1959): 324–48.

———. 1973. The Philosophical Basis of Intuitionistic Logic. In *Proceedings of the Bristol Logic Colloquium*, edited by R. Gandy. Amsterdam: North-Holland.

———. 1977. *The Elements of Intuitionism.* Oxford: Oxford University Press.

Dunmore, C. 1992. Meta-level Revolutions in Mathematics. In Gillies 1992.

Eco, U. 1984. *Semiotics and the Philosophy of Language*. Bloomington: Indiana University Press.

Ernest, P. 1977. Review of *Proofs and Refutations*, by I. Lakatos. *Mathematical Reviews*.

————. 1985. Equivalence Relations: A Unifying Topic. *CASTME Journal* 5, 3: 12–16.

————. 1987a. A Model of the Cognitive Meaning of Mathematical Expressions. *British Journal of Educational Psychology* 57: 343–70.

————. 1987b. Understanding the Language of Mathematics. *CASTME Journal* 7, no. 2: 10–15.

————, ed. 1989. *Mathematics Teaching: The State of the Art*. Basingstoke: Falmer Press.

————. 1991. *The Philosophy of Mathematics Education*. London: Falmer Press.

————. 1992. Are there Revolutions in Mathematics? *Philosophy of Mathematics Education Newsletter* 4/5: 14–18. Reprinted in *Humanistic Mathematics Network Journal* 8 (1993): 63–65.

————. 1993a. Epistemology and the Relationship between Subjective and Objective Knowledge of Mathematics. Paper presented at Invitation Conference on the Cultural Context of the Mathematics Classroom, University of Bielefeld, Germany, 11–15 October 1993.

————. 1993b. Mathematical Activity and Rhetoric: Towards a Social Constructivist Account. In *Proceedings of 17th International Conference on the Psychology of Mathematics Education*, edited by N. Nohda. Tsukuba, Japan: University of Tsukuba.

————. 1994a. The Dialogical Nature of Mathematics. In Ernest 1994d.

————. 1994b. Social Constructivism and the Psychology of Mathematics Education. In Ernest 1994c.

————, ed. 1994c. *Constructing Mathematical Knowledge: Epistemology and Mathematics Education*. London: Falmer Press.

————. 1994d. *Mathematics, Education, and Philosophy: An International Perspective*. London: Falmer Press.

————. 1995. The Mythic Quest of the Hero: A Semiotic Analysis of Mathematical Proof. Paper presented at 19th Annual Conference of the International Group for the Psychology of Mathematics Education, Recife, Brazil, July 1995.

Everitt, N., and A. Fisher. 1995. *Modern Epistemology*. London: McGraw-Hill.

Eves, H. 1964. *An Introduction to the History of Mathematics*. Rev. ed. New York: Holt, Rinehart and Winston.

Faust, D. 1984. *The Limits of Scientific Reasoning*. Minneapolis: University of Minnesota Press.

Feferman, S. 1981. The Logic of Mathematical Discovery vs. the Logical Structure of Mathematics. In *Proceedings of the Philosophy of Science Association Annual Conference 1978*, vol. 2. Illinois: Philosophy of Science Association.

Feigl, H., and W. Sellars, eds. 1949. *Readings in Philosophical Analysis*. New York: Appleton-Century-Crofts.

Ferguson, J. 1970. *Socrates*. London: Macmillan.

Feyerabend, P. 1975. *Against Method*. London: New Left Books.

Field, H. 1989. *Realism, Mathematics & Modality*. Oxford: Blackwell.

Firestone, W. 1987. Meaning in Method: The Rhetoric of Quantitative and Qualitative Research. *Educational Researcher* 16: 16–20.

Fisher, C. S. 1966. The Death of a Mathematical Theory: A Study in the Sociology of Knowledge. *Archive for History of Exact Sciences* 3: 137–59.

Foucault, M. 1972. *The Archaeology of Knowledge*. London: Tavistock.

———. 1980. *Power/Knowledge*. Edited by C. Gordon. New York: Pantheon Books.

———. 1981. *The History of Sexuality*. Part 1. Harmondsworth: Penguin Books.

———. 1984. *The Foucault Reader*. Edited by P. Rabinow. London: Penguin Books.

Frankenstein, M. 1983. Critical Mathematics Education: An Application of Paulo Freire's Epistemology. *Journal of Education* 165, no. 4: 315–39.

Frege, G. [1879] 1967. *Begriffsschrift*. Translated in Heijenoort 1967.

———. [1884] 1968. *The Foundations of Arithmetic*. Translated by J. L. Austin. Oxford: Blackwell.

———. [1892] 1966. On Sense and Reference. In *Translations from the Philosophical Writings of Gottlob Frege*, edited by P. Geach and M. Black. Oxford: Blackwell.

———. [1893] 1964. *Grundgesetze der Arithmetik*. Translated selections in Furth 1964.

———. [1903] 1968. On the Foundations of Geometry. Translated by M. E. Szabo. In *Essays on Frege*, ed. E. D. Klemke. Urbana: University of Illinois Press.

———. 1980. *Philosophical and Mathematical Correspondence.* Edited by B. McGuiness. Translated by H. Kaal. Oxford: Blackwell.

Fritz, K. von. 1955. Die APXAI in der griechischen Mathematik. *Archiv fur Begriffsgeschichte.* Vol. 1. Bonn. Cited in Szabo 1966.

Fuller, S. 1988. *Social Epistemology.* Bloomington: Indiana University Press.

———. 1993. *Philosophy of Science and its Discontents.* 2d ed. New York: Guilford Press.

Furth, M., ed. 1964. *Gottlob Frege: The Basic Laws of Arithmetic.* Berkeley and Los Angeles: University of California Press.

Gadamer, H. G. 1979. *Truth and Method.* Translated by W. Glen-Doepler. London: Sheed and Ward.

Gavroglu, K., Y. Goudaroulis, and P. Nicolacopoulos, eds. 1989. *Imre Lakatos and Theories of Scientific Change.* Boston Studies in the Philosophy of Science, vol. 111. Dordrecht: Kluwer.

Gellner, E. 1959. *Words and Things.* London: Gollancz.

Gentzen, G. 1936. Die Widerspruchfreiheit der reinen Zahlentheorie. *Mathematische Annalen* 112: 493–565.

Gergen K. J. 1988. Feminist Critique of Science and the Challenge of Social Epistemology. In *Feminist Thought and the Structure of Knowledge,* edited by M. M. Gergen. New York: New York University Press.

Gergen, K. J. 1993. From Construction to Context to Reconstruction in Education. In *Constructivism in Education,* edited by L. P. Steffe. Hillsdale, N.J.: Erlbaum.

Giedymin, J. (1982) *Science and Convention.* Oxford: Pergamon Press.

Gillies, D. A. 1996. Personal Communication, 28 March 1996.

———, ed. 1992. *Revolutions in Mathematics.* Oxford: Clarendon Press.

Glas, E. 1988. Beyond Form and Function: Social Issues in Mathematics Change. *Philosophica* 42, no. 2: 21–41.

Glasersfeld, E. von. 1995. *Radical Constructivism: A Way of Knowing and Learning.* London: Falmer Press.

Gödel, K. 1930. The Completeness of the Axioms of the Functional Calculus in Logic. In Heijenoort 1967.

———. [1931] 1967. Über formal unentscheidbare Sätze der Principia Mathematica und verwandter Systeme I. Translation in Heijenoort 1967. Originally published in *Monatshefte fur Mathematik und Physik* 38: 173–98.

————. 1964. *What is Cantor's Continuum Problem?* In Benacerraf and Putnam 1964.

————. 1967. *Note.* In Heijenoort (1967).

Goldman, A. I. 1980. What is Justified Belief? In *Justification and Knowledge*, edited by G. Pappas. Dordrecht: Reidel.

Gowri, A. 1994. Review of *The Philosophy of Mathematics Education*, by P. Ernest. *Social Epistemology* 8, no. 2: 139–50.

Grene, M. 1966. *The Knower and the Known*. London: Faber and Faber.

Grice, H. P. 1975. Logic and Conversation. In *Speech Acts*, edited by P. Cole and J. L. Morgan. New York: Academic Press.

Grouws, D. A., ed. 1992. *Handbook of Research on Mathematics Teaching and Learning*. New York: Macmillan.

Haack, S. 1974. *Deviant Logic*. Cambridge: Cambridge University Press.

————. 1978. *The Philosophy of Logic*. Cambridge: Cambridge University Press.

————. 1979–80. Epistemology with a Knowing Subject. *Review of Metaphysics* 33: 309–35.

Habermas, J. 1987. *The Philosophical Discourse of Modernity*. Translated by F. Lawrence. Cambridge: Polity Press.

————. 1987–91. *The Theory of Communicative Action*. 2 vols. Translated by T. McCarthy. Cambridge: Polity Press.

Hacking, I. 1979. Imre Lakatos's Philosophy of Science. *British Journal for the Philosophy of Science* 30, no. 4: 381–402.

————. 1984. Wittgenstein Rules. *Social Studies of Science* 14: 469–76.

Hadamard, J. 1954. *The Psychology of Invention in the Mathematical Field*. Princeton: Princeton University Press, 1945. Reprint, New York: Dover Press.

Hadden, R. W. 1994. *On the Shoulders of Merchants: Exchange and the Mathematical Conception of Nature in Early Modern Europe*. Albany, N.Y.: SUNY Press.

Hallett, M. 1979. Towards a Theory of Mathematical Research Programmes I & II. *British Journal for the Philosophy of Science* 30, no. 1: 1–25; no. 2: 135–59.

————. 1984. *Cantorian Set Theory and Limitation of Size*. Oxford: Oxford University Press.

Halliday, M. A. K. 1978. *Language as a Social Semiotic*. London: Edward Arnold.

Hamlyn, D. W. 1978. *Experience and the Growth of Understanding*. London: Routledge and Kegan Paul.

Hammer, P. 1964. The Role and Nature of Mathematics. *The Mathematics Teacher* 57: 514–21.

Hanson, N. R. 1958. *Patterns of Discovery*. Cambridge: Cambridge University Press.

Harding, S. 1986. *The Science Question in Feminism*. Milton Keynes: Open University Press.

———. 1991. *Whose Science? Whose Knowledge?* Milton Keynes: Open University Press.

Harding, S., and M. B. Hintikka, eds. 1983. *Discovering Reality; Feminist Perspectives on Epistemology, Metaphysics, Methodology, and Philosophy of Science*. Dordrecht: Reidel.

Hardy, G. H. 1941. *A Mathematician's Apology*. Cambridge: Cambridge University Press.

Harré, R. 1979. *Social Being*. Oxford: Blackwell.

———. 1983. *Personal Being*. Oxford: Blackwell.

———. 1987. *Physical Being*. Oxford: Blackwell.

Harré, R., and M. Krausz. 1996. *Varieties of Relativism*. Oxford: Blackwell.

Harris, R. 1986. *The Origin of Writing*. LaSalle, Ill.: Open Court.

Heijenoort, J. van, ed. 1967. *From Frege to Gödel: A Source Book in Mathematical Logic*. Cambridge: Harvard University Press.

Henkin, L. [1949] 1969a. The Completeness of the First-Order Functional Calculus. In Hintikka 1969. Originally published in *Journal of Symbolic Logic* 14 (1949): 159–66.

———. [1950] 1969b. Completeness in the Theory of Types. In Hintikka 1969. Originally published in *Journal of Symbolic Logic* 15 (1950): 81–91.

Henle, J. M. 1991. The Happy Formalist. *Mathematical Intelligencer* 13, no. 1: 12–18.

Henriques, J., W. Holloway, C. Urwin, C. Venn, and V. Walkerdine. 1984. *Changing the Subject: Psychology, Social Regulation, and Subjectivity*. London: Methuen.

Her Majesty's Inspectorate. 1985. *Mathematics from 5 to 16*. London: Her Majesty's Stationery Office.

Hersh, R. 1978a. Introducing Imre Lakatos. *Mathematical Intelligencer* no. 1: 148–51.

———. 1978b. Review of *Proofs and Refutations*, by Imre Lakatos. *Advances in Mathematics* 29, no. 1: 131–33.

———. 1979. Some Proposals for Reviving the Philosophy of Mathematics. *Advances in Mathematics* 31: 31–50.

————. 1988. Mathematics Has a Front and a Back. Paper presented at Sixth International Congress of Mathematics Education, Budapest, 27 July–4 August 1988.

Heyting, A. [1931] 1964. The Intuitionist Foundations of Mathematics. In Benacerraf and Putnam 1964. Originally published in *Erkenntnis* 1931: 91–121.

————. 1956. *Intuitionism: An Introduction.* Amsterdam: North-Holland.

Hilbert, D. 1902. *The Foundations of Geometry.* Lasalle, Ill.: Open Court. Originally published as *Grundlagen der Geometrie* (1899).

————. 1964. *On the Infinite.* In Benacerraf and Putnam 1964. Originally published in *Mathematische Annalen* 95 (1925): 161–90.

Hintikka, J. 1973. *Logic, Language Games, and Information.* Oxford: Clarendon Press.

Hintikka, J., ed. 1969. *The Philosophy of Mathematics.* Oxford: Oxford University Press.

Hobbes, T. [1651] 1962. *Leviathan.* Glasgow: William Collins, Fontana Library.

Horn, J. 1995. Constatives. In *The Oxford Companion to Philosophy*, edited by T. Honderich. Oxford: Oxford University Press.

Howson, A. G., and J.-P. Kahane. 1990. *The Popularization of Mathematics.* Cambridge: Cambridge University Press.

Høyrup, J. 1987. Influences of Institutionalized Mathematics Teaching on the Development and Organisation of Mathematical Thought in the Pre-Modern Period. Extract printed in *The History of Mathematics: A Reader*, edited by J. Fauvel and J. Gray. London: Macmillan, 1987.

————. 1994. *In Measure, Number, and Weight.* Albany, N.Y.: SUNY Press.

Hughes, G. E., and M. J. Cresswell. 1968. *An Introduction to Modal Logic.* London: Methuen.

James, W. 1912. *Essays in Radical Empricism.* London: Longmans, Green and Company.

Johnson, M. 1987. *The Body in the Mind.* Chicago: University of Chicago Press.

Joseph, G. G. 1991. *The Crest of the Peacock.* London: I. B. Tauris.

Kadvany, J. 1989. A Mathematical Bildungsroman. *History and Theory* 28: 25–42.

Kalmar, L. 1967. Foundations of Mathematics—Whither Now? In Lakatos 1967.

Kant, I. [1781] 1961. *Critique of Pure Reason.* Translated by N. Kemp Smith. London: Macmillan.

————. [1783] 1950. *Prolegomena to Any Future Metaphysics.* Edited by L. W. Beck. Library of Liberal Arts. Indianapolis: Bobbs-Merrill.

Kenny, A. 1973. *Wittgenstein*. Harmondsworth: Penguin Books.

Kielkopf, C. F. 1970. *Strict Finitism*. The Hague: Mouton.

Kieren, C. 1992. On the Learning and Teaching of School Algebra. In Grouws 1992.

Kilpatrick, J. 1992. A History of Research in Mathematics Education. In Grouws 1992.

Kitcher, P. 1979. Frege's Epistemology. *Philosophical Review* 88: 235–66.

———. 1984. *The Nature of Mathematical Knowledge*. Oxford: Oxford University Press.

———. 1988. Mathematical Naturalism. In Aspray and Kitcher 1988.

———. 1991. Persuasion. In Pera and Shea 1991.

Kitcher, P., and W. Aspray. 1988. An Opinionated Introduction. In Aspray and Kitcher 1988.

Klenk, V. H. 1976. *Wittgenstein's Philosophy of Mathematics*. The Hague: Martinus Nijhoff.

Kline, M. 1980. *Mathematics the Loss of Certainty*. Oxford: Oxford University Press.

Kneale, W., and Kneale, M. 1962. *The Development of Logic*. Oxford: Oxford University Press.

Kneebone, G. T. 1963. *Mathematical Logic and the Foundations of Mathematics*. London: Van Nostrand.

Knorr, W. 1975. *The Evolution of the Euclidean Elements*. Dordrecht: Reidel.

Knowles, M. H. 1995. Transfinite Set Theory is Trivially Inconsistent. Paid advertisement. *The Mathematical Intelligencer* 17, no. 3: 5.

Knuth, D. E. 1985. Algorithmic Thinking and Mathematical Thinking. *American Mathematical Monthly* 43: 170–81.

Koetsier, T. 1991. *Lakatos's Philosophy of Mathematics: A Historical Approach*. Amsterdam: North-Holland.

Kolakowski, L. 1972. *Positivist Philosophy*. London: Pelican Books.

Körner, S. 1960. *The Philosophy of Mathematics*. London: Hutchinson.

Kreisel, G. 1958. Wittgenstein's Remarks on the Foundations of Mathematics. *British Journal for the Philosophy of Science* 9: 135–58.

———. 1965. Mathematical Logic. In *Lectures on Modern Mathematics*, vol. 3, edited by T. L. Saaty. New York: Wiley.

Kreisel, G., and J. L. Krivine. 1967. *Elements of Mathematical Logic*. Amsterdam: North-Holland.

Kripke, S. 1980. *Naming and Necessity*. Cambridge: Harvard University Press.

———. 1982. *Wittgenstein: On Rules and Private Language*. Oxford: Blackwell.

Krulik, S., and R. E. Reys, eds. 1980. *Problem Solving in School Mathematics*. 1980 Yearbook. Reston, Va.: National Council of Teachers of Mathematics.

Kuhn, T. S. 1962. *The Structure of Scientific Revolutions*. Chicago: Chicago University Press.

———. 1970. *The Structure of Scientific Revolutions*. 2d ed. Chicago: Chicago University Press.

———. 1977. *The Essential Tension*. Chicago: University of Chicago Press.

Kvasz, L. 1995. On Classification of Scientific Revolutions. Paper presented at Tenth Logic Methodology and Philosophy of Science conference, Florence, 19–25 August 1995.

Lachterman, D. 1989. *The Ethics of Geometry*. New York and London: Routledge.

Lakatos, I. 1961. Essays in the Logic of Mathematical Discovery. Ph.D. diss., King's College, University of Cambridge.

———. 1963–64. Proofs and Refutations. *British Journal for the Philosophy of Science* 14: 1–25, 120–39, 221–43, 296–342.

———. 1976. *Proofs and Refutations: The Logic of Mathematical Discovery*. Edited by J. Worrall and E. Zahar. Cambridge: Cambridge University Press.

———. 1978a. Cauchy and the Continuum. In Lakatos 1978b.

———. 1978b. Infinite Regress and the Foundations of Mathematics. In Lakatos 1978. Revised version of a paper published in *Aristotelian Society Proceedings*, supplementary vol. 36 (1962), 155–84.

———. 1978c. *Mathematics, Science, and Epistemology*. Philosophical Papers, vol. 2. Cambridge: Cambridge University Press.

———. 1978d. *The Methodology of Scientific Research Programmes*. Philosophical Papers, vol. 1. Cambridge: Cambridge University Press.

———, ed. 1967. *Problems in the Philosophy of Mathematics*. Amsterdam: North-Holland.

———. 1968. *The Problem of Inductive Logic*. Amsterdam: North-Holland.

Lakatos, I., and A. Musgrave, eds. 1968. *Problems in the Philosophy of Science*. Amsterdam: North-Holland.

———. 1970. *Criticism and the Growth of Knowledge*. Cambridge: Cambridge University Press.

Laudan, L. 1977. *Progress and Its Problems*. Berkeley and Los Angeles: University of California Press.

Lave, J. 1988. *Cognition in Practice*. Cambridge: Cambridge University Press.

Lave, J., and E. Wenger. 1991. *Situated Learning: Legitimate Peripheral Participation*. Cambridge: Cambridge University Press.

Lear, J. 1982. Leaving the World Alone. *Journal of Philosophy* 79: 382–403.

Lefebvre, H. 1972. *The Sociology of Marx*. Harmondsworth: Penguin Books.

Lemay, E. C., and J. A. Pitts. 1994. *Heidegger for Beginners*. London: Writers and Readers.

Lerman, S. 1989. Investigations: Where to Now? In Ernest 1989.

Livingston, E. 1986. *The Ethnomethodological Foundations of Mathematics*. London: Routledge and Kegan Paul.

Lloyd, G. E. R. 1990. *Demystifying Mentalities*. Cambridge: Cambridge University Press.

Lorenzen, P. 1970. Scientismus versus Dialektik. In *Hermeneutik und Dialektik*, vol. 1, edited by R. Bubner, K. Cramer, and R. Wiehl. Tübingen, 1970.

Losee, J. 1980. *A Historical Introduction to the Philosophy of Science*. 2d ed. Oxford: Oxford University Press.

——— . 1987. *Philosophy of Science and Historical Enquiry*. Oxford: Clarendon Press.

Lotman, Y. 1988. Text within a Text. *Soviet Psychology* 24, no. 3: 32–51.

Lukes, S. 1970. Methodological Individualism Reconsidered. In *Sociological Theory and Philosophical Analysis*, edited by D. Emmet and A. MacIntyre (London: Macmillan). Originally published in *The British Journal of Sociology* vol. 19 (1968).

Lyotard, J. F. 1984. *The Postmodern Condition: A Report on Knowledge*. Manchester: Manchester University Press.

Machover, M. 1983. Towards a New Philosophy of Mathematics. *British Journal for the Philosophy of Science* 34: 1–11.

MacKenzie, D. 1993. Negotiating Arithmetic, Constructing Proof: The Sociology of Mathematics and Information Technology. *Social Studies of Science* 23: 37–65.

Maddy, P. 1984. New Directions in the Philosophy of Mathematics. *Philosophy of Science Proceedings 1984*. Volume 2. East Lansing, Mich.: Philosophy of Science Association.

————. 1990. *Realism in Mathematics*. Oxford: Clarendon Press.

————. 1992. Wittgenstein's Anti-Philosophy of Mathematics. Paper presented at International Conference on Wittgenstein's Philosophy of Mathematics, Kirchberg, August 1992.

Maher, P. 1994. Potential Space and Mathematical Reality. In Ernest 1994c.

Malcolm, N. 1958. *Ludwig Wittgenstein: A Memoir*. With a biographical sketch by G. H. von Wright. Oxford: Oxford University Press.

Manin, Y. I. 1977. *A Course in Mathematical Logic*. New York: Springer.

Mannheim, K. 1936. *Ideology and Utopia*. London: Routledge and Kegan Paul.

Marchi, P. 1976. Mathematics as a Critical Enterprise. In Cohen *et al.* 1976.

Markus, G. 1987. Why Is There No Hermeneutics of Natural Sciences? Some Preliminary Theses. *Science in Context* 1: 5–51.

Marx, K. [1867] 1967. *Capital*. Vol. 1. New York: International Publishers.

Masterman, M. 1970. The Nature of a Paradigm. In Lakatos and Musgrave 1970.

McBride, M. 1994. The Theme of Individualism in Mathematics Education: An Examination of Mathematics Textbooks. *For the Learning of Mathematics* 14, no. 3: 36–42.

McCleary, J., and McKinney, A. 1986. What Philosophy of Mathematics Isn't. *The Mathematical Intelligencer* 8, no. 3: 51–53, 77.

McCloskey, D. 1985. *The Rhetoric of Economics*. Madison: University of Wisconsin Press.

Mead, G. H. [1913] 1964. The Social Self. In Mead 1964b. Originally published in *Journal of Philosophy, Psychology and Scientific Methods* 10: 374–80.

————. 1934. *Mind, Self and Society*. Chicago: University of Chicago Press.

————. 1964a. *George Herbert Mead on Social Psychology*. Rev. ed. Chicago: University of Chicago Press.

————. 1964b. *Selected Writings*. Edited by A. J. Reck. Chicago: University of Chicago Press.

Mellin-Olsen, S. 1987. *The Politics of Mathematics Education*. Dordrecht: Reidel.

Merleau-Ponty, M. [1945] 1962. *The Phenomenology of Perception*. Translated by C. Smith. London: Routledge and Kegan Paul.

Miller, G. 1964. Language and Psychology, In *New Directions in the Study of Language*, edited by E. H. Lenneberg. Cambridge: MIT Press.

Mills, C. W. 1963. Language, Logic, and Culture. In C. W. Mills, *Collected Essays*. New York: Oxford University Press. Reprinted in *Language in Education*, edited by A. Cashdan and E. Grugeon. (London: Routledge and Kegan Paul, 1972).

Monk, R. 1990. *Wittgenstein: The Duty of Genius*. London: Jonathan Cape.

Morgan, C. R. 1995. An Analysis of the Discourse of Written Reports of Investigative Work in GCSE Mathematics. Ph.D. diss., University of London Institute of Education, London.

Morris, C. R. 1963. *Locke Berkeley Hume*. Oxford: Oxford University Press.

Moser, P. 1992. The Gettier Problem. In Dancy and Sosa 1992.

Moulton, J. 1983. A Paradigm of Philosophy: The Adversary Method. In Harding and Hintikka 1983.

Nagel, E. 1956. Symbolic Notation, Haddocks Eyes and the Dog-Walking Ordinance. In Newman 1956.

———. 1961. *The Structure of Science*. London: Routledge and Kegan Paul.

National Council of Teachers of Mathematics. 1980. *An Agenda for Action*. Reston, Va.: National Council of Teachers of Mathematics.

———. 1989. *Curriculum and Evaluation Standards for School Mathematics*. Reston, Va.: National Council of Teachers of Mathematics.

Nelson, J., A. Megill, and D. McCloskey. 1987a. Rhetoric of Inquiry. In Nelson, Megill, and McCloskey 1987b.

———, eds. 1987b. *The Rhetoric of the Human Sciences*. Madison: University of Wisconsin Press.

Neumann, J. von. [1931] 1964. The Formalist Foundations of Mathematics. In Benacerraf and Putnam 1964. Originally published in *Erkenntnis* 1931: 91–121.

Newman, J. R., ed. 1956. *The World of Mathematics*. 4 vols. New York: Simon and Schuster.

Norris, C. 1983. *The Deconstructive Turn*. London: Methuen.

Nye, A. 1989. *Words of Power*. London: Routledge.

O'Hear, A. 1992. Fallibilism. In Dancy and Sosa 1992.

Orwell, G. 1949. *1984*. London: Martin Secker and Warburg.

Palmer, R. E. 1969. *Hermeneutics*. Evanston: Northwestern University Press.

Passmore, J. 1957. *A Hundred Years of Philosophy*. London: Duckworth.

Peano, G. [1889] 1967. *Arithmetices principia, nova methodo exposita.* Translated extracts in Heijenoort 1967.

Peirce, C. S. [1868] 1931–58. Some Consequences of Four Incapacities. In Peirce 1931–58, vol. 5.

———. 1931–58. *Collected Papers.* 8 vols. Cambridge: Harvard University Press.

Pera, M., and W. R. Shea, eds. 1991. *Persuading Science: The Art of Scientific Rhetoric.* New York: Science History Publications.

Perry, W. G. 1970. *Forms of Intellectual and Ethical Development in the College Years: A Scheme.* New York: Holt, Rinehart and Winston.

Peursen, C. A. van. 1969. *Ludwig Wittgenstein: An Introduction to his Philosophy.* London: Faber and Faber.

Philosophy of Science Association. 1981. *Proceedings of PSA Conference 1978.* LaSalle, Ill.: Philosophy of Science Association.

Piaget, J. 1972. *Psychology and Epistemology: Towards a Theory of Knowledge.* Harmondsworth: Penguin Books.

Pimm, D. 1987. *Speaking Mathematically.* London: Routledge.

Pimm, D., and E. Love, eds. 1991. *Teaching and Learning School Mathematics.* London: Hodder and Stoughton.

Plato 1961. *Parmenides, Theaitetos, Sophist, Statesman.* Translated by J. Warrington. Everyman's Library. London: Dent.

Poincaré, H. 1905. *Science and Hypothesis.* Translated by W. J. G. London: Walter Scott Publishing Company.

Polanyi, M. 1964. *Personal Knowledge.* Rev. ed. New York: Harper and Row.

———. 1966. *The Tacit Dimension.* London: Routledge and Kegan Paul.

———. 1969. *Knowing and Being.* Edited by M. Grene. Chicago: Chicago University Press.

Pole, D. 1958. *The Later Philosophy of Wittgenstein.* London: University of London, Athlone Press.

Polya, G. 1945. *How to Solve It.* Princeton: Princeton University Press.

———. 1954. *Mathematics and Plausible Reasoning.* Vol. 1, *Induction and Analogy in Mathematics.* Vol. 2, *Patterns of Plausible Inference.* Princeton: Princeton University Press.

Popper, K. 1957. *The Poverty of Historicism.* London: Routledge and Kegan Paul.

———. 1959. *The Logic of Scientific Discovery.* London: Hutchinson.

——. 1960. On the Sources of Knowledge and of Ignorance. *Proceedings of the British Academy* 46: 39–71.

——. 1962. *The Open Society and its Enemies.* Vol. 2, *Hegel and Marx.* 4th rev. ed., with 1961 addendum. London: Routledge.

——. 1972. *Conjectures and Refutations.* Rev. 4th ed. London: Routledge and Kegan Paul.

——. 1976. *Unended Quest.* Glasgow: Fontana-Collins.

Popper, K. R. 1979. *Objective Knowledge.* Rev. ed. Oxford: Oxford University Press.

Post, J. F. 1992. Infinite Regress Argument. In Dancy and Sosa 1992.

Priest, G. 1973. A Bedside Reader's Guide to the Conventionalist Philosophy of Mathematics. In Bell et al. 1973.

Prigogine, I., and I. Stengers. 1984. *Order Out of Chaos.* London: Heinemann.

Putnam, H. 1972. *Philosophy of Logic.* London: George Allen and Unwin.

——. 1975. *Mathematics, Matter, and Method.* Philosophical Papers, vol. 1. Cambridge: Cambridge University Press.

Quine, W. V. O. 1949. Truth by Convention. In Feigl and Sellars 1949.

——. 1953a. *From a Logical Point of View.* New York: Harper Torchbooks.

——. 1953b. Two Dogmas of Empiricism. In Quine 1953a.

——. 1953c. On What There Is. In Quine 1953a.

——. 1960. *Word and Object.* Cambridge: Massachusetts Institute of Technology Press.

——. 1969. *Ontological Relativity and Other Essays.* New York: Columbia University Press.

——. 1970. *The Philosophy of Logic.* Englewood Cliffs, N.J.: Prentice-Hall.

Quinton, A. 1963. The A Priori and the Analytic. *Proceedings of the Aristotelian Society* 64: 31–54.

Rav, Y. 1989. Philosophical Problems of Mathematics in the Light of Evolutionary Epistemology. *Philosophica* 43, no. 1: 49–78.

Reichenbach, H. 1951. *The Rise of Scientific Philosophy.* Berkeley and Los Angeles: University of California Press.

Restivo, S. 1984. Representations and the Sociology of Mathematical Knowledge. In *Les Savoirs Dans Les Practiques Quotidiennes*, edited by C. Belisle and B. Schiele. Paris: Editions du Centre National De La Recherche Scientifique.

———. 1985. *The Social Relations of Physics, Mysticism, and Mathematics*. Dordrecht: Reidel, Pallas Paperbacks.

———. 1992. *Mathematics in Society and History*. Dordrecht: Kluwer.

———. 1993. The Promethean Task of Bringing Mathematics to Earth. In Restivo, Van Bendegem, and Fischer 1993.

Restivo, S., and R. Collins. 1991. A Sociological Theory of Mind. Unpublished paper.

Restivo, S., J. P. Van Bendegem, and R. Fischer, eds. 1993. *Math Worlds: Philosophical and Social Studies of Mathematics and Mathematics Education*. Albany, N.Y.: SUNY Press.

Richards, J. L. 1980. The Art and Science of British Algebra: A Study in the Perception of Mathematical Truth. *Historia Mathematica* 7, no. 3: 343–65.

———. 1987. Augustus De Morgan, The History of Mathematics, and the Foundations of Algebra. *Isis* 78, no. 291: 7–30.

———. 1989. *Mathematical Visions*. London: Academic Press.

Ricoeur, P. 1981. *Hermeneutics and the Human Sciences*. Cambridge: Cambridge University Press.

Roberts, J. 1992. *The Logic of Reflection*. New Haven: Yale University Press.

Robinson, A. 1966. *Non-Standard Analysis*. Amsterdam: North-Holland.

———. 1967. The Metaphysics of the Calculus. In Lakatos 1967. Reprinted in Hintikka 1969.

Rorty, R. 1979. *Philosophy and the Mirror of Nature*. Princeton: Princeton University Press.

———. 1991. *Contingency, Irony and Solidarity*. Philosophical Papers, vol. 2. Cambridge: Cambridge University Press.

Rosen, S. 1989. *The Ancients and the Moderns: Rethinking Modernity*. New Haven: Yale University Press.

Rosenblatt, M., ed. 1984. *Errett Bishop: Reflections on Him and His Research*. Contemporary Mathematics, vol. 39. Providence: American Mathematical Society.

Rotman, B. 1987. *Signifying Nothing: The Semiotics of Zero*. London: Routledge.

———. 1988. Towards a Semiotics of Mathematics. *Semiotica* 72, nos. 1/2: 1–35.

———. 1993. *Ad Infinitum—The Ghost in Turing's Machine: Taking God Out of Mathematics and Putting the Body Back In*. Stanford: Stanford University Press.

————. 1994. Mathematical Writing, Thinking, and Virtual Reality. In Ernest 1994d.

Routley, R., with R. K. Meyer, V. Plumwood, and R. Brady. 1982. *Relevant Logics and their Rivals 1.* Atscadero, Calif.: Ridgeview.

Russell, B. [1902] 1967. Letter to Frege. In Heijenoort 1967.

————. 1919. *Introduction to Mathematical Philosophy.* London: George Allen and Unwin.

————. 1940. *An Inquiry into Meaning and Truth.* London: George Allen and Unwin.

————. 1959. *My Philosophical Development.* London: George Allen and Unwin.

Ryle, G. 1949. *The Concept of Mind.* London: Hutchinson.

Samuels, P. 1993. A Case Self-Study of How Mathematicians Work. *How Mathematicians Work Newsletter* 3 (July): 6–11.

Sangalli, A. 1990. The Computer Search for a Projective Plane of Order 10. *New Scientist* 3 February, 34.

Sapir, E. 1949. *Language.* New York: Harcourt, Brace and Company.

Saxe, G. B. 1991. *Culture and Cognitive Development: Studies in Mathematical Understanding.* Hillsdale, N.J.: Erlbaum.

Schoenfeld, J. R. 1967. *Mathematical Logic.* Reading, Mass.: Addison-Wesley.

Schubring, G. 1989. Pure and Applied Mathematics in Divergent Institutional Settings in Germany: The Role and Impact of Felix Klein. In *The History of Modern Mathematics*, vol. 2, *Institutions and Applications*, edited by D. E. Rowe and J. McCleary. London: Academic Press.

Searle, J. R. 1995. *The Construction of Social Reality.* London: Penguin Press, Allen Lane.

Shanker, S. G. 1987. *Wittgenstein and the Turning Point in the Philosophy of Mathematics.* London: Croom Helm.

Sheffler, I. 1965. *Conditions of Knowledge: An Introduction to Epistemology and Education.* Chicago: Scott Foresman.

Shotter, J. 1991a. Rhetoric and the Social Construction of Cognitivism. *Theory and Psychology* 1, no. 4: 1–18.

————. 1991b. Rom Harré: Realism and the Turn to Social Constructionism. In Bhaskar 1991.

Simons, H., ed. 1989. *Rhetoric in the Human Sciences.* London: Sage.

Skemp, R. R. 1982. Communicating Mathematics: Surface Structures and Deep Structures. *Visible Language* 16, no. 3: 281–88.

Skovsmose, O. 1994. *Towards a Philosophy of Critical Mathematics Education*. Dordrecht: Kluwer.

Smullyan, R. M. 1968. *First-Order Logic*. Heidelberg: Springer-Verlag.

Solomon, Y. 1989. *The Practice of Mathematics*. London: Routledge.

Specht, E. 1969. *The Foundations of Wittgenstein's Late Philosophy*. Translated by D. E. Walford. Manchester: Manchester University Press.

Spengler, O. [1927] 1956. Meaning of Numbers. In Newman 1956. Originally published in O. Spengler, *The Decline of the West* (New York: Alfred A. Knopf, 1927).

Sperber, D., and D. Wilson. 1986. *Relevance*. Oxford: Blackwell.

Stabler, E. R. 1953. *Introduction to Mathematical Thought*. Reading, Mass.: Addison-Wesley.

Steen, L. A. 1988. The Science of Patterns. *Science* 240, no. 4852: 611–16.

Steiner, M. 1975. *Mathematical Knowledge*. Ithaca, N.Y.: Cornell University Press.

Szabo, A. 1967. Greek Dialectic and Euclid's Axiomatics. In Lakatos 1967.

———. 1969. *Anfange der Griechischen Mathematik*. Budapest: Akademiai Kiado.

———. 1978. *The Beginnings of Greek Mathematics*. Translated by A. M. Ungar. Dordrecht: Reidel.

Tarski, A. 1936. Der Wahrheitsbegriff in den formaliesierten Sprachen. *Studia Philosphica* 1: 261–405.

———. 1954. *Logic, Semantics, and Metamathematics*. Edited by A. Tarski. Oxford: Oxford University Press.

Thomas, R. S. D. 1996. Private communication. 1 September 1996.

Tiles, M. 1991. *Mathematics and the Image of Reason*. London: Routledge.

Toulmin, S. 1972. *Human Understanding*, vol. 1. Oxford: Clarendon Press.

———. 1976. History, Praxis, and the "Third World." In Cohen, Feyerabend, and Wartofsky 1976.

Trevarthen, C. 1987. Brain Development. In *The Oxford Companion to the Mind*, edited by R. L. Gregory. Oxford: Oxford University Press.

Troelstra, A., and D. van Dalen. 1988. *Constructivism in Mathematics: An Introduction*. Vol. 1. Amsterdam: North-Holland.

Tymoczko, T. 1979. The Four-Color Problem and its Philosophical Significance. *The Journal of Philosophy* 76, no. 2: 57–83.

———. 1985. Gödel, Wittgenstein, and the Nature of Mathematical Knowledge. In *Philosophy of Science Association Proceedings 1985*, vol. 2. East Lansing, Mich.: Philosophy of Science Association.

———. 1986a. Making Room for Mathematicians in the Philosophy of Mathematics. *Mathematical Intelligencer* 8, no. 3: 44–50.

———, ed. 1986b. *New Directions in the Philosophy of Mathematics*. Boston: Birkhauser.

Urmson, J. O., and J. Rée, eds. 1989. *The Concise Encycloedia of Western Philosophy and Philosophers*. London: Unwin Hyman.

Van Bendegem, J. P. 1987. Fermat's Last Theorem Seen as an Exercise in Evolutionary Epistemology. In Callebaut and Pinxten 1987b.

———, ed. 1988–89. *Recent Issues in the Philosophy of Mathematics*. *Philosophica* 43, nos. 1 and 2.

Varela, F. J., E. Thompson, and E. Rosch. 1991. *The Embodied Mind*. Cambridge: MIT Press.

Vico, G-B. [1710] 1858. *De antiquissima Italorum sapientia*. Latin original and Italian translation by Pomodoro. Naples: Stamperia de'Classici Latini.

———. [1744] 1961. *The New Science*. Translated by T. G. Bergin and M. H. Fisch. Garden City, N.Y.: Anchor Books.

Volosinov, V. N. 1973. *Marxism and the Philosophy of Language*. Translated by L. Maejka and I. R. Titunik. New York: Seminar Press. Originally published Leningrad, 1930.

Vygotsky, L. 1978. *Mind in Society*. Cambridge: Harvard University Press.

———. 1979. The Instrumental Method in Psychology. In Wertsch 1979.

———. 1986. *Thought and Language*. Translated by A. Kozulin. Cambridge: MIT Press.

Waismann, F. 1951. *Introduction to Mathematical Thinking*. London: Hafner Publishing Company.

———. 1967. *Ludwig Wittgenstein und der Wiener Kreis*. Oxford: Blackwell.

———. 1979. *Ludwig Wittgenstein and the Vienna Circle*. Oxford: Blackwell.

Walkerdine, V. 1988. *The Mastery of Reason*. London: Routledge.

Walkerdine, V., and the Girls and Mathematics Unit. 1989. *Counting Girls Out*. London: Virago Press.

Wartofsky, M. W. 1976. Lakatos's Philosophy of Science. In Cohen, Feyerabend, and Wartofsky 1976.

Watkins, J. W. N. 1968. Historical Explanation in the Social Sciences. In *Readings in the Philosophy of the Social Sciences*, edited by M. Brodbeck (New York: Macmillan). Originally published in *British Journal for the Philosophy of Science* 8 (1957): 104–17.

Wertheimer, M. 1945. *Productive Thinking*. New York: Harper.

Wertsch, J. V. 1991. *Voices of the Mind*. London: Harvester Wheatsheaf.

———, ed. 1979. *The Concept of Activity in Soviet Psychology*. Armonk, N.Y.: M. E. Sharpe.

Weyl, H. 1947. *Philosophy of Mathematics and Natural Science*. Princeton: Princeton University Press.

White, L. A. 1947. The Locus of Mathematical Reality: An Anthropological Footnote. In Newman 1956. Originally published in *Philosophy of Science* October 1947.

White, M. 1950. *The Analytic and the Synthetic: An Untenable Dualism*. In *John Dewey: Philosopher of Science and Freedom*, ed. S. Hook. New York: Dial Press.

Whitehead, A. N., and B. Russell. 1910–13. *Principia Mathematica*. 3 vols. Cambridge: Cambridge University Press.

———. 1962. *Principia Mathematica to *56*. Cambridge: Cambridge University Press.

Whorf, B. L. 1956. *Language, Thought, and Reality*. London: MIT Press.

Wigner, E. P. 1969. The Unreasonable Effectiveness of Mathematics in the Physical Sciences. In *The Spirit and Uses of the Mathematical Sciences*, edited by T. L. Saaty and F. J. Weyl. New York: McGraw-Hill.

Wilder, R. L. 1965. *Introduction to the Foundations of Mathematics*. New York: Wiley.

———. 1974. *Evolution of Mathematical Concepts*. London: Transworld Books.

———. 1981. *Mathematics as a Cultural System*. Oxford: Pergamon Press.

Williams, R. 1983. *Keywords*. Rev. 2d ed. Glasgow: Fontana-Collins.

Winch, P. 1958. *The Idea of a Social Science*. London: Routledge and Kegan Paul.

———, ed. 1969. *Studies in the Philosophy of Wittgenstein*. London: Routledge and Kegan Paul.

Winnicott, D. 1971. *Playing and Reality*. London: Penguin Books.

Wittgenstein, L. 1922. *Tractatus Logico-Philosophicus*. London: Routledge and Kegan Paul.

————. 1953. *Philosophical Investigations*. Translated by G. E. M. Anscombe. Oxford: Blackwell.

————. 1956. *Remarks on the Foundations of Mathematics*. Oxford: Blackwell.

————. 1969. *Philosophische Grammatik*. Oxford: Blackwell.

————. 1976. *Wittgenstein's Lectures on the Foundations of Mathematics*. Edited by C. Diamond. Ithaca: Cornell University Press.

————. 1978. *Remarks on the Foundations of Mathematics*. Rev. ed. Cambridge: MIT Press.

Womack, C. A. 1995. Ersatz Falsification and the Case Against Fallibilism. Paper presented at 10th Logic Methodology and Philosophy of Science conference, Florence, 19–25 August 1995.

Woolgar, S. 1988. *Science: The Very Idea*. London: Tavistock, Ellis Horwood.

Woozley, A. D. 1949. *Theory of Knowledge*. London: Hutchinson.

Worrall, J. 1976. Imre Lakatos (1922–1974): Philosopher of Mathematics and Philosopher of Science. In Cohen, Feyerabend, and Wartofsky 1976.

Wright, C. 1980. *Wittgenstein on the Foundations of Mathematics*. London: Duckworth.

Yackel, E. 1987. A Year in the Life of a Second Grade Class: A Small Group Perspective. In Bergeron, Herscovics, and Kieran 1987.

Yackel, E., P. Cobb, and T. Wood. 1991. Small-Group Interactions as a Source of Learning Opportunities in Second-Grade Mathematics. *Journal for Research in Mathematics Education* 22, no. 5: 390–408.

Yessenin-Volpin, A. S. 1980. The Ultra-Intuitionist Criticism and the Antitraditional Program for the Foundations of Mathematics. In *Intuitionism and Proof Theory*, edited by A. Kino, J. Myhill, and E. Vesley. Amsterdam: North-Holland.

Young, K. G. 1987. *Taleworlds and Storyrealms*. Dordrecht: Martinus Nijhoff.

Young, J. S. 1995. *Young Children's Apprenticeship in Number*. Ph.D. diss. University of North London, London.

Yuxin, Z. 1990. From the Logic of Mathematical Discovery to the Methodology of Scientific Research Programmes. *British Journal for the Philosophy of Science* 41: 377–99.

Zaslavsky, C. 1973. *Africa Counts*. Boston: Prindle, Weber and Schmidt.

INDEX